NEW PERSPECTIVES ON
Microsoft® Excel® 2010

BRIEF

June Jamrich Parsons
Dan Oja
Roy Ageloff
Patrick Carey

COURSE TECHNOLOGY
CENGAGE Learning™

Australia • Brazil • Japan • Korea • Mexico • Singapore • Spain • United Kingdom • United States

COURSE TECHNOLOGY
CENGAGE Learning™

New Perspectives on Microsoft Excel 2010, Brief

Vice President, Publisher: Nicole Jones Pinard

Executive Editor: Marie L. Lee

Associate Acquisitions Editor: Brandi Shailer

Senior Product Manager: Kathy Finnegan

Product Manager: Leigh Hefferon

Associate Product Manager: Julia Leroux-Lindsey

Editorial Assistant: Jacqueline Lacaire

Director of Marketing: Cheryl Costantini

Senior Marketing Manager: Ryan DeGrote

Marketing Coordinator: Kristen Panciocco

Developmental Editor: Robin M. Romer

Senior Content Project Manager:
  Jennifer Goguen McGrail

Composition: GEX Publishing Services

Art Director: Marissa Falco

Text Designer: Althea Chen

Cover Designer: Roycroft Design

Cover Art: © David Jordan Williams/Corbis

Copyeditor: Suzanne Huizenga

Proofreader: Andrea Schein

Indexer: Alexandra Nickerson

Some of the product names and company names used in this book have been used for identification purposes only and may be trademarks or registered trademarks of their respective manufacturers and sellers.

Microsoft and the Office logo are either registered trademarks or trademarks of Microsoft Corporation in the United States and/or other countries. Course Technology, Cengage Learning is an independent entity from the Microsoft Corporation, and not affiliated with Microsoft in any manner.

Disclaimer: Any fictional data related to persons or companies or URLs used throughout this book is intended for instructional purposes only. At the time this book was printed, any such data was fictional and not belonging to any real persons or companies.

Library of Congress Control Number: 2010929431

ISBN-13: 978-0-538-74292-4

ISBN-10: 0-538-74292-5

Course Technology
20 Channel Center Street
Boston, MA 02210
USA

Cengage Learning is a leading provider of customized learning solutions with office locations around the globe, including Singapore, the United Kingdom, Australia, Mexico, Brazil, and Japan. Locate your local office at:
international.cengage.com/global

Cengage Learning products are represented in Canada by Nelson Education, Ltd.

To learn more about Course Technology, visit **www.cengage.com/course technology**

To learn more about Cengage Learning, visit **www.cengage.com**

Purchase any of our products at your local college store or at our preferred online store **www.cengagebrain.com**

Printed in the United States of America
3 4 5 6 7 8 9 14 13 12 11

Preface

The New Perspectives Series' critical-thinking, problem-solving approach is the ideal way to prepare students to transcend point-and-click skills and take advantage of all that Microsoft Office 2010 has to offer.

In developing the New Perspectives Series, our goal was to create books that give students the software concepts and practical skills they need to succeed beyond the classroom. We've updated our proven case-based pedagogy with more practical content to make learning skills more meaningful to students.

With the New Perspectives Series, students understand *why* they are learning *what* they are learning, and are fully prepared to apply their skills to real-life situations.

About This Book

This book provides essential coverage of Microsoft Excel 2010, and includes the following:

- Detailed, hands-on instruction of Microsoft Excel 2010 basics, including creating and formatting a workbook, working with formulas and functions, and creating charts
- Coverage of important spreadsheet concepts, including order of precedence in formulas, function syntax, and absolute and relative cell references
- Exploration of the exciting new features in Excel 2010, including working in Backstage view and adding sparklines for compact graphing

New for this edition!

- Each session begins with a Visual Overview, a new two-page spread that includes colorful, enlarged screenshots with numerous callouts and key term definitions, giving students a comprehensive preview of the topics covered in the session, as well as a handy study guide.
- New ProSkills boxes provide guidance for how to use the software in real-world, professional situations, and related ProSkills exercises integrate the technology skills students learn with one or more of the following soft skills: decision making, problem solving, teamwork, verbal communication, and written communication.
- Important steps are now highlighted in yellow with attached margin notes to help students pay close attention to completing the steps correctly and avoid time-consuming rework.

System Requirements

This book assumes a typical installation of Microsoft Excel 2010 and Microsoft Windows 7 Ultimate using an Aero theme. (You can also complete the material in this text using another version of Windows 7, such as Home Premium, or earlier versions of the Windows operating system. You will see only minor differences in how some windows look.) The browser used for any steps that require a browser is Internet Explorer 8.

www.cengage.com/ct/newperspectives

The New Perspectives Approach

Context

Each tutorial begins with a problem presented in a "real-world" case that is meaningful to students. The case sets the scene to help students understand what they will do in the tutorial.

Hands-on Approach

Each tutorial is divided into manageable sessions that combine reading and hands-on, step-by-step work. Colorful screenshots help guide students through the steps. **Trouble?** tips anticipate common mistakes or problems to help students stay on track and continue with the tutorial.

VISUAL OVERVIEW

Visual Overviews

New for this edition! Each session begins with a Visual Overview, a new two-page spread that includes colorful, enlarged screenshots with numerous callouts and key term definitions, giving students a comprehensive preview of the topics covered in the session, as well as a handy study guide.

PROSKILLS

ProSkills Boxes and Exercises

New for this edition! ProSkills boxes provide guidance for how to use the software in real-world, professional situations, and related ProSkills exercises integrate the technology skills students learn with one or more of the following soft skills: decision making, problem solving, teamwork, verbal communication, and written communication.

KEY STEP

Key Steps

New for this edition! Important steps are highlighted in yellow with attached margin notes to help students pay close attention to completing the steps correctly and avoid time-consuming rework.

INSIGHT

InSight Boxes

InSight boxes offer expert advice and best practices to help students achieve a deeper understanding of the concepts behind the software features and skills.

TIP

Margin Tips

Margin Tips provide helpful hints and shortcuts for more efficient use of the software. The Tips appear in the margin at key points throughout each tutorial, giving students extra information when and where they need it.

REVIEW
APPLY

Assessment

Retention is a key component to learning. At the end of each session, a series of Quick Check questions helps students test their understanding of the material before moving on. Engaging end-of-tutorial Review Assignments and Case Problems have always been a hallmark feature of the New Perspectives Series. Colorful bars and brief descriptions accompany the exercises, making it easy to understand both the goal and level of challenge a particular assignment holds.

REFERENCE
TASK REFERENCE
GLOSSARY/INDEX

Reference

Within each tutorial, Reference boxes appear before a set of steps to provide a succinct summary and preview of how to perform a task. In addition, a complete Task Reference at the back of the book provides quick access to information on how to carry out common tasks. Finally, each book includes a combination Glossary/Index to promote easy reference of material.

www.cengage.com/ct/newperspectives

Our Complete System of Instruction

Coverage To Meet Your Needs
Whether you're looking for just a small amount of coverage or enough to fill a semester-long class, we can provide you with a textbook that meets your needs.

- Brief books typically cover the essential skills in just 2 to 4 tutorials.
- Introductory books build and expand on those skills and contain an average of 5 to 8 tutorials.
- Comprehensive books are great for a full-semester class, and contain 9 to 12+ tutorials.

So if the book you're holding does not provide the right amount of coverage for you, there's probably another offering available. Go to our Web site or contact your Course Technology sales representative to find out what else we offer.

CourseCasts – Learning on the Go. Always available...always relevant.
Want to keep up with the latest technology trends relevant to you? Visit our site to find a library of podcasts, CourseCasts, featuring a "CourseCast of the Week," and download them to your mp3 player at http://coursecasts.course.com.

Our fast-paced world is driven by technology. You know because you're an active participant—always on the go, always keeping up with technological trends, and always learning new ways to embrace technology to power your life.

Ken Baldauf, host of CourseCasts, is a faculty member of the Florida State University Computer Science Department where he is responsible for teaching technology classes to thousands of FSU students each year. Ken is an expert in the latest technology trends; he gathers and sorts through the most pertinent news and information for CourseCasts so your students can spend their time enjoying technology, rather than trying to figure it out. Open or close your lecture with a discussion based on the latest CourseCast.

Visit us at http://coursecasts.course.com to learn on the go!

Instructor Resources
We offer more than just a book. We have all the tools you need to enhance your lectures, check students' work, and generate exams in a new, easier-to-use and completely revised package. This book's Instructor's Manual, ExamView testbank, PowerPoint presentations, data files, solution files, figure files, and a sample syllabus are all available on a single CD-ROM or for downloading at http://www.cengage.com/coursetechnology.

SAM: Skills Assessment Manager

SAM is designed to help bring students from the classroom to the real world. It allows students to train and test on important computer skills in an active, hands-on environment.

SAM's easy-to-use system includes powerful interactive exams, training, and projects on the most commonly used Microsoft Office applications. SAM simulates the Office application environment, allowing students to demonstrate their knowledge and think through the skills by performing real-world tasks, such as bolding text or setting up slide transitions. Add in live-in-the-application projects, and students are on their way to truly learning and applying skills to business-centric documents.

Designed to be used with the New Perspectives Series, SAM includes handy page references, so students can print helpful study guides that match the New Perspectives textbooks used in class. For instructors, SAM also includes robust scheduling and reporting features.

Content for Online Learning

Course Technology has partnered with the leading distance learning solution providers and class-management platforms today. To access this material, visit www.cengage.com/webtutor and search for your title. Instructor resources include the following: additional case projects, sample syllabi, PowerPoint presentations, and more. For students to access this material, they must have purchased a WebTutor PIN-code specific to this title and your campus platform. The resources for students might include (based on instructor preferences): topic reviews, review questions, practice tests, and more. For additional information, please contact your sales representative.

Acknowledgments

We would like to thank the many people whose invaluable contributions made this book possible. First, sincere thanks go to our reviewers: Carol DesJardins, St. Clair County Community College; Kristen Hockman, University of Missouri–Columbia; Dana Hooper, The University of Alabama; Ahmed Kamel, Concordia College; Peter Ross, University at Albany; Diane Shingledecker, Portland Community College; Kelly Swain, Humber College; Karen Toreson, Shoreline Community College; Mary Voehl, Caldwell College; Raymond Yu, Douglas College; and Violet Zhang, George Brown College. At Course Technology we would like to thank Marie Lee, Executive Editor; Kathy Finnegan, Senior Product Manager; Brandi Shailer, Associate Acquisitions Editor; Julia Leroux-Lindsey, Associate Product Manager; Jacqueline Lacaire, Editorial Assistant; Jennifer Goguen McGrail, Senior Content Project Manager; Christian Kunciw, Manuscript Quality Assurance Supervisor; and John Freitas and Susan Whalen, MQA Testers. Special thanks to Robin Romer, Developmental Editor, for her exceptional efforts, keeping us focused and providing guidance and encouragement as we worked to complete this text.
– June Jamrich Parsons
– Dan Oja
– Roy Ageloff
– Patrick Carey

TABLE OF CONTENTS

OBJECTIVES

- Explore the programs in Microsoft Office
- Start programs and switch between them
- Explore common window elements
- Minimize, maximize, and restore windows
- Use the Ribbon, tabs, and buttons
- Use the contextual tabs, the Mini toolbar, and shortcut menus
- Save, close, and open a file
- Learn how to share files using SkyDrive
- Use the Help system
- Preview and print a file
- Exit programs

Getting Started with Microsoft Office 2010

Preparing a Meeting Agenda

Case | *Recycled Palette*

Recycled Palette, a company in Oregon founded by Ean Nogella in 2006, sells 100 percent recycled latex paint to both individuals and businesses in the area. The high-quality recycled paint is filtered to industry standards and tested for performance and environmental safety. The paint is available in both 1 gallon cans and 5 gallon pails, and comes in colors ranging from white to shades of brown, blue, green, and red. The demand for affordable recycled paint has been growing each year. Ean and all his employees use Microsoft Office 2010, which provides everyone in the company with the power and flexibility to store a variety of information, create consistent files, and share data. In this tutorial, you'll review how the company's employees use Microsoft Office 2010.

STARTING DATA FILES

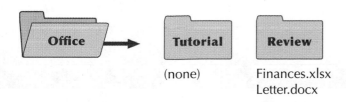

Office → Tutorial   Review

(none)   Finances.xlsx
Letter.docx

VISUAL OVERVIEW

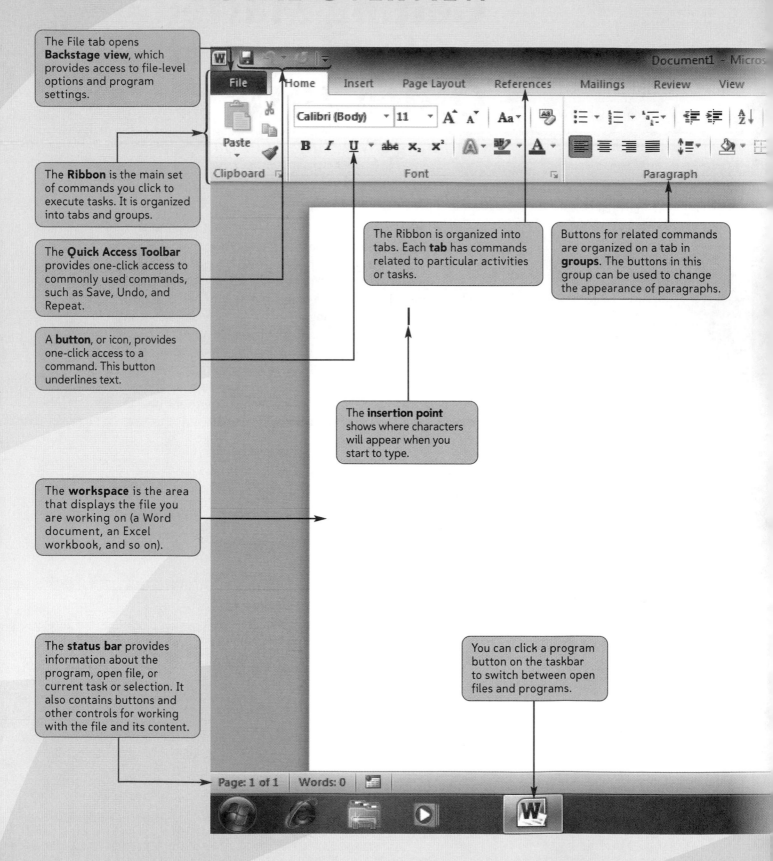

The File tab opens **Backstage view**, which provides access to file-level options and program settings.

The **Ribbon** is the main set of commands you click to execute tasks. It is organized into tabs and groups.

The **Quick Access Toolbar** provides one-click access to commonly used commands, such as Save, Undo, and Repeat.

A **button**, or icon, provides one-click access to a command. This button underlines text.

The **workspace** is the area that displays the file you are working on (a Word document, an Excel workbook, and so on).

The **status bar** provides information about the program, open file, or current task or selection. It also contains buttons and other controls for working with the file and its content.

The Ribbon is organized into tabs. Each **tab** has commands related to particular activities or tasks.

Buttons for related commands are organized on a tab in **groups**. The buttons in this group can be used to change the appearance of paragraphs.

The **insertion point** shows where characters will appear when you start to type.

You can click a program button on the taskbar to switch between open files and programs.

COMMON WINDOW ELEMENTS

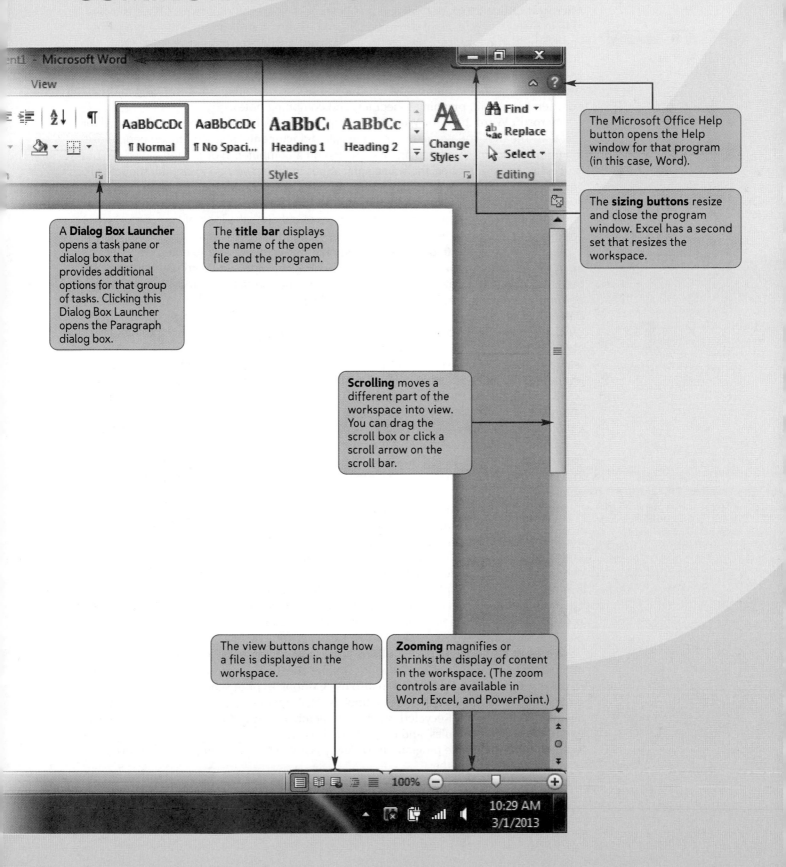

The Microsoft Office Help button opens the Help window for that program (in this case, Word).

The **sizing buttons** resize and close the program window. Excel has a second set that resizes the workspace.

A **Dialog Box Launcher** opens a task pane or dialog box that provides additional options for that group of tasks. Clicking this Dialog Box Launcher opens the Paragraph dialog box.

The **title bar** displays the name of the open file and the program.

Scrolling moves a different part of the workspace into view. You can drag the scroll box or click a scroll arrow on the scroll bar.

The view buttons change how a file is displayed in the workspace.

Zooming magnifies or shrinks the display of content in the workspace. (The zoom controls are available in Word, Excel, and PowerPoint.)

View

AaBbCcDc AaBbCcDc AaBbC AaBbCc
¶ Normal   ¶ No Spaci... Heading 1 Heading 2

Change Styles ▾
Styles

🔍 Find ▾
ab Replace
Select ▾
Editing

100%

10:29 AM
3/1/2013

Exploring Microsoft Office 2010

Microsoft Office 2010, or **Office**, is a collection of Microsoft programs. Office is available in many suites, each of which contains a different combination of these programs. For example, the Professional suite includes Word, Excel, PowerPoint, Access, Outlook, Publisher, and OneNote. Other suites are available and can include more or fewer programs. Each Office program contains valuable tools to help you accomplish many tasks, such as composing reports, analyzing data, preparing presentations, compiling information, sending email, planning schedules, and compiling notes.

Microsoft Word 2010, or **Word**, is a computer program you use to enter, edit, and format text. The files you create in Word are called **documents**, although many people use the term *document* to refer to any file created on a computer. Word, often called a word-processing program, offers many special features that help you compose and update all types of documents, ranging from letters and newsletters to reports, brochures, faxes, and even books, in attractive and readable formats. You can also use Word to create, insert, and position figures, tables, and other graphics to enhance the look of your documents. For example, the Recycled Palette employees create business letters using Word.

Microsoft Excel 2010, or **Excel**, is a computer program you use to enter, calculate, analyze, and present numerical data. You can do some of this in Word with tables, but Excel provides many more tools for recording and formatting numbers as well as performing calculations. The graphics capabilities in Excel also enable you to display data visually. You might, for example, generate a pie chart or a bar chart to help people quickly see the significance of and the connections between information. The files you create in Excel are called **workbooks** (commonly referred to as spreadsheets), and Excel is often called a spreadsheet program. The Recycled Palette accounting department uses a line chart in an Excel workbook to visually track the company's financial performance.

Microsoft Access 2010, or **Access**, is a computer program used to enter, maintain, and retrieve related information (or data) in a format known as a database. The files you create in Access are called **databases**, and Access is often referred to as a database or relational database program. With Access, you can create forms to make data entry easier, and you can create professional reports to improve the readability of your data. The Recycled Palette operations department tracks the company's inventory in an Access database.

Microsoft PowerPoint 2010, or **PowerPoint**, is a computer program you use to create a collection of slides that can contain text, charts, pictures, sound, movies, multimedia, and so on. The files you create in PowerPoint are called **presentations**, and PowerPoint is often called a presentation graphics program. You can show these presentations on your computer monitor, project them onto a screen as a slide show, print them, share them over the Internet, or display them on the Web. You can also use PowerPoint to generate presentation-related documents such as audience handouts, outlines, and speakers' notes. The Recycled Palette marketing department uses a PowerPoint slide presentation to promote its paints.

Microsoft Outlook 2010, or **Outlook**, is a computer program you use to send, receive, and organize email; plan your schedule; arrange meetings; organize contacts; create a to-do list; and record notes. You can also use Outlook to print schedules, task lists, phone directories, and other documents. Outlook is often referred to as an information management program. The Recycled Palette staff members use Outlook to send and receive email, plan their schedules, and create to-do lists.

Although each Office program individually is a strong tool, their potential is even greater when used together.

TIP

For additional information about the available suites, go to the Microsoft Web site.

PROSKILLS

Teamwork: Integrating Office Programs

One of the main advantages of Office is **integration**, the ability to share information between programs. Integration ensures consistency and accuracy, and it saves time because you don't have to reenter the same information in several Office programs. It also means that team members can effortlessly share Office files. Team members can create files based on their skills and information that can be used by others as needed. The staff at Recycled Palette uses the integration features of Office every day, as described in the following examples:

- The accounting department created an Excel bar chart on fourth-quarter results for the previous two years, and inserted it into the quarterly financial report created in Word. The Word report includes a hyperlink that employees can click to open the Excel workbook and view the original data.
- The operations department included an Excel pie chart of sales percentages by paint colors on a PowerPoint slide, which is part of a presentation to stockholders.
- The marketing department produced a mailing to promote its recycled paints to local contractors and designers by combining a form letter created in Word with an Access database that stores the names and addresses of these potential customers.
- A sales representative merged the upcoming promotion letter that the marketing department created in Word with an Outlook contact list containing the names and addresses of prospective customers.

Even these few examples of how information from one Office program can be integrated with another illustrate how integration can save time and effort. Each team member can focus on creating files in the program best suited to convey the information he or she is responsible for. Yet, everyone can share the files, using them as needed for their specific purpose.

Starting Office Programs

You can start any Office program from the Start menu on the taskbar. As soon as the program starts, you can immediately begin to create new files or work with existing ones.

REFERENCE

Starting an Office Program

- On the taskbar, click the Start button.
- On the Start menu, click All Programs, click Microsoft Office, and then click the name of the program to start.

or

- Click the name of the program to start in the left pane of the Start menu.

You'll start Word using the Start button.

To start Word and open a new, blank document:

▶ **1.** Make sure your computer is on and the Windows desktop appears on your screen.

Trouble? If your screen varies slightly from those shown in the figures, your computer might be set up differently. The figures in this book were created while running Windows 7 with the Aero feature turned on, but how your screen looks depends on the version of Windows you are using, the resolution of your screen, and other settings.

▶ **2.** On the taskbar, click the **Start** button 🔵, and then click **All Programs** to display the All Programs list.

▶ **3.** Click **Microsoft Office**, and then point to **Microsoft Word 2010**. Depending on how your computer is set up, your desktop and menu might contain different icons and commands. See Figure 1.

Figure 1	Start menu with All Programs list displayed

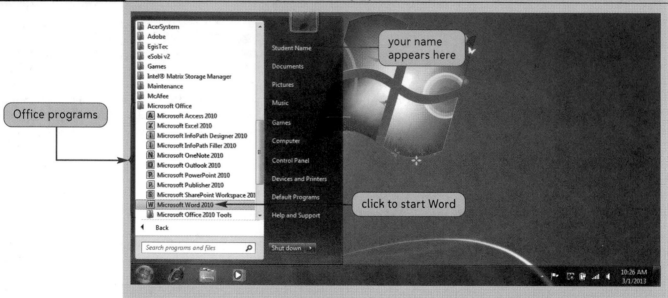

Trouble? If you don't see Microsoft Office on the All Programs list, point to Microsoft Word 2010 on the All Programs menu. If you still don't see Microsoft Word 2010, ask your instructor or technical support person for help.

▶ **4.** Click **Microsoft Word 2010**. Word starts and a new, blank document opens. Refer to the Visual Overview to review the common program window elements.

Trouble? If the Word window doesn't fill your entire screen as shown in the Visual Overview, the window is not maximized, or expanded to its full size. You'll maximize the window shortly.

You can have more than one Office program open at once. You'll use this same method to start Excel and open a new, blank workbook.

To start Excel and open a new, blank workbook:

1. On the taskbar, click the **Start** button , click **All Programs** to display the All Programs list, and then click **Microsoft Office**.

   Trouble? If you don't see Microsoft Office on the All Programs list, point to Microsoft Excel 2010 on the All Programs list. If you still don't see Microsoft Excel 2010, ask your instructor or technical support person for help.

2. Click **Microsoft Excel 2010**. Excel starts and a new, blank workbook opens. See Figure 2.

Figure 2   **New, blank Excel workbook**

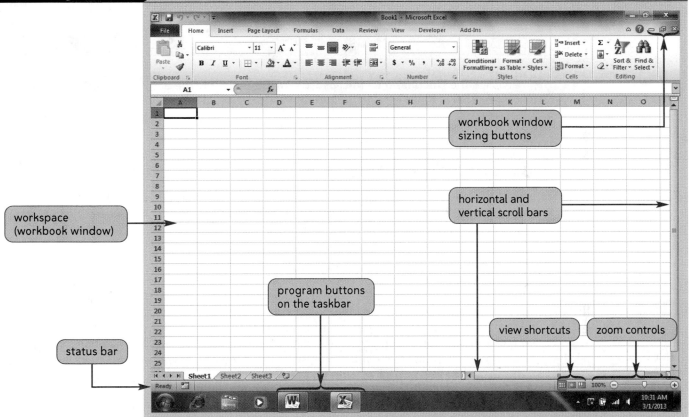

Trouble? If the Excel window doesn't fill your entire screen, the window is not maximized, or expanded to its full size. You'll maximize the window shortly.

Switching Between Open Programs and Files

Two programs are running at the same time—Word and Excel. The taskbar contains buttons for both programs. When you have two or more programs running or two files within the same program open, you can click the program buttons on the taskbar to switch from one program or file to another. When you point to a program button, a thumbnail (or small picture) of each open file in that program is displayed. You can then click the thumbnail of the file you want to make active. The employees at Recycled Palette often work in several programs and files at once.

To switch between the open Word and Excel files:

1. On the taskbar, point to the **Microsoft Word** program button 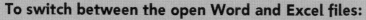. A thumbnail of the open Word document appears. See Figure 3.

Figure 3 **Thumbnail of the open Word document**

click the thumbnail that appears to make the file active

point to the Word program button

Excel program button

2. Click the **Document1 - Microsoft Word** thumbnail. The active program switches from Excel to Word.

Exploring Common Window Elements

As you can see, many elements in both the Word and Excel program windows are the same. In fact, most Office programs have these same elements. Because these elements are the same in each program, after you've learned one program, it's easy to learn the others.

Resizing the Program Window and Workspace

TIP

Excel has two sets of sizing buttons. The top set controls the program window and the bottom set controls the workspace.

There are three different sizing buttons that appear on the right side of a program window's title bar. The Minimize button ▬, which is the left button, hides a window so that only its program button is visible on the taskbar. The middle button changes name and function depending on the status of the window—the Maximize button ☐ expands the window to the full screen size or to the program window size, and the Restore Down button ❐ returns the window to a predefined size. The Close button ✕, on the right, exits the program or closes the file.

The sizing buttons give you the flexibility to arrange the program and file windows to best fit your needs. Most often, you'll want to maximize the program window and workspace to take advantage of the full screen size you have available. If you have several files open, you might want to restore down their windows so that you can see more than one window at a time, or you might want to minimize programs or files you are not working on at the moment.

To resize the windows and workspaces:

1. On the Word title bar, click the **Minimize** button ▬. The Word program window is reduced to a taskbar button. The Excel program window is visible again.

2. On the Excel title bar, click the **Maximize** button ☐ to expand the Excel program window to fill the screen, if necessary.

3. In the bottom set of Excel sizing buttons, click the **Restore Window** button ⊡. The workspace is resized smaller than the full program window. See Figure 4.

Figure 4 **Resized Excel window and workspace**

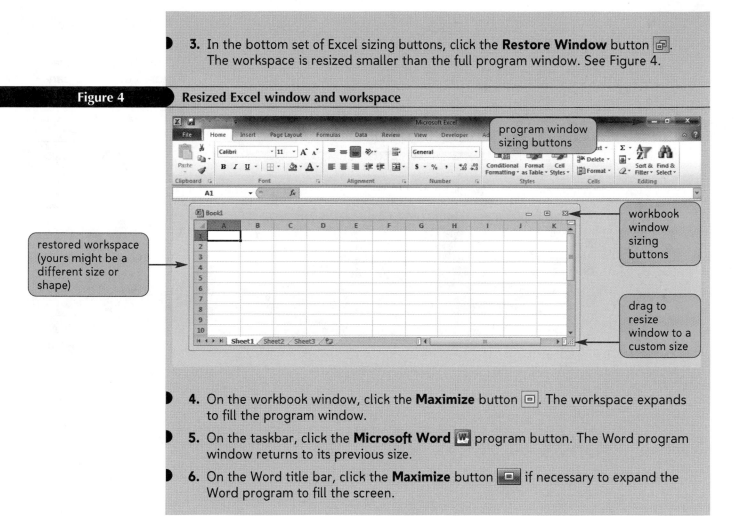

program window sizing buttons

restored workspace (yours might be a different size or shape)

workbook window sizing buttons

drag to resize window to a custom size

4. On the workbook window, click the **Maximize** button ▫. The workspace expands to fill the program window.

5. On the taskbar, click the **Microsoft Word** 📄 program button. The Word program window returns to its previous size.

6. On the Word title bar, click the **Maximize** button ▫ if necessary to expand the Word program to fill the screen.

Switching Views

Each program has a variety of views, or ways to display the file in the workspace. For example, Word has five views: Print Layout, Full Screen Reading, Web Layout, Outline, and Draft. The content of the file doesn't change from view to view, although the presentation of the content does. In Word, for example, Print Layout view shows how the document would appear as a printed page, whereas Web Layout view shows how the document would appear as a Web page. You'll change views in later tutorials.

Zooming and Scrolling

You can zoom in to get a closer look at the content of an open document, worksheet, slide, or database report. Likewise, you can zoom out to see more of the content at a smaller size. You can select a specific percentage or size based on your file. The zoom percentage can range from 10 percent to 400 percent (Excel and PowerPoint) or 500 percent (Word). The figures shown in these tutorials show the workspace zoomed in to enhance readability. Zooming can shift part of the workspace out of view. To change which area of the workspace is visible in the program window, you can use the scroll bars. A scroll bar has arrow buttons that you can click to shift the workspace a small amount in the specified direction and a scroll box that you can drag to shift the workspace a larger amount in the direction you drag. Depending on the program and zoom level, you might see a vertical scroll bar, a horizontal scroll bar, or both.

To zoom and scroll in Word and Excel:

1. On the Word status bar, drag the **Zoom slider** ▽ to the left until the percentage is **10%**. The document is reduced to its smallest size, which makes the entire page visible but unreadable. See Figure 5.

| Figure 5 | Word zoom level set to 10% |

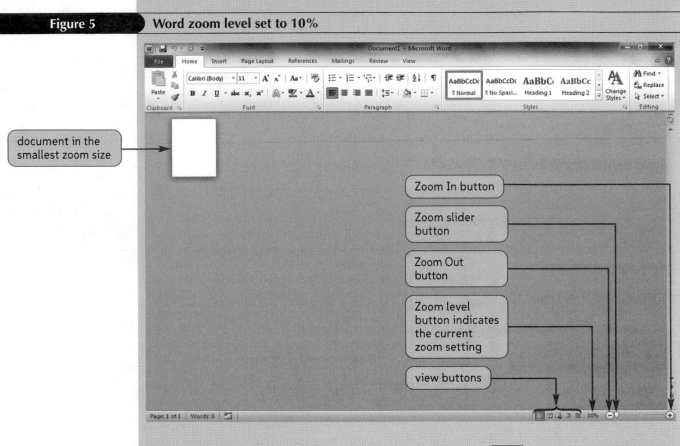

document in the smallest zoom size

Zoom In button

Zoom slider button

Zoom Out button

Zoom level button indicates the current zoom setting

view buttons

2. On the Word status bar, click the **Zoom level** button 10%. The Zoom dialog box opens. See Figure 6.

| Figure 6 | Zoom dialog box |

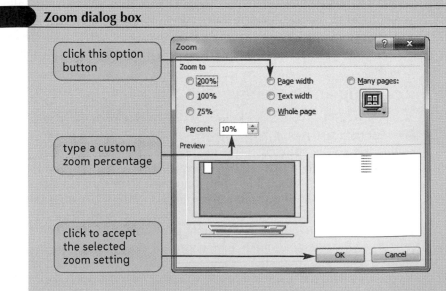

click this option button

type a custom zoom percentage

click to accept the selected zoom setting

3. Click the **Page width** option button, and then click the **OK** button. The Word document is magnified to its page width, which matches how the Word figures appear in the tutorials.

4. On the taskbar, click the **Microsoft Excel** program button 🔣. The Excel program window is displayed.

5. On the status bar, click the **Zoom In** button ⊕ twice. The worksheet is magnified to 120%, which is the zoom level that matches the Excel figures shown in the tutorials.

6. On the horizontal scroll bar, click the **right arrow** button ▶ twice. The worksheet shifts two columns to the right. Columns A and B (labeled by letter at the top of the columns) shift out of view and two other columns shift into view.

7. On the horizontal scroll bar, drag the **scroll box** all the way to the left. The worksheet shifts left to display columns A and B again.

8. On the taskbar, click the **Microsoft Word** program button 📝. The Word program window is displayed.

Using the Ribbon

TIP

To view more workspace, click the Minimize the Ribbon button, located below the sizing buttons, to reduce the Ribbon to a single line. Click the Expand the Ribbon button to redisplay the full Ribbon.

Although the tabs on the Ribbon differ from program to program, each program has two tabs in common. The first tab on the Ribbon, the File tab, opens Backstage view. Backstage view provides access to file-level features, such as creating new files, opening existing files, saving files, printing files, and closing files, as well as the most common program options. The second tab in each program—called the Home tab—contains the commands for the most frequently performed activities, including cutting and pasting, changing fonts, and using editing tools. In addition, the Insert, Review, and View tabs appear on the Ribbon in all Office programs except Access, although the commands they include might differ from program to program. Other tabs are program specific, such as the Design tab in PowerPoint and the Datasheet Tools tab in Access.

To use the Ribbon tabs:

1. In Word, point to the **Insert** tab on the Ribbon. The Insert tab is highlighted, though the Home tab with the options for using the Clipboard and formatting text remains visible.

2. Click the **Insert** tab. The Insert tab is displayed on the Ribbon. This tab provides access to all the options for adding objects such as shapes, pages, tables, illustrations, text, and symbols to a document. See Figure 7.

Figure 7	Insert tab on the Ribbon in Word

Insert tab selected

3. Click the **Home** tab. The Home tab options appear on the Ribbon.

Clicking Buttons

For the most part, when you click a button, something happens in the file. For example, the Clipboard group on the Home tab includes the Cut, Copy, Paste, and Format Painter buttons, which you can click to move or copy text, objects, and formatting.

Buttons can be **toggles**: one click turns the feature on and the next click turns the feature off. While the feature is on, the button remains colored or highlighted. For example, on the Home tab in Word, the Show/Hide ¶ button in the Paragraph group displays the nonprinting characters when toggled on and hides them when toggled off.

Some buttons have two parts: a button that accesses a command, and an arrow that opens a menu of all the commands or options available for that task. For example, the Paste button in the Clipboard group on the Home tab includes the Paste command and an arrow to access all the Paste commands and options. To select one of these commands or options, you click the button arrow and then click the command or option.

INSIGHT

How Buttons and Groups Appear on the Ribbon

The buttons and groups on the Ribbon change based on your monitor size, your screen resolution, and the size of the program window. With smaller monitors, lower screen resolutions, and reduced program windows, buttons can appear as icons without labels and a group can be condensed into a button that you click to display the group options. The figures in these tutorials were created using a screen resolution of 1024 × 768 and, unless otherwise specified, the program and workspace windows are maximized. If you are using a different screen resolution or window size, the buttons on the Ribbon might show more or fewer button names, and some groups might be reduced to a button.

You'll type text in the Word document, and then use the buttons on the Ribbon.

To use buttons on the Ribbon:

1. Type **Meeting Agenda** and then press the **Enter** key. The text appears in the first line of the document and the insertion point moves to the second line.

   Trouble? If you make a typing error, press the Backspace key to delete the incorrect letters, and then retype the text.

2. In the Paragraph group on the Home tab, click the **Show/Hide ¶** button ¶. The nonprinting characters appear in the document, and the Show/Hide ¶ button remains toggled on. See Figure 8.

Figure 8   **Button toggled on**

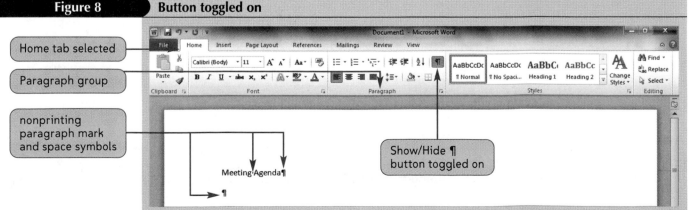

Home tab selected

Paragraph group

nonprinting paragraph mark and space symbols

Show/Hide ¶ button toggled on

Meeting·Agenda¶

Trouble? If the nonprinting characters disappear from your screen, the Show/Hide ¶ button was already on. Repeat Step 2 to show nonprinting characters.

▶ **3.** Position the insertion point to the left of the word "Meeting," press and hold the left mouse button, drag the pointer across the text of the first line but not the paragraph mark to highlight the text, and then release the mouse button. All the text in the first line of the document (but not the paragraph mark ¶) is selected.

▶ **4.** In the Clipboard group on the Home tab, click the **Copy** button 📋. The selected text is copied to the Clipboard.

▶ **5.** Press the ↓ key. The text is deselected (no longer highlighted), and the insertion point moves to the second line in the document.

▶ **6.** In the Clipboard group on the Home tab, point to the top part of the **Paste** button 📋. Both parts of the Paste button are outlined in yellow, but the icon at the top is highlighted to indicate that it will be selected if you click the mouse button.

▶ **7.** Point to the **Paste button arrow**. The button is outlined and the button arrow is highlighted.

▶ **8.** Click the **Paste button arrow**. The paste commands and options are displayed. See Figure 9.

Figure 9	Two-part Paste button

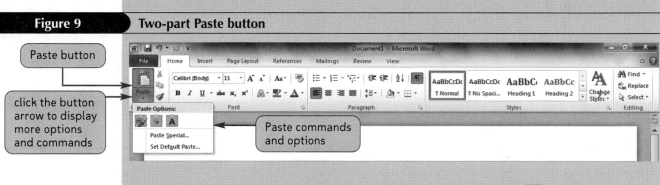

Paste button

click the button arrow to display more options and commands

Paste commands and options

▶ **9.** On the Paste Options menu, click the **Keep Text Only** button Ⓐ. The menu closes, and the text is duplicated in the second line of the document. The Paste Options button 📋(Ctrl)▾ appears below the duplicated text, providing access to the same paste commands and options.

Using Keyboard Shortcuts and Key Tips

INSIGHT

Keyboard shortcuts can help you work faster and more efficiently. A **keyboard shortcut** is a key or combination of keys you press to access a feature or perform a command. You can use these shortcuts to access options on the Ribbon, on the Quick Access Toolbar, and in Backstage view without removing your hands from the keyboard. To access the options on the Ribbon, press the Alt key. A label, called a Key Tip, appears over each tab. To select a tab, press the corresponding key. The tab is displayed on the Ribbon and Key Tips appear over each available button or option on that tab. Press the appropriate key or keys to select a button.

You can also press combinations of keys to perform specific commands. For example, Ctrl+S is the keyboard shortcut for the Save command (you press and hold the Ctrl key while you press the S key). This type of keyboard shortcut appears in ScreenTips next to the command's name. Not all commands have this type of keyboard shortcut. Identical commands in each Office program use the same keyboard shortcut.

Using Galleries and Live Preview

Galleries and Live Preview let you quickly see how your file will be affected by a selection. A **gallery** is a menu or grid that shows a visual representation of the options available for a button. For example, the Bullet Library gallery in Word shows an icon of each bullet style you can select. Some galleries include a More button ⬇ that you click to expand the gallery to see all the options it contains. When you point to an option in a gallery, **Live Preview** shows the results that would occur in your file if you clicked that option. To continue the bullets example, when you point to a bullet style in the Bullet Library gallery, the selected text or the paragraph in which the insertion point is located appears with that bullet style. By moving the pointer from option to option, you can quickly see the text set with different bullet styles; you can then click the style you want.

To use the Bullet Library gallery and Live Preview:

1. In the Paragraph group on the Home tab, click the **Bullets button arrow** ☰ ▾. The Bullet Library gallery opens.

2. Point to the **check mark bullet** style ✓. Live Preview shows the selected bullet style in your document. See Figure 10.

Figure 10	Live Preview of bullet icon

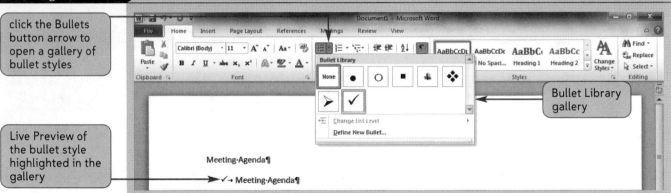

click the Bullets button arrow to open a gallery of bullet styles

Bullet Library gallery

Live Preview of the bullet style highlighted in the gallery

3. Place the pointer over each of the remaining bullet styles and preview them in your document.

4. Click the **check mark bullet** style ✓. The Bullet Library gallery closes, and the check mark bullet is added to the line, which is indented. The Bullets button remains toggled on when the insertion point is in the line with the bullet.

5. On the second line, next to the check mark bullet, select **Meeting Agenda**. The two words are highlighted to indicate they are selected.

6. Type **Brainstorm names for the new paint colors.** to replace the selected text with an agenda item.

7. Press the **Enter** key twice to end the bulleted list.

Opening Dialog Boxes and Task Panes

The button to the right of some group names is the Dialog Box Launcher 🔲, which opens a task pane or dialog box related to that group of tasks. A **task pane** is a window that helps you navigate through a complex task or feature. For example, you can use the Clipboard task pane to paste some or all of the items that were cut or copied from any Office program during the current work session. A **dialog box** is a window from which you enter or choose settings for how you want to perform a task. For example, the Page Setup dialog box in Word contains options to change how the document looks. Some dialog boxes organize related information into tabs, and related options and settings are organized into groups, just as they are on the Ribbon. You select settings in a dialog box using option buttons, check boxes, text boxes, and lists to specify how you want to perform a task. In Excel, you'll use the Dialog Box Launcher to open the Page Setup dialog box.

To open the Page Setup dialog box using the Dialog Box Launcher:

1. On the taskbar, click the **Microsoft Excel** program button 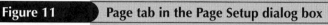 to switch from Word to Excel.

2. On the Ribbon, click the **Page Layout** tab. The page layout options appear on the Ribbon.

3. In the Page Setup group, click the **Dialog Box Launcher**. The Page Setup dialog box opens with the Page tab displayed. See Figure 11.

| Figure 11 | Page tab in the Page Setup dialog box |

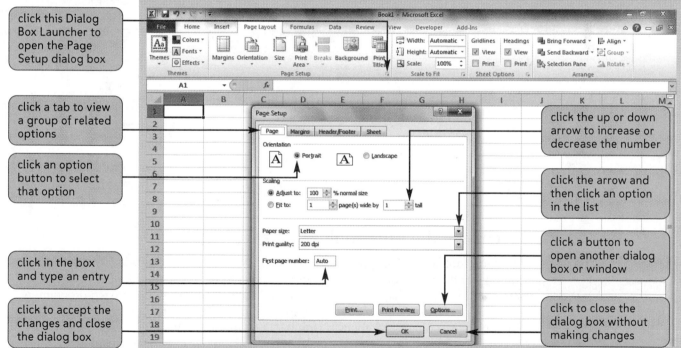

click this Dialog Box Launcher to open the Page Setup dialog box

click a tab to view a group of related options

click an option button to select that option

click in the box and type an entry

click to accept the changes and close the dialog box

click the up or down arrow to increase or decrease the number

click the arrow and then click an option in the list

click a button to open another dialog box or window

click to close the dialog box without making changes

4. Click the **Landscape** option button. The workbook's page orientation changes to a page wider than it is long.

5. Click the **Sheet** tab. The dialog box displays options related to the worksheet. You can click a check box to turn an option on (checked) or off (unchecked).

6. In the Print section of the dialog box, click the **Gridlines** check box and the **Row and column headings** check box. Check marks appear in both check boxes, indicating that these options are selected.

7. Click the **Cancel** button. The dialog box closes without making any changes to the page setup.

TIP

You can check more than one check box in a group, but you can select only one option button in a group.

Using Contextual Tools

Some tabs, toolbars, and menus come into view as you work. Because these tools become available only as you might need them, the workspace remains less cluttered. However, tools that appear and disappear as you work can take some getting used to.

Displaying Contextual Tabs

Any object that you can select in a file has a related contextual tab. An **object** is anything that appears on your screen that can be selected and manipulated, such as a table, a picture, a shape, a chart, or an equation. A **contextual tab** is a Ribbon tab that contains commands related to the selected object so you can manipulate, edit, and format that object. Contextual tabs appear to the right of the standard Ribbon tabs just below a title label. For example, Figure 12 shows the Table Tools contextual tabs that appear when you select a table in a Word document. Although contextual tabs appear only when you select an object, they function in the same way as standard tabs on the Ribbon. Contextual tabs disappear when you click elsewhere on the screen, deselecting the object. Contextual tabs can also appear as you switch views. You'll use contextual tabs in later tutorials.

Figure 12 Table Tools contextual tabs

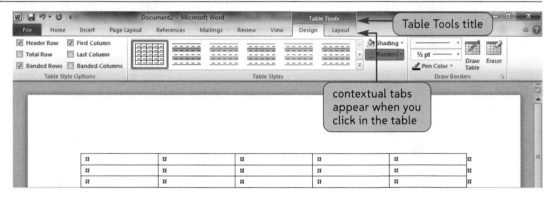

Accessing the Mini Toolbar

The **Mini toolbar**, which appears next to the pointer whenever you select text, contains buttons for the most commonly used formatting commands, such as font, font size, styles, color, alignment, and indents. The Mini toolbar buttons differ in each program. A transparent version of the Mini toolbar appears immediately after you select text. When you move the pointer over the Mini toolbar, it comes into full view so you can click the appropriate formatting button or buttons. The Mini toolbar disappears if you move the pointer away from the toolbar, press a key, or click in the workspace. The Mini toolbar can help you format your text faster, but initially you might find that the toolbar disappears unexpectedly. All the commands on the Mini toolbar are also available on the Ribbon. Note that Live Preview does not work with the Mini toolbar.

You'll use the Mini toolbar to format text you enter in the workbook.

To use the Mini toolbar to format text:

1. If necessary, click cell **A1** (the rectangle in the upper-left corner of the worksheet).

2. Type **Budget**. The text appears in the cell.

3. Press the **Enter** key. The text is entered in cell A1 and cell A2 is selected.

4. Type **2013** and then press the **Enter** key. The year is entered in cell A2 and cell A3 is selected.

5. Double-click cell **A1** to place the insertion point in the cell. Now you can select the text you typed.

6. Double-click **Budget** in cell A1. The selected text appears white with a black background, and the transparent Mini toolbar appears directly above the selected text. See Figure 13.

| Figure 13 | Transparent Mini toolbar |

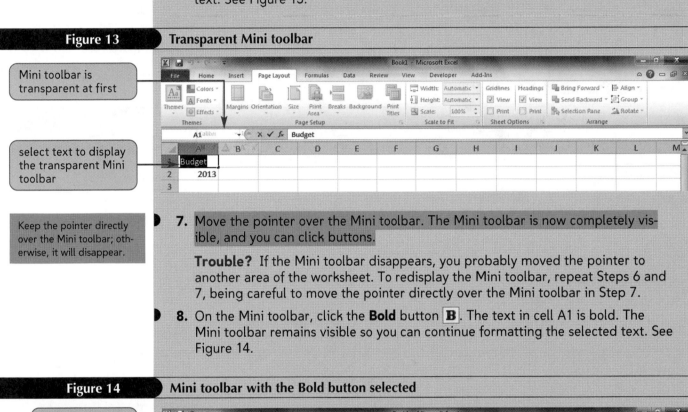

Mini toolbar is transparent at first

select text to display the transparent Mini toolbar

Keep the pointer directly over the Mini toolbar; otherwise, it will disappear.

7. Move the pointer over the Mini toolbar. The Mini toolbar is now completely visible, and you can click buttons.

   Trouble? If the Mini toolbar disappears, you probably moved the pointer to another area of the worksheet. To redisplay the Mini toolbar, repeat Steps 6 and 7, being careful to move the pointer directly over the Mini toolbar in Step 7.

8. On the Mini toolbar, click the **Bold** button **B**. The text in cell A1 is bold. The Mini toolbar remains visible so you can continue formatting the selected text. See Figure 14.

| Figure 14 | Mini toolbar with the Bold button selected |

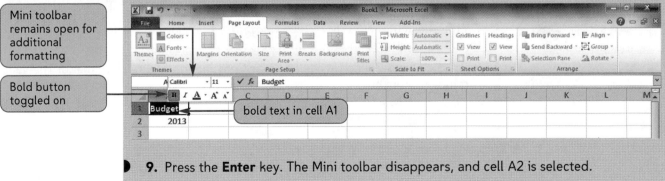

Mini toolbar remains open for additional formatting

Bold button toggled on

bold text in cell A1

9. Press the **Enter** key. The Mini toolbar disappears, and cell A2 is selected.

Opening Shortcut Menus

A **shortcut menu** is a list of commands related to a selection that opens when you click the right mouse button. Shortcut menus enable you to quickly access commands that you're most likely to need in the context of the task you're performing without using the tabs on the Ribbon. The shortcut menu includes commands that perform actions, commands that open dialog boxes, and galleries of options that provide Live Preview. The Mini toolbar also opens when you right-click. If you click a button on the Mini toolbar, the rest of the shortcut menu closes while the Mini toolbar remains open so you can continue formatting the selection. For example, you can right-click selected text to open a shortcut menu with a Mini toolbar; the menu will contain text-related commands such as Cut, Copy, and Paste, as well as other program-specific commands.

You'll use a shortcut menu to delete the content you entered in cell A1.

To use a shortcut menu to delete content:

1. Right-click cell **A1**. A shortcut menu opens, listing commands related to common tasks you'd perform in a cell, along with the Mini toolbar. See Figure 15.

Figure 15   Shortcut menu with Mini toolbar

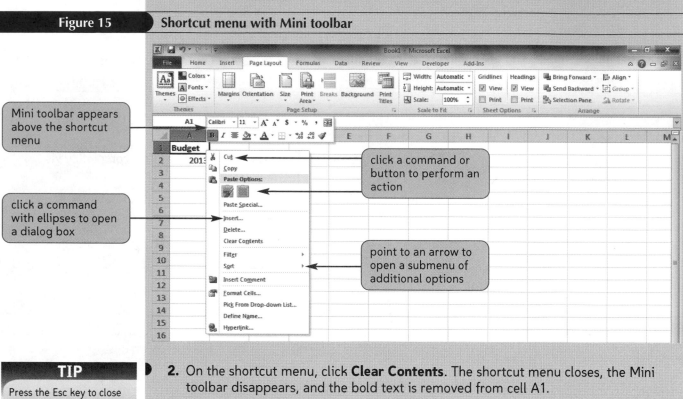

Mini toolbar appears above the shortcut menu

click a command with ellipses to open a dialog box

click a command or button to perform an action

point to an arrow to open a submenu of additional options

TIP
Press the Esc key to close an open menu, shortcut menu, list, or gallery without selecting an option.

2. On the shortcut menu, click **Clear Contents**. The shortcut menu closes, the Mini toolbar disappears, and the bold text is removed from cell A1.

3. Right-click cell **A2**, and then click **Clear Contents** on the shortcut menu. The year is removed from cell A2.

Working with Files

The most common tasks you perform in any Office program are to create, open, save, and close files. All of these tasks can be done from Backstage view, and the processes for these tasks are basically the same in all Office programs. To begin working in a program, you need to create a new file or open an existing file. When you start Word, Excel, or PowerPoint, the program opens along with a blank file—ready for you to begin working on a new document, workbook, or presentation. When you start Access, the New tab in Backstage view opens, displaying options for creating a new database or opening an existing one.

Saving a File

As you create and modify an Office file, your work is stored only in the computer's temporary memory, not on a hard drive. If you were to exit the program without saving, turn off your computer, or experience a power failure, your work would be lost. To prevent losing work, save your file frequently—at least every 10 minutes. You can save files to the hard drive located inside your computer, an external hard drive, a network storage drive, or a portable storage drive such as a USB flash drive.

To save a file, you can click either the Save button on the Quick Access Toolbar or the Save command in Backstage view. If it is the first time you are saving a file, the Save As dialog box will open so that you can specify save options. You can also click the Save As command in Backstage view to open the Save As dialog box, in which you can name the file you are saving and specify a location to save it.

The first time you save a file, you need to name it. This **filename** includes a title you specify and a file extension assigned by Office to indicate the file type. You should specify a descriptive title that accurately reflects the content of the document, workbook, presentation, or database, such as "Shipping Options Letter" or "Fourth Quarter Financial Analysis." Your descriptive title can include uppercase and lowercase letters, numbers, hyphens, and spaces in any combination, but not the special characters ? " / \ < > * | and :. Each filename ends with a **file extension**, which is a period followed by several characters that Office adds to your descriptive title to identify the program in which that file was created. The default file extensions for Office 2010 are .docx for Word, .xlsx for Excel, .pptx for PowerPoint, and .accdb for Access. Filenames (the descriptive title and extension) can include a maximum of 255 characters. You might see file extensions depending on how Windows is set up on your computer. The figures in these tutorials do not show file extensions.

You also need to decide where to save the file—on which drive and in what folder. A **folder** is a container for your files. Just as you organize paper documents within folders stored in a filing cabinet, you can organize your files within folders stored on your computer's hard drive or on a removable drive such as a USB flash drive. Store each file in a logical location that you will remember whenever you want to use the file again. The default storage location for Office files is the Documents folder; you can create additional storage folders within that folder or navigate to a new location.

REFERENCE

Saving a File

To save a file the first time or with a new name or location:
- Click the File tab to open Backstage view, and then click the Save As command in the navigation bar (for an unnamed file, click the Save command or click the Save button on the Quick Access Toolbar).
- In the Save As dialog box, navigate to the location where you want to save the file.
- Type a descriptive title in the File name box, and then click the Save button.

To resave a named file to the same location with the same name:
- On the Quick Access Toolbar, click the Save button.

The text you typed in the Word window needs to be saved.

To save a file for the first time:

1. On the taskbar, click the **Microsoft Word** program button [W]. Word becomes the active program.

2. On the Ribbon, click the **File** tab. Backstage view opens with commands and tabs for creating new files, opening existing files, and saving, printing, and closing files. See Figure 16.

Figure 16	Backstage view

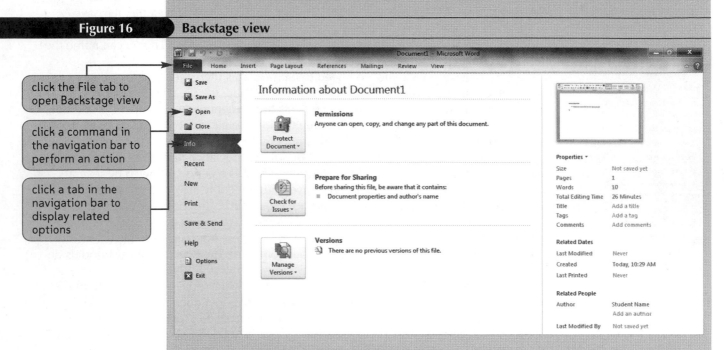

click the File tab to open Backstage view

click a command in the navigation bar to perform an action

click a tab in the navigation bar to display related options

3. In the navigation bar, click the **Save As** command. The Save As dialog box opens because you have not yet saved the file and need to specify a storage location and filename. The default location is set to the Documents folder, and the first few words of the first line appear in the File name box as a suggested title.

4. In the Navigation pane along the left side of the dialog box, click the link for the location that contains your Data Files, if necessary.

   Trouble? If you don't have the starting Data Files, you need to get them before you can proceed. Your instructor will either give you the Data Files or ask you to obtain them from a specified location (such as a network drive). In either case, make a backup copy of the Data Files before you start so that you will have the original files available in case you need to start over. If you have any questions about the Data Files, see your instructor or technical support person for assistance.

5. In the file list, double-click the **Office** folder, and then double-click the **Tutorial** folder. This is the location where you want to save the document.

6. Type **Agenda** in the File name box. This descriptive filename will help you more easily identify the file. See Figure 17 (your file path may differ).

Figure 17   **Completed Save As dialog box**

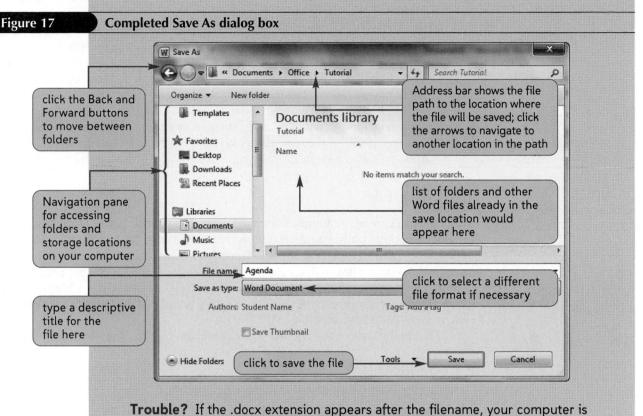

click the Back and Forward buttons to move between folders

Navigation pane for accessing folders and storage locations on your computer

type a descriptive title for the file here

Address bar shows the file path to the location where the file will be saved; click the arrows to navigate to another location in the path

list of folders and other Word files already in the save location would appear here

click to select a different file format if necessary

click to save the file

Trouble? If the .docx extension appears after the filename, your computer is configured to show file extensions. Continue with Step 7.

▶ **7.** Click the **Save** button. The Save As dialog box closes, and the name of your file appears in the Word window title bar.

The saved file includes everything in the document at the time you last saved it. Any new edits or additions you make to the document exist only in the computer's memory and are not saved in the file on the drive. As you work, remember to save frequently so that the file is updated to reflect the latest content.

Because you already named the document and selected a storage location, you don't need to use the Save As dialog box unless you want to save a copy of the file with a different filename or to a different location. If you do, the previous version of the file remains on your drive as well.

You need to add your name to the agenda. Then, you'll save your changes.

To modify and save the Agenda document:

▶ **1.** Type your name, and then press the **Enter** key. The text you typed appears on the next line.

▶ **2.** On the Quick Access Toolbar, click the **Save** button 🖫. The changes you made to the document are saved in the file stored on the drive.

Saving Files Before Closing

As a standard practice, you should save files before closing them. However, Office has an added safeguard: if you attempt to close a file without saving your changes, a dialog box opens, asking whether you want to save the file. Click the Save button to save the changes to the file before closing the file and program. Click the Don't Save button to close the file and program without saving changes. Click the Cancel button to return to the program window without saving changes or closing the file and program. This feature helps to ensure that you always save the most current version of any file.

Closing a File

Although you can keep multiple files open at one time, you should close any file you are no longer working on to conserve system resources as well as to ensure that you don't inadvertently make changes to the file. You can close a file by clicking the Close command in Backstage view. If that's the only file open for the program, the program window remains open and no file appears in the window. You can also close a file by clicking the Close button in the upper-right corner of the title bar. If that's the only file open for the program, the program also closes.

You'll add the date to the agenda. Then, you'll attempt to close it without saving.

To modify and close the Agenda document:

▶ **1.** Type today's date, and then press the **Enter** key. The text you typed appears below your name in the document.

▶ **2.** On the Ribbon, click the **File** tab to open Backstage view, and then click the **Close** command in the navigation bar. A dialog box opens, asking whether you want to save the changes you made to the document.

▶ **3.** Click the **Save** button. The current version of the document is saved to the file, and then the document closes. Word is still open, so you can create additional new files in the open program or you can open previously created and saved files.

Opening a File

When you want to open a blank document, workbook, presentation, or database, you create a new file. When you want to work on a previously created file, you must first open it. Opening a file transfers a copy of the file from the storage location (either a hard drive or a portable drive) to the computer's memory and displays it on your screen. The file is then in your computer's memory and on the drive.

REFERENCE

Opening an Existing File

- Click the File tab to open Backstage view, and then click the Open command in the navigation bar.
- In the Open dialog box, navigate to the storage location of the file you want to open.
- Click the filename of the file you want to open.
- Click the Open button.
- If necessary, click the Enable Editing button in the Information Bar.

or

- Click the File tab, and then click the Recent tab in the navigation bar.
- Click a filename in the Recent list.

Any file you open that was downloaded from the Internet, accessed from a shared network, or received as an email attachment might open in a read-only format, called **Protected View**. In Protected View, you can see the file contents, but you cannot edit, save, or print them until you enable editing. To do so, click the Enable Editing button on the Information Bar, as shown in Figure 18.

Figure 18 **Protected View warning**

You need to print the meeting agenda you typed for Ean. To do that, you'll reopen the Agenda document.

To open the Agenda document:

1. On the Ribbon, click the **File** tab to display Backstage view.

2. In the navigation bar, click the **Open** command. The Open dialog box, which works similarly to the Save As dialog box, opens.

3. In the Open dialog box, use the Navigation pane or the Address bar to navigate to the **Office\Tutorial** folder included with your Data Files. This is the location where you saved the Agenda document.

4. In the file list, click **Agenda**. See Figure 19.

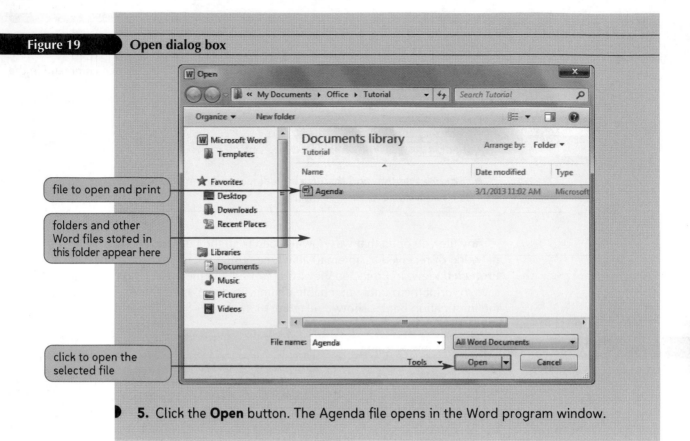

Figure 19   Open dialog box

file to open and print

folders and other Word files stored in this folder appear here

click to open the selected file

5. Click the **Open** button. The Agenda file opens in the Word program window.

Sharing Files Using Windows Live SkyDrive

Often the purpose of creating a file is to share it with other people—sending it attached to an email message for someone else to read or use, collaborating with others on the same document, or posting it as a blog for others to review. You can do all of these things in Backstage view from the Save & Send tab.

When you send a file using email, you can attach a copy of the file, send a link to the file, or attach a copy of the file in a PDF or another file format. You can also save to online workspaces where you can make the file available to others for review and collaboration. The Save to Web option on the Save & Send tab in Backstage view gives you access to **Windows Live SkyDrive**, which is an online workspace provided by Microsoft; your personal workspace comes with a Public folder for saving files to share as well as a My Documents folder for saving files you want to keep private. (SkyDrive is not available for Access.) Figure 20 shows the Save to Web options on the Save & Send tab in Backstage view of Word. SharePoint is an online workspace set up by an organization, such as a school, business, or nonprofit group.

Files saved to an online workspace can be worked on by more than one person at the same time. The changes are recorded in the files with each author's name and the date of the change. A Web browser is used to access and edit the files. You choose who can have access to the files.

| Figure 20 | Save to Web options on the Save & Send tab |

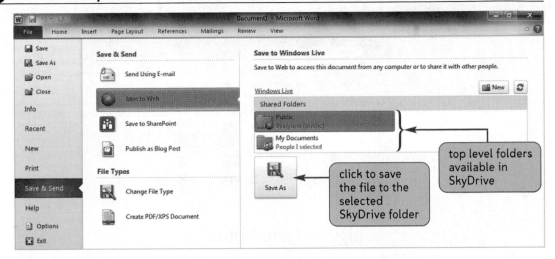

Saving a File to SkyDrive

- Click the File tab to open Backstage view, and then click the Save & Send tab in the navigation bar.
- In the center pane, click Save to Web.
- In the right pane, click the Sign In button, and then use your Windows Live ID to log on to your Windows Live SkyDrive account.

Getting Help

If you don't know how to perform a task or want more information about a feature, you can turn to Office itself for information on how to use it. This information is referred to simply as **Help**. You can get Help in ScreenTips and from the Help window.

Viewing ScreenTips

ScreenTips are a fast and simple method you can use to get information about objects you see on the screen. A **ScreenTip** is a box with descriptive text about an object or button. Just point to a button or object to display its ScreenTip. In addition to the button's name, a ScreenTip might include the button's keyboard shortcut if it has one, a description of the command's function, and, in some cases, a link to more information so that you can press the F1 key while the ScreenTip is displayed to open the Help window with the relevant topic displayed.

To view ScreenTips:

1. Point to the **Microsoft Office Word Help** button 🔘. The ScreenTip shows the button's name, its keyboard shortcut, and a brief description. See Figure 21.

Figure 21   **ScreenTip for the Help button**

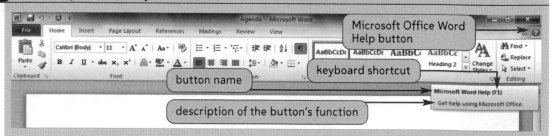

2. Point to other buttons on the Ribbon to display their ScreenTips.

Using the Help Window

For more detailed information, you can use the **Help window** to access all the Help topics, templates, and training installed on your computer with Office and available on Office.com. **Office.com** is a Web site maintained by Microsoft that provides access to the latest information and additional Help resources. For example, you can access current Help topics and training for Office. To connect to Office.com, you need to be able to access the Internet from your computer. Otherwise, you see only topics that are stored on your computer.

Each program has its own Help window from which you can find information about all of the Office commands and features as well as step-by-step instructions for using them. There are two ways to find Help topics—the search function and a topic list.

The Type words to search for box enables you to search the Help system for a task or a topic you need help with. You can click a link to open a Help topic with explanations and step-by-step instructions for a specific procedure. The Table of Contents pane displays the Help system content organized by subjects and topics, similar to a book's table of contents. You click main subject links to display related topic links. You click a topic link to display that Help topic in the Help window.

REFERENCE

Getting Help

- Click the Microsoft Office Help button (the button name depends on the Office program).
- Type a keyword or phrase in the Type words to search for box, click the Search button, and then click a Help topic in the search results list.
  or
  In the Table of Contents pane, click a "book," and then click a Help topic.
- Read the information in the Help window and then click other topics or links.
- On the Help window title bar, click the Close button.

You'll use Help to get information about printing a document in Word.

To search Help for information about printing:

1. Click the **Microsoft Office Word Help** button ⬛. The Word Help window opens.

2. If the Table of Contents pane is not open on the left side of the Help window, click the **Show Table of Contents** button 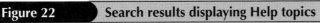 on the toolbar to display the pane.

3. Click the **Type words to search for** box, if necessary, and then type **print document**. You can specify where you want to search.

4. Click the **Search button arrow**. The Search menu shows the online and local content available.

5. If your computer is connected to the Internet, click **All Word** in the Content from Office.com list. If your computer is not connected to the Internet, click **Word Help** in the Content from this computer list.

6. Click the **Search** button. The Help window displays a list of topics related to the keywords "print document" in the left pane. See Figure 22.

Figure 22	Search results displaying Help topics

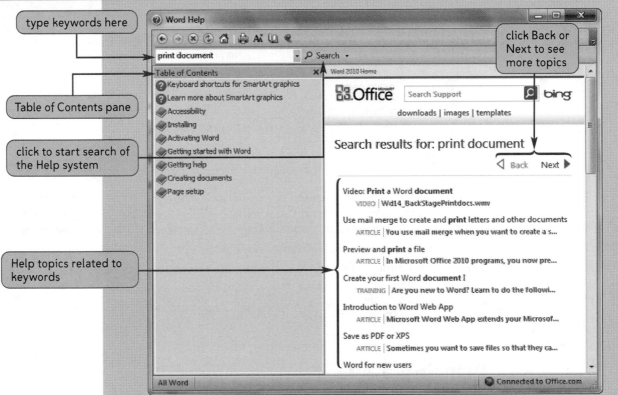

Trouble? If your search results list differs from the one shown in Figure 22, your computer is not connected to the Internet or Microsoft has updated the list of available Help topics since this book was published. Continue with Step 7.

7. Scroll through the list to review the Help topics.

8. Click **Preview and print a file**. The topic content is displayed in the Help window so you can learn more about how to print a document. See Figure 23.

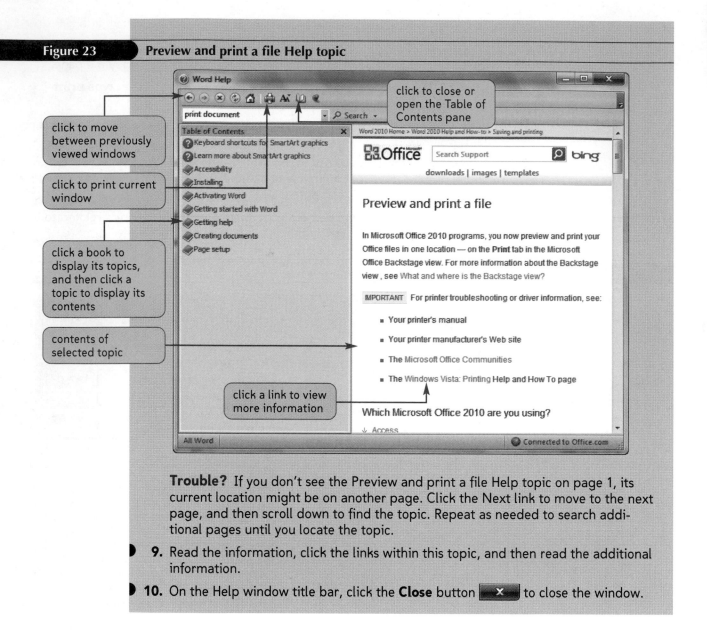

Figure 23   Preview and print a file Help topic

Trouble? If you don't see the Preview and print a file Help topic on page 1, its current location might be on another page. Click the Next link to move to the next page, and then scroll down to find the topic. Repeat as needed to search additional pages until you locate the topic.

9. Read the information, click the links within this topic, and then read the additional information.

10. On the Help window title bar, click the **Close** button [X] to close the window.

Printing a File

At times, you'll want a paper copy of Office files. Whenever you print, you should review and adjust the printing settings as needed. You can select the number of copies to print, the printer, the portion of the file to print, and so forth; the printing settings vary slightly from program to program. You should also check the file's print preview to ensure that the file will print as you intended. This simple review will help you to avoid reprinting, which requires additional paper, ink, and energy resources.

Printing a File

- On the Ribbon, click the File tab to open Backstage view.
- In the navigation bar, click the Print tab.
- Verify the print settings and review the print preview.
- Click the Print button.

You will print the agenda for Ean.

To print the Agenda document:

1. Make sure your printer is turned on and contains paper.

2. On the Ribbon, click the **File** tab to open Backstage view.

3. In the navigation bar, click the **Print** tab. The print settings and preview appear. See Figure 24.

Figure 24 | **Print tab in Backstage view**

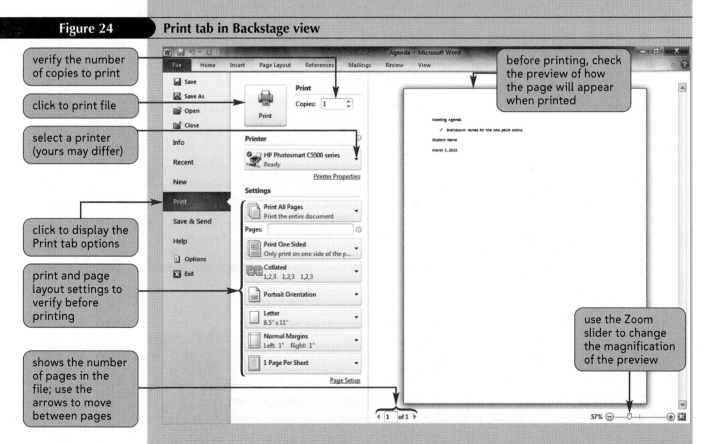

- verify the number of copies to print
- click to print file
- select a printer (yours may differ)
- click to display the Print tab options
- print and page layout settings to verify before printing
- shows the number of pages in the file; use the arrows to move between pages
- before printing, check the preview of how the page will appear when printed
- use the Zoom slider to change the magnification of the preview

4. Verify that **1** appears in the Copies box.

5. Verify that the correct printer appears on the Printer button. If it doesn't, click the **Printer** button, and then click the correct printer from the list of available printers.

6. Click the **Print** button to print the document.

Trouble? If the document does not print, see your instructor or technical support person for help.

Exiting Programs

When you finish working with a program, you should exit it. As with many other aspects of Office, you can exit programs with a button or a command. You'll use both methods to exit Word and Excel. You can use the Exit command to exit a program and close an open file in one step. If you haven't saved the final version of the open file, a dialog box opens, asking whether you want to save your changes. Clicking the Save button in this dialog box saves the open file, closes the file, and then exits the program.

To exit the Word and Excel programs:

▶ 1. On the Word title bar, click the **Close** button ⊠. Both the Word document and the Word program close. The Excel window is visible again.

   Trouble? If a dialog box opens asking if you want to save the document, you might have inadvertently made a change to the document. Click the Don't Save button.

▶ 2. On the Ribbon, click the **File** tab to open Backstage view, and then click the **Exit** command in the navigation bar. A dialog box opens asking whether you want to save the changes you made to the workbook. If you click the Save button, the Save As dialog box opens and Excel exits after you finish saving the workbook. This time, you don't want to save the workbook.

▶ 3. Click the **Don't Save** button. The workbook closes without saving a copy, and the Excel program closes.

Exiting programs after you are done using them keeps your Windows desktop uncluttered for the next person using the computer, frees up your system's resources, and prevents data from being lost accidentally.

Quick Check

REVIEW

1. What Office program would be best to use to write a letter?
2. How do you start an Office program?
3. What is the purpose of Live Preview?
4. What is Backstage view?
5. Explain the difference between Save and Save As.
6. True or False. In Protected View, you can see file contents, but you cannot edit, save, or print them until you enable editing.
7. What happens if you open a file, make edits, and then attempt to close the file or exit the program without saving the current version of the file?
8. What are the two ways to get Help in Office?

*Practice the skills
you learned in
the tutorial.*

PRACTICE

Review Assignments

Data Files needed for the Review Assignments: Finances.xlsx, Letter.docx

You need to prepare for an upcoming meeting at Recycled Palette. You'll open and print documents for the meeting. Complete the following:

1. Start PowerPoint, and then start Excel.
2. Switch to the PowerPoint window, and then close the presentation but leave the PowerPoint program open. (*Hint*: Use the Close command in Backstage view.)
3. Open a blank PowerPoint presentation from the New tab in Backstage view. (*Hint*: Make sure Blank presentation is selected in the Available Templates and Themes section, and then click the Create button.)
4. Close the PowerPoint presentation and program using the Close button on the PowerPoint title bar; do not save changes if asked.
5. Open the **Finances** workbook located in the Office\Review folder. If the workbook opens in Protected View, click the Enable Editing button.
6. Use the Save As command to save the workbook as **Recycled Palette Finances** in the Office\Review folder.
7. In cell A1, type your name, press the Enter key to insert your name at the top of the worksheet, and then save the workbook.
8. Preview and print one copy of the worksheet using the Print tab in Backstage view.
9. Exit Excel using the Exit command in Backstage view.
10. Start Word, and then open the **Letter** document located in the Office\Review folder. If the document opens in Protected View, click the Enable Editing button.
11. Use the Save As command to save the document with the filename **Recycled Palette Letter** in the Office\Review folder.
12. Press and hold the Ctrl key, press the End key, and then release both keys to move the insertion point to the end of the letter, and then type your name.
13. Use the Save button to save the change to the Recycled Palette Letter document.
14. Preview and print one copy of the document using the Print tab in Backstage view.
15. Close the document, and then exit the Word program.
16. Submit the finished files to your instructor.

ASSESS

SAM: Skills Assessment Manager

For current SAM information, including versions and content details, visit SAM Central (http://samcentral.course.com). If you have a SAM user profile, you may have access to hands-on instruction, practice, and assessment of the skills covered in this tutorial. Since various versions of SAM are supported throughout the life of this text, check with your instructor for the correct instructions and URL/Web site for accessing assignments.

ENDING DATA FILES

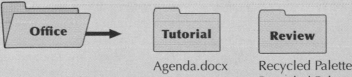

Office → Tutorial   Review

Agenda.docx   Recycled Palette Finances.xlsx
Recycled Palette Letter.docx

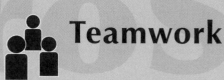

Teamwork

Working on a Team

Teams consist of individuals who have skills, talents, and abilities that complement each other and, when joined, produce synergy—results greater than those a single individual could achieve. It is this sense of shared mission and responsibility for results that makes a team successful in its efforts to reach its goals. Teams are everywhere. In the workplace, a team might develop a presentation to introduce products. In the classroom, a team might complete a research project.

Teams meet face to face or virtually. A virtual team rarely, if ever, meets in person. Instead, technology makes it possible for members to work as if everyone was in the same room. Some common technologies used in virtual teamwork are corporate networks, email, teleconferencing, and collaboration and integration tools, such as those found in Office 2010.

Even for teams in the same location, technology is a valuable tool. For example, teams commonly collaborate on a copy of a file posted to an online shared storage space, such as SkyDrive. In addition, team members can compile data in the program that best suits the information related to their part of the project. Later, that information can be integrated into a finished report, presentation, email message, and so on.

Collaborate with Others

At home, school, or work, you probably collaborate with others to complete many types of tasks—such as planning an event, creating a report, or developing a presentation. You can use Microsoft Office to streamline many of these tasks. Consider a project that you might need to work on with a team. Complete the following steps:

1. Start Word, and open a new document, if necessary.
2. In the document, type a list of all the tasks the team needs to accomplish. If you are working with a team, identify which team member would complete each task.
3. For each task, identify the type of Office file you would create to complete that task. For example, you would create a Word document to write a letter.
4. For each file, identify the Office program you would use to create that file, and explain why you would use that program.
5. Save the document with an appropriate filename in an appropriate folder location.
6. Use a Web browser to visit the Microsoft site at *www.microsoft.com* and research the different Office 2010 suites available. Determine which suite includes all the programs needed for the team to complete the tasks on the list.
7. In the document, type which Office suite you selected and a brief explanation of why.
8. Determine how the team can integrate the different programs in the Office suite you selected to create the files that complete the team's goal or task. Include this information at the end of the Word document. Save the document.
9. Develop an efficient way to organize the files that the team will create to complete the goal or task. Add this information at the end of the Word document.
10. If possible, sign in to SkyDrive, and then save a copy of the file in an appropriate subfolder within your Public folder. If you are working with a team, have your teammates access your file, review your notes, and add a paragraph with their comments and name.
11. Preview and print the finished document, and then submit it to your instructor.

EXCEL

OBJECTIVES

Session 1.1
- Understand the use of spreadsheets and Excel
- Learn the parts of the Excel window
- Scroll through a worksheet and navigate between worksheets
- Create and save a workbook file
- Enter text, numbers, and dates into a worksheet
- Resize, insert, and remove columns and rows

Session 1.2
- Select and move cell ranges
- Insert formulas and functions
- Insert, delete, move, and rename worksheets
- Work with editing tools
- Preview and print a workbook

Getting Started with Excel

Creating an Order Report

Case | *RipCity Digital*

When Amanda Dunn purchased a DVD burner a few years ago, one of her first tasks was to convert her home videos into DVDs. After she saw how simple it was, she upgraded her hardware and software, and proceeded to create DVDs from home movies and slides for her parents and friends. Based on her success, Amanda decided to make a business out of her hobby and founded RipCity Digital, an online service specializing in creating DVDs from the home movies, photos, and slides sent to her from customers. Amanda wants to list the weekly orders from her customers, tracking the names and addresses of her clients, the number of DVDs that she creates, and finally the cost of creating and shipping the DVDs.

Amanda is so busy creating DVDs that she asks you to record her orders. You'll do this in **Microsoft Excel 2010** (or **Excel**), a computer program used to enter, analyze, and present quantitative data. You'll also enter the latest orders she received for her new business.

STARTING DATA FILES

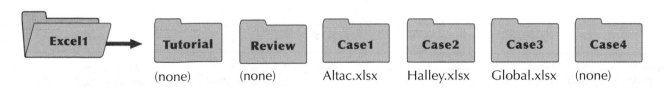

Excel1 →	Tutorial	Review	Case1	Case2	Case3	Case4
	(none)	(none)	Altac.xlsx	Halley.xlsx	Global.xlsx	(none)

SESSION 1.1 VISUAL OVERVIEW

Excel stores spreadsheets in files called **workbooks**. The contents of a workbook are shown in a workbook window.

The **Name box** displays the cell reference of the active cell.

The **Select All button** is used to select all of the cells in the active worksheet.

The **formula bar** displays the value or formula entered in the active cell.

The **row headings** are the numbers along the left side of the worksheet window that identify the different rows in the worksheet. You click a row heading to select the entire worksheet row.

A workbook is made up of individual **sheets**. Each sheet is identified by a sheet name, which appears in the **sheet tab**.

The **sheet tab scrolling buttons** scroll the list of sheet tabs in the worksheet.

The sheet currently displayed in the workbook window is the **active sheet**; its sheet tab is white.

The other sheets in the workbook are not visible. The sheet tabs for these inactive sheets are gray.

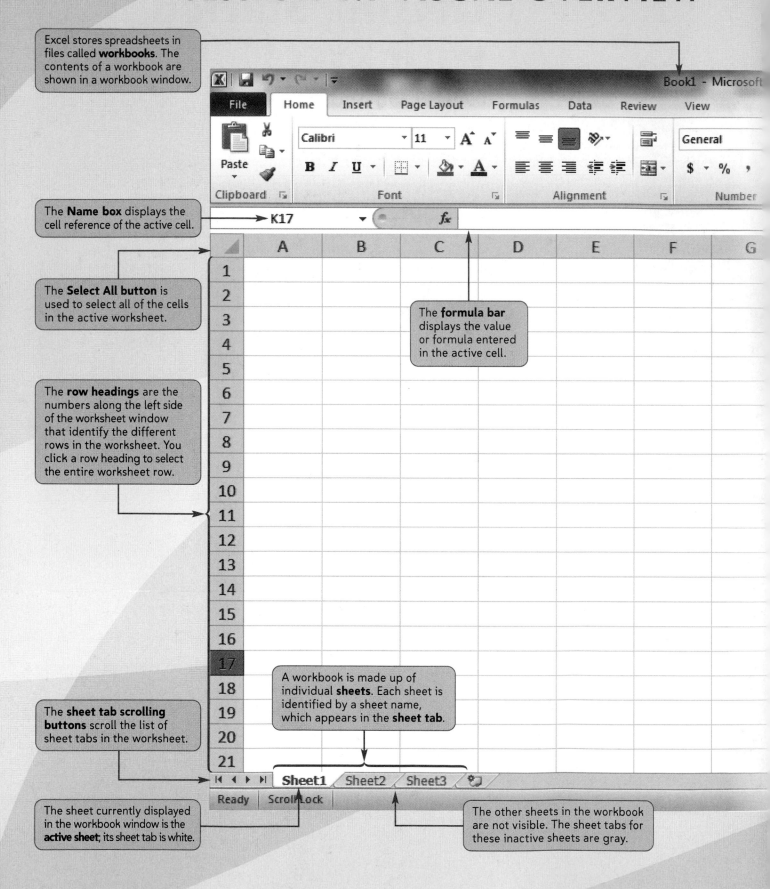

THE EXCEL WINDOW

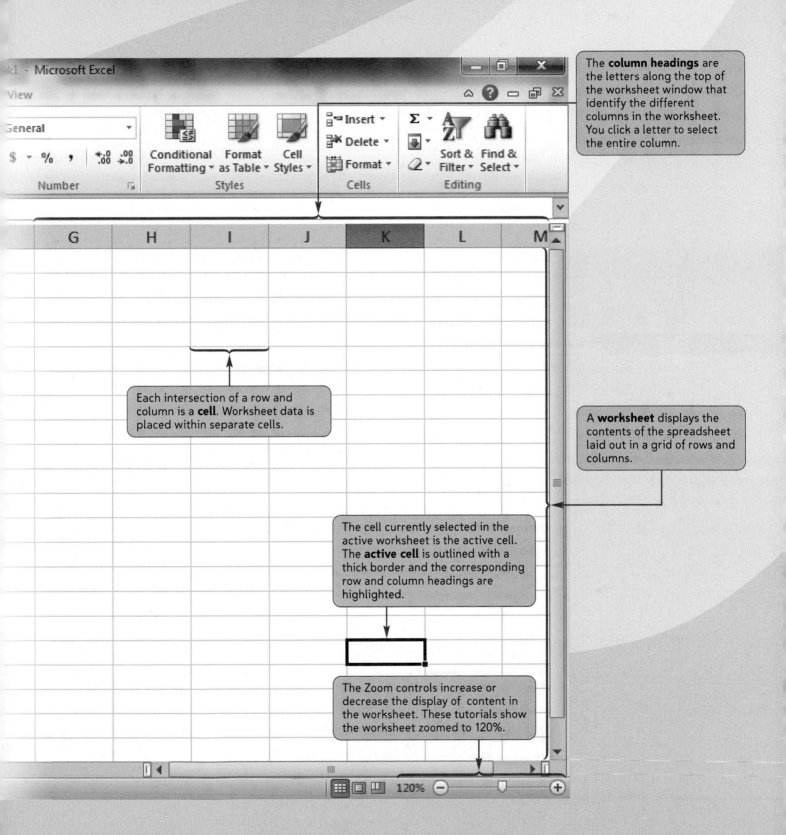

The **column headings** are the letters along the top of the worksheet window that identify the different columns in the worksheet. You click a letter to select the entire column.

Each intersection of a row and column is a **cell**. Worksheet data is placed within separate cells.

A **worksheet** displays the contents of the spreadsheet laid out in a grid of rows and columns.

The cell currently selected in the active worksheet is the active cell. The **active cell** is outlined with a thick border and the corresponding row and column headings are highlighted.

The Zoom controls increase or decrease the display of content in the worksheet. These tutorials show the worksheet zoomed to 120%.

Introducing Excel

Before you begin working in Excel, you will review some of the features, key terms, and concepts associated with spreadsheets.

Understanding Spreadsheets

A **spreadsheet** is a collection of text and numbers laid out in a rectangular grid. Spreadsheets are often used in business for budgeting, inventory management, and decision making. They can also be used to manage personal budgets and track household assets. Excel is a computer program used to create electronic versions of spreadsheets. For example, the spreadsheet in Figure 1-1 shows a cash flow report. The spreadsheet records the estimated and actual cash flow for the month of January. Each line, or row, displays a different value, such as the starting cash balance or cash sales for the month. Each column displays the budgeted or actual numbers, or text that describes those values. The total cash expenditures, net cash flow, and closing cash balance for the month are not entered directly, but calculated from other numbers in the spreadsheet. For example, the total cash expenditure is equal to the expenditures on advertising, wages, and supplies. This allows you to use Excel to perform a **what-if analysis** in which you change one or more values in a spreadsheet and then assess the effect those changes have on the calculated values. You can also use Excel to store data, generate reports, and analyze data values using a variety of statistical tools.

| Figure 1-1 | Spreadsheet data in Excel |

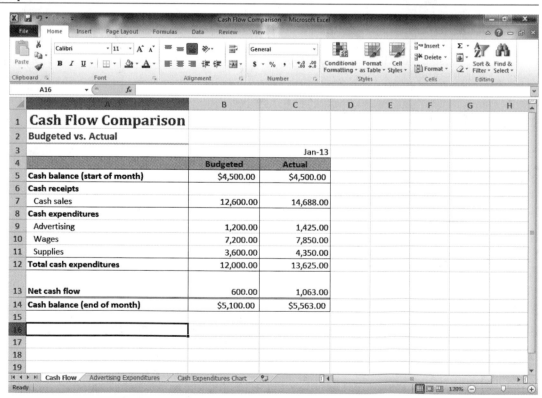

Exploring the Excel Window

Before entering Amanda's data, you'll review the different parts of the Excel window. The Excel window contains many of the elements that you find in other Office 2010 programs, including a title bar, the Ribbon, scroll bars, and a status bar. The Excel window also contains features that are unique to Excel.

To start Excel:

1. Click the **Start** button ⊙ on the taskbar, click **All Programs**, click **Microsoft Office**, and then point to **Microsoft Excel 2010**.

   Trouble? If you don't see Microsoft Excel 2010 on the Microsoft Office submenu, look for it on a different submenu or on the All Programs menu. If you still cannot find Microsoft Excel 2010, ask your instructor or technical support person for help.

2. Click **Microsoft Excel 2010**. The Excel window opens.

   All the figures showing the Excel window in these tutorials are zoomed to 120% for better readability. If you want to zoom your Excel window to match the figures, complete Step 3. If you prefer to work in the default zoom of 100% or at another zoom level, continue with Step 4; you might see more or less of the worksheet on your screen, but this does not affect your work in the tutorials.

3. If you want your Excel window zoomed to match the figures, click the **Zoom In** button ⊕ on the status bar twice to increase the zoom level to 120%. The 120% magnification increases the screen size of each cell, but reduces the number of worksheet cells visible in the workbook window.

4. If necessary, click the **Maximize** button ▣ on the Excel window title bar. The Excel window fills the screen.

By default, Excel starts with a blank workbook maximized to fill the Excel window. The name of the active workbook, Book1, appears in the title bar. You can open more than one workbook window at a time to display the contents of different workbooks. You can also open multiple workbook windows for one workbook to display different views of the workbook's contents.

Navigating Between Worksheets

A workbook can have two kinds of sheets: worksheets and chart sheets. A worksheet contains a grid of rows and columns into which the user enters data values and formulas. A **chart sheet** contains an Excel chart that provides a visual representation of worksheet data. Charts can also be embedded within worksheets, displaying both the data and charts in one sheet. By default, all new Excel workbooks are created with three worksheets named Sheet1, Sheet2, and Sheet3. The Sheet1 worksheet is the active sheet.

Multiple sheets enable you to better organize data in the workbook. For example, a sales report workbook might have a different worksheet for each sales region and another worksheet that summarizes the results from all the regions.

Some workbooks contain so many sheets that their sheet tabs cannot all be displayed at the same time in the workbook window. For these workbooks, you can scroll through the sheet tabs using the sheet tab scrolling buttons. Scrolling through the sheet tabs does not change the active sheet. To change the active sheet, you must click a sheet tab.

TIP

You can also move to the previous or next sheet by pressing the Ctrl+Page Up or Ctrl+Page Down keys.

To change the active sheet:

1. Click the **Sheet2** sheet tab. The Sheet2 worksheet, which is also blank, becomes the active worksheet. The Sheet2 tab is white, indicating this worksheet is active.

2. Click the **Sheet3** sheet tab. The Sheet3 worksheet becomes the active worksheet.

3. Click the **Sheet1** sheet tab to return to the first worksheet.

Navigating Within a Worksheet

Each cell within a worksheet is identified by a **cell reference**, which indicates its column and row location. For example, the cell reference B6 refers to the cell located where column B intersects row 6. The column letter always appears before the row number in any cell reference. Row numbers range from 1 to 1,048,576. The first 26 column letters range in alphabetical order from A to Z. After Z, the next column headings are labeled AA, AB, AC, and so forth. Excel allows a maximum of 16,385 columns in a worksheet (the last column has the heading XFD). When Excel starts, cell A1 is the active cell.

As you work, you'll need to change which cell is the active cell. You can use your mouse to click a cell to make it the active cell, or you can use the keyboard to move between cells, as described in Figure 1-2.

Figure 1-2   **Excel navigation keys**

Press	To move the active cell
↑ ↓ ← →	Up, down, left, or right one cell
Home	To column A of the current row
Ctrl+Home	To cell A1
Ctrl+End	To the last cell in the worksheet that contains data
Enter	Down one row or to the start of the next row of data
Shift+Enter	Up one row
Tab	One column to the right
Shift+Tab	One column to the left
Page Up, Page Down	Up or down one screen
Ctrl+Page Up, Ctrl+Page Down	To the previous or next sheet in the workbook

You'll use both your mouse and your keyboard to change the active cell in the Sheet1 worksheet.

To change the active cell:

1. Move your pointer over cell **A5**, and then click the mouse button. The active cell moves from cell A1 to cell A5, and the cell reference in the Name box changes from A1 to A5. The column heading for column A and the row heading for row 5 are both highlighted.

2. Press the → key on your keyboard. The active cell moves one cell to the right to cell B5.

3. Press the **Page Down** key. The active cell moves down one full screen.

4. Press the **Page Up** key. The active cell moves up one full screen, back to cell B5.

5. Press the **Ctrl+Home** keys. The active cell returns to the first cell in the worksheet, cell A1.

The mouse and keyboard provide quick ways to navigate the active worksheet. For larger worksheets that span several screens, you can move directly to a specific cell using the Go To dialog box or by typing a cell reference in the Name box. You'll try both of these methods.

To use the Go To dialog box and Name box:

TIP

You can also open the Go To dialog box by pressing the F5 key or the Ctrl+G keys.

1. Click the **Home** tab on the Ribbon, if necessary. The button to open the Go To dialog box is in the Editing group.

2. In the Editing group, click the **Find & Select** button, and then click **Go To** on the menu that opens. The Go To dialog box opens.

3. Type **C14** in the Reference box. See Figure 1-3.

Figure 1-3	Go To dialog box

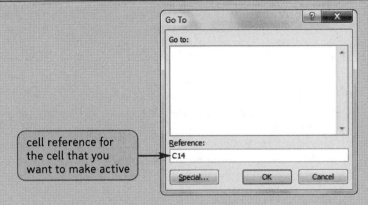

cell reference for the cell that you want to make active

Trouble? If your screen varies slightly from those shown in the figures, your computer might be set up differently. The figures in this book were created while running Windows 7 using the default Windows 7 settings, but how your screen looks depends on a variety of things, including the version of Windows, background settings, monitor resolution, and so forth.

4. Click the **OK** button. Cell C14 is the active cell and its cell reference appears in the Name box. You'll use the Name box to make a different cell active.

5. Click in the **Name** box, type **A1**, and then press the **Enter** key. Cell A1 is once again the active cell.

To view more of the active worksheet, you can use the horizontal and vertical scroll bars, located at the bottom and right side of the workbook window, respectively, to move through the worksheet horizontally and vertically. You can scroll one row or column at a time, or you can scroll several rows and columns. Scrolling through the worksheet does not change the location of the active cell.

To scroll through the worksheet:

1. Click the **down arrow** on the vertical scroll bar three times. The worksheet scrolls down three rows, but the active cell remains cell A1.

2. Click the **right arrow** on the horizontal scroll bar twice. The worksheet scrolls two columns to the right. The active cell still remains cell A1, although that cell is scrolled out of view.

3. Drag the vertical scroll box up until you can see the first row in the worksheet.

4. Drag the horizontal scroll box to the left until you can see the first column in the worksheet.

Planning a Workbook

Before you begin to enter data into a workbook, you should develop a plan. You can do this by using a **planning analysis sheet**, which includes the following questions that help you think about the workbook's purpose and how to achieve your desired results:

1. **What problems do I want to solve?** The answer defines the goal or purpose of the workbook.
2. **What data do I need?** The answer defines the type of data that you need to collect and enter into the workbook.
3. **What calculations do I need to enter?** The answer defines the formulas you need to apply to the data you've collected and entered.
4. **What form should my solution take?** The answer defines the appearance of the workbook content and how it should be presented to others.

Amanda carefully considered these questions and developed the following plan as a guide for entering data in her workbook:

1. I need to know contact information for each customer, how many DVDs I create for customers, how much I charge customers, and how much revenue RipCity Digital is generating.
2. I need each customer's name and contact information, the order date, the number of DVDs created for each customer, and the cost of creating each DVD.
3. I need to calculate the total charge for each order, the total number of DVDs for all orders, and the total revenue generated from all orders.
4. Customer orders should be placed in a table with each row containing data on a different customer. Information about each customer should be placed in separate columns. The last column should contain the total charge for each customer. The last row should contain the total number of DVDs created and the total revenue from all customer orders.

PROSKILLS

Written Communication: Creating Effective Workbooks

Workbooks convey information in written form. As with any writing, the final product creates an impression and provides an indicator of your interest, knowledge, and attention to detail. To create the best impression, all workbooks—especially those you intend to share with others such as coworkers and clients—should be well planned, well organized, and well written.

A well-designed workbook should clearly identify its overall goal and present information in an organized format. The data it includes should be accurate both in the entered values and calculated values. Developing an effective workbook includes the following steps:

- Determine the workbook's purpose, content, and organization before you start.
- Create a list of the sheets used in the workbook, making note of each sheet's purpose.
- Insert a documentation sheet that describes the workbook's purpose and organization. Include the name of the workbook author, the date the workbook was created, and any additional information that will help others to track the workbook to its source.
- Enter all of the data in the workbook. Add text to indicate what the values represent and, if possible, where they originated so others can view the source of your data.
- Enter formulas for calculated items rather than entering the calculated values into the workbook. For more complicated calculations, provide documentation explaining them.
- Test the workbook with a variety of values; edit the data and formulas to correct errors.
- Save the workbook and create a backup copy when the project is completed. Print the workbook's contents if you need to provide a hard-copy version to others or for your files.
- Maintain a history of your workbook as it goes through different versions, so that you and others can quickly see how the workbook has changed during revisions.

By including clearly written documentation, explanatory text, a logical organization, and accurate data and formulas, you'll create effective workbooks that others can use easily.

Entering Text, Numbers, and Dates

Worksheet cells can contain text, numbers, or dates and times. **Text data** is any combination of letters, numbers, and symbols that form words and sentences. Text data is often referred to as a **text string** because it contains a string of text characters. **Number data** is any numerical value that can be used in a mathematical calculation. **Date** and **time data** are commonly recognized formats for date and time values. For example, Excel interprets the cell entry April 15, 2013 as a date and not as text. By default, text is left-aligned in cells, whereas numbers, dates, and times are right-aligned.

Entering Text

New data values are placed into the cell that is currently active in the worksheet. As you enter data, the entry appears in both the active cell and the formula bar. Amanda wants you to enter some of the information from the planning analysis sheet into the first sheet of the workbook. This worksheet will document the workbook's purpose and content.

To enter the text for the documentation sheet:

1. Press the **Ctrl+Home** keys to make cell A1 the active cell on the Sheet1 worksheet, if necessary.

2. Type **RipCity Digital Customer Orders** in cell A1. As you type, the text appears both in cell A1 and in the formula bar.

3. Press the **Enter** key twice. Excel enters the text into cell A1 and moves the active cell down two cells to cell A3.

4. Type **Author** in cell A3, and then press the **Tab** key. The text is entered and the active cell moves one cell to the right to cell B3.

5. Type your name in cell B3, and then press the **Enter** key. The text is entered and the active cell moves one cell down and to the left to cell A4.

6. Type **Date** in cell A4, and then press the **Tab** key. The text is entered and the active cell moves one cell to the right to cell B4, where you would enter the date you created the worksheet. For now, you'll leave the cell for the date blank.

7. Click cell **A5** to make it the active cell, type **Purpose** in the cell, and then press the **Tab** key. The active cell moves one cell to the right to cell B5.

8. Type **To record orders from RipCity Digital customers** in cell B5, and then press the **Enter** key. Figure 1-4 shows the text entered in the Sheet1 worksheet.

Figure 1-4   Documentation sheet

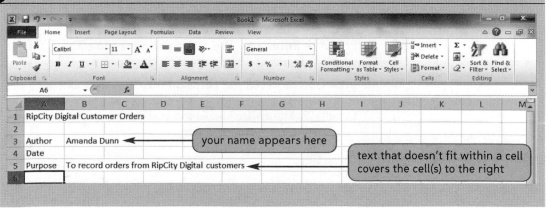

- your name appears here
- text that doesn't fit within a cell covers the cell(s) to the right

The text you entered in cell A1 is so long that it appears to flow into cells B1 and C1. The same is true for the text you entered in cells B3 and B5. Any text you enter in a cell that doesn't fit within that cell covers the adjacent cells to the right as long as they are empty. If the adjacent cells contain text or data, only the text that fits into the cell is displayed. The rest of the text entry is hidden, or **truncated**, from the view. The text itself is not affected. The complete text is still entered in the cell; it's just not displayed. To display all of the text, you must increase the cell's width, which you'll learn how to do in the next session.

Next, you'll enter the RipCity Digital customer orders. As shown in Figure 1-5, the orders will contain the name and address of each customer, the order date, the number of DVDs created from the customer's home videos, and the price per DVD. Amanda's price per DVD decreases for larger orders.

Figure 1-5 Customer orders

Last	First	Address	Date	DVDs	Price per DVD
Dawes	Gregory	402 Elm St. Merrill, MI 48637	3/13/2013	7	$17.29
Garcia	Susan	1025 Drake Ave. Exeter, NH 03833	3/14/2013	25	$15.79
Torbet	Dr. Lilla	5 North Ln. Oswego, NY 13126	3/17/2013	32	$12.99
Rhoden	Tony	24 Mountain Dr. Auburn, ME 04210	3/24/2013	20	$15.79

You'll enter this data in the Sheet2 worksheet.

To enter the text labels and customer names:

1. Click the **Sheet2** sheet tab. Sheet2 becomes the active worksheet. You'll enter the column labels in cells A1, B1, C1, D1, E1, and F1.

2. Type **Last** in cell A1, and then press the **Tab** key. The label is entered in cell A1 and the active cell moves to cell B1.

3. Type **First** in cell B1, and then press the **Tab** key. The label is entered in cell B1 and the active cell moves to cell C1.

4. Type **Address** in cell C1, and then press the **Tab** key.

5. Type **Date** in cell D1, and then press the **Tab** key.

6. Type **DVDs** in cell E1, press the **Tab** key, and then type **Price per DVD** in cell F1. You've typed all the labels for the customer orders.

7. Press the **Enter** key. The active cell moves to cell A2, the start of the next row where you want to begin entering the customer data.

8. Type **Dawes** in cell A2, press the **Tab** key, type **Gregory** in cell B2, and then press the **Tab** key. You've entered the first customer's name and moved the active cell to cell C2. Figure 1-6 shows the text you've entered so far.

| Figure 1-6 | Text entered for customer orders |

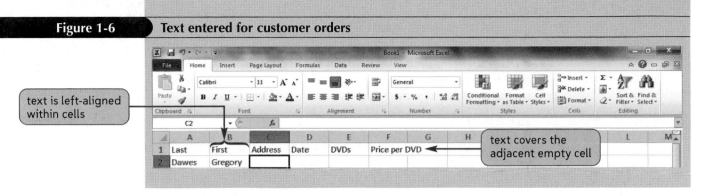

text is left-aligned within cells

text covers the adjacent empty cell

As you type text into the active cell, Excel tries to anticipate the remaining characters by displaying text that begins with the same letters as a previous entry in the same column. This feature, known as **AutoComplete**, helps make entering repetitive text easier. To accept the suggested text, press the Tab or Enter key. To override the suggested text, continue to type the text you want to enter in the cell. AutoComplete does not work with dates or numbers, or when a blank cell is between the previous entry and the text you're typing.

Entering Multiple Lines of Text Within a Cell

Addresses are often entered on two or more separate lines. Amanda wants you to follow that convention with her customers' addresses. To place text on separate lines within the same cell, you press and hold the Alt key while you press the Enter key. This creates a line break within the cell.

You'll enter the address for the first RipCity Digital customer, which will occupy two lines within the same cell.

To enter multiple lines of text within a cell:

1. Type **402 Elm St.** in cell C2, but do not press the Tab or Enter key. Instead, you'll insert a new line break.

2. Hold down the **Alt** key and press the **Enter** key, and then release both keys. The insertion point moves to a new line within cell C2.

   Be sure to hold down the Alt key as you press Enter; otherwise, only the first address line will be entered in cell C2.

3. Type **Merrill, MI 48637** on the new line, and then press the **Tab** key. The two lines of text are entered in cell C2, and cell D2 becomes the active cell. See Figure 1-7.

| Figure 1-7 | Multiple lines of text entered in cell C2 |

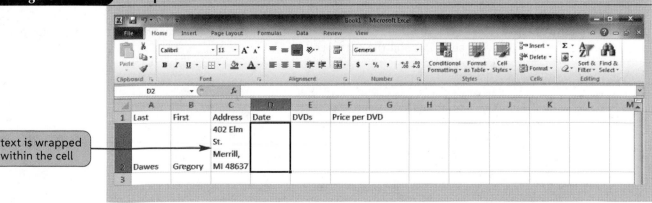

text is wrapped within the cell

TIP

To force text that extends beyond a cell's border to fit within the cell, click the Wrap Text button in the Alignment group on the Home tab. The row height increases as needed to wrap all the text within the cell.

When you enter multiple lines of text within a cell, Excel confines the text within the cell's borders, increasing the cell's height, if necessary, to show all of the text. As you can see, the text in cell C2 appears on four lines even though you entered the address on two lines. The automatic reflow of text within a cell is referred to as wrapping. If the cell's width were increased, the text would then appear on two lines as Amanda wants. You'll do this in the next session.

Entering Dates

You can enter dates in any of the standard date formats. For example, you can enter the date April 6, 2013 in any of the following date formats (and many others) and Excel recognizes each entry as representing the same date:

- 4/6/2013
- 4/6/13
- 4-6-2013
- April 6, 2013
- 6-Apr-13

Even though you enter a date as text, Excel stores the date as a numeric value equal to the number of days between the specified date and January 0, 1900. This means that the date January 1, 1900 has a value of 1 and so forth. Times are also entered as text and are stored as fractional parts of a 24-hour day. Storing dates and times as numeric values allows Excel to perform date and time calculations, such as determining the elapsed time between one date and another.

Based on the default date format your computer uses, Excel might alter the date format you type. For example, if you enter the date 4/6/13 into the active cell, Excel might display the date with the four-digit year value, 4/6/2013; if you enter the text April 6, 2013, Excel might convert the date format to 6-Apr-13. Changing the date or time format doesn't affect the underlying date or time value.

For Amanda's workbook, you'll enter the dates in the format *m/d/yyyy*, where *m* is the 1- or 2-digit month number, *d* is the 1- or 2-digit day number, and *yyyy* is the 4-digit year number. You will enter the order date on the Sheet2 worksheet and the current date in the Sheet1 worksheet.

To enter the dates for the customer orders:

1. Type **3/13/2013** in cell D2, and then press the **Tab** key to move to cell E2. The date of Gregory Dawes's order appears in cell D2, and cell E2 becomes the active cell. The width of column D expands to display the full date.

2. Click the **Sheet1** sheet tab. The Sheet1 worksheet is the active worksheet.

3. Click cell **B4** to make it active, insert the current date using the format *m/d/yyyy*, and then press the **Enter** key.

4. Click the **Sheet2** sheet tab. The Sheet2 worksheet is the active worksheet, and cell E2 is still the active cell.

International Date Formats

As business transactions become more international in scope, you may need to adopt international standards for expressing dates, times, and currency values in your workbooks. For example, a worksheet cell might contain 06/05/12. This format could represent any of the following dates:

- The 5th of June, 2012
- The 6th of May, 2012
- The 12th of May, 2006

The date depends on which country the workbook has been designed for. You can avoid this problem by entering the full date as in the example June 5, 2012. However, this will not work with documents written in foreign languages such as Japanese that use different character symbols.

To solve this problem, many international businesses adopt ISO (International Organization for Standardization) dates in the format *yyyy-mm-dd*, where *yyyy* is the four-digit year value, *mm* is the two-digit month value, and *dd* is the two-digit day value. So, a date such as June 5, 2012 is entered as 2012/06/05. If you choose to use this international date format, make sure that people using your workbook understand this format so they do not misinterpret the dates. You can include information about the date format in the documentation sheet.

Entering Numbers

In Excel, numbers can be integers such as 378, decimals such as 1.95, or negatives such as −5.2. In the case of currency and percentages, you can include the currency symbol and percent sign when you enter the value. Excel treats a currency value such as $87.25 as the number 87.25, and a percentage such as 95% as the decimal 0.95. Currency and percentages, like dates, are formatted in a convenient way for you to read. Excel right-aligns numbers within each cell.

You'll complete the information for Gregory Dawes's order by entering the number of DVDs Amanda created for him and the price she charged him for each DVD.

To enter numbers for the first customer order:

1. Type **7** in cell E2, and then press the **Tab** key. The order quantity for Gregory Dawes is entered and the active cell is cell F2.

2. Type **$17.29** in cell F2, and then press the **Enter** key. The currency value is entered in cell F2. Note that Excel enters the number 17.29 in the cell and formats it as currency.

3. Click cell **A3**, which is where you want to enter the information for the next customer. See Figure 1-8.

Figure 1-8	First customer order data

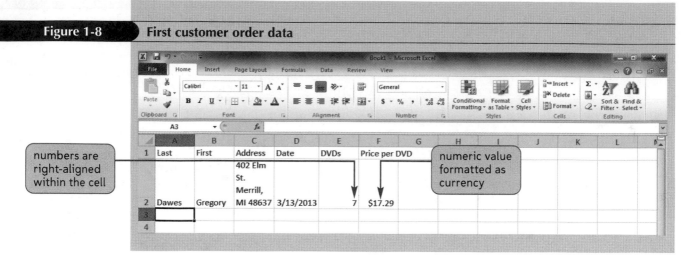

You've completed the data entry for Amanda's first customer. You still need to enter the data for three more customers into the worksheet. You'll use the same techniques you used to enter Gregory Dawes's order to enter their data.

To enter the remaining customer order data:

1. Type **Garcia** in cell A3, press the **Tab** key, type **Susan** in cell B3, and then press the **Tab** key. The second customer name is entered.

2. Type **1025 Drake Ave.** in cell C3, press the **Alt+Enter** keys, type **Exeter, NH 03833** on the next line, and then press the **Tab** key. The second customer's address is entered in the cell on two lines.

3. Type **3/14/2013** in cell D3, press the **Tab** key, type **25** in cell E3, press the **Tab** key, type **$15.79** in cell F3, and then press the **Enter** key. The rest of the second customer's data is entered.

4. Enter the following data for the remaining two customers in rows 4 and 5, making sure that you press the Alt+Enter keys to enter the addresses on two lines. Because column C is not wide enough to display the entire address text, it wraps within the cell and the zip code may be hidden. You'll correct this shortly. See Figure 1-9.

   Torbet, Dr. Lilla
   5 North Ln.
   Oswego, NY 13126
   3/17/2013, 32, $12.99

   Rhoden, Tony
   24 Mountain Dr.
   Auburn, ME 04210
   3/24/2013, 20, $15.79

Figure 1-9   **Customer orders for RipCity Digital**

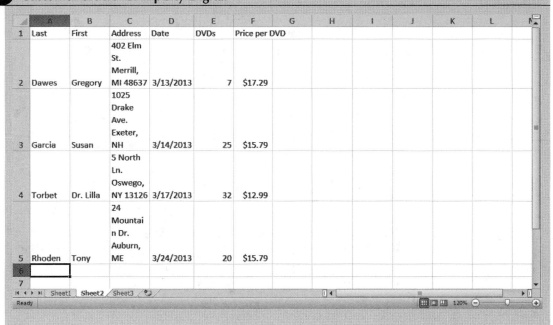

	A	B	C	D	E	F	G	H	I	J	K	L	M
1	Last	First	Address	Date	DVDs	Price per DVD							
2	Dawes	Gregory	402 Elm St. Merrill, MI 48637	3/13/2013	7	$17.29							
3	Garcia	Susan	1025 Drake Ave. Exeter, NH	3/14/2013	25	$15.79							
4	Torbet	Dr. Lilla	5 North Ln. Oswego, NY 13126	3/17/2013	32	$12.99							
5	Rhoden	Tony	24 Mountai n Dr. Auburn, ME	3/24/2013	20	$15.79							
6													
7													

Sheet1 Sheet2 Sheet3

Ready   120%

Working with Columns and Rows

Amanda has reviewed the customer order data you entered in the worksheet. She asks you to make the data easier to read. You can do this by modifying the size of the columns and rows in the worksheet.

REFERENCE

Changing the Column Width or Row Height

- Drag the right border of the column heading left to decrease the column width or right to increase the column width.
- Drag the bottom border of the row heading up to decrease the row height or down to increase the row height.

or

- Double-click the right border of a column heading or the bottom border of a row heading to autofit the column or row to the cell contents (or select one or more columns or rows, click the Home tab on the Ribbon, click the Format button in the Cells group, and then click AutoFit Column Width or AutoFit Row Height).

or

- Select one or more columns or rows.
- Click the Home tab on the Ribbon, click the Format button in the Cells group, and then click Column Width or Row Height.
- Enter the column width or row height you want, and then click the OK button.

Setting Column Widths

The default sizes of the columns and rows in a worksheet might not always accommodate the information you need to enter. This is what happened with the addresses you entered in the worksheet when Excel wrapped the text in ways that made the text difficult to read. Other times, long cell content might be truncated, hiding text or numeric values from the user. To make the cell content easier to read, you can resize the columns and rows in the worksheet.

Column widths are expressed in terms of the number of characters the column can contain. The default column width is 8.43 standard-sized characters. This means that, in general, you can type eight characters in a cell before that entry is truncated, overlaps the adjacent cell, or is wrapped to a new line within the cell. If the font size of the text in the cell is reduced, you can insert more characters within the cell.

Column widths are also expressed in terms of pixels. A **pixel** is a single point on a computer monitor or printout. A column width of 8.43 characters equals 64 pixels.

INSIGHT

Setting Column Widths

Pixel size is based on screen resolution. As a result, cell contents that look fine on one screen might be truncated when viewed on a screen with different resolution. If you work on multiple computers or share your workbooks with others, you should set column widths based on the maximum number of characters you want to display in the cells rather than pixel size. This ensures that everyone sees the cell contents the way you intended.

You will increase the width of the Address column to allow the addresses to appear on two lines in the cells without additional line wrapping.

To increase the width of column C:

1. Move the pointer over the right border of the column C heading until the pointer changes to ↔.

2. Click and drag to the right until the width of the column heading reaches **20** characters, but do not release the mouse button. The ScreenTip that appears as you resize the column shows the measurements of the new column width first as the number of characters and second in parentheses as pixels.

3. Release the mouse button. The width of column C expands to 20 characters and all the addresses fit on two lines with no extra line wrapping. See Figure 1-10.

Figure 1-10 **Increased column width**

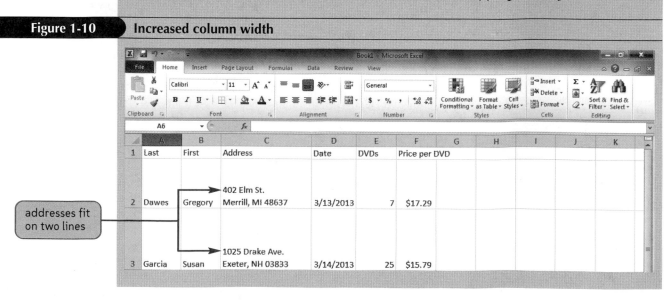

addresses fit on two lines

Amanda also wants you to increase the widths of columns A and B to 15 characters to accommodate longer names. Rather than resizing each column separately, you can select both columns and adjust their widths at the same time.

TIP

To select multiple columns, you can also click and drag the pointer over multiple column headings.

To increase the widths of columns A and B:

1. Click the **column A** heading. The entire column is selected.

2. Hold down the **Ctrl** key, click the **column B** heading, and then release the **Ctrl** key. Both columns A and B are selected.

3. Move the pointer to the right border of the column B heading until the pointer changes to ↔.

4. Drag to the right until the column width changes to **15** characters, and then release the mouse button. Both columns are wide enough to display longer names.

The text in cell F1, Price per DVD, overflows the cell borders. This column would look better if you increased the width of column F to 12 characters. You can set the column width using the Format command on the Home tab. The Format command gives you precise control in setting column widths and row heights.

To set the width of column F to 12 characters:

1. Click the **column F** heading. The entire column is selected.

2. In the Cells group on the Home tab, click the **Format** button, and then click **Column Width**. The Column Width dialog box opens.

3. Type **12** in the Column width box, and then click the **OK** button. The width of column F changes to 12 characters, placing the text in cell F1 entirely within the borders of the cell.

Setting Row Heights

The height of an Excel row is measured in points or pixels. A **point** is approximately 1/72 of an inch. The default row height is 15 points or 20 pixels. Row heights are set in the same way as column widths. You can drag the bottom border of the row to a new row height or define a specific row height using the Format command. Another option is to autofit the row's height (or the column's width) to match its content. **Autofitting** eliminates empty space by matching the row height or column width to its tallest or longest cell entry. If the row or column is blank, Excel restores its default height or width.

The row heights didn't change after you resized the columns, which leaves a lot of blank space in the four rows of customer data. This extra blank space makes the data difficult to read and extends the content out of view. Amanda wants you to autofit the heights of these rows to remove that empty space.

To autofit the second row to match its contents:

▶ **1.** Move the pointer over the bottom border of the row 2 heading until the pointer changes to ╫.

▶ **2.** Double-click the bottom border of row 2. The height of row 2 shrinks to match the content of cell C2, which is the tallest entry in the row, with two lines of text.

You could continue to resize the remaining rows one at a time, but a quicker way is to select the rows you want to resize and then autofit all the selected rows simultaneously.

To autofit rows 3 through 5:

▶ **1.** Drag the pointer across the row headings for rows 3, 4, and 5. The contents of rows 3 through 5 are selected.

▶ **2.** In the Cells group on the Home tab, click the **Format** button. A menu of commands opens.

▶ **3.** Click **AutoFit Row Height**. The height of each of the three rows autofits to its contents, and all the empty space is removed.

▶ **4.** Click cell **A1** to make it the active cell. The other cells in the worksheet are deselected. Figure 1-11 shows the worksheet with the revised row heights.

| Figure 1-11 | Row heights after autofitting to contents |

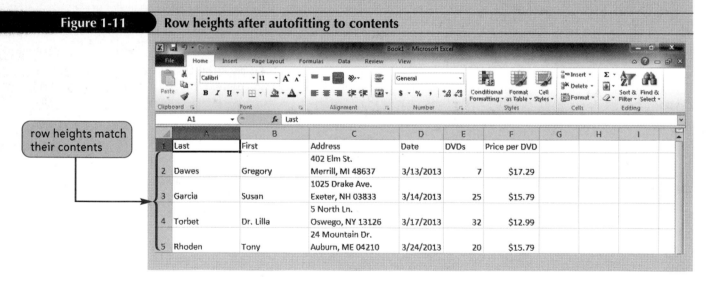

row heights match their contents

Inserting a Column or Row

You can insert a new column or row anywhere within a worksheet. When you insert a new column, the existing columns are shifted to the right and the new column has the same width as the column directly to its left. When you insert a new row, the existing rows are shifted down and the new row has the same height as the row above it.

Inserting a Column or Row

- Select the column(s) or row(s) where you want to insert the new column(s) or row(s); Excel will insert the same number of columns or rows as you select to the left of the selected columns or above the selected rows.
- In the Cells group on the Home tab, click the Insert button (or right-click a column or row heading or selected column and row headings, and then click Insert on the short-cut menu).

You will insert a column for customer phone numbers between the Address column and the Date column, and then enter the customer phone numbers in the new column.

To insert the new column:

1. Click the **column D** heading to select the entire column.

2. In the Cells group on the Home tab, click the **Insert** button. A new column D is inserted into the worksheet and the rest of the columns shift to the right. The new column has the same width as column C.

3. Reduce the width of column D to **15** characters.

4. Click cell **D1** to make it the active cell, type **Phone** as the label, and then press the **Enter** key. The new column label is entered in cell D1, and cell D2 becomes the active cell.

5. Enter the phone numbers in cells D2, D3, D4, and D5, as shown in Figure 1-12, pressing the **Enter** key after each entry.

Figure 1-12   New column inserted into the worksheet

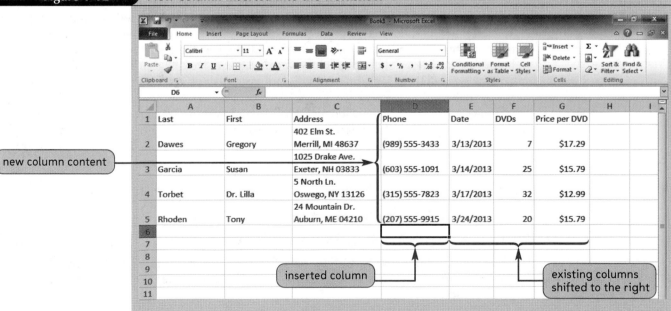

new column content

inserted column

existing columns shifted to the right

Amanda neglected to include a customer order. Because the customer was RipCity Digital's first customer, Amanda wants this order inserted at the top of the list. To add this new order, you need to insert a new row in the worksheet below the column labels.

To insert the new row:

▶ **1.** Click the **row 2** heading. The entire second row is selected.

▶ **2.** In the Cells group on the Home tab, click the **Insert** button. A new row 2 is inserted, and the remaining rows shift down.

▶ **3.** Enter the new customer order shown in Figure 1-13 into row 2.

Figure 1-13 New row inserted into the worksheet

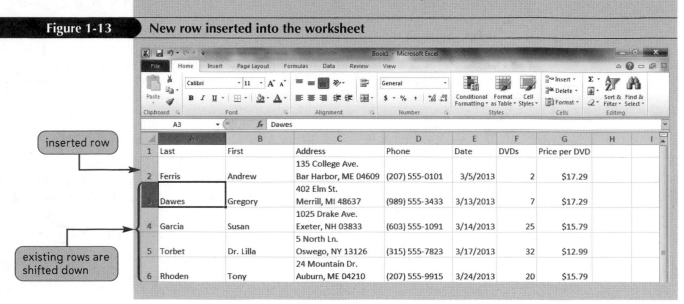

Deleting and Clearing a Row or Column

You can remove data in two ways: clearing and deleting. **Clearing** data from a worksheet removes the data, leaving blank cells where the data had been. **Deleting** data from the worksheet removes both the data and the cells. When a cell is deleted, the remaining cells in the worksheet shift into the deleted location. For example, when you delete a column, the columns to the right shift left to fill the vacated space. Similarly, the rows below a deleted row shift up to fill the vacated space. Note that pressing the Delete key does not *delete* the selected row or column; instead, it *clears* the contents, leaving the row or column in place.

Gregory Dawes just canceled his order. Amanda wants you to remove this order from the worksheet. You'll first clear Gregory Dawes's data from the worksheet and then delete the row that contained the data. Usually, you would do this in one step by simply deleting the row, but this will highlight the difference between clearing and deleting.

To clear and delete the third row:

▶ **1.** Click the **row 3** heading. The entire row 3 with Gregory Dawes's order is selected.

▶ **2.** Right-click the **row 3** heading, and then click **Clear Contents** on the shortcut menu. Excel clears the values in the third row, but leaves the blank row in that space.

▶ **3.** Verify that the third row is still selected.

▶ **4.** In the Cells group on the Home tab, click the **Delete** button. The third row is deleted, and the rows below it shift up. Only four customer orders remain in the worksheet.

Before continuing, you'll save your workbook with a descriptive name.

To save the current workbook:

1. Click the **File** tab on the Ribbon to display Backstage view.

2. Click the **Save** command in the navigation bar. The Save As dialog box opens because this is the first time you are saving this workbook.

3. Navigate to the **Excel1\Tutorial** folder included with your Data Files.

   Trouble? If you don't have the starting Data Files, you need to get them before you can proceed. Your instructor will either give you the Data Files or ask you to obtain them from a specified location (such as a network drive). In either case, make a backup copy of the Data Files before you start so that you will have the original files available in case you need to start over. If you have any questions about the Data Files, see your instructor or technical support person for assistance.

4. Verify that **Excel Workbook** appears in the Save as type box.

   Trouble? If your computer is set up to show filename extensions, you will see the Excel file extension .xlsx in the Save as type box as well.

5. Select **Book1** in the File name box, and then type **RipCity Digital Orders**. The default filename Book1 is replaced with the name you entered.

6. Click the **Save** button. The Save As dialog box closes and the workbook file is saved with its descriptive filename.

So far, you have entered the customer order data. In the process, you worked with rows and columns. In the next session, you'll learn how to work with individual cells and groups of cells. You will also add calculations to the worksheet to determine how much revenue Amanda will generate from these orders.

Session 1.1 Quick Check

REVIEW

1. What are the two types of sheets used in a workbook?
2. List two ways of identifying the active cell in the worksheet.
3. What is the cell reference for the cell located in the fourth column and third row of a worksheet?
4. What keyboard shortcut changes the active cell to cell A1?
5. What is text data?
6. What keys do you press to start a new line of text within a cell?
7. Cell A4 contains May 3, 2013; why doesn't Excel consider this entry a text string?
8. Explain the difference between clearing a row and deleting a row.

SESSION 1.2 VISUAL OVERVIEW

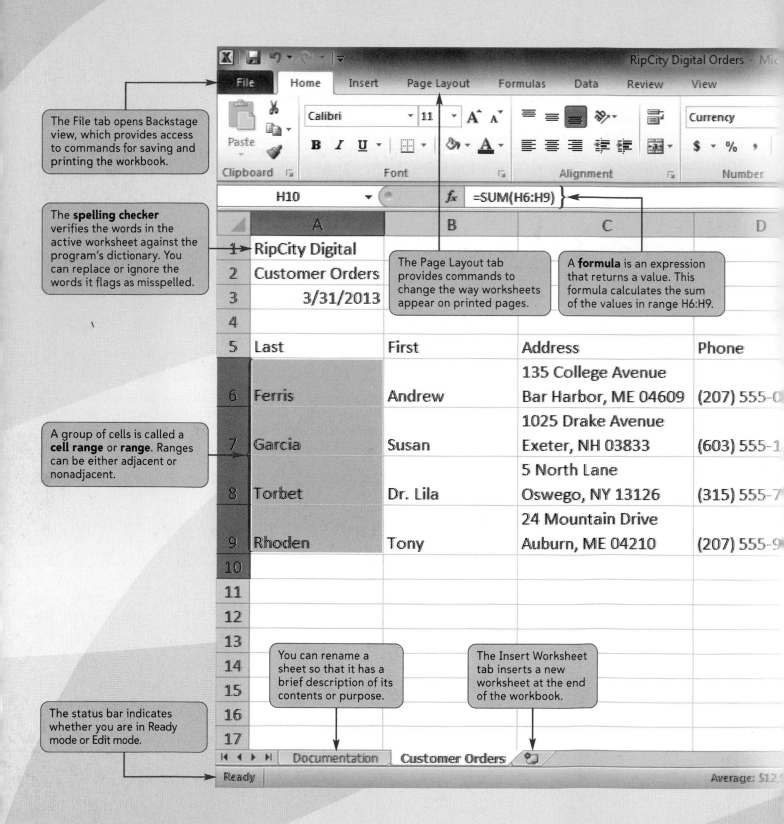

The File tab opens Backstage view, which provides access to commands for saving and printing the workbook.

The **spelling checker** verifies the words in the active worksheet against the program's dictionary. You can replace or ignore the words it flags as misspelled.

A group of cells is called a **cell range** or **range**. Ranges can be either adjacent or nonadjacent.

The status bar indicates whether you are in Ready mode or Edit mode.

The Page Layout tab provides commands to change the way worksheets appear on printed pages.

A **formula** is an expression that returns a value. This formula calculates the sum of the values in range H6:H9.

You can rename a sheet so that it has a brief description of its contents or purpose.

The Insert Worksheet tab inserts a new worksheet at the end of the workbook.

RipCity Digital Orders - Mic

File   Home   Insert   Page Layout   Formulas   Data   Review   View

Calibri   11

B I U

Clipboard   Font   Alignment   Number

Currency

$ % ,

H10   =SUM(H6:H9)

	A	B	C	D
1	RipCity Digital			
2	Customer Orders			
3	3/31/2013			
4				
5	Last	First	Address	Phone
6	Ferris	Andrew	135 College Avenue Bar Harbor, ME 04609	(207) 555-0
7	Garcia	Susan	1025 Drake Avenue Exeter, NH 03833	(603) 555-1
8	Torbet	Dr. Lila	5 North Lane Oswego, NY 13126	(315) 555-7
9	Rhoden	Tony	24 Mountain Drive Auburn, ME 04210	(207) 555-9
10				
11				
12				
13				
14				
15				
16				
17				

Documentation   Customer Orders

Ready   Average: $12.9

WORKSHEET DATA

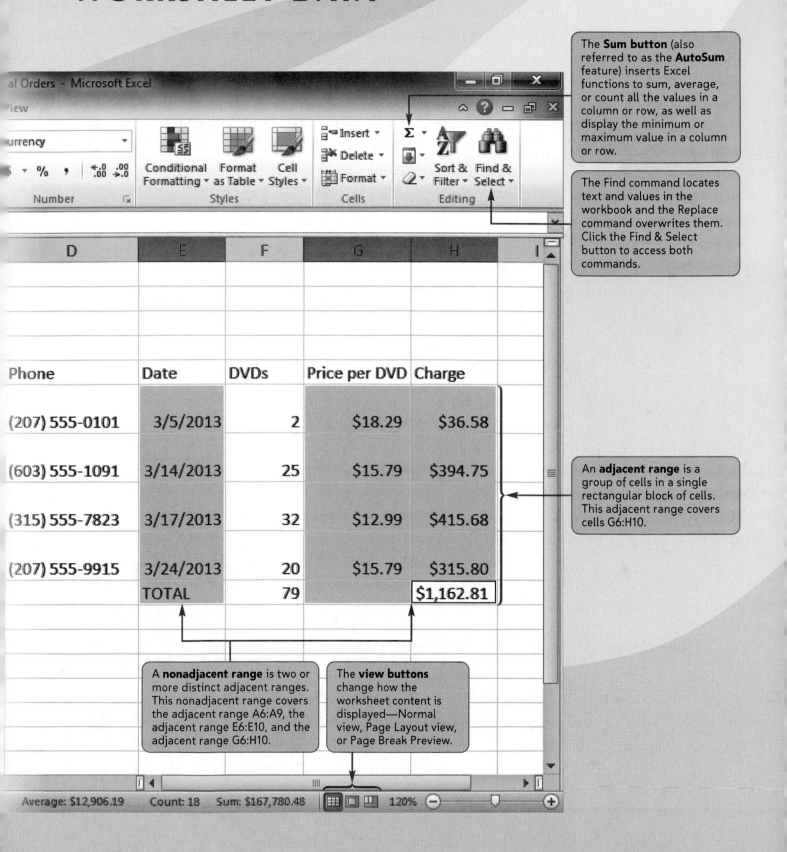

The **Sum button** (also referred to as the **AutoSum** feature) inserts Excel functions to sum, average, or count all the values in a column or row, as well as display the minimum or maximum value in a column or row.

The Find command locates text and values in the workbook and the Replace command overwrites them. Click the Find & Select button to access both commands.

An **adjacent range** is a group of cells in a single rectangular block of cells. This adjacent range covers cells G6:H10.

A **nonadjacent range** is two or more distinct adjacent ranges. This nonadjacent range covers the adjacent range A6:A9, the adjacent range E6:E10, and the adjacent range G6:H10.

The **view buttons** change how the worksheet content is displayed—Normal view, Page Layout view, or Page Break Preview.

al Orders - Microsoft Excel

Phone	Date	DVDs	Price per DVD	Charge
(207) 555-0101	3/5/2013	2	$18.29	$36.58
(603) 555-1091	3/14/2013	25	$15.79	$394.75
(315) 555-7823	3/17/2013	32	$12.99	$415.68
(207) 555-9915	3/24/2013	20	$15.79	$315.80
	TOTAL	79		$1,162.81

Average: $12,906.19   Count: 18   Sum: $167,780.48   120%

Working with Cells and Ranges

In the previous session, you worked with entire columns or rows of cells. In this session you'll work with groups of worksheet cells, or ranges. The customer order data you entered in cells A1 through G5 forms an adjacent range because it covers one rectangular block of cells. All the last names in cells A1 through A5 and all the numbers in cells F1 through G5 together form a nonadjacent range because they are two distinct rectangular blocks of cells.

Just as a cell reference indicates the location of an individual worksheet cell, a **range reference** indicates the location and size of a cell range. For adjacent ranges, the range reference includes the cell reference of the upper-left and lower-right cells in the rectangular block separated by a colon. For example, the range reference A1:G5 refers to all the cells in the rectangular block from cells A1 through G5. The range reference for nonadjacent ranges separates each adjacent range reference by a semicolon. For example, the cell reference A1:A5;F1:G5 references two rectangular blocks of cells: one covering cells A1 through A5 and the other covering cells F1 through G5.

Selecting a Range

You can select adjacent and nonadjacent ranges of cells with your mouse, just as you selected individual cells. Selecting a range enables you to work with all of the cells in the range as a group. This means you can move the groups of cells, delete them, or clear all their contents at the same time.

REFERENCE

Selecting Ranges

To select an adjacent range:
- Click the cell in the upper-left corner of the adjacent range, drag the pointer to the cell in the lower-right corner of the adjacent range, and then release the mouse button.

or
- Click the cell in the upper-left corner of the adjacent range, press the Shift key as you click the cell in the lower-right corner of the adjacent range, and then release the Shift key.

To select a nonadjacent range of cells:
- Select a cell or an adjacent range, press the Ctrl key as you select each additional cell or adjacent range, and then release the Ctrl key.

To select all the cells in a worksheet:
- Click the Select All button located at the intersection of the row and column headings (or press the Ctrl+A keys).

To select an entire row or entire rows:
- Click a row heading to select a single row. To select multiple rows, click and drag the pointer over multiple row headings.

To select an entire column or entire columns:
- Click a column heading to select a single column. To select multiple columns, click and drag the pointer over multiple column headings.

You'll use the pointer to select the adjacent range A1:G5, which includes all the content you entered in the orders worksheet.

To select the adjacent range A1:G5:

1. If you took a break at the end of the previous session, make sure the RipCity Digital Orders workbook is open and the Sheet2 worksheet is active.

2. Click cell **A1** to select that cell, and then with the mouse button still pressed, drag the pointer to cell **G5**, which is the cell in the lower-right corner of the range A1:G5.

3. Release the mouse button. As shown in Figure 1-14, all the cells in the adjacent range A1:G5 are selected. The selected cells are highlighted with color and surrounded by a black border. The first cell you selected, cell A1, is still the active cell in the worksheet.

Figure 1-14   Selected adjacent range A1:G5

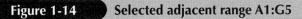

the active cell in the selected range is white

selected range is highlighted in the worksheet

4. Click any cell in the worksheet to deselect the range.

Next, you'll use the pointer to select the nonadjacent range A1:A5;F1:G5.

To select the nonadjacent range A1:A5;F1:G5:

1. Select the adjacent range **A1:A5** with your mouse.

2. Hold down the **Ctrl** key, and then select the adjacent range **F1:G5**.

3. Release the **Ctrl** key. As shown in Figure 1-15, all the cells in the nonadjacent range A1:A5;F1:G5 are selected.

| Figure 1-15 | Selected nonadjacent range A1:A5;F1:G5 |

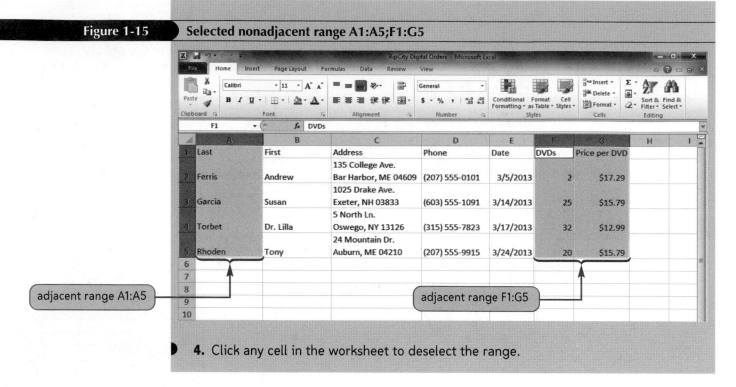

adjacent range A1:A5

adjacent range F1:G5

4. Click any cell in the worksheet to deselect the range.

Moving and Copying a Range

Amanda wants you to insert titles into the worksheet that describe the customer order data you have entered. Including the company name, a descriptive title, and the current date is part of good worksheet design, enabling others to quickly see the *who, what,* and *when* of the data. The current worksheet has no space to add this information. You could insert several blank rows at the top of the worksheet for this information. Another option is to select and then move the customer data lower in the worksheet, freeing up the rows at the top for the new text.

REFERENCE

Moving or Copying a Cell or Range

- Select the cell or range you want to move or copy.
- Move the pointer over the border of the selection until the pointer changes shape.
- To move the range, click the border and drag the selection to a new location (or to copy the range, hold down the Ctrl key and drag the selection to a new location).

or

- Select the cell or range you want to move or copy.
- In the Clipboard group on the Home tab, click the Cut button or the Copy button (or right-click the selection, and then click Cut or Copy on the shortcut menu).
- Select the cell or upper-left cell of the range where you want to move or copy the content.
- In the Clipboard group, click the Paste button (or right-click the selection, and then click Paste on the shortcut menu).

TIP

To move to a location that is not visible, drag the selection to the edge of the worksheet window until it scrolls down or across, and then drop the selection into the new location.

One way to move a cell or range is to select it, position the pointer over the bottom border of the selection, and then drag the selection to a new location. This technique is called **drag and drop** because you are dragging the range and dropping it in a new location. You can also use the drag-and-drop technique to copy cells by pressing the Ctrl key as you drag the selected range to its new location. A copy of the original range is placed in the new location without removing the original range from the worksheet.

You'll use the drag-and-drop method to move the customer order data to a new location in the worksheet.

To drag and drop the customer order data:

1. Select the range **A1:G5**.

2. Move the pointer over the bottom border of the selected range so that the pointer changes to ⌖.

3. Press and hold the mouse button to change the pointer to ⬚, and then drag the selection down three rows. Do not release the mouse button. A ScreenTip appears, indicating the new range reference of the selected cells. See Figure 1-16.

| Figure 1-16 | Selected range being moved |

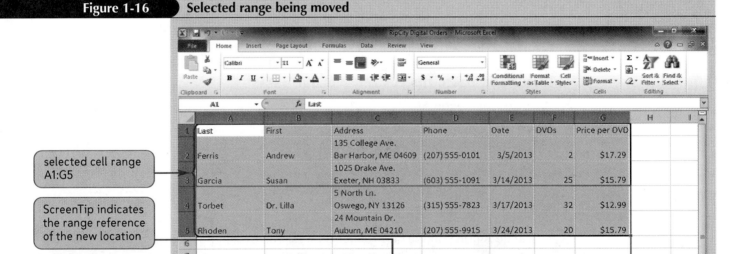

4. When the ScreenTip displays the range A4:G8, release the mouse button. The selected cells move to their new location.

5. Enter the title information shown in Figure 1-17 in the range A1:A3, pressing the **Enter** key after each entry.

Figure 1-17   **Titles added to the worksheet**

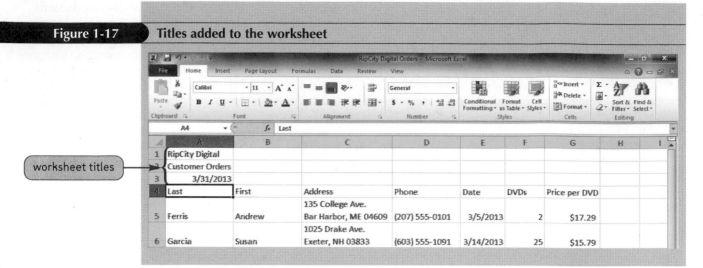

worksheet titles

Some people find dragging and dropping a difficult and awkward way to move a selection, particularly if the worksheet is large and complex. In those situations, it's often more efficient to cut and paste the cell contents. **Cutting** places the cell contents into computer memory or on the Clipboard. The contents can then be pasted from the Clipboard into a new location in the worksheet. You'll cut and paste a range now.

To cut and paste the customer order data:

1. Select the range **A4:G8**.

2. In the Clipboard group on the Home tab, click the **Cut** button ✂. The selected range is surrounded by a blinking border, which indicates that its contents are stored on the Clipboard.

3. Click cell **A11**. This cell is the upper-left corner of the range where you want to paste the data.

4. In the Clipboard group, click the **Paste** button. Excel pastes the contents of the range A4:G8 into the new range A11:G15. The blinking border disappears as a visual clue that the Clipboard is now empty.

5. With the range **A11:G15** still selected, click the **Cut** button ✂ in the Clipboard group.

6. Click cell **A4**, and then click the **Paste** button in the Clipboard group. The customer order data is pasted into its original location in the range A4:G8.

Inserting and Deleting a Range

Amanda wants more space between the three title rows you just entered and the table of customer orders. You could simply move the range A4:G8 down one more row, but another way is to insert new cells between the titles and the order data.

When you insert a new range of cells with the Insert button, the existing cells shift down when the selected range is wider than it is long, and they shift right when the selected range is longer than it is wide (as shown in Figure 1-18). When you use the Insert Cells command, you specify whether the existing cells shift right or down, or whether to insert an entire row or column into the new range.

Figure 1-18 Cells being inserted into a worksheet

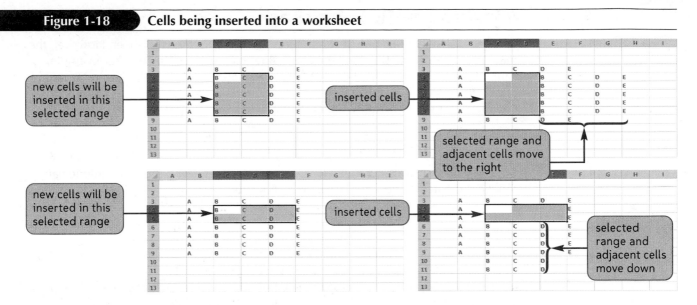

new cells will be inserted in this selected range

inserted cells

selected range and adjacent cells move to the right

new cells will be inserted in this selected range

inserted cells

selected range and adjacent cells move down

The process works in reverse when you delete a range. As with deleting a row or column, the cells adjacent to the deleted range either move up or left to fill in the space left by the deleted cells. The Delete Cells command lets you specify whether you want to shift the adjacent cells left or up, or whether to delete the entire column or row.

REFERENCE

Inserting or Deleting a Range

- Select a range that matches the range you want to insert or delete.
- In the Cells group on the Home tab, click the Insert button or the Delete button.

or

- Select the range that matches the range you want to insert or delete.
- In the Cells group on the Home tab, click the Insert button arrow and then click Insert Cells, or click the Delete button arrow and then click Delete Cells (or right-click the selected range, and then click Insert or Delete on the shortcut menu).
- Click the option button for the direction to shift the cells, columns, or rows.
- Click the OK button.

You will insert a blank range of cells between the worksheet titles and the table of customer orders.

To insert the cell range:

1. Select the range **A4:G4**. You want to insert blank cells in this range.

2. In the Cells group on the Home tab, click the **Insert button arrow**, and then click **Insert Cells**. The Insert dialog box opens.

3. Verify that the **Shift cells down** option button is selected.

4. Click the **OK** button. The existing cells shift down and the new cells are inserted into the range A4:G4.

Working with Formulas

So far you have entered only text, numbers, and dates in the worksheet. However, the main reason for using Excel is to display values calculated from data. For example, Amanda wants the workbook to determine the number of DVDs she has to create for her customers and how much revenue these orders will generate. Such calculations are added to a worksheet using formulas and functions.

Entering a Formula

A formula is an expression that returns a value. In most cases, this is a numeric value though it could also be a text string, a yes/no value, or a date. Every Excel formula begins with an equal sign (=) followed by an expression describing the operation that returns the value. Note that if you don't begin the formula with the equal sign, Excel assumes that you are entering text and will not treat the cell contents as a formula.

A formula is written using **operators** that combine different values, resulting in a single value that is then displayed within the cell. The most commonly used operators are **arithmetic operators** that perform addition, subtraction, multiplication, division, and exponentiation. For example, the following formula adds 5 and 7, returning a value of 12:

=5+7

Most Excel formulas contain references to cells rather than specific values. This allows you to change the values being used in the calculation without having to modify the formula itself. For example, the following formula returns the result of adding the values stored in cells A1 and B2:

=A1+B2

If the value 5 is stored in cell A1 and the value 7 is stored in cell B2, this formula would also return a value of 12. If you then changed the value in cell A1 to 10, the formula returns a value of 17. Figure 1-19 describes the different arithmetic operators and provides examples of formulas.

Figure 1-19　**Excel arithmetic operators**

Operation	Arithmetic Operator	Example	Description
Addition	+	=10+A1	Adds 10 to the value in cell A1
		=B1+B2+B3	Adds the values in cells B1, B2, and B3
Subtraction	–	=C9–B2	Subtracts the value in cell B2 from the value in cell C9
		=1–D2	Subtracts the value in cell D2 from 1
Multiplication	*	=C9*B9	Multiplies the values in cells C9 and B9
		=E5*0.06	Multiplies the value in cell E5 by 0.06
Division	/	=C9/B9	Divides the value in cell C9 by the value in cell B9
		=D15/12	Divides the value in cell D15 by 12
Exponentiation	^	=B5^3	Raises the value of cell B5 to the third power
		=3^B5	Raises 3 to the value in cell B5

If a formula contains more than one arithmetic operator, Excel performs the calculation using the same order of precedence you might have already seen in math classes. The **order of precedence** is a set of predefined rules used to determine the sequence in which operators are applied in a calculation. Excel first calculates the value of any operation within parentheses, then it applies exponentiation (^), multiplication (*), and division (/), and finally it performs addition (+) and subtraction (–). For example, the following formula returns the value 23 because multiplying 4 by 5 takes precedence over adding 3:

=3+4*5

If a formula contains two or more operators with the same level of precedence, the operators are applied in order from left to right. In the following formula, Excel first multiplies 4 by 10 and then divides that result by 8 to return the value 5:

=4*10/8

When parentheses are used, the value inside them is calculated first. In the following formula, Excel calculates the (3+4) and then multiplies that result by 5 to return the value 35:

=(3+4)*5

Figure 1-20 shows how slight changes in a formula affect the order of precedence and the result of the formula.

Figure 1-20   **Order of precedence applied to Excel formulas**

Formula	Application of the Order of Precedence	Result
=50+10*5	10*5 calculated first and then 50 is added	100
=(50+10)*5	(50+10) calculated first and then multiplied by 5	300
=50/10–5	50/10 calculated first and then 5 is subtracted	0
=50/(10–5)	(10–5) calculated first and then 50 is divided by that value	10
=50/10*5	Two operators at same precedence level, so the calculation is done left to right in the expression	25
=50/(10*5)	(10*5) calculated first and then 50 is divided by that value	1

REFERENCE

Inserting a Formula

- Click the cell in which you want the formula results to appear.
- Type = and a formula that calculates a value using cell references and arithmetic operators.
- Press the Enter key or press the Tab key to complete the formula.

Amanda wants the worksheet to include the total amount she charged for creating each customer's DVDs. The charge is equal to the number of DVDs created multiplied by the price per DVD. You've already entered this information for each customer in columns F and G. You'll enter a formula to calculate the charge for each customer in column H.

To enter the formula into the worksheet:

▶ **1.** Click cell **H5** to make it the active cell, type **Charge** for the column label, and then press the **Enter** key. The column label is entered in cell H5. Cell H6, where you want to enter the formula, is the active cell.

▶ **2.** Type **=F6*G6** (the number of DVDs created multiplied by the price per DVD). As you type the formula, a list of Excel function names appears in a ScreenTip, which provides a quick method for entering functions. The list will close when you complete the formula. You'll learn more about Excel functions shortly.

▶ **3.** Press the **Enter** key. The formula is entered in cell H6, which displays the value $34.58. The result is displayed as currency because cell G6 referenced in the formula contains a currency value.

After a formula has been entered into a cell, the worksheet displays the value returned by the formula. If the results are not what you expect, you might have entered the formula incorrectly. You can view the formula by selecting the cell and reviewing the expression displayed in the formula bar. One challenge with formulas, particularly long formulas, is interpreting the cell references. Excel makes this simpler by color coding each cell reference in the formula and its corresponding cell in the worksheet. You'll see this when you view the formula you just entered.

To view the formula:

▶ **1.** Click cell **H6** to make it the active cell. The formula you entered appears in the formula bar, whereas the value returned by the formula appears in the cell.

▶ **2.** Click in the formula bar. Each cell used in the formula has a different colored border that matches the color of its cell reference in the formula. This provides a visual cue to the formula, so you can quickly match cell references with their locations in the worksheet. See Figure 1-21.

Figure 1-21 Formula in the formula bar

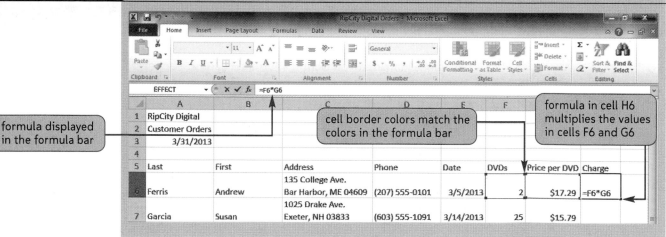

formula displayed in the formula bar

cell border colors match the colors in the formula bar

formula in cell H6 multiplies the values in cells F6 and G6

For Amanda's first customer, you entered the formula by typing each cell reference in the expression. You can also insert a cell reference by clicking the cell as you type the formula. This technique reduces the possibility of error caused by typing an incorrect cell reference. You'll use this method to enter the formula to calculate the charge for the second customer.

TIP

Be sure to type = as the first part of the entry in any cell containing a formula; otherwise, Excel will not interpret the entry as a formula.

To enter a cell reference using the mouse:

1. Click cell **H7** to make it the active cell, and then type =. When you type the equal sign, Excel knows that you're entering a formula. Any cell that you click from now on causes Excel to insert the cell reference of the selected cell into the formula until you complete the formula by pressing the Enter or Tab key.

2. Click cell **F7**. The cell reference is inserted into the formula in the formula bar. At this point, any cell you click changes the cell reference used in the formula. The cell reference isn't locked until you type an operator.

3. Type * to enter the multiplication operator. The cell reference for cell F7 is locked in the formula, and the next cell you click will be inserted after the operator.

4. Click cell **G7** to enter its cell reference in the formula, and then press the **Enter** key. Cell H7 displays the value $394.75, which is the total charge for the second customer.

Copying and Pasting Formulas

Sometimes you'll need to repeat the same formula throughout your worksheet. Rather than retyping the formula, you can copy a formula from one cell and paste it into another cell. Pasting a formula is different from pasting a value. With formulas, Excel adjusts the formula's cell references to reflect the new location of the formula in the worksheet. This is because you usually want to copy the actions of a formula rather than the specific value the formula generates. In this case, the formula's action is to multiply the number of DVDs Amanda created for a customer by the price she is charging for creating each DVD. By copying and pasting the formula, you can quickly repeat that action for every customer in the worksheet.

You will see how this works as you copy the formula you just entered in cell H7 to cells H8 and H9 to calculate Amanda's charges to the two remaining customers listed in the worksheet.

To copy and paste the formula that calculates charges:

1. Click cell **H7** to select the cell that contains the formula you want to copy.

2. In the Clipboard group on the Home tab, click the **Copy** button. Excel copies the formula to the Clipboard. The cell from which the formula was copied has a dotted border to remind you that cell is being copied.

3. Select the range **H8:H9**. These are the cells in which you want to paste the formula.

4. In the Clipboard group, click the **Paste** button. Excel pastes the formula into the selected range. A shortcut button appears below the selected range, providing options for pasting formulas and values. See Figure 1-22.

| Figure 1-22 | Formula copied and pasted |

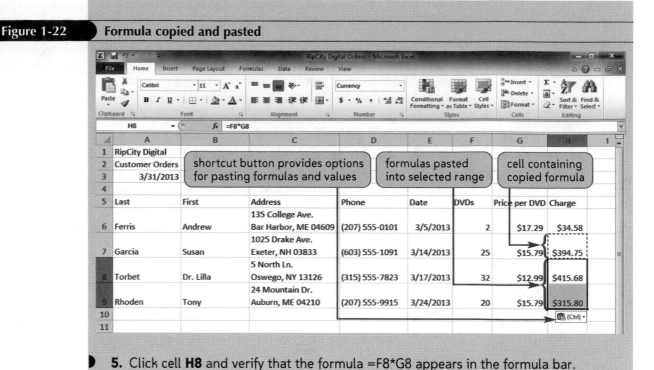

5. Click cell **H8** and verify that the formula =F8*G8 appears in the formula bar.

6. Click cell **H9** and verify that the formula =F9*G9 appears in the formula bar.

When you pasted the formulas into cells H8 and H9, Excel automatically adjusted the formulas so that the total charges calculated for the customers in rows 8 and 9 use the cell values from rows 8 and 9. By copying and pasting the formula, you have saved time and avoided potential mistakes in retyping the same formula again and again.

Introducing Functions

In addition to cell references and operators, formulas can also contain functions. A **function** is a named operation that returns a value. Functions are used to simplify formulas, reducing what might be a long formula into a compact statement. For example, to add the values in the range A1:A10, you could enter the following long formula:

```
=A1+A2+A3+A4+A5+A6+A7+A8+A9+A10
```

Or, you could use the SUM function to calculate the sum of cell values found within a specified range. In this case, the formula would appear as:

```
=SUM(A1:A10)
```

In both instances, Excel adds the values in cells A1 through A10, but the SUM function is faster and simpler to enter and less prone to a typing error. You should always use a function, if one is available, in place of a long, complex formula.

Excel supports more than 300 different functions from the fields of finance, business, science, and engineering. Excel provides functions that work with numbers, text, and dates.

Entering a Function

Amanda wants to calculate the total number of DVDs she needs to create for her customers. To do that, you'll use the SUM function to add the values in the range F6:F9.

To enter the SUM function to add the values in the range F6:F9:

1. Click cell **E10**, type **TOTAL** in all uppercase letters as the label, and then press the **Tab** key. The label is entered in cell E10, and cell F10 is the active cell.

2. Type **=SUM(F6:F9** in cell F10. As you begin to type the function, a ScreenTip lists the names of all functions that start with the letter "S." When you type the cell references, Excel highlights all the cells in the specified range to provide a visual reminder of exactly which cells the SUM function is using. See Figure 1-23.

Figure 1-23   **SUM function being entered**

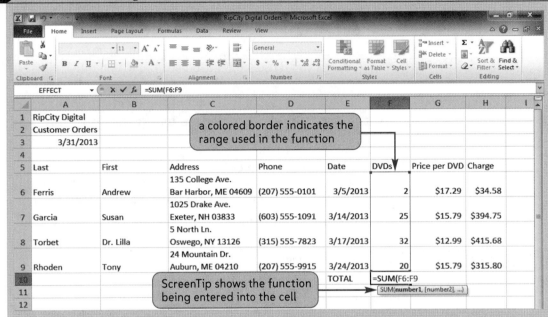

3. Type **)** to complete the function, and then press the **Tab** key. The value of the SUM function appears in cell F10, indicating that Amanda has to create 79 DVDs to complete all of her current orders.

Entering Functions with the AutoSum Feature

A fast and convenient way to enter commonly used functions is with the AutoSum feature. The AutoSum feature includes buttons to quickly insert the SUM, AVERAGE, COUNT, MIN, and MAX functions to generate the following:

- Sum of the values in the column or row
- Average value in the column or row
- Total count of numeric values in the column or row
- Minimum value in the column or row
- Maximum value in the column or row

The Sum button automatically inserts both the function name and the range reference to the row or column of data to which the summary function is being applied.

INSIGHT

How AutoSum Works

Excel determines the range reference needed for the function being inserted by the AutoSum feature by examining the layout of the data and choosing what seems to be the most likely range. When you use the Sum button, Excel highlights the range it thinks you want to use. For example, if you use the Sum button in a cell that is below a column of numbers, Excel assumes that you want to summarize the values in the column. You can change that range by typing a different range reference or selecting a different range.

Make sure to always verify the range AutoSum selected, especially when a worksheet's column or row titles contain numbers. AutoSum cannot differentiate between numbers used as titles (such as years) and numbers used as data for the calculation.

Amanda wants to calculate the total revenue she'll generate after she fulfills her customer orders. You'll use the AutoSum feature to enter the SUM function.

To calculate the total revenue using the AutoSum feature:

1. Click cell **H10** to make it the active cell.

2. In the Editing group on the Home tab, click the **Sum button arrow** Σ ▾. The button's menu opens and displays five common summary functions: Sum, Average, Count Numbers, Max (for maximum), and Min (for minimum).

3. Click **Sum** to enter the SUM function. See Figure 1-24.

| Figure 1-24 | SUM function being entered with AutoSum |

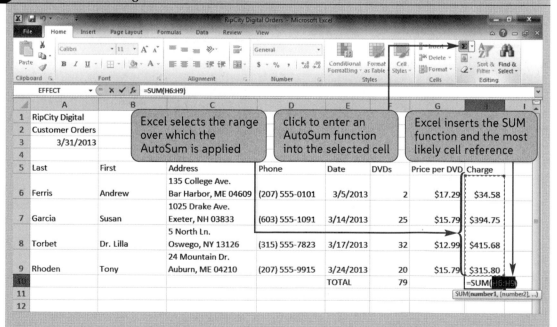

4. Verify that the range **H6:H9** appears in the SUM function and is highlighted with a dotted border. The dotted border shows what will be included in the SUM function.

5. Press the **Enter** key to accept the automatically generated formula. The total charge for all of Amanda's customers, shown in cell H10, is $1,160.81.

PROSKILLS

Problem Solving: Writing Effective Formulas

You can use formulas to quickly perform calculations and solve problems. First, identify the problem you need to solve. Then, gather the data needed to solve the problem. Finally, create accurate and effective formulas that use the data to answer or resolve the problem. Follow these guidelines:

- **Keep formulas simple.** Use functions in place of long, complex formulas whenever possible. For example, use the SUM function instead of entering a formula that adds individual cells, which makes it easier to confirm that the formula is making an accurate calculation as it provides answers needed to evaluate the problem.
- **Do not hide data values within formulas.** The worksheet displays formula results, not the actual formula. For example, to calculate a 5% interest rate on a currency value in cell A5, you could enter the formula =0.05*A5. However, this doesn't show how the value is calculated. A better approach places the value 0.05 in a cell accompanied by a descriptive label and uses the cell reference in the formula. If you place 0.05 in cell A6, the formula =A6*A5 would calculate the interest value. Other people can then easily see the interest rate as well as the resulting interest, ensuring that the formula is solving the right problem.
- **Break up formulas to show intermediate results.** When a worksheet contains complex computations, other people can more easily comprehend how the formula results are calculated when different parts of the formula are distinguished. For example, the formula =SUM(A1:A10)/SUM(B1:B10) calculates the ratio of two sums, but hides the two sum values. Instead, enter each SUM function in a separate cell, such as cells A11 and B11, and use the formula =A11/B11 to calculate the ratio. Other people can see both sums and the value of their ratio in the worksheet and better understand the final result, which makes it more likely that the best problem resolution will be selected.

Finding a solution to a problem requires accurate data and analysis. With workbooks, this means using formulas that are easy to understand, clearly show the data being used in the calculations, and demonstrate how the results are calculated. Only then can you be confident that you are choosing the best problem resolution.

Working with Worksheets

You've seen that new workbooks are created with three initial worksheets labeled Sheet1, Sheet2, and Sheet3. If needed, you can add new worksheets to a workbook and remove unused sheets. You can also give worksheets more descriptive and meaningful names.

Inserting or Deleting a Worksheet

TIP

To insert a new worksheet to the left of the active sheet, right-click a sheet tab, click Insert on the shortcut menu, select a sheet type, and then click the OK button.

When you insert a new worksheet in a workbook, the new sheet is named based on the number and names of the other sheets in the workbook. For example, if a workbook has four worksheets named Sheet1 through Sheet4, the next inserted worksheet is named Sheet5. You'll add a new, blank worksheet to the RipCity Digital Orders workbook.

To insert a new worksheet:

1. Locate the three sheet tabs in the lower-left corner of the worksheet window.

2. To the right of the Sheet3 sheet tab, click the **Insert Worksheet** tab 🗐. A new worksheet named Sheet4 appears at the end of the workbook and is active.

The workbook now includes two empty worksheets: Sheet3 and Sheet4. Because you don't plan to use these sheets, it's a good idea to remove them.

To delete the Sheet3 and Sheet4 worksheets:

1. Right-click the **Sheet3** sheet tab, and then click **Delete** on the shortcut menu. The Sheet3 worksheet is removed from the workbook.

2. If necessary, click the **Sheet4** sheet tab to make it the active sheet.

3. In the Cells group on the Home tab, click the **Delete button arrow**, and then click **Delete Sheet**. The Sheet4 worksheet is removed from the workbook.

Renaming a Worksheet

The remaining worksheets, Sheet1 and Sheet2, do not have very descriptive names. You can rename them so that they better describe their contents. Keep in mind that sheet names cannot exceed 31 characters in length, including blank spaces. The width of the sheet tab adjusts to the length of the name you enter. You'll rename Sheet1 and Sheet2.

TIP

You can also rename a sheet by right-clicking the sheet tab and clicking Rename on the shortcut menu.

To rename the two worksheets:

1. Double-click the **Sheet2** sheet tab. The sheet name is selected in the sheet tab.

2. Type **Customer Orders** and then press the **Enter** key. The width of the sheet tab expands to match the longer sheet name.

3. Double-click the **Sheet1** sheet tab, type **Documentation**, and then press the **Enter** key. Both sheets are renamed.

Moving and Copying a Worksheet

You can change the placement of the worksheets in a workbook. A good practice is to place the most important worksheets at the beginning of the workbook (the leftmost sheet tabs) and less important worksheets toward the end (the rightmost tabs). You'll move the Documentation sheet to the end of the workbook and then return it to the beginning.

TIP

To copy a worksheet, hold down the Ctrl key as you drag and drop the sheet tab. The copy appears where you drop the sheet tab; the original remains in its initial position.

To move the Documentation sheet:

1. If necessary, click the **Documentation** sheet tab to make that worksheet active.

2. Press and hold the mouse button so the pointer changes to ▯ and a small triangle appears in the upper-left corner of the tab.

3. Drag the pointer to the right of the Customer Orders sheet tab, and then release the mouse button. The Documentation worksheet is now the second sheet in the workbook.

4. Drag the **Documentation** worksheet back to be the first sheet in the workbook.

Editing Worksheet Content

As you work, you might make mistakes that you want to correct or undo, or you might need to replace a value based on more current information. The price per DVD for Andrew Ferris's order should be $18.29, not $17.29 as entered in cell G6. You could simply clear the value in the cell and then type the correct value. However, sometimes you need to edit only a portion of an entry rather than change the entire contents of a cell, especially if the cell contains a large block of text or a complex formula. To edit the cell contents, you can work in **Edit mode**.

When you work in Edit mode, some of the keyboard shortcuts you've been using work differently because they apply only to the text within the selected cell. For example, the Home, End, Backspace, Delete, and arrow keys move the insertion point to different locations within the cell. The Home key moves the insertion point to the beginning of the cell's content. The End key moves the insertion point to the end of the cell's content. The left and right arrow keys move the insertion point backward and forward through the cell's content. The Backspace key deletes the character immediately to the left of the insertion point, and the Delete key deletes the character to the right of the insertion point. You'll change one digit of the value in cell G6 to correct the price per DVD.

TIP

To change the active cell to Edit mode, press the F2 key or click in the formula bar. To cancel all changes made in Edit mode, press the Esc key or click the Cancel button in the formula bar.

To edit the value in cell G6:

1. Click the **Customer Orders** sheet tab to make it the active worksheet.
2. Double-click cell **G6**. The mode indicator on the status bar switches from Ready to Edit, indicating that you are in Edit mode.
3. Press the **End** key. The insertion point moves to the end of the cell.
4. Press the ← key three times. The insertion point moves to the right of the 7.
5. Press the **Backspace** key to delete the 7, and then type **8**. The value in cell G6 changes to 18.29. See Figure 1-25.

Figure 1-25 Cell being edited in Edit mode

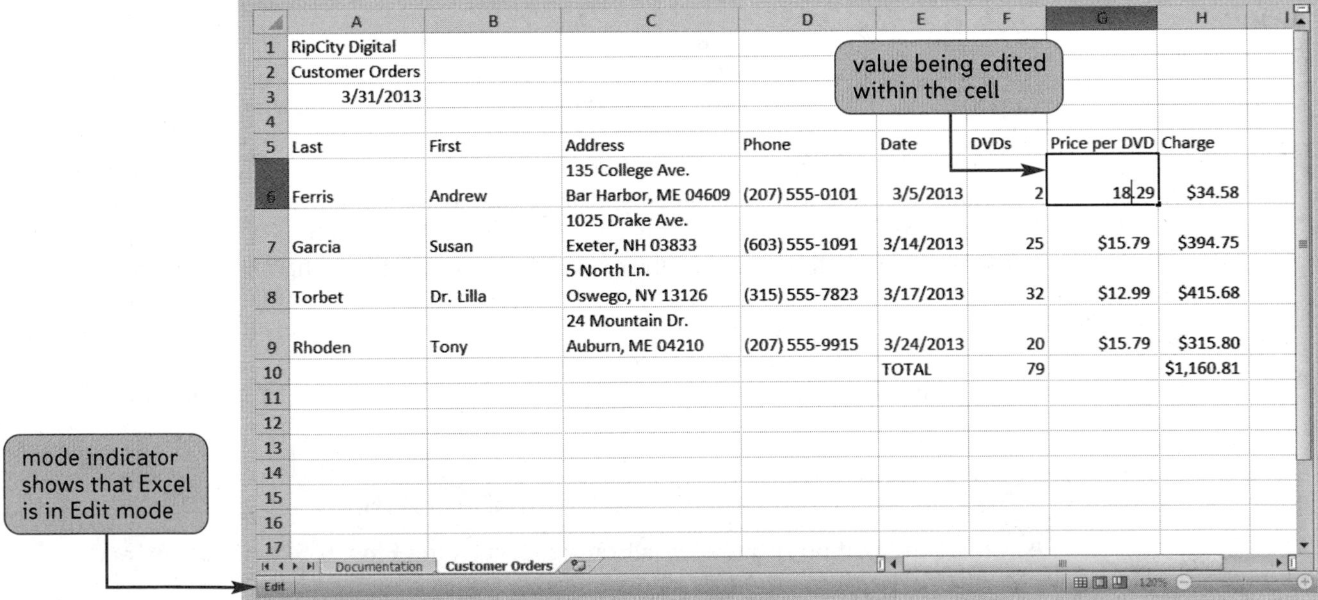

	A	B	C	D	E	F	G	H
1	RipCity Digital							
2	Customer Orders							
3	3/31/2013							
4								
5	Last	First	Address	Phone	Date	DVDs	Price per DVD	Charge
6	Ferris	Andrew	135 College Ave. Bar Harbor, ME 04609	(207) 555-0101	3/5/2013	2	18.29	$34.58
7	Garcia	Susan	1025 Drake Ave. Exeter, NH 03833	(603) 555-1091	3/14/2013	25	$15.79	$394.75
8	Torbet	Dr. Lilla	5 North Ln. Oswego, NY 13126	(315) 555-7823	3/17/2013	32	$12.99	$415.68
9	Rhoden	Tony	24 Mountain Dr. Auburn, ME 04210	(207) 555-9915	3/24/2013	20	$15.79	$315.80
10					TOTAL	79		$1,160.81

6. Press the **Enter** key to accept the edit in cell G6. The value $18.29 appears in cell G6, the active cell is cell G7, and the mode indicator on the status bar changes from Edit to Ready to indicate that you are no longer in Edit mode.

Undoing and Redoing an Action

As you revise a workbook, you might need to undo a previous action. Excel maintains a list of the actions you perform in a workbook during the current session, so you can undo most of these actions. You can reverse the most recent action or you can reverse more than one action. If you undo more than one action, all actions subsequent to the earliest action you select are also undone. You'll undo the edit to cell G6.

To undo the edit to cell G6:

▶ **1.** On the Quick Access Toolbar, click the **Undo** button ↺.

▶ **2.** Verify that $17.29 appears again in cell G6, indicating that your last action—editing the value of this cell—has been undone.

If you find that you have gone too far in undoing previous actions, you can go forward in the action list and redo those actions. As with the Undo feature, you can redo more than one action at a time. You'll use Redo to restore the value of cell G6.

To redo the edit to cell G6:

▶ **1.** On the Quick Access Toolbar, click the **Redo** button ↻.

▶ **2.** Verify that the value in cell G6 returns to $18.29.

Using Find and Replace

Amanda wants you to replace all the street title abbreviations with their full names. Specifically, "Ave." should be "Avenue," "Ln." should be "Lane," and "Dr." should be "Drive." Although you could read through the worksheet to locate each occurrence, this can be time-consuming with larger workbooks. For greater speed and accuracy, you can use the Find command to locate a string of characters known as a **search string** and replace that text with a **replacement string** of new text characters.

You can limit the search to the current worksheet or search the entire workbook. You can specify whether to match the capitalization in the Find what box and whether the search text should match the entire cell contents or part of the cell contents. You can choose to review each occurrence of the search value and decide whether to replace it, or you can replace all occurrences at once.

You'll use the Find and Replace commands to replace each street title abbreviation.

To find and replace the street title abbreviations:

▶ **1.** In the Editing group on the Home tab, click the **Find & Select** button, and then click **Replace**. The Find and Replace dialog box opens.

▶ **2.** Type **Ave.** in the Find what box, press the **Tab** key, and then type **Avenue** in the Replace with box.

▶ **3.** Click the **Options** button. The dialog box expands to display additional Find and Replace options. See Figure 1-26.

Figure 1-26   Find and Replace dialog box

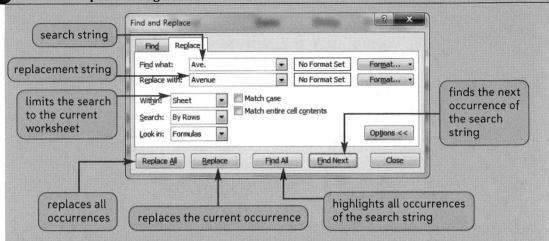

4. Verify that **Sheet** appears in the Within box to limit the find and replace to the current worksheet only.

5. Click the **Replace All** button. Excel finds and replaces the search string wherever it appears in the current worksheet. A dialog box opens, indicating that Excel has completed its search and made two replacements.

6. Click the **OK** button to close the dialog box.

7. Select the text in the Find what box, type **Ln.** as the new search string, press the **Tab** key, and then type **Lane** in the Replace with box. You want to replace all instances of this search string.

8. Click the **Replace All** button to make the replacement wherever it appears in the worksheet, and then click the **OK** button to close the dialog box that indicates Excel has completed its search and made one replacement.

9. Select the text in the Find what box, type **Dr.** as the new search string, press the **Tab** key, and then type **Drive** in the Replace with box. Because "Dr." is also the abbreviation for "Doctor," you must review each "Dr." abbreviation and replace only the ones within an address.

10. Click the **Find Next** button. The next occurrence of "Dr." in the worksheet occurs in cell B8 with the text, "Dr. Lilla."

11. Click the **Find Next** button to ignore this occurrence. The next occurrence of "Dr." is in the mailing address for Tony Rhoden.

12. Click the **Replace** button to replace this text. The only other occurrence of "Dr." in the worksheet—"Dr. Lilla"—is highlighted again. You've finished finding and replacing text in the worksheet.

13. Click the **Close** button to close the Find and Replace dialog box.

Using the Spelling Checker

Another editing tool is the spelling checker. Although the spelling checker's dictionary includes a large number of words, as well as common first and last names and places, many words you use in workbooks might not be included. If the spelling checker finds a word that is not in its dictionary, the word appears in a dialog box along with a list of suggested replacements. You can replace the word with one from the list, or you can ignore the word and go to the next possible misspelling. You can also add words to the dictionary to prevent them from being flagged as misspellings in the future. Note that the spelling checker will not find a correctly spelled word used incorrectly, such as "there" instead of "their" or "your" instead of "you're." The best way to catch these types of errors is to proofread your worksheets.

Before giving the workbook to Amanda, you'll check the spelling in the Customer Orders worksheet.

To check the spelling in the Customer Orders worksheet:

1. Click cell **A1** to start the spell check from the upper-left corner of the sheet.

2. Click the **Review** tab on the Ribbon, and then click the **Spelling** button in the Proofing group. The Spelling dialog box opens and flags "RipCity" as a possible spelling error. Excel suggests two alternatives. See Figure 1-27.

Figure 1-27 Spelling dialog box

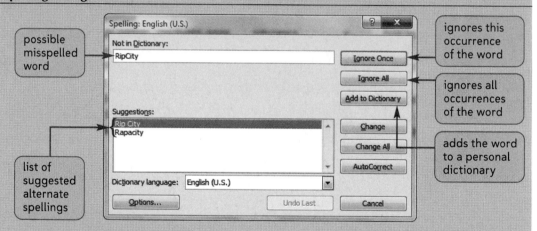

3. Click the **Ignore All** button. You ignored all the occurrences of this spelling because "RipCity" is the name of Amanda's company. The spelling checker flags "Torbet," a last name that is not in the program's dictionary.

4. Click the **Ignore All** button to ignore the spelling of this name. The next potential spelling error is the name "Lilla" in cell B8. The name should have been entered as "Lila," a first name that the spelling checker recognizes.

5. Click **Lila** in the Suggestions box, if necessary, and then click the **Change** button. The text is changed within the cell. The spelling checker is finished.

   Trouble? If the spelling checker finds another error, you might have another typing error in your worksheet. Use the spelling checker to find and correct any other errors in your workbook, and then continue with Step 6.

6. Click the **OK** button to close the Microsoft Excel dialog box.

7. Proofread the worksheet and correct any other spelling errors you find. You do not have to check the spelling in the Documentation worksheet at this time.

Previewing and Printing a Workbook

Now that you have finished the final edit of the workbook, you are ready to print a hard copy of the customer orders list for Amanda. However, before you print the workbook, you should preview it to ensure that it will print correctly.

Changing Worksheet Views

You can view a worksheet in three ways. **Normal view**, which you've been using throughout this tutorial, shows the contents of the worksheet. **Page Layout view** shows how the worksheet will appear when printed. **Page Break Preview** displays the location of the different page breaks within the worksheet. This is useful when a worksheet will span several printed pages and you need to control what content appears on each page.

You'll switch between these views to see how the Customer Orders worksheet will appear on printed pages.

To switch the worksheet views:

▶ **1.** Click the **Page Layout** button 🔲 on the status bar. The page layout of the worksheet appears in the program window. You want to see the rest of the data, which extends to a second page.

▶ **2.** Use the Zoom slider to reduce the zoom level to **60%**. See Figure 1-28.

| Figure 1-28 | Worksheet displayed in Page Layout view |

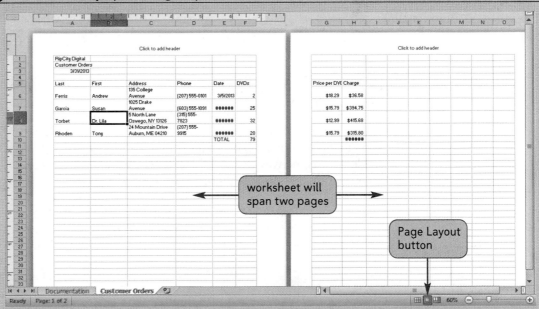

▶ **3.** Click the **Page Break Preview** button 🔲 on the status bar. The view switches to Page Break Preview, which shows only those parts of the current worksheet that will print. A dotted blue border separates one page from another.

Trouble? If the Welcome to Page Break Preview dialog box opens, this is the first time you've switched to Page Break Preview. Click the OK button to close the dialog box and continue with Step 4.

4. Zoom the worksheet to **120%** so that you can more easily read the contents of the worksheet. See Figure 1-29.

Figure 1-29   Worksheet displayed in Page Break Preview

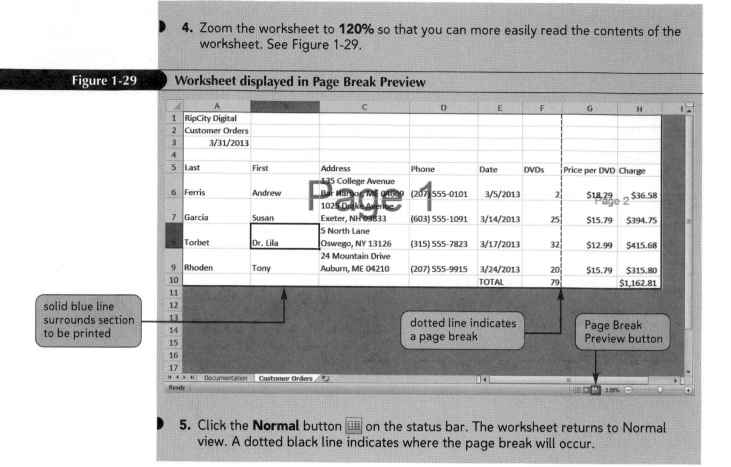

solid blue line surrounds section to be printed

dotted line indicates a page break

Page Break Preview button

5. Click the **Normal** button ⊞ on the status bar. The worksheet returns to Normal view. A dotted black line indicates where the page break will occur.

Working with Portrait and Landscape Orientation

As you saw in Page Layout view and Page Break Preview, the Customer Orders worksheet will print on two pages—columns A through F will print on one page and columns G and H will print on a second page. Amanda wants the entire worksheet printed on a single page. One way to accomplish this is to change the page orientation from portrait to landscape. In **portrait orientation**, the page is taller than it is wide. In **landscape orientation**, the page is wider than it is tall. By default, Excel displays pages in portrait orientation. In many cases, however, you will want to print the page in landscape orientation. Changing the page orientation affects only the active worksheet.

You'll change the orientation of the Customer Orders worksheet to landscape.

To change the page orientation of the worksheet:

1. Click the **Page Layout** tab on the Ribbon.

2. In the Page Setup group, click the **Orientation** button, and then click **Landscape**. The orientation switches to landscape, and the worksheet contents fit on one page.

3. Click the **Page Layout** button 🔲 on the status bar, and then verify that all the worksheet contents fit on one page.

4. Click the **Documentation** sheet tab, and then click the **Page Layout** button 🔲. The Documentation sheet remains in portrait orientation.

5. Verify that the entire contents of the Documentation worksheet fit on one page.

Printing the Workbook

You can print the contents of a workbook by using the Print tab in Backstage view. The Print tab provides options for choosing what to print and how to print. For example, you can specify the number of copies to print, which printer to use, and what to print. You can choose to print only the selected cells, the active sheets, or all worksheets in the workbook that contain data. The printout will include only the data in the worksheet. The other elements in the worksheet, such as the row and column headings and the gridlines around the worksheet cells, will not print by default. You also see a preview of the workbook so you can see exactly how printed pages will look with the settings you've chosen before you print. A good practice is to always review the print preview before printing to ensure that the printout looks exactly as you intended and avoid unnecessary reprinting.

You'll preview and print the RipCity Digital Orders workbook now.

To preview and print the workbook:

1. Click the File tab on the Ribbon to display Backstage view.

2. Click the **Print** tab in the navigation bar to display the print options and preview of the first sheet in the workbook (the Documentation worksheet). See Figure 1-30.

Figure 1-30	Print tab in Backstage view

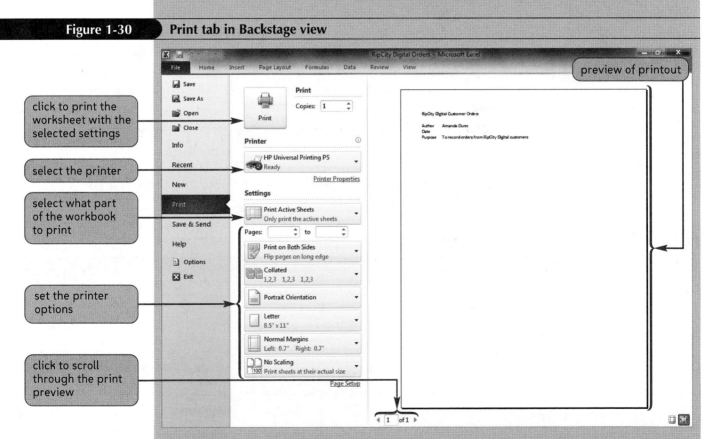

click to print the worksheet with the selected settings

select the printer

select what part of the workbook to print

set the printer options

click to scroll through the print preview

preview of printout

3. Click the **Printer** button, and then click the printer to which you want to print if it is not already selected.

4. In the Settings group, click the top button, and then click **Print Entire Workbook**. This will print both the Documentation worksheet and the Customer Orders worksheet.

5. Below the preview, click the **Next Page** button ▶. The first page of the print job contains the contents of the Documentation worksheet in portrait orientation, and the second page contains the Customer Orders worksheet in landscape orientation.

6. Click the **Print** button. The worksheet prints.

Viewing and Printing Worksheet Formulas

The printout of the Customer Orders worksheet displays only the worksheet values and none of the formulas. Most of the time, you will be interested in only the final results of the worksheet, not the formulas used to calculate those results. However, in some cases, you might want to view the formulas used to develop the workbook. This is particularly useful when you encounter unexpected results and you want to examine the underlying formulas, or you want to discuss your formulas with a colleague. You can view the formulas in a workbook by switching to **formula view**, a view of the worksheet contents that displays formulas instead of the resulting values.

You'll look at the Customer Orders worksheet in formula view now.

To view the formulas in the Customer Orders worksheet:

TIP

To toggle in and out of formula view, press the Ctrl+` keys. The ` grave accent symbol is usually located above the Tab key on your keyboard.

1. Click the **Customer Orders** sheet tab, if necessary, and then click the **Normal** button ▦ on the status bar. The Customer Orders worksheet is active and displayed in Normal view.

2. Press the **Ctrl+`** keys. The worksheet changes to formula view.

3. Scroll the worksheet to the right to view the formulas in columns F and H. The column widths are wider to display the entire formula in each cell. As long as you don't resize the column widths while in formula view, they remain unchanged in other views. See Figure 1-31.

Figure 1-31 **Worksheet in formula view**

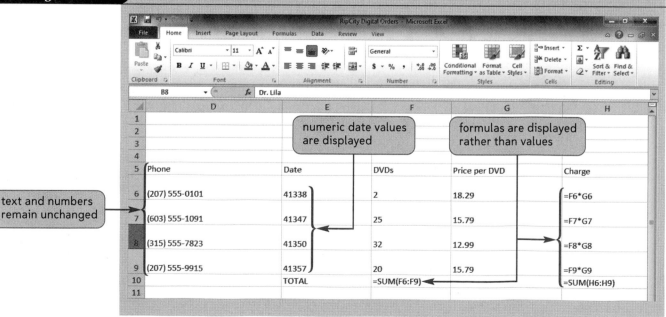

Amanda wants a printout of the formula view. The Customer Orders worksheet will not fit on one page because of the expanded column widths. You can scale the worksheet to force the contents to fit on a single page. **Scaling** a printout reduces the width and the height of the printout to fit the number of pages you specify by shrinking the text size as needed. You can also scale a printout proportionally to a percentage of its actual size. You'll scale the Customer Orders worksheet to a width and height of one page.

To scale the worksheet formulas to print on one page:

1. Click the **Page Layout** tab on the Ribbon.

2. In the Scale to Fit group, click the **Width arrow**, and then click **1 page**.

3. In the Scale to Fit group, click the **Height arrow**, and then click **1 page**. You'll verify that the worksheet formula view fits on a single page.

4. Click the **Page Layout** button 📖 on the status bar, and then zoom the worksheet to **50%**. The formula view of the worksheet fits on one page. See Figure 1-32.

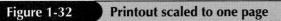
Figure 1-32   **Printout scaled to one page**

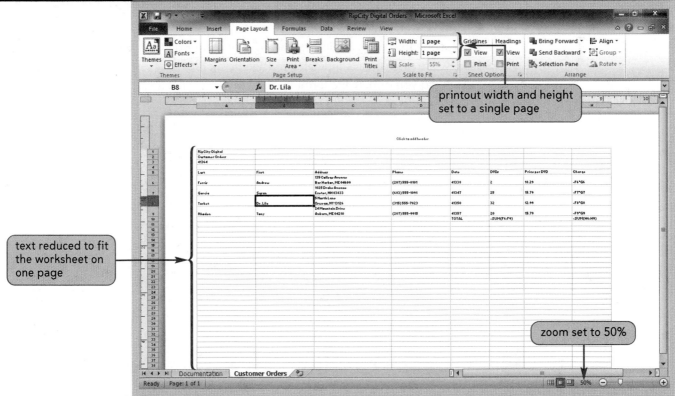

5. Click the **File** tab on the Ribbon to display Backstage view, and then click the **Print** tab in the navigation bar to view the print options.

6. In the Settings group, click the top button, and then click **Print Active Sheets** to print only the Customer Orders worksheet.

7. Click the **Print** button. The active sheet, the Customer Orders worksheet, prints.

At this point, you've completed your work for Amanda. Before closing the workbook, you'll change the view of the workbook contents back to Normal view.

To save and close the workbook:

▶ 1. Press the **Ctrl+`** keys to switch the worksheet out of formula view.

▶ 2. Click the **Normal** button ⊞ on the status bar to return the worksheet to Normal view.

▶ 3. Save your changes to the workbook, and then close it.

Amanda is pleased with the workbook you created for her. All the customers and orders appear on one worksheet, and she can easily add new customers and orders. The formulas quickly update the calculations that show her income from burning DVDs.

REVIEW

Session 1.2 Quick Check

1. Describe the two types of ranges in Excel.
2. What is the range reference for cells A3 through G5 and J3 through M5?
3. What formula would you enter to add the values in cells B4, B5, and B6? What function would you enter to achieve the same result?
4. How do you rename a worksheet?
5. Describe four ways of viewing the content of an Excel workbook.
6. How are page breaks indicated in Page Break Preview?
7. How do you display the formulas used in a worksheet?
8. Why would you scale a worksheet?

Review Assignments

There are no Data Files needed for the Review Assignments.

Amanda has another set of orders for you to enter on the Customer Orders worksheet. In addition to calculating the charge for creating the DVDs, Amanda also wants to include the cost of shipping in the total charged to each customer. Complete the following:

1. Open a blank workbook, and then save the workbook as **Order Report** in the Excel1\Review folder.
2. Rename the Sheet1 worksheet as **Documentation**, and then enter the following data into the specified cells:
   Cell A1: **RipCity Digital**
   Cell A3: **Author**   Cell B3: your name
   Cell A4: **Date**   Cell B4: the current date
   Cell A5: **Purpose**   Cell B5: **To track customer orders for RipCity Digital**
3. Rename the Sheet2 worksheet as **Customer Orders**.
4. Delete the Sheet3 worksheet.
5. On the Customer Orders worksheet, enter the following data into the specified cells:
   Cell A1: **RipCity Digital**
   Cell A3: **Customer Orders Report**
   Cell A4: **March 27 to April 17, 2013**
6. In cells A5 through H10, enter the column titles and data from Figure 1-33. The address text in column D should be set on two lines within each cell.

Figure 1-33   New customer order data

Date	Last	First	Address	Phone	DVDs	Price per DVD	Shipping Charge
3/27/2013	Fleming	Doris	25 Lee St. Bedford, VA 24523	(540) 555-5681	7	$18.29	$7.49
4/4/2013	Ortiz	Thomas	28 Ridge Ln. Newfane, VT 05345	(802) 555-7710	13	$16.55	$9.89
4/8/2013	Dexter	Kay	150 Main St. Greenbelt, MD 20770	(301) 555-8823	25	$15.79	$7.23
4/9/2013	Sisk	Norman	250 East Maple Ln. Cranston, RI 02910	(401) 555-3350	15	$16.55	$10.55
4/17/2013	Romano	June	207 Jackston Ave. Westport, IN 47283	(812) 555-2681	22	$15.79	$13.95

7. Set the width of column A to 10 characters, columns B and C to 12 characters, column D to 20 characters, and columns E, G, and H to 16 characters.
8. Autofit all of the rows in the worksheet to the cell contents.
9. In cell I5, enter **Total Charge**. In cell I6, insert a formula that calculates the total charge for the first customer (the number of DVDs multiplied by the price per DVD and then added to the shipping charge). Increase the width of column I to 11 characters.
10. Copy the formula in cell I6 and paste it into the range I7:I10.

11. In cell E11, enter **Total DVDs**. In cell F11, use the SUM function to calculate the total number of DVDs created for all customers. In cell I11, use the AutoSum feature to insert the SUM function to calculate the total charges for all of the customer orders.

12. Use Edit mode to make the following corrections:

   a. In cell D6, change the street address from "25 Lee St." to **2500 Lee St.**

   b. In cell F9, change the number of DVDs from "15" to **17**.

   c. In cell H8, change the shipping charge from "$7.23" to **$8.23**.

13. Use the Find and Replace commands to replace all occurrences of "St." with **Street**, "Ln." with **Lane**, and "Ave." with **Avenue**.

14. Change the page layout of the Customer Orders worksheet to print in landscape orientation on a single page.

15. Preview and print the contents of the entire workbook.

16. Change the Customer Orders worksheet to formula view, landscape orientation, and scaled to fit on a single page. Preview and print the Customer Orders worksheet.

17. Return the view of the Customer Orders worksheet to Normal view, save your changes to the Order Report workbook, and then save the current workbook as **Revised Report** in the Excel1\Review folder. (*Hint*: Use the Save As command in Backstage view to save the existing workbook with a new name.)

18. Remove Kay Dexter's order from the Customer Orders worksheet.

19. Add the following order directly after the order placed by June Romano: date **4/22/2013**; name **Patrick Crawford**; address **200 Valley View Road, Rome, GA 30161**; phone **(706) 555-0998**; DVDs **14**; price per DVD **$16.55**; shipping charge **$12.45**.

20. Use Edit mode to change the ending date of the report in cell A4 from "April 17" to **April 22**.

21. Save the workbook, preview and print the contents and formulas of the revised Customer Orders worksheet, close the workbook, and then submit the finished workbooks and printouts to your instructor.

Case Problem 1

If you have a SAM 2010 user profile, your instructor may have assigned an autogradable version of this assignment. If so, log into the SAM 2010 Web site at www.cengage.com/sam2010 to download the instructions and start files.

APPLY

Data File needed for this Case Problem: Altac.xlsx

Altac Bicycles   Deborah York is a financial consultant for Altac Bicycles, an online seller of bicycles and bicycle equipment based in Silver City, New Mexico. She has entered some financial information in an Excel workbook for an income statement she is preparing for the company. You will enter the remaining data and formulas. Complete the following:

1. Open the **Altac** workbook located in the Excel1\Case1 folder, and then save the workbook as **Altac Bicycles** in the same folder.

2. Insert three new rows at the top of the Sheet1 worksheet, and then enter the following text on two lines within cell A1:

   Altac Bicycles
   Income Statement*

3. In cell A2, enter **For the Years Ended December 31, 2011 through December 31, 2013**.

4. In the range C6:E7, enter the following net sales and cost of sales figures:

	2013	2012	2011
Net Sales	13,520	10,981	9,034
Cost of Sales	4,140	3,960	3,011

5. In the range C11:E14, enter the following expense figures (expand the column widths as necessary to show the text and data values):

	2013	2012	2011
Salaries and Wages	1,632	1,481	1,392
Sales and Marketing	2,631	2,112	1,840
Administrative	521	410	375
Research and Development	501	404	281

6. In the nonadjacent range C18:E18;C20:E20;C24:E24, enter the following values for Other Income, Income Taxes, and Shares, pressing the Enter or Tab key to navigate from cell to cell in the selected range:

	2013	2012	2011
Other Income	341	302	239
Income Taxes	1,225	1,008	821
Shares	3,621	3,001	2,844

7. In the range C8:E8, enter a formula to calculate the gross margin for each year, where the gross margin is equal to the net sales minus the cost of sales.

8. In the range C15:E15, enter the SUM function to calculate the total operating expenses for each year, where the total operating expenses equal the sum of the four expense categories.

9. In the range C17:E17, enter a formula to calculate the operating income for each year, where operating income is equal to the gross margin minus the total operating expenses.

10. In the range C19:E19, enter a formula to calculate the pretax income for each year, where pretax income is equal to the operating income plus other income.

11. In the range C22:E22, enter a formula to calculate the company's net income for each year, where net income is equal to the pretax income minus income taxes.

12. In the range C25:E25, enter a formula to calculate the earnings per share for each year, where earnings per share is equal to the net income divided by the number of shares.

13. Use the spelling checker to correct and replace any spelling errors in the worksheet. Ignore the spelling of "Altac."

14. In cell A18, use Edit mode to capitalize the word "income."

15. Increase the width of column A to 18 characters and increase the width of column B to 25 characters. Autofit the height of row 1.

16. Rename the Sheet1 worksheet as **Income Statement**, rename the Sheet2 worksheet as **Documentation** and move it to the beginning of the workbook, and then delete the Sheet3 worksheet.

17. In the Documentation worksheet, enter the following text and values:

    Cell A1: **Altac Bicycles**

    Cell A3: **Author**   Cell B3: your name

    Cell A4: **Date**   Cell B4: the current date

    Cell A5: **Purpose**   Cell B5: **Income statement for Altac Bicycles for 2011 through 2013**

18. Save the workbook, preview the workbook and make sure each worksheet in portrait orientation fits on one page in the printout, and then print the entire workbook. Close the workbook, and then submit the finished workbook and printouts to your instructor.

Use the skills you learned to complete a balance sheet for a food retailer.

APPLY

Case Problem 2

Data File needed for this Case Problem: Halley.xlsx

Halley Foods   Michael Li is working on the annual financial report for Halley Foods of Norman, Oklahoma. One part of the financial report will be the company's balance sheet for the previous three years. Michael has entered some of the labels for the balance sheet. You will finish the job by entering the actual values and formulas. Complete the following:

1. Open the **Halley** workbook located in the Excel1\Case2 folder, and then save the workbook as **Halley Foods** in the same folder.
2. Rename the Sheet1 worksheet as **Balance Sheet**, and then delete the Sheet2 and Sheet3 worksheets.
3. Insert two new rows at the top of the worksheet, and then enter the following text on four lines within cell A1:

   Halley Foods

   Balance Sheet

   As of December 31

   For the years 2011 through 2013
4. Change the width of column A to 30 characters, the width of column B to 20 characters, and the width of column C to 26 characters. Autofit the height of row 1.
5. Enter the asset and liability values shown in Figure 1-34 into the corresponding cells in the Balance Sheet worksheet for each of the last three years.

Figure 1-34	Halley Foods assets and liabilities

		2013	2012	2011
Current Assets	Cash and equivalents	806	589	423
	Short-term investments	1,194	1,029	738
	Accounts receivable	1,283	1,151	847
	Net inventories	683	563	463
	Deferred taxes	510	366	332
	Other current assets	162	153	128
Other Assets	Investments	7,077	5,811	4,330
	Restricted investments	910	797	681
	Property and equipment	779	696	420
	Other assets	1,178	484	485
Current Liabilities	Accounts payable	350	293	192
	Income taxes payable	608	442	352
	Accrued payroll	661	564	389
	Other accrued liabilities	1,397	1,250	775
Minority Interest		44	43	36
Shareholders' Equity	Preferred and common stock	5,557	4837	3,515
	Retained earnings	5,666	4,007	3,401
	Other comprehensive income	299	203	187

6. Use AutoSum to calculate the total current assets, other assets, current liabilities, and shareholders' equity in the ranges D11:F11, D17:F17, D25:F25, and D33:F33, respectively, for each of the previous three years.

7. Insert a formula in the range D19:F19 to calculate the total assets (current assets plus other assets) for each year.

8. Insert a formula in the range D36:F36 to calculate the value of the total current liabilities plus the minority interest plus the total shareholders' equity for each year.

9. Use the spelling checker to correct any spelling mistakes in the Balance Sheet worksheet, and then proofread the worksheet.

10. Change the zoom level of the Balance Sheet worksheet to 70% in Normal view to view the entire contents of the sheet in the workbook window.

11. View the Balance Sheet worksheet in Page Layout view zoomed to 80%, and then scale the height and width of the worksheet to fit on one page.

12. Insert a new worksheet named **Documentation** at the beginning of the workbook.

13. In the Documentation worksheet, enter the following data:

    Cell A1: **Halley Foods**

    Cell A3: **Author**   Cell B3: your name

    Cell A4: **Date**   Cell B4: the current date

    Cell A5: **Purpose**   Cell B5: **Balance Sheet for Halley Foods for 2011 through 2013**

14. Save, preview, and then print the entire Halley Foods workbook.

15. Print the formula view of the Balance Sheet worksheet on two pages in landscape orientation. Return the Balance Sheet worksheet to Page Layout view when you're finished.

16. Save and close the workbook, and then submit the finished workbook and printouts to your instructor.

Explore using AutoSum to calculate production statistics.

CHALLENGE

Case Problem 3

Data File needed for this Case Problem: Global.xlsx

Global Site GPS   Kevin Hodge is a production assistant at Global Site GPS, a leading manufacturer of GPS devices located in Crestwood, Missouri. One of Kevin's jobs is to monitor output at the company's five regional plants. He wants to create an Excel workbook that reports the monthly production at the five sites, including the monthly average, minimum and maximum production, and total production for the previous year. You will create the workbook that reports these statistics. Complete the following:

1. Open the **Global** workbook located in the Excel1\Case3 folder, and then save the workbook as **Global Site** in the same folder.

2. Rename the Sheet1 worksheet as **Production History**, and then insert 12 new rows at the top of the worksheet.

3. Increase the width of column A to 23 characters and the width of columns B through F to 14 characters.

4. In the range B7:F7, enter the titles **Plant1**, **Plant2**, **Plant3**, **Plant4**, and **Plant5**, respectively.

5. In the range A8:A11, enter **Total Units Produced**, **Average per Month**, **Maximum**, and **Minimum**, respectively.

⊕ EXPLORE   6. Select the range B26:F26, use AutoSum to calculate the sum of the production values for each of the five plants, and then drag and drop the selected cells to the range B8:F8.

⊕ EXPLORE   7. Select the range B26:F26, use AutoSum to calculate the average of the production values for each of the five plants, and then drag and drop the selected cells to the range B9:F9.

⊕ EXPLORE

8. Repeat Step 7 to calculate the maximum values for each of the five plants and move those calculated values to the range B10:F10, and then repeat to calculate the minimum production values and drag and drop those calculated values to the range B11:F11.

9. In the Production History worksheet, enter the following data:

Cell A1: **Global Site GPS**
Cell A2: **Production Report**
Cell A3: **Model**   Cell B3: **MapTracker 201**
Cell A4: **Year**   Cell B4: **2013**
Cell A5: **Total Units Produced**

10. In cell B5, use the SUM function to add the values in the range B8:F8.

11. Insert a new worksheet named **Plant Directory**, and then move it to be the first worksheet in the workbook.

12. In cells A1 and A2, enter **Global Site GPS** and **Plant Directory**, respectively, and then enter the text shown in Figure 1-35 in the range A4:D9, making sure that the address is entered on two lines within the cell.

| Figure 1-35 | Plant directory data |

Plant	Plant Manager	Address	Phone
1	Karen Brookers	300 Commerce Avenue Crestwood, MO 63126	(314) 555-3881
2	Daniel Gomez	15 North Main Street Edison, NJ 08837	(732) 555-0012
3	Jody Hetrick	3572 Howard Lane Weston, FL 33326	(954) 555-4817
4	Yong Jo	900 South Street Kirkland, WA 98033	(425) 555-8775
5	Sandy Nisbett	3771 Water Street Helena, MT 59623	(406) 555-4114

13. Set the width of column B to 15 characters, the width of column C to 30 characters, and the width of column D to 16 characters. Autofit the height of each row to its content.

14. Insert a new worksheet named **Documentation**, move it to be the first worksheet in the workbook, and then enter the following data:

Cell A1: **Global Site GPS**
Cell A3: **Author**   Cell B3: your name
Cell A4: **Date**   Cell B4: the current date
Cell A5: **Purpose**   Cell B5: **Production report for Global Site GPS**

15. Switch the Production History worksheet to Page Layout view, change the orientation to landscape, and then verify that the worksheet fits on a single page.

16. Save your workbook, preview and print the workbook, close the workbook, and then submit the finished workbook and printouts to your instructor.

Create an Excel workbook to record service calls for a lawn service agency.

CREATE

Case Problem 4

There are no Data Files needed for this Case Problem.

Green Lawns   Green Lawns provides yard service and maintenance for homes in and around Mount Vernon, Ohio. Gary Taylor manages the accounts for Green Lawns and wants to use Excel to record weekly service calls made by the company. Gary provides you with the list of service calls made in the first week of August. You will use this data to create the workbook for Gary. Complete the following:

1. Open a blank workbook, and then save it as **Green Lawns** in the Excel1\Case4 folder included with your Data Files.
2. Rename the Sheet1 worksheet as **Documentation**, and then enter information documenting the workbook. Include the name of the company, your name, the current date, and a brief description of the purpose of the workbook. The layout and appearance of the worksheet are up to you.
3. In the Sheet2 worksheet, enter the service calls shown in Figure 1-36, and then enter appropriate formulas to calculate the service charge for each customer. Green Lawns charges each customer a base fee plus a working fee that is equal to the hourly rate multiplied by the number of hours worked. Also, enter a formula to calculate the total charges for all customer calls. The layout and appearance of the page are up to you.

Figure 1-36   **August service calls (week 1)**

Customer	Address	Phone	Last Service	Hours	Base Fee	Hourly Rate
David Lane	391 Country Drive Mount Vernon, OH 43050	(740) 555-4439	8/2/2013	3	$35	$17.50
Robert Gomez	151 Apple Lane Mount Vernon, OH 43051	(740) 555-0988	8/2/2013	3.5	$35	$17.50
Sandra Lee	112 Main Street Mount Vernon, OH 43050	(740) 555-3773	8/3/2013	1.5	$20	$14.50
Gregory Sands	305 Country Drive Mount Vernon, OH 43050	(740) 555-4189	8/3/2013	5	$35	$21.50
Betty Oaks	205 Second Street Mount Vernon, OH 43049	(740) 555-0088	8/3/2013	1.5	$20	$14.50

4. Rename the Sheet2 worksheet as **Service Calls**, and then delete any unused sheets from the workbook.
5. Check the spelling in the workbook, correcting any spelling errors, and then proofread the workbook.
6. Save the workbook, preview the worksheets to ensure that each fits onto a single page, and then print the entire workbook. Close the workbook, and then submit the finished workbook and printouts to your instructor.

SAM: Skills Assessment Manager

ASSESS

For current SAM information, including versions and content details, visit SAM Central (http://samcentral.course.com). If you have a SAM user profile, you may have access to hands-on instruction, practice, and assessment of the skills covered in this tutorial. Since various versions of SAM are supported throughout the life of this text, check with your instructor for the correct instructions and URL/Web site for accessing assignments.

ENDING FILES

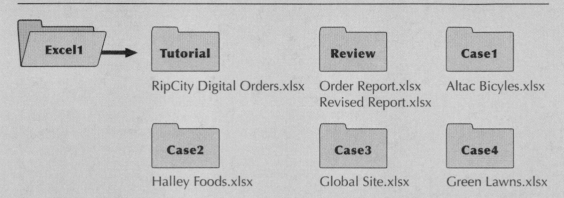

| Excel1 → | Tutorial | Review | Case1 |
| | RipCity Digital Orders.xlsx | Order Report.xlsx Revised Report.xlsx | Altac Bicyles.xlsx |

| Case2 | Case3 | Case4 |
| Halley Foods.xlsx | Global Site.xlsx | Green Lawns.xlsx |

Formatting a Workbook

Designing a Financial Report

OBJECTIVES

Session 2.1
- Format text, numbers, and dates
- Change fonts and font colors
- Add fill colors and background images
- Create formulas to add, subtract, and divide values
- Apply number formats
- Align, indent, and rotate cell contents
- Merge a range into a single cell
- Copy and paste formats

Session 2.2
- Apply built-in cell styles
- Change the theme of a workbook
- Create formulas to add and subtract values
- Apply a built-in table style and select table style options
- Highlight cells with conditional formats
- Hide worksheet rows
- Define the print area, insert page breaks, and add print titles
- Create headers and footers
- Select page margins

Case | *ExerComp Exercise Equipment*

ExerComp, based in Mason, Ohio, manufactures electronic and computer components for fitness machines and sporting goods. At the upcoming annual sales meeting, sales managers will present reports that detail the sales history of different ExerComp products. Sales manager Tom Uhen will report on the recent sales history of the X310 heart rate monitor.

Tom has already created a workbook and entered the sales figures for the past two years. He wants you to enter formulas to calculate total sales and increases in sales. He also wants you to make the data more readable and informative. To do this, you will work with formatting tools to modify the appearance of the data in each cell, the cell itself, and the entire worksheet. Because much of Tom's data has been stored in tables, you will also use some special formatting tools designed for tables.

STARTING DATA FILES

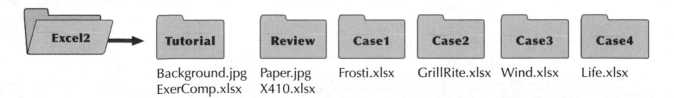

Excel2 →	Tutorial	Review	Case1	Case2	Case3	Case4
	Background.jpg ExerComp.xlsx	Paper.jpg X410.xlsx	Frosti.xlsx	GrillRite.xlsx	Wind.xlsx	Life.xlsx

SESSION 2.1 VISUAL OVERVIEW

The **Format Painter** copies and pastes formatting from one cell or range to another without duplicating any data.

You can format a text string within a cell in Edit mode.

The appearance of text is determined by its **typeface**, which is the specific design of a set of characters, including letters, numbers, punctuation marks, and symbols.

Every font can be formatted with a font style such as *italic*, **bold**, or ***bold italic*** and special effects such as underline, strikethrough, and color.

You can rotate content in the cell.

The Comma style adds a thousands separator and two decimal places to the right of the decimal point, and lines up values by their decimal points. You can change how many decimal places are displayed.

A **font** is a set of characters that employ the same typeface, such as Arial, Times New Roman, and Courier.

The Accounting style lines up currency values by their currency symbol and decimal point; negative numbers are enclosed in parentheses.

The Alignment group has buttons for setting the horizontal and vertical alignment, the orientation, indents, and text wrapping of text in a cell, as well as merging cells.

You can **merge**, or combine, several cells into one cell. This content is merged and centered across the range A4:F4.

You can set the **font size** to increase or decrease the size of the text. Font sizes are measured in **points**, where one point is approximately 1/72 of an inch.

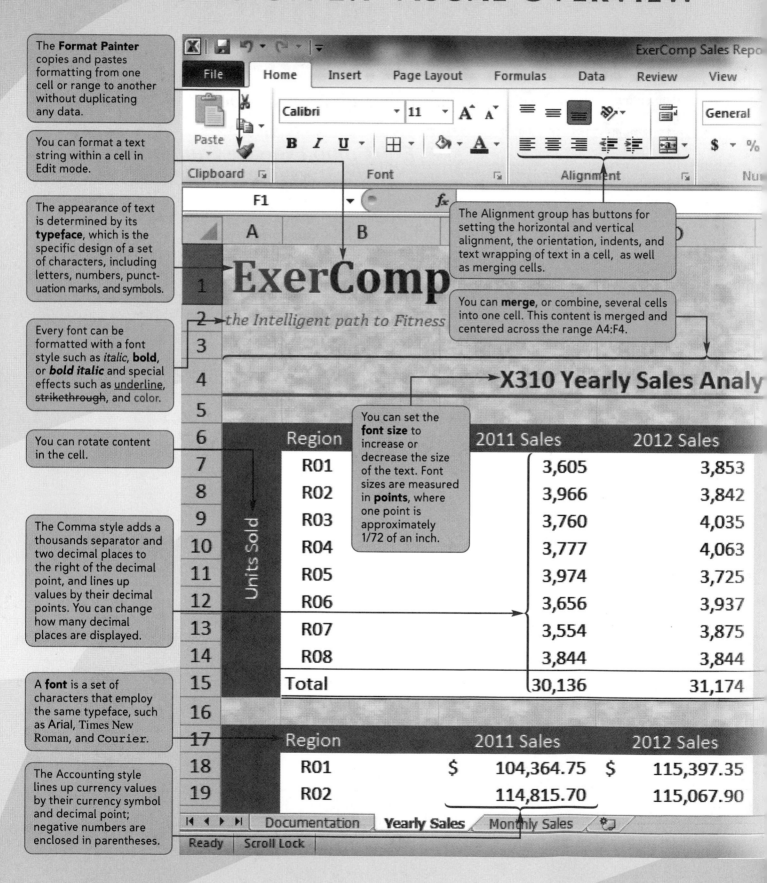

Region	2011 Sales	2012 Sales
R01	3,605	3,853
R02	3,966	3,842
R03	3,760	4,035
R04	3,777	4,063
R05	3,974	3,725
R06	3,656	3,937
R07	3,554	3,875
R08	3,844	3,844
Total	30,136	31,174

Region	2011 Sales	2012 Sales
R01	$ 104,364.75	$ 115,397.35
R02	114,815.70	115,067.90

X310 Yearly Sales Analy

ExerComp Sales Repo

the Intelligent path to Fitness

WORKSHEET FORMATTING

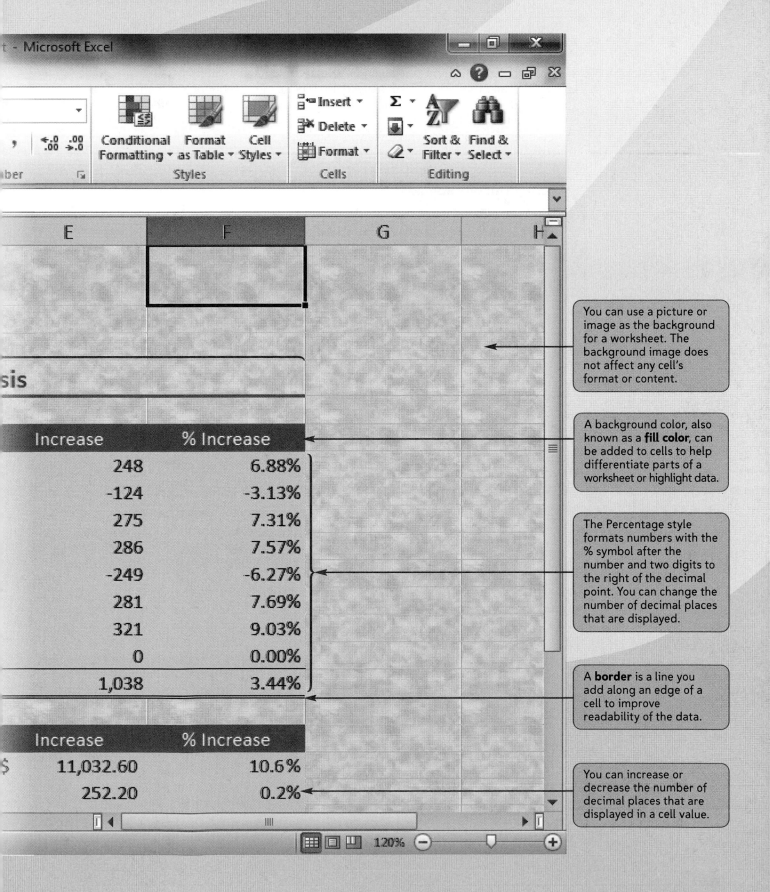

You can use a picture or image as the background for a worksheet. The background image does not affect any cell's format or content.

A background color, also known as a **fill color**, can be added to cells to help differentiate parts of a worksheet or highlight data.

The Percentage style formats numbers with the % symbol after the number and two digits to the right of the decimal point. You can change the number of decimal places that are displayed.

A **border** is a line you add along an edge of a cell to improve readability of the data.

You can increase or decrease the number of decimal places that are displayed in a cell value.

Formatting Cell Text

Tom has already entered the data and some formulas in a workbook, which is only a rough draft of what he wants to submit to the company. The Documentation sheet describes the workbook's purpose and content. The Yearly Sales sheet displays the sales history of the X310 heart rate monitor including the total number of units sold per sales region (labeled R01 through R08) and the total revenue generated by those sales in the past two years. The Monthly Sales sheet also reports the number of X310 units sold by region and month. In its current form, the data is difficult to read and interpret. Tom wants you to format the workbook contents to improve its readability and visual appeal. You'll open the workbook and review its content.

To open the workbook:

1. Open the **ExerComp** workbook located in the **Excel2\Tutorial** folder included with your Data Files, and then save the workbook as **ExerComp Sales Report**.

2. In the Documentation sheet, enter your name in cell B4 and the date in cell B5.

3. Review the contents of the three worksheets.

Formatting is the process of changing a workbook's appearance by defining the fonts, styles, colors, and decorative features. Formatting changes only the appearance of data—it does not affect the data itself. Excel organizes its formatting tools in terms of themes. A **theme** is a collection of formats for text, colors, images, and graphical effects applied throughout a workbook. Each theme has a name. The Office theme is the default, although you can apply other themes or create your own. You can also use fonts and colors that are not part of the current theme. As you format a workbook, Live Preview shows the effects of the formats on the workbook's appearance.

PROSKILLS

Written Communication: Formatting Workbooks for Readability and Appeal

Designing a workbook requires the same care as designing any written document or report. A well-formatted workbook is easier to read and establishes a sense of professionalism with readers. Do the following to improve the appearance of your workbooks:

- Clearly identify each worksheet's purpose with column or row titles and a descriptive sheet name.
- Don't crowd individual worksheets with too much information. Each worksheet should deal with only one or two topics. Place extra topics on separate sheets. Readers should be able to interpret each worksheet with a minimal amount of horizontal and vertical scrolling.
- Place worksheets containing the most important information first in the workbook. Position worksheets summarizing your findings near the front of the workbook. Position worksheets with detailed and involved analysis near the end as an appendix.
- Use consistent formatting throughout the workbook. If negative values appear in red on one worksheet, format them in the same way on all sheets. Also, be consistent in the use of thousands separators, decimal places, and percentages.
- Pay attention to the format of the printed workbook. Make sure your printouts are legible with informative headers and footers. Check that the content of the printout is scaled correctly to the page size and that page breaks divide the information into logical sections.

Excel provides many formatting tools. However, too much formatting can be intrusive, overwhelm data, and make the document difficult to read. Always remember, the goal of formatting is not simply to make a "pretty workbook," but also to accentuate important trends and relationships in the data. A well-formatted workbook should seamlessly convey your data to the reader. If the reader is thinking about how your workbook looks, it means he or she is not thinking about your data.

Applying Fonts and Font Styles

Excel organizes fonts into theme and non-theme fonts. A **theme font** is associated with a particular theme and used for headings and body text in the workbook. These fonts change automatically when you change the theme applied to the workbook. When you don't want to apply a font associated with a particular design, you use a **non-theme font**. Text formatted with a non-theme font retains its appearance no matter what theme is used with the workbook.

Fonts appear in different character styles. **Serif fonts**, such as Times New Roman, have extra decorative strokes at the end of each character. **Sans serif fonts**, such as Arial, do not include these decorative strokes. Other fonts are purely decorative such as a font used for specialized logos.

Every font can be further formatted with a font style such as *italic*, **bold**, or ***bold italic***, and special effects such as underline, ~~strikethrough~~, and color. Finally, you can set the font size to increase or decrease the size of the text.

You'll format the company name displayed at the top of each worksheet to appear in large, bold letters using the default heading font from the Office theme. Tom wants the slogan "The Intelligent Path to Fitness" displayed below the company name to appear in the heading font, but in smaller, italicized letters.

To format text in the Documentation worksheet:

1. Click the **Documentation** sheet tab to make it the active worksheet, and then click cell **A1** to make it the active cell.

2. In the Font group on the Home tab, click the **Font arrow** to display a list of fonts available on your computer. The first two fonts are the theme fonts for headings and body text—Cambria and Calibri. See Figure 2-1.

Figure 2-1	Theme and non-theme fonts in the font list

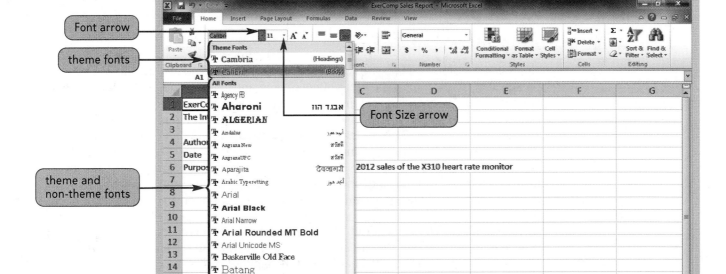

3. Click **Cambria**. The company name in cell A1 changes to the Cambria font, the default headings font in the current theme.

TIP

You can also change the font size incrementally by clicking the Increase Font Size or Decrease Font Size button in the Font group on the Home tab.

4. In the Font group, click the **Font Size arrow** to display a list of font sizes, and then click **26**. The company name changes to 26 points.

5. In the Font group, click the **Bold** button **B**. The company name is boldfaced. Next, you'll format the company slogan.

6. Click cell **A2** to make it active. The slogan text is selected.

7. In the Font group, click the **Font arrow**, and then click **Cambria**. The slogan text changes to the Cambria font.

8. In the Font group, click the **Font Size arrow**, and then click **10**. The slogan text changes to 10 points.

9. In the Font group, click the **Italic** button **I**. The slogan in cell A2 is italicized.

10. Select the range **A4:A6**, click the **Bold** button **B** in the Font group, and then click cell **A7**. The column labels are bolded. The formatted text is shown in Figure 2-2.

Figure 2-2	Formatted cell text

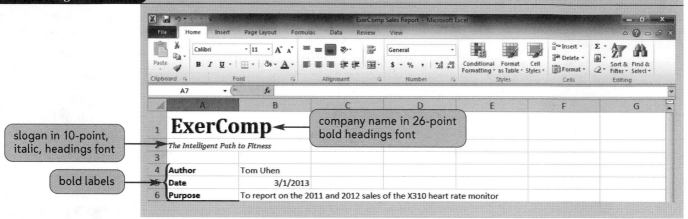

slogan in 10-point, italic, headings font

company name in 26-point bold headings font

bold labels

Applying a Font Color

Color can transform a plain workbook filled with numbers and text into a powerful presentation that captures the user's attention and adds visual emphasis to the points you want to make. By default, Excel displays text in a black color font.

Just as it did with fonts, Excel organizes colors into theme and non-theme colors. **Theme colors** are the 12 colors that belong to the workbook's theme. Four colors are designated for text and backgrounds, six colors are used for accents and highlights, and two colors are used for hyperlinks (followed and not followed links). These 12 colors are designed to work well together and to remain readable in all combinations. Each theme color has five variations, or **accents**, in which a different tint or shading is applied to the theme color.

Ten **standard colors**—dark red, red, orange, yellow, light green, green, light blue, blue, dark blue, and purple—are always available regardless of the workbook's theme. You can also open an extended palette of 134 standard colors. You can create a **custom color** by specifying a mixture of red, blue, and green color values, making available 16.7 million custom colors—more colors than the human eye can distinguish. Some dialog boxes have an **automatic color** option that uses your Windows default text and background colors, usually black text on a white background.

Tom wants the labels in the Documentation worksheet to stand out so you will change the ExerComp title and slogan to blue.

To change the title and slogan font color:

1. Select the range **A1:A2**.

2. In the Font group, click the **Font Color button arrow** to display the theme and standard colors. (The two colors for hyperlinked text are not shown.)

3. Point to the **Blue** color (the eighth color) in the Standard Colors section. The color name appears in a ScreenTip and you see a Live Preview of the text with the blue font color. See Figure 2-3.

Figure 2-3 | Available font colors

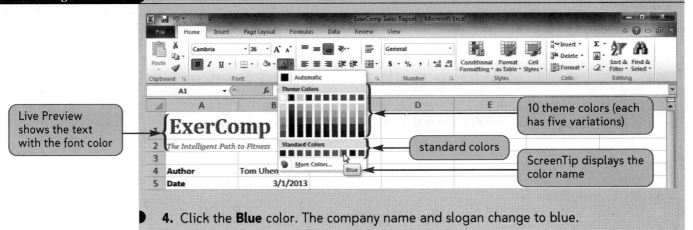

4. Click the **Blue** color. The company name and slogan change to blue.

Formatting Text Selections

In the ExerComp logo, "Exer" appears in blue text and "Comp" appears in red text. You'll need to format part of the contents in cell A1 one way and the rest a different way. When you select text in Edit mode, you can format the selection with a different font, size, style, and color. You'll format "Comp" in a red font.

TIP

You can also use the buttons on the Mini toolbar to change the font, size, style, and color of selected text within a cell.

To format the Comp text selection:

1. Double-click cell **A1** to select the cell and go into Edit mode, and then select **Comp**.

2. In the Font group on the Home tab, click the **Font Color button arrow**, and then click the **Red** color in the Standard Colors section. The text color changes. See Figure 2-4.

Figure 2-4 | Text selection being formatted

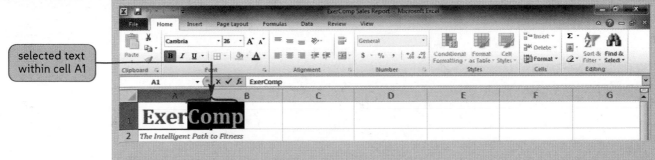

3. Click cell **A7** to deselect the cell. The text "ExerComp" in cell A1 is blue and red.

REFERENCE

Formatting Cell Content

- To change the font, select the cell or range. In the Font group on the Home tab, click the Font arrow, and then click a font.
- To change the font size, select the cell or range. In the Font group on the Home tab, click the Font Size arrow, and then click a font size.
- To change a font style, select the cell or range. In the Font group on the Home tab, click the Bold, Italic, or Underline button.
- To change a font color, select the cell or range. In the Font group on the Home tab, click the Font Color button arrow, and then click a color.
- To format a text selection, double-click the cell to enter Edit mode, select the text to format, change the font, size, style, or color, and then press the Enter key.

Working with Colors and Backgrounds

Another way to distinguish sections of a worksheet is by formatting the cell background. You can fill the cell background with color or an image. Tom wants you to format the Documentation worksheet by adding fill colors and background images.

Changing a Fill Color

TIP

You can add a fill color to a sheet tab. In the Cells group on the Home tab, click the Format button, point to Tab Color, and then click a color.

By default, Excel does not add any background color to worksheet cells; but background colors, also known as fill colors, can be added using the same color palette you use for font colors. The labels in the Documentation worksheet should be in a white font on a blue background. The author's name, current date, and purpose of the worksheet should be in a blue font on a white background. You will make both of these changes to the Documentation worksheet.

To change the background fill color:

1. Select the range **A4:A6**.

2. In the Font group on the Home tab, click the **Fill Color button arrow** 🎨 ▾, and then click the **Blue** color (the eighth color) in the Standard Colors section.

3. In the Font group, click the **Font Color button arrow** 🅰 ▾, and then click the **White** color in the Theme Colors section.

4. Select the range **B4:B6**, and then format the cells with a blue font on a white background.

5. Increase the width of column B to **55** characters.

6. Click cell **A7**. See Figure 2-5.

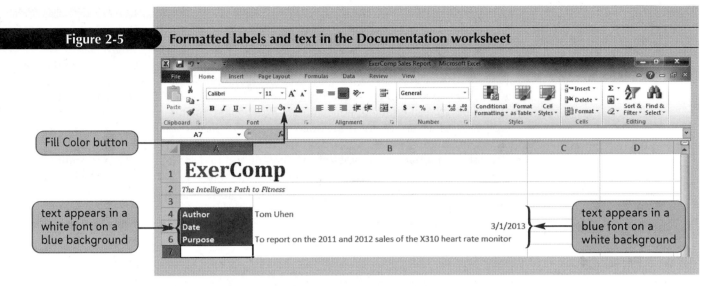

Figure 2-5   **Formatted labels and text in the Documentation worksheet**

Fill Color button

text appears in a white font on a blue background

text appears in a blue font on a white background

Adding a Background Image

You can use a picture or an image as the background for a worksheet. An image can give the worksheet a textured appearance, like that of granite, wood, or fibered paper. The image is repeated until it fills the entire worksheet. The background image does not affect any cell's format or content. Background colors applied to cells appear on top of the image, covering that portion of the image. Background images do not print.

Tom has provided an image for you to use as the background of the Documentation worksheet.

To add a background image to the Documentation worksheet:

1. Click the **Page Layout** tab on the Ribbon. The page layout options appear on the Ribbon.

2. In the Page Setup group, click the **Background** button. The Sheet Background dialog box opens.

3. Navigate to the **Excel2\Tutorial** folder included with your Data Files, click the **Background** JPEG image file, and then click the **Insert** button. The image is added to the background of the Documentation worksheet. See Figure 2-6.

Figure 2-6   **Background image added to the worksheet**

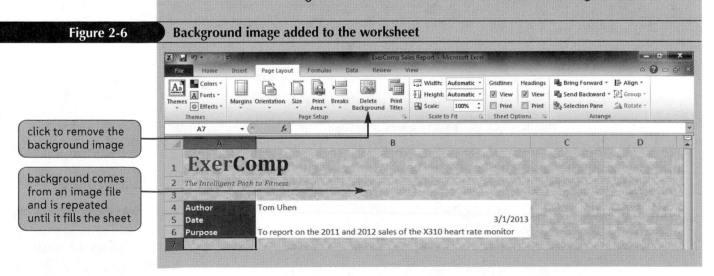

click to remove the background image

background comes from an image file and is repeated until it fills the sheet

Using Color to Enhance a Workbook

When used wisely, color can enhance any workbook. However, when used improperly, color can distract the user, making the workbook more difficult to read. As you format a workbook, keep in mind the following tips:

- Use colors from the same theme within a workbook to maintain a consistent look and feel across the worksheets. If the built-in themes do not fit your needs, you can create a custom theme.
- Use colors to differentiate types of cell content and to direct users where to enter data. For example, format a worksheet so that formula results appear in cells without a fill color and users enter data in cells with a light gray fill color.
- Avoid garish color combinations that can annoy the reader and be difficult to read.
- Print the workbook on both color and black-and-white printers to ensure that the printed copy is readable in both versions.
- Understand your printer's limitations and features. Colors that look good on your monitor might not look as good when printed.
- Be sensitive to your audience. About 8 percent of all men and 0.5 percent of all women have some type of color blindness and might not be able to see the text when certain color combinations are used. Red-green color blindness is the most common, so avoid using red text on a green background or green text on a red background.

Formatting Calculated Values

When you format numeric values, the goal is to make the workbook easier for the reader to interpret (which is same goal of any formatting you apply to a workbook). For example, adding a comma as a thousands separator, controlling the number of decimal places, and using percentage and currency symbols can make a large table of numbers easier to read and understand.

For Tom's report, you'll format the values in the worksheets that contain the sales figures for the past two years.

Creating Formulas to Add, Subtract, and Divide Values

The Yearly Sales worksheet contains the annual sales figures from 2011 and 2012 for the X310 heart rate monitor. The upper section of the worksheet displays the number of units sold in each sales region per year, and the lower section displays the revenue generated by sales region per year in dollars. You will add formulas to the worksheet to calculate the total sales for each year as well as the net and percent change in sales from one year to another.

To calculate the total yearly sales:

1. Click the **Yearly Sales** sheet tab. The Yearly Sales worksheet is now the active sheet in the workbook.

2. In cells B15 and B26, enter the label **Total**.

3. Select the range **C15:D15**. You'll insert the SUM function in both cells at once.

4. Click the **Home** tab on the Ribbon.

5. In the Editing group, click the **Sum** button Σ. The formulas inserted in these cells, =SUM(C7:C14) in cell C15 and =SUM(D7:D14) in cell D15, calculate the total units sold for 2011 and 2012, which are 30136 and 31174, respectively.

6. In the Clipboard group on the Home tab, click the **Copy** button 📋. The formulas are copied to the Clipboard.

7. Scroll down and select the range **C26:D26**. These are the cells in which you want to paste the copied formulas.

8. In the Clipboard group, click the **Paste** button 📋. The formulas to calculate the total annual revenues are pasted in the selected range, displaying totals of 872437.2 in 2011 and 933661.3 in 2012. See Figure 2-7.

Figure 2-7   **Formulas calculate the total units sold and total revenue**

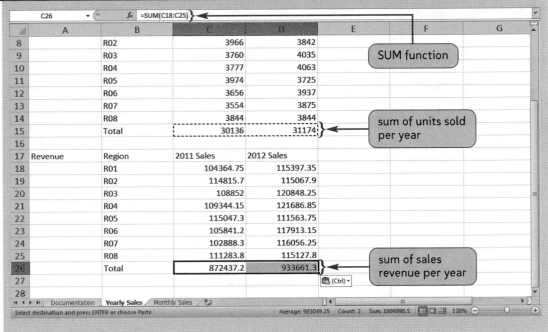

The formula results are difficult to read in their current form. You'll correct that problem shortly.

To calculate the net change in units sold and revenue from 2011 to 2012, you'll subtract the 2011 figures from the 2012 figures. To calculate the percent change, you'll divide the net change by the 2011 units sold and revenue figures for each sales region as well as across all sales regions.

To calculate the net and percent change from 2011 to 2012:

1. In cells E6 and E17, enter the label **Increase**, and then, in cells F6 and F17, enter the label **% Increase**.

2. In cell E7, enter the formula **=D7–C7** to calculate the increase in units sold from 2011 to 2012.

3. In cell F7, enter the formula **=E7/C7** to calculate the percent increase in units sold from 2011 to 2012. When calculating a percent increase, always divide the amount of increase by the starting value and not the ending value.

4. Select the range **E7:F7**. Rather than reenter the formulas in cells E7 and F7, you'll copy and paste them into the rest of the worksheet.

5. In the Clipboard group on the Home tab, click the **Copy** button. The range is copied to the Clipboard.

6. Select the nonadjacent range **E8:F15;E18:F26**. You want to paste the formulas in these cells.

7. In the Clipboard group, click the **Paste** button. The formulas are pasted in the selected ranges.

8. Click cell **A6** to deselect the range. The formulas calculate the values for the net and percent increase in units sold and revenue from 2011 to 2012. See Figure 2-8.

Figure 2-8   **Net and percent increase in sales and revenue**

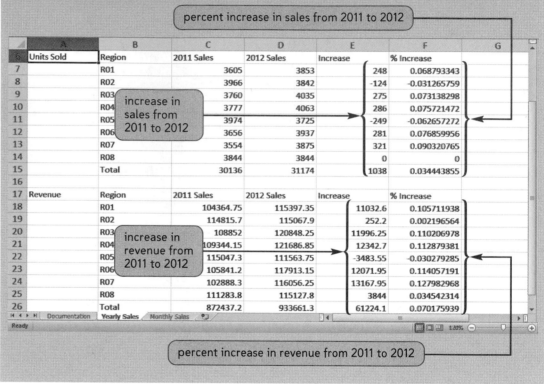

Applying Number Formats

You can format values using a **number format**, which displays the values in a way that makes it easy for the reader to quickly understand and interpret them. You can change the number format for the displayed value without affecting the underlying stored value. Excel formats numbers by default in the **General number format**, which, for the most part, displays values exactly as they are typed by the user. If the value is calculated from a formula or function, Excel shows as many digits after the decimal point as will fit in the cell with the last displayed digit rounded. Calculated values too large to fit into the cell are displayed in scientific notation.

The General number format is good for simple calculations, but some values require additional formatting to make the numbers easier to interpret. Using Excel, you can:

- Set the number of digits displayed to the right of the decimal point
- Add commas to act as a thousands separator for large values
- Apply currency or accounting symbols to numeric values to identify the monetary unit being used
- Display percentages using the % symbol

The values in the Yearly Sales worksheet are difficult to interpret. For example, it is unclear whether a particular value represents sales revenue or units sold, and it is hard to determine, without study, whether a revenue value is expressed in millions or hundreds of thousands of dollars. You will format these values to make them easier to read.

To apply a thousands separator to the units sold values:

▶ **1.** Select the range **C7:E15**.

▶ **2.** In the Number group on the Home tab, click the **Comma Style** button ⬚. Each value in the selected range now includes a thousands separator. Two digits were also added to the right of the decimal point. Because the units sold values are expressed in integers, you will remove the digits to the right of the decimal place.

▶ **3.** In the Number group, click the **Decrease Decimal** button ⬚ twice. The two extra digits are removed. See Figure 2-9.

Figure 2-9 | **Units sold values formatted**

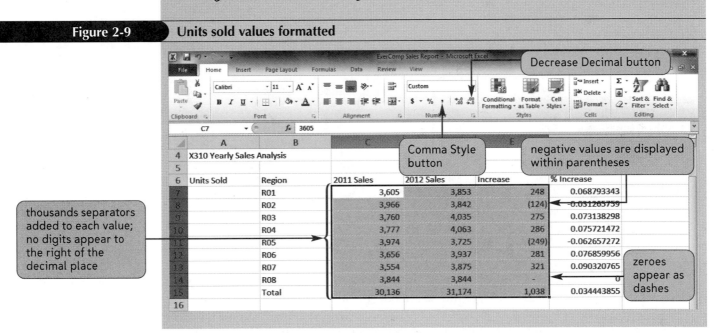

Though you used the Comma Style button to add the thousands separator, the button actually applies an accounting style used for currency values to the values in the columns. This accounting style lines up currency values within a column by the currency symbol and decimal point. When the values do not have a currency symbol, the values are aligned by the decimal point. The accounting style also encloses negative numbers, such as –124 in cell E8, within parentheses, such as (124). This is a standard format used in accounting documents. If you prefer to display negative numbers in a different way, you can modify this format. Another standard accounting practice is to add a currency symbol to only the first and last entries within a column of values.

You will display the revenue values in columns C through E using the same accounting style, but with two decimal places and with the currency symbol appearing only in rows 18 and 26.

To format the revenue values:

1. Select the range **C18:E26**.

2. In the Number group on the Home tab, click the **Comma Style** button .

3. Select the nonadjacent range **C18:E18;C26:E26**.

4. In the Number group, click the **Accounting Number Format** button $. As shown in Figure 2-10, $ symbols are added to the revenue values in the first and last row.

Figure 2-10   **Revenue values formatted**

Accounting Number Format button

$ symbols added to the revenue values in the first and last rows

$ symbols and decimal points are lined up within each column

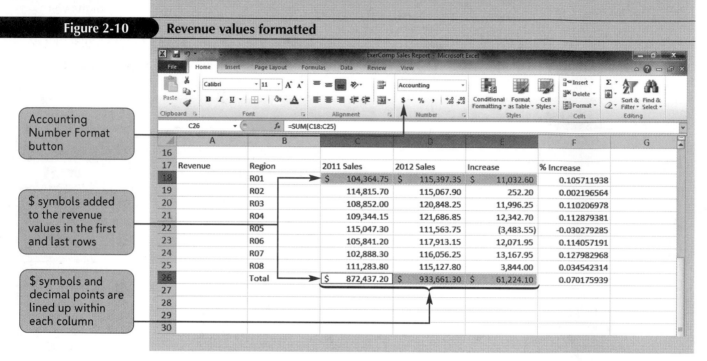

Next, you'll format the percent change values in column F. When you format values as percentages, the % symbol appears after the number and no digits appear to the right of the decimal point. You can change how many decimal places are displayed in the cell. Tom wants the percentages in column F to display the % symbol with two decimal places.

To format the percentages in column F:

1. Select the nonadjacent range **F7:F15;F18:F26**.

2. In the Number group on the Home tab, click the **Percent Style** button %.

3. In the Number group, click the **Increase Decimal** button twice to display the percentages to two decimal places.

4. Scroll up and click cell **A6** to deselect the range. Figure 2-11 shows the formatted numbers in the worksheet.

Figure 2-11   **Percent increase values formatted**

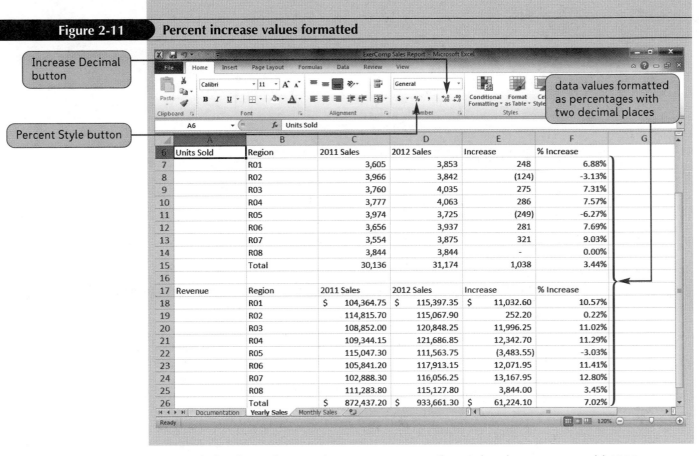

With the data reformatted, Tom can more easily see that the company sold 1038 more units in 2012 than in 2011—an increase of 3.44 percent, which increased revenue by $61,224.10, or 7.02 percent. This was not uniform across all sales regions. Total units sold and revenue for Region R05, for example, decreased between 2011 and 2012.

Formatting Dates and Times

The date in the Documentation sheet is displayed in an abbreviated format, *mm/dd/yyyy*. Tom wants you to use an extended format that includes the day of the week, the full month name, the day, and the year.

Because Excel stores dates and times as numbers and not as text, you can apply different formats without affecting the date and time value. The abbreviated format entered into the Documentation sheet is referred to as the Short Date format. You can also apply a Long Date format that displays the day of the week and the full month name in addition to the day of the month and the year. Other built-in Excel formats include formats for displaying time values in 12- or 24-hour time.

You will change the date in the Documentation sheet to the Long Date format.

To format the date in the Long Date format:

1. Click the **Documentation** sheet tab to make the Documentation worksheet active, and then select cell **B5**.

2. In the Number group on the Home tab, click the **Number Format** arrow, and then click **Long Date**. The date format changes to show the weekday name, month name, day, and year. See Figure 2-12.

Figure 2-12 **Formatted date**

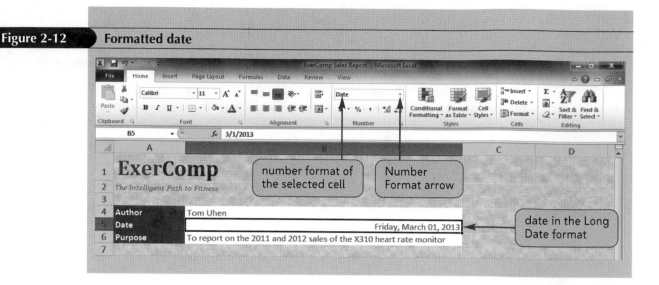

Excel Dates and Times as Numeric Values

INSIGHT

Although dates and times entered into a cell usually are displayed as text, they are actually stored by Excel as numbers measuring the interval between the specified date and time and January 1, 1900 at 12:00 a.m. For example, the date April 1, 2013 is stored as 41,365, which is the number of days between April 1, 2013 and January 1, 1900.

Times are stored as fractional parts of one day. A time of 6:00 a.m. is stored as 0.25 because that represents one-fourth of a 24-hour day (starting the day from 12:00 a.m.). Similarly, a cell containing the date and time of April 1, 2013 at 6:00 a.m. would be stored as 41,365.25.

Excel stores dates and times as numbers to make it easier to calculate time intervals. For example, to calculate the difference between one date and another, you just subtract the earlier date from the later date. If you subtract the date and time of March 30, 2013 at 12:00 p.m. from April 1, 2013 at 6:00 a.m., Excel displays 1.75—or one and three quarters of a day.

You can always view the actual date and time by selecting the cell that contains the date/time entry and applying the General number format, or by switching the workbook window to Formula view.

Formatting Worksheet Cells

You can format the appearance of individual cells by modifying the alignment of text within the cell, indenting cell text, or adding borders of different styles and colors to individual cells or ranges. You'll make these changes to the cells in Tom's workbook.

Aligning Cell Content

By default, cell text is aligned with the left and bottom borders of a cell and cell values are aligned with the right and bottom borders. In some cases, you might want to change the text alignment to make the text more readable or visually appealing. In general, you should center column titles, left-align other cell text, and align numbers to keep their decimal places lined up within a column. The buttons to set these alignment options are located in the Alignment group on the Home tab. Figure 2-13 describes the operations of these buttons.

| Figure 2-13 | Alignment buttons |

Button	Description
≡	Aligns the cell content with the cell's top edge
≡	Vertically centers the cell content within the cell
≡	Aligns the cell content with the cell's bottom edge
≡	Aligns the cell content with the cell's left edge
≡	Horizontally centers the cell content within the cell
≡	Aligns the cell content with the cell's right edge
建	Decreases the size of the indentation used in the cell
建	Increases the size of the indentation used in the cell
≫	Rotates the cell content to any angle within the cell
🖹	Forces the cell text to wrap within the cell borders
🔳	Merges the selected cells into a single cell

Although the date in the Documentation worksheet is formatted to display as text, it is right-aligned in the cell (because Excel treats dates and times as numbers). You'll use the Alignment group buttons to left-align the date in the Documentation worksheet and center the column titles in the Yearly Sales worksheet.

To left-align the date and center the column titles:

1. If necessary, select cell **B5**.

2. In the Alignment group on the Home tab, click the **Align Text Left** button ≡. The date shifts to the left edge of the cell.

3. Click the **Yearly Sales** sheet tab to make that worksheet active, and then select the nonadjacent range **C6:F6;C17:F17**.

4. In the Alignment group, click the **Center** button ≡. The column titles in columns C, D, E, and F are centered.

Indenting Cell Content

Sometimes you want a cell's content moved a few spaces from the cell left edge. This is particularly useful for entries that are considered subsections of a worksheet. For example, Tom recorded sales for eight regions and then added the totals. Each region can be considered a subsection, and Tom thinks it would look better if the region labels were indented a few spaces. You increase the indentation by roughly one character space each time you click the Increase Indent button in the Alignment group on the Home tab. To decrease or remove an indentation, click the Decrease Indent button.

You'll increase the indent for the region labels.

To indent the region labels:

1. Select the nonadjacent range **B7:B14;B18:B25**.

2. In the Alignment group on the Home tab, click the **Increase Indent** button 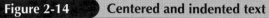. Each region label indents one character space.

3. Click cell **A6** to deselect the range. See Figure 2-14.

Figure 2-14   **Centered and indented text**

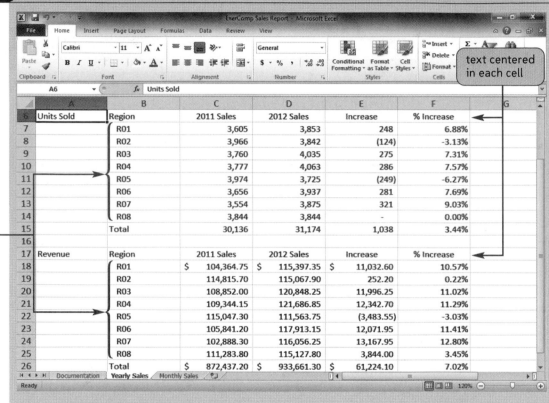

Merging Cells

In the Yearly Sales worksheet, Tom wants the title "X310 Yearly Sales Analysis" in cell A4 centered over columns A through F. One way to align text over several columns or rows is to merge several cells into one cell. When you merge cells, only the content from the upper-left cell in the range is retained. The cell reference for the merged cell is the upper-left cell reference. So, if you merge cells A1 and A2, the merged cell reference is cell A1.

After you merge a range into a single cell, you can realign its content. The Merge button in the Alignment group on the Home tab includes the following options:

- **Merge & Center** merges the range into one cell and horizontally centers the content.
- **Merge Across** merges each of the rows in the selected range across the columns in the range.
- **Merge Cells** merges the range into a single cell, but does not horizontally center the cell content.
- **Unmerge Cells** reverses a merge, returning the merged cell back into a range of individual cells.

You will merge and center the title in cell A4 across the range A4:F4.

To merge and center the title across a cell range:

1. Select the range **A4:F4** in the Yearly Sales worksheet.

2. In the Alignment group on the Home tab, click the **Merge & Center** button ⊞. The range A4:F4 merges into one cell with a cell reference of A4 and the text is centered within the cell.

3. Select the range **A6:A15**, and then click the **Merge & Center** button ⊞. The cells are merged vertically into a single cell, displaying the text "Units Sold" aligned with the bottom cell border.

4. Select the range **A17:A26**, and then click the **Merge & Center** button ⊞. The cells in the range are also merged vertically into a single cell.

5. Click cell **A3**. Figure 2-15 shows the merged cells in the Yearly Sales worksheet.

Figure 2-15   **Merged ranges with centered text**

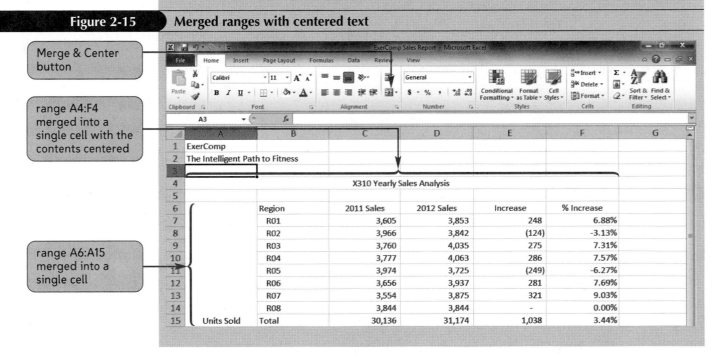

Merge & Center button

range A4:F4 merged into a single cell with the contents centered

range A6:A15 merged into a single cell

Rotating Cell Contents

Text and numbers are displayed within cells horizontally. However, you can rotate cell text to any angle to save space or to provide visual interest to a worksheet. The Units Sold and Revenue titles were placed at the bottom of their respective merged cells, which makes them difficult to read. The titles would look better and take up less room if they were rotated vertically within their cells. You will rotate the titles.

To rotate the titles:

1. Click the merged cell **A6** to select it.

2. In the Alignment group on the Home tab, click the **Orientation** button ✏, and then click **Rotate Text Up**. The cell text rotates 90 degrees counterclockwise.

3. In the Alignment group, click the **Middle Align** button ≡. The rotated text vertically aligns within the merged cell.

4. Click the merged cell **A17** to select it, and then repeat Steps 1 through 3 to rotate and align the text.

5. Reduce the width of column A to **5** characters. See Figure 2-16.

Figure 2-16	Rotated cell text

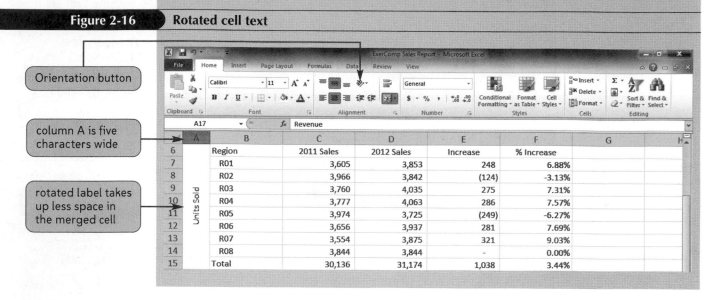

Adding Cell Borders

TIP

You set the gridlines or the row and column headings to print by clicking the appropriate Print check box in the Sheet Options group on the Page Layout tab.

When a worksheet is printed, the gridlines that surround the cells are not printed by default. They only appear on the worksheet as a guide. Sometimes you want to include lines along the edges of cells to enhance the readability of the rows and columns of data. One way to do this is by adding a border to a cell or range. You can add borders to the left, top, right, or bottom of a cell or range; around an entire cell; or around the outside edges of a range. You can also specify the thickness of and the number of lines in the border.

Tom wants you to add borders to the column titles and Total rows. Standard accounting practice is to add a single top border and a double bottom border to the Total rows to clearly differentiate them from financial data.

To add cell borders to the column labels and Total rows:

1. Select the nonadjacent range **B6:F6;B17:F17**. You'll add a bottom border to these column labels.

2. In the Font group on the Home tab, click the **Border button arrow** ⊞ ▼, and then click **Bottom Border**. A border is added to the bottom of the selected cells.

3. Select the nonadjacent range **B15:F15;B26:F26**. You'll add top and bottom borders to these Total rows.

4. In the Font group, click the **Border button arrow** ⊞ ▼, and then click **Top and Double Bottom Border**. The Total rows both have a single top border and a double bottom border, following standard accounting practice.

5. Click cell **A5** to deselect the range. See Figure 2-17.

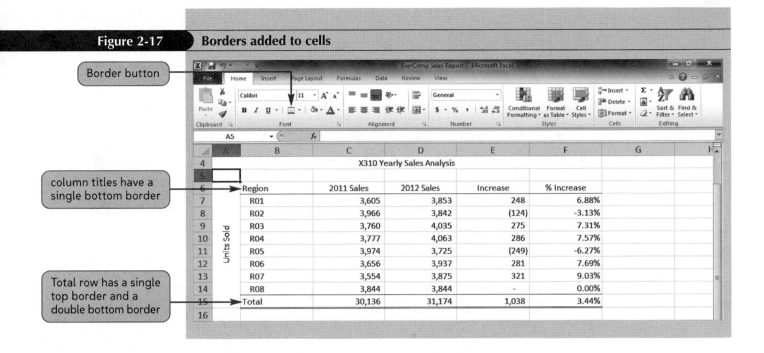

Figure 2-17 — Borders added to cells

Border button

column titles have a single bottom border

Total row has a single top border and a double bottom border

Exploring Options in the Format Cells Dialog Box

The buttons on the Home tab provide quick access to the most commonly used formatting choices. For more options, you can use the Format Cells dialog box. For example, the numbers in cells E8 and E11 are displayed in parentheses to indicate that they are negative. Although parentheses are common in accounting to indicate negative currency values, Tom wants you to reformat the units sold numbers to display negative numbers with a minus symbol. You can do this in the Format Cells dialog box.

TIP

You can also open the Format Cells dialog box by right-clicking a cell or selected range, and then clicking Format Cells on the shortcut menu.

To open the Format Cells dialog box:

1. Select the range **E7:E15**.

2. In the Number group on the Home tab, click the **Dialog Box Launcher**. The Format Cells dialog box opens with the Number tab active.

The Format Cells dialog box has six tabs, each focusing on a different set of formatting options, as described below. You can apply the formats in this dialog box to selected worksheet cells.

- **Number** provides options for formatting the appearance of numbers, including dates and numbers treated as text (for example, telephone or Social Security numbers).
- **Alignment** provides options for how data is aligned within a cell.
- **Font** provides options for selecting font types, sizes, styles, and other formatting attributes such as underlining and font colors.
- **Border** provides options for adding and removing cell borders as well as selecting a line style and color.
- **Fill** provides options for creating and applying background colors and patterns to cells.
- **Protection** provides options for locking or hiding cells to prevent other users from modifying their contents.

Although you've applied many of these formats from the Home tab, the Format Cells dialog box presents them in a different way and provides more choices. You'll use the Number tab to change the number format for the selected cells. Remember, modifying the number format does not affect the value stored in the workbook.

To set the format for negative values:

1. In the Category box on the left side of the Format Cells dialog box, click **Number**.

2. Verify that **0** (zero) appears in the Decimal places box.

3. Verify that the **Use 1000 Separator (,)** check box contains a check mark.

4. In the Negative numbers box, verify that **−1,234** (the first option) is selected. See Figure 2-18.

Figure 2-18   **Number tab in the Format Cells dialog box**

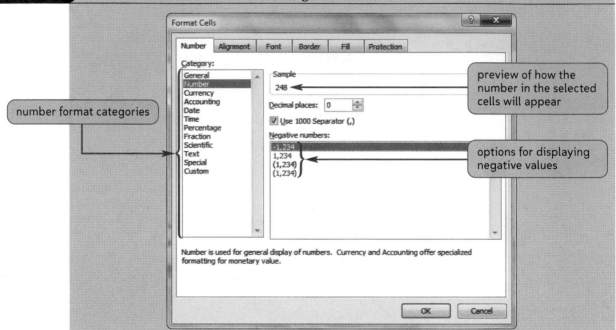

5. Click the **OK** button. The Format Cells dialog box closes and the negative numbers in the range E7:E15 appear with a minus symbol, a comma as the thousands separator, and no decimal places.

Tom wants the bottom border color used for the column titles changed from black to green. You'll use the Border tab in the Format Cells dialog box to set the border line color and make this change. On the Border tab, you can select a line style ranging from thick to thin, choose double to dotted lines, and place these lines anywhere around the cells in the selected range.

To set the border color for the column labels:

1. Select the nonadjacent range **B6:F6;B17:F17**.

2. In the Font group on the Home tab, click the **Borders button arrow** ⊞ ▾, and then click **More Borders**. The Format Cells dialog box opens with the Border tab active.

   3. In the Line group, click the **Color arrow** to display the color palette, and then
       click **Green** (the sixth color) in the Standard Colors section.

   4. Click the bottom border of the border preview. A green bottom border is shown
       in the preview. See Figure 2-19.

Figure 2-19   **Border tab in the Format Cells dialog box**

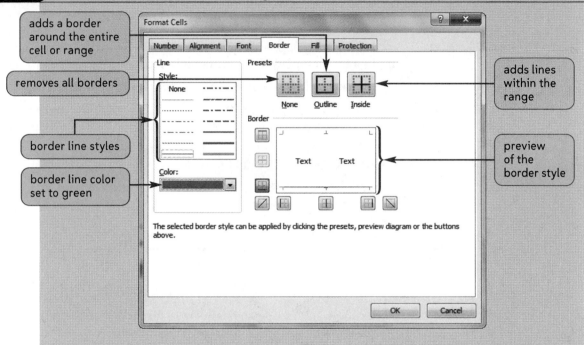

adds a border around the entire cell or range

removes all borders

border line styles

border line color set to green

adds lines within the range

preview of the border style

   5. Click the **OK** button. The dialog box closes and the cells with column titles have a
       green bottom border.

Copying and Pasting Formats

You have not yet formatted the titles in cells A1 and A2 of the Yearly Sales worksheet
to match the style you used for the Documentation worksheet. You could repeat the
same steps to format these cells, but a quicker method is to copy those formats from the
Documentation worksheet into the Yearly Sales worksheet.

Copying Formats with the Format Painter

Using the Format Painter is a fast and efficient way of maintaining a consistent look and
feel throughout a workbook. So, after you set the formatting in one cell, you can copy
that formatting to another cell or range without duplicating the data.

   You'll use the Format Painter to copy the cell formats from the range A1:A2 in the
Documentation worksheet into the same range in the Yearly Sales worksheet.

TIP

You can double-click the Format Painter button to paste the same format multiple times. Click the Format Painter button again to turn it off.

To copy and paste a format:

1. Click the **Documentation** sheet tab to make that worksheet active, and then select the range **A1:A2**.

2. In the Clipboard group on the Home tab, click the **Format Painter** button. The formats from the selected cells are copied to the Clipboard.

3. Click the **Yearly Sales** sheet tab to make that worksheet active, and then select the range **A1:A2**. The formatting from the Documentation worksheet is removed from the Clipboard and applied to the selected cells. Format Painter does not copy formatting applied to text selections within a cell, so the red color you applied to "Comp" was not included in the pasted formatting.

4. Double-click cell **A1** to switch to Edit mode, and then select **Comp** in the cell.

5. In the Font group on the Home tab, click the **Font Color button arrow**, and then click **Red** (the second color) in the Standard Colors section. The selected text changes to red.

6. Press the **Enter** key to exit Edit mode.

7. Select the range **A1:A2** in the Yearly Sales worksheet, and then repeat Steps 2 through 6 to copy the formatting to the range A1:A2 in the Monthly Sales worksheet.

Copying Formats with the Paste Options Button

Sometimes you want to copy and paste more than a cell's formatting. When you want to paste the formatting from a copied range along with its contents, you can use the Paste Options button. As shown in Figure 2-20, each time you paste, the Paste Options button appears in the lower-right corner of the pasted cell or range. When you click the Paste Options button, you can choose from a list of pasting options, such as pasting only the values or only the formatting.

Figure 2-20 Paste Options button

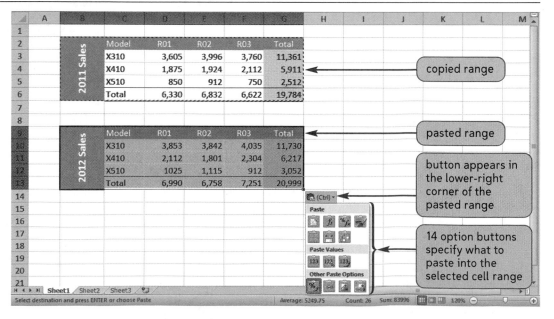

Copying Formats with Paste Special

The Paste Special command is another way to control what you paste from the Clipboard. To use Paste Special, select and copy a range, select the range where you want to paste the Clipboard contents, click the Paste button arrow in the Clipboard group on the Home tab, and then click Paste Special to open the dialog box shown in Figure 2-21. From the Paste Special dialog box, you can control exactly how to paste the copied range.

Figure 2-21   **Paste Special dialog box**

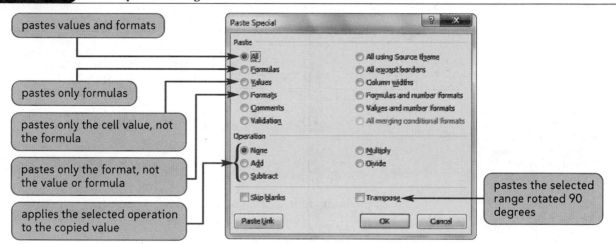

pastes values and formats

pastes only formulas

pastes only the cell value, not the formula

pastes only the format, not the value or formula

applies the selected operation to the copied value

pastes the selected range rotated 90 degrees

So far, you have formatted cells and ranges in Tom's workbook. In the next session, you'll work with built-in styles, themes, table styles, conditional formatting, and page layout tools.

Session 2.1 Quick Check

REVIEW

1. What is the difference between a serif font and a sans serif font?
2. What is the difference between a theme color and a standard color?
3. What is the General number format?
4. Why are dates right-aligned within a worksheet cell by default?
5. The range A1:C5 is merged into a single cell. What is the cell reference of this merged cell?
6. Where can you access all the formatting options for worksheet cells?
7. What are three tools you can use to copy and paste only the formatting of a cell?
8. Describe how you would use the Paste Special dialog box to multiply every value in a selected range by 2.

SESSION 2.2 VISUAL OVERVIEW

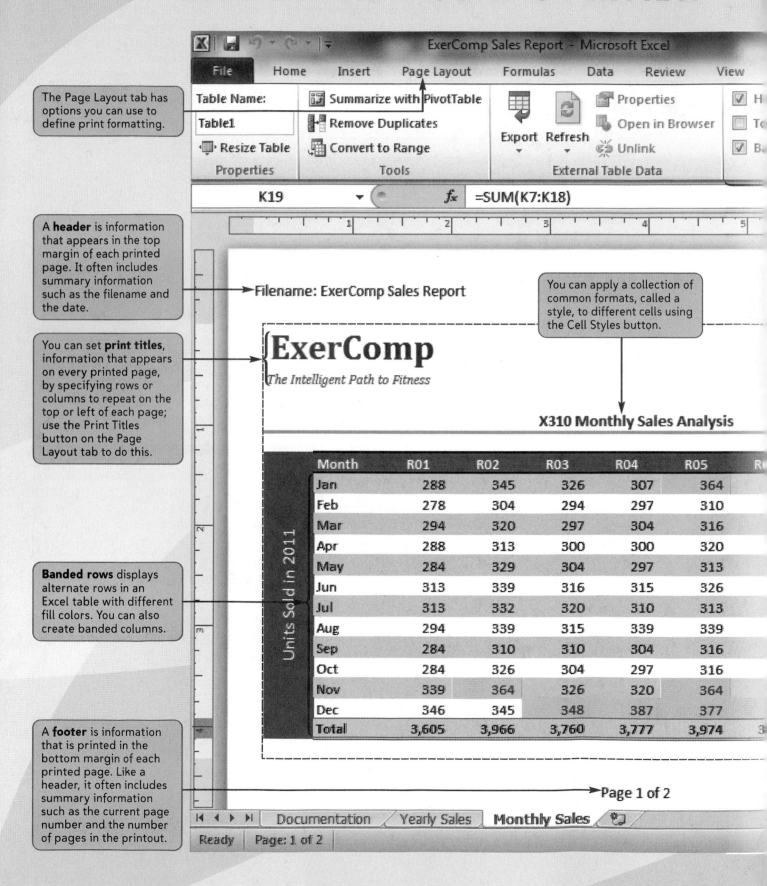

The Page Layout tab has options you can use to define print formatting.

A **header** is information that appears in the top margin of each printed page. It often includes summary information such as the filename and the date.

You can set **print titles**, information that appears on every printed page, by specifying rows or columns to repeat on the top or left of each page; use the Print Titles button on the Page Layout tab to do this.

Banded rows displays alternate rows in an Excel table with different fill colors. You can also create banded columns.

A **footer** is information that is printed in the bottom margin of each printed page. Like a header, it often includes summary information such as the current page number and the number of pages in the printout.

You can apply a collection of common formats, called a style, to different cells using the Cell Styles button.

ExerComp Sales Report - Microsoft Excel

| File | Home | Insert | Page Layout | Formulas | Data | Review | View |

Table Name:
Table1
Resize Table
Properties

Summarize with PivotTable
Remove Duplicates
Convert to Range
Tools

Export Refresh

Properties
Open in Browser
Unlink
External Table Data

K19   fx   =SUM(K7:K18)

Filename: ExerComp Sales Report

ExerComp
The Intelligent Path to Fitness

X310 Monthly Sales Analysis

Units Sold in 2011

Month	R01	R02	R03	R04	R05	R
Jan	288	345	326	307	364	
Feb	278	304	294	297	310	
Mar	294	320	297	304	316	
Apr	288	313	300	300	320	
May	284	329	304	297	313	
Jun	313	339	316	315	326	
Jul	313	332	320	310	313	
Aug	294	339	315	339	339	
Sep	284	310	310	304	316	
Oct	284	326	304	297	316	
Nov	339	364	326	320	364	
Dec	346	345	348	387	377	
Total	3,605	3,966	3,760	3,777	3,974	3

Page 1 of 2

Documentation / Yearly Sales / **Monthly Sales**

Ready   Page: 1 of 2

TABLE STYLES AND PAGE FORMATTING

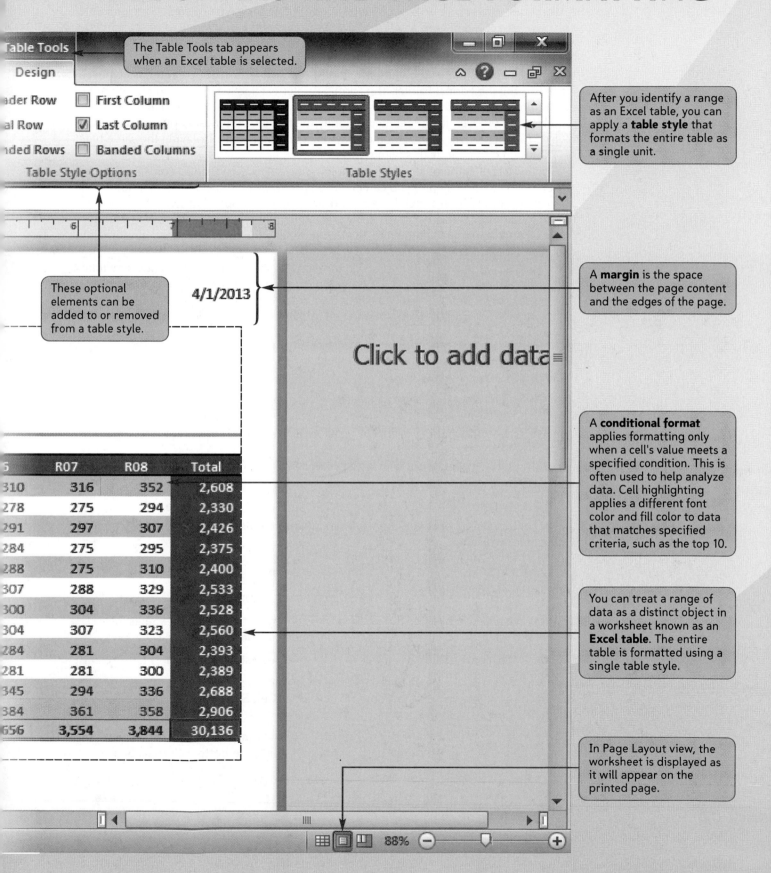

The Table Tools tab appears when an Excel table is selected.

After you identify a range as an Excel table, you can apply a **table style** that formats the entire table as a single unit.

These optional elements can be added to or removed from a table style.

A **margin** is the space between the page content and the edges of the page.

A **conditional format** applies formatting only when a cell's value meets a specified condition. This is often used to help analyze data. Cell highlighting applies a different font color and fill color to data that matches specified criteria, such as the top 10.

You can treat a range of data as a distinct object in a worksheet known as an **Excel table**. The entire table is formatted using a single table style.

In Page Layout view, the worksheet is displayed as it will appear on the printed page.

Table Tools

Design

der Row   ☐ First Column

al Row   ☑ Last Column

ded Rows   ☐ Banded Columns

Table Style Options   Table Styles

4/1/2013

Click to add data

	R07	R08	Total
310	316	352	2,608
278	275	294	2,330
291	297	307	2,426
284	275	295	2,375
288	275	310	2,400
307	288	329	2,533
300	304	336	2,528
304	307	323	2,560
284	281	304	2,393
281	281	300	2,389
345	294	336	2,688
384	361	358	2,906
656	3,554	3,844	30,136

88%

Applying Cell Styles

A workbook often contains several cells that store the same type of data. For example, each worksheet might have a cell displaying the sheet title, or a range of financial data might have several cells containing summary totals. It's good design practice to apply the same format to worksheet cells that contain the same type of data.

One way to ensure that you are using consistent formats is to copy and paste your formats using the Format Painter. The Format Painter is effective, but it can also be time consuming if you need to copy the same format to several cells scattered across the workbook. Moreover, if you decide to modify the format, you must copy and paste the revised format all over again. Another way to ensure that cells displaying the same type of data use the same format is with styles.

A style is a selection of formatting options using a specific font and color from the current theme. For example, you can create a style to display sheet titles in a bold, white, 20-point Calibri font on a blue background. You can then apply that style to any sheet title in a workbook. If you later revise the style, the appearance of any cell formatted with that style is updated automatically. This saves you the time and effort of reformatting each cell individually.

Excel has a variety of built-in styles to format worksheet titles, column and row totals, and cells with emphasis. You used the built-in Currency and Percent styles when you formatted data in the Yearly Sales worksheet as currency and percentages. Some styles are based on the workbook's current theme and may change if the theme is changed.

REFERENCE

Applying a Cell Style

- Select the cell or range to which you want to apply a style.
- In the Styles group on the Home tab, click the Cell Styles button.
- Point to each style in the Cell Styles gallery to see a Live Preview of that style on the selected cell or range.
- Click the style you want to apply to the selected cell or range.

You will use some of the built-in styles to add more color and visual interest to the Yearly Sales worksheet.

To apply built-in styles to the Yearly Sales worksheet:

1. If you took a break after the previous session, open the ExerComp Sales Report workbook located in the Excel2\Tutorial folder included with your Data Files.

2. Click the **Yearly Sales** sheet tab to make that worksheet active, and then select the merged cell **A4**.

3. In the Styles group on the Home tab, click the **Cell Styles** button. The Cell Styles gallery opens.

4. Point to the **Heading 1** style in the Titles and Headings section. Live Preview shows cell A4 in a 15-point, bold font with a solid blue bottom border. See Figure 2-22.

Figure 2-22 Cell Styles gallery

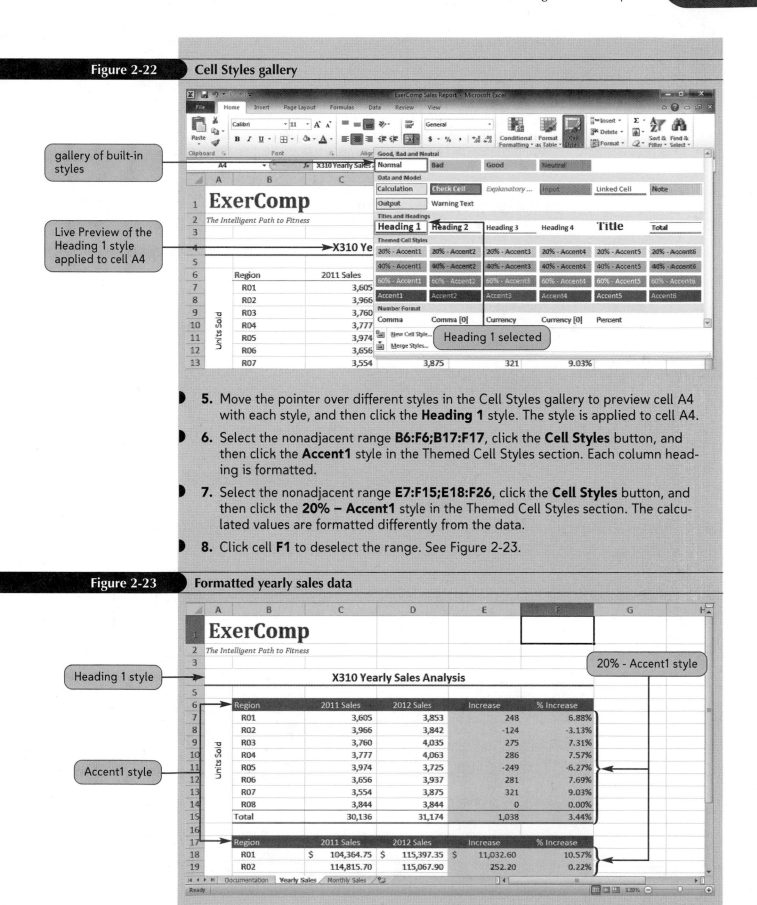

gallery of built-in styles

Live Preview of the Heading 1 style applied to cell A4

Heading 1 selected

5. Move the pointer over different styles in the Cell Styles gallery to preview cell A4 with each style, and then click the **Heading 1** style. The style is applied to cell A4.

6. Select the nonadjacent range **B6:F6;B17:F17**, click the **Cell Styles** button, and then click the **Accent1** style in the Themed Cell Styles section. Each column heading is formatted.

7. Select the nonadjacent range **E7:F15;E18:F26**, click the **Cell Styles** button, and then click the **20% – Accent1** style in the Themed Cell Styles section. The calculated values are formatted differently from the data.

8. Click cell **F1** to deselect the range. See Figure 2-23.

Figure 2-23 Formatted yearly sales data

Heading 1 style

20% - Accent1 style

Accent1 style

	Region	2011 Sales	2012 Sales	Increase	% Increase
R01		3,605	3,853	248	6.88%
R02		3,966	3,842	-124	-3.13%
R03		3,760	4,035	275	7.31%
R04		3,777	4,063	286	7.57%
R05		3,974	3,725	-249	-6.27%
R06		3,656	3,937	281	7.69%
R07		3,554	3,875	321	9.03%
R08		3,844	3,844	0	0.00%
Total		30,136	31,174	1,038	3.44%

X310 Yearly Sales Analysis

Region	2011 Sales	2012 Sales	Increase	% Increase
R01	$ 104,364.75	$ 115,397.35	$ 11,032.60	10.57%
R02	114,815.70	115,067.90	252.20	0.22%

Working with Themes

Most of the formatting you have applied so far is based on the workbook's current theme—the default Office theme. As you've seen, fonts, colors, and cell styles are organized in theme and non-theme categories. The appearance of these fonts, colors, and cell styles depends on the workbook's current theme. If you change the theme, the formatting of these elements also changes throughout the entire workbook.

You'll change the workbook's theme to see its effect on the workbook's appearance.

To change the workbook's theme:

▶ 1. Click the **Page Layout** tab on the Ribbon.

▶ 2. In the Themes group, click the **Themes** button. The Themes gallery opens. Office—the current theme—is the default.

▶ 3. Point to each theme in the Themes gallery. Live Preview shows how each theme changes the appearance of the Yearly Sales worksheet.

▶ 4. Click the **Apex** theme to apply that theme to the workbook. See Figure 2-24.

Figure 2-24   Apex theme applied to the yearly sales data

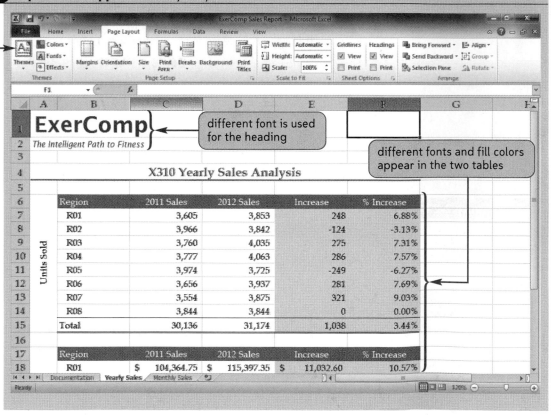

Changing the theme made a significant difference in the worksheet's appearance. The most obvious changes are the fill colors and the fonts. Only elements directly tied to a theme change when you select a different theme. The cells you formatted with the Accent1 cell style changed because the Accent1 color is blue in the Office theme and orange in the Apex theme. The Heading 1 style you applied to the titles in cells A1 and A2 uses the Cambria typeface in the Office theme and the Lucida Sans typeface in the Apex theme. The Apex theme also uses a different font for body text, which is why the rest of the text changed size and appearance.

The logo colors in cell A1 did not change because you used two standard colors, blue and red, which are not part of a theme. Changing the theme does not affect these colors.

Tom prefers the default Office theme, so you'll reapply that theme.

To select the Office theme:

▶ **1.** In the Themes group on the Page Layout tab, click the **Themes** button, and then click the **Office** theme from the gallery of themes.

PROSKILLS

Teamwork: Sharing Styles and Themes

Using a common style and design theme for all the files you create in Microsoft Office is a simple way to give your files a consistent look and feel and project a professional image. This consistency is especially important when a team of workers is collaborating on a set of documents. When all team members work from a common set of style and design themes, readers will not be distracted by inconsistent or clashing styles.

To quickly copy the styles from one workbook to another, open the workbook with the styles you want to copy, and then open the workbook in which you want to copy those styles. In the Styles group on the Home tab, click the Cell Styles button, and then click Merge Styles. The Merge Styles dialog box opens, listing the currently open workbooks. Select the workbook with the styles you want to copy, and then click the OK button to copy those styles into the current workbook. If you modify any styles, you must copy the styles to the other workbook; Excel does not update styles between workbooks.

Because other Office files, including those created with Word or PowerPoint, use the same file format for themes, you can create one theme to use with all the Office files you create. To save a theme, in the Themes group on the Page Layout tab, click the Themes button, and then click Save Current Theme. The Save Current Theme dialog box opens. Select a save location (in a default Theme folder on your computer or another folder), type a descriptive name in the File name box, and then click the Save button. If you saved the theme file in a default Theme folder, the theme appears in the Themes gallery, and any changes made to the theme are reflected in any Office file that uses that theme.

By creating a library of styles and themes, you can create a report containing pages generated from different Office programs and those pages will still share a consistent set of design elements. Employees with expertise in page design can design a theme for the rest of the team to use. If those styles and themes are changed or modified, the new design style can be quickly applied to new and existing documents without having to reformat each document. Through careful planning, a well-designed theme can save you and your colleagues a lot of effort later on.

Creating Formulas to Add and Subtract Values

Next, you'll work with the Monthly Sales worksheet, which contains the sales results by month for the eight sales regions over the past two years. Tom wants to use this data to identify trends. He's more interested in the "big picture" than in specific numbers. He wants to know which sales regions are performing well and which are underperforming. He also wants to explore the pattern of monthly sales throughout the year.

Creating Formulas to Calculate Totals

The top of the worksheet contains annual sales for the previous two years. The bottom of the worksheet displays the increase in annual sales for each region and month. Tom wants you to calculate the monthly totals broken down by region. You'll start with the 2011 sales values.

To calculate the monthly and regional totals for 2011:

1. Click the **Monthly Sales** sheet tab to make the worksheet active.

2. In cells K6 and B19, enter the label **Total**.

3. Select the nonadjacent range **K7:K18;C19:K19**. You'll add the formula to calculate the total in these cells.

4. In the Editing group on the Home tab, click the **Sum** button Σ. The 2011 monthly and regional sales totals are entered in the selected range. See Figure 2-25.

Figure 2-25 Monthly and regional sales totals for 2011

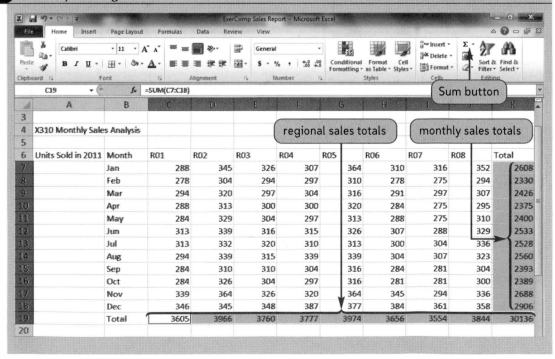

Next, you will calculate the monthly and regional sales totals for 2012. Rather than retyping the text and formulas, you can copy and paste them from 2011.

To calculate the monthly and regional totals for 2012:

▶ 1. Select the range **K6:K19**, and then click the **Copy** button 🖹 in the Clipboard group on the Home tab. The cell contents are copied to the Clipboard.

▶ 2. Click cell **K21**, and then click the **Paste** button 🖺. Excel inserts formulas to calculate the 2012 monthly sales totals into the range K21:K34.

▶ 3. Select the range **B19:J19**, and then click the **Copy** button 🖹.

▶ 4. Click cell **B34**, and then click the **Paste** button 🖺. Excel inserts formulas to calculate the 2012 regional sales totals into the range B34:J34. See Figure 2-26.

Figure 2-26 | Monthly and regional sales totals for 2012

Annotations: text and formulas to copy → Total row 19; monthly sales totals → Total column K21:K34; regional sales totals → Total row 34

Creating Formulas to Subtract Values

Tom also wants you to calculate the change in sales from one year to another, broken down by region and month. You'll use the copy and paste features to quickly add this third table to the Monthly Sales worksheet. Then you will add formulas to calculate the increase in units sold between 2011 and 2012.

To calculate the change in sales from one year to the next:

▶ 1. In cell A36, enter the label **Net Increase**.

▶ 2. Copy the range **B21:K21**, and then paste it into the range **B36:K36**.

▶ 3. Copy the range **B22:B34**, and then paste it into the range **B37:B49**.

▶ 4. In cell C37, enter the formula **=C22–C7**. After you press the Enter key, the value 64 appears in the cell; this is the increase in January sales for region R01.

▶ 5. Copy cell **C37**, and then paste it into the range **C37:K49**. The formula =C22–C7 is copied and pasted into the range of cells with the remaining months and regions.

▶ 6. Click cell **A36** to deselect the range. Figure 2-27 shows the completed table.

Figure 2-27 **Net increase in sales by region and month**

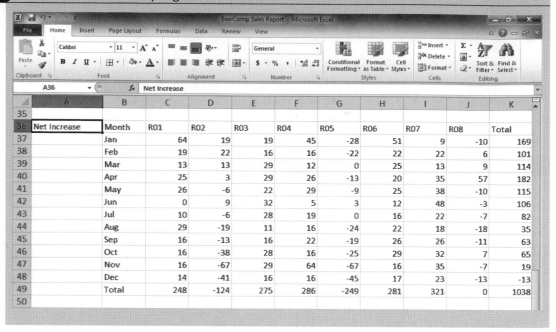

Next, you'll format the row and column titles for these tables. You'll use the formatting options on the Home tab and in the Format Cells dialog box to format the new table to match the other tables.

To format the titles:

1. Select the range **A4:K4**, and then click the **Merge & Center** button ⊞ in the Alignment group on the Home tab. The title is centered in the merged cell.

2. In the Styles group, click the **Cell Styles** button, and then click the **Heading 1** style. The Heading 1 style is applied to the title.

3. Select the range **A6:A19**, and then click the **Merge & Center** button ⊞ in the Alignment group. The label is centered in the merged cell.

4. In the Alignment group, click the **Orientation** button ⤸▾, and then click **Rotate Text Up**. The text in the cell rotates 90 degrees.

5. In the Alignment group, click the **Middle Align** button ≡. The text is centered both horizontally and vertically in the cells.

6. Reduce the width of column A to **5** characters.

7. Select the range **C7:K19**, and then, in the Number group on the Home tab, click the **Dialog Box Launcher**. The Format Cells dialog box opens with the Number tab displayed.

8. Click **Number** in the Category box, type **0** (a zero) in the Decimal places box, click the **Use 1000 Separator (,)** check box to insert a check mark, verify that the **−1,234** option is selected, and then click the **OK** button. The numbers display a thousands separator and use a minus symbol for negatives.

   Next you'll copy this format to the two other tables on the worksheet.

9. Select the range **A6:K19**.

Be sure to double-click the
Format Painter button so
you can paste the copied
format into multiple cells.

10. In the Clipboard group, double-click the **Format Painter** button 🖌.

11. Click cell **A21**. All of the formats in the range A6:K19 are applied to the cell.

12. Click cell **A36**. Once again, all of the formats are applied to the selected cell.

13. In the Clipboard group, click the **Format Painter** button 🖌 to turn off the Format Painter.

14. Scroll up to the top of the worksheet and select cell **A1**. Figure 2-28 shows the formatted values for the first table.

Figure 2-28   **Formatted table**

Month	R01	R02	R03	R04	R05	R06	R07	R08	Total
Jan	288	345	326	307	364	310	316	352	2,608
Feb	278	304	294	297	310	278	275	294	2,330
Mar	294	320	297	304	316	291	297	307	2,426
Apr	288	313	300	300	320	284	275	295	2,375
May	284	329	304	297	313	288	275	310	2,400
Jun	313	339	316	315	326	307	288	329	2,533
Jul	313	332	320	310	313	300	304	336	2,528
Aug	294	339	315	339	339	304	307	323	2,560
Sep	284	310	310	304	316	284	281	304	2,393
Oct	284	326	304	297	316	281	281	300	2,389
Nov	339	364	326	320	364	345	294	336	2,688
Dec	346	345	348	387	377	384	361	358	2,906
Total	3,605	3,966	3,760	3,777	3,974	3,656	3,554	3,844	30,136

ExerComp
The Intelligent Path to Fitness

X310 Monthly Sales Analysis

Units Sold in 2011

Documentation   Yearly Sales   Monthly Sales

Ready   120%

Working with Table Styles

You can identify a range as an Excel table, which makes available tools designed for analyzing tabular data, such as the ability to sort data, transfer data to and from an external file, and filter the data to show only those rows that match specified criteria. Excel tables can include optional elements such as a header row that contains titles for the different columns in the table, and a total row that contains formulas summarizing the values in the table's data. You can also apply a table style, which specifies formats such as font color, fill color, and so on for each of these elements. Formatting an entire table with a table style is more efficient than formatting individual cells in the table. (This tutorial covers only the styles associated with Excel tables.

TIP

Applying a table style also
marks the range as an
Excel table.

In addition, using a table style ensures that the table's formatting reflects any changes made to the table, such as adding or deleting table rows or columns. For example, many tables display alternate rows with different fill colors. This banded rows effect makes the data easier to read, especially in large tables with many rows. You could create the banded rows effect by applying a cell style with a background fill to every other row in the table; but if you later add or delete a row from the table, the banded rows effect might be lost. A table style, on the other hand, applies alternating row colors to the entire Excel table and adjusts the banded rows effect as needed if you add or delete rows. This is because a table style treats the table as a single object rather than a collection of cells. Figure 2-29 shows the banded rows effect applied both manually and with a table style.

Figure 2-29   **Banded rows in a table**

	A	B	C	D
1	Region	Year 1 Sales	Year 2 Sales	Difference
2	R01	3,605	3,853	248
3	R02	3,966	3,842	-124
4	R03	3,760	4,035	275
5	R04	3,777	4,063	286
6	R05	3,974	3,725	-249
7	R06	3,656	3,937	281
8	R07	3,554	3,875	321
9	R08	3,844	3,844	0
10	Total	30,136	31,174	1,038
11				

original table with banded rows

	A	B	C	D
1	Region	Year 1 Sales	Year 2 Sales	Difference
2	R01	3,605	3,853	248
3	R02	3,966	3,842	-124
4	R03	3,760	4,035	275
5	R07	3,554	3,875	321
6	R08	3,844	3,844	0
7	Total	18,729	19,449	720
8				

after deleting a row from a
table formatted manually,
the banded effect is lost

	A	B	C	D
1	Region	Year 1 Sales	Year 2 Sales	Difference
2	R01	3,605	3,853	248
3	R02	3,966	3,842	-124
4	R03	3,760	4,035	275
5	R07	3,554	3,875	321
6	R08	3,844	3,844	0
7	Total	18,729	19,449	720
8				

after deleting a row from a table
formatted with a table style, the
table formatting adjusts to keep
banded rows

Tom wants you to format the sales data in the Monthly Sales worksheet as Excel
tables. First, you'll apply a table style to the units sold in 2011 data.

To apply a table style to the 2011 sales data:

1. Select the range **B6:K19**.

2. In the Styles group on the Home tab, click the **Format as Table** button, and then
   click **Table Style Medium 2** (the second style in the first row in the Medium section).
   The Format As Table dialog box opens, confirming the range you selected for the
   table and whether the table includes header rows.

3. Verify that the range is **=$B$6:$K$19** and then verify that the **My table has
   headers** check box contains a check mark to include the text labels in the table.

4. Click the **OK** button to apply the table style to the selected range, and then click
   cell **A5** to deselect the range. See Figure 2-30.

Figure 2-30   **Range formatted with a table style**

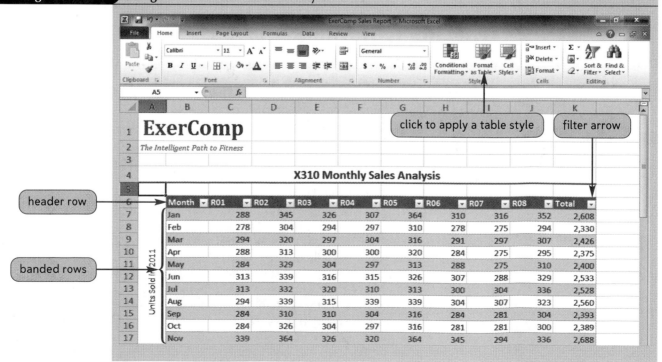

The table style treated the range as a single unit and modified its overall appearance. In this case, Table Style Medium 2 formatted the range so the header row appears in a white font on a blue fill and the remaining rows are formatted as banded rows. In addition, filter arrows appear next to the column titles in the header row. These filter arrows are applied when the user wants to hide or filter out different table rows that contain certain data.

Tom doesn't want to filter the data right now, so you will remove the arrows and work only with elements related to the table style.

To remove the filter arrows from the table:

▶ 1. Click cell **B6** to make the table active.

▶ 2. Click the **Data** tab on the Ribbon.

▶ 3. In the Sort & Filter group, click the **Filter** button. The filter arrows disappear from the header row.

Selecting Table Style Options

After you apply a table style, you can choose which table elements to include in the style. Table styles have the following six elements that can be turned on or off:

- **Header Row**, which formats the first row of the table
- **Total Row**, which inserts a new row at the bottom of the table that adds the column values
- **First Column**, which formats the first column of the table
- **Last Column**, which formats the last column of the table
- **Banded Rows**, which formats alternating rows in different colors
- **Banded Columns**, which formats alternating columns in different colors

For example, if you turn on the Header Row option, you can specify a format for the table's first row, which usually contains text that describes the contents of each table column. If you insert a new row at the top of the table, the new row becomes the header row and is formatted with the table style.

In the table style you just used, only the Header Row and Banded Rows options are on. Although the other elements are still part of the table structure, the current style does not format them. Tom wants you to format the table's last column and header row as well as remove the banded rows effect.

To modify the table style:

TIP
You can click any cell within a table to make the table active; you do not need to select all of the table cells.

▶ 1. If necessary, click cell **B6** to make the table active. The Table Tools contextual tab appears on the Ribbon.

▶ 2. Click the **Design** tab on the Ribbon. The table design options appear on the Ribbon.

▶ 3. In the Table Style Options group, click the **Last Column** check box to insert a check mark. The last column is formatted.

▶ 4. In the Table Style Options group, click the **Banded Rows** check box to remove the check mark. The banded rows are removed from the table.

Only the Header Row and Last Column elements appear in the table. You'll use a built-in table style to format them.

▶ 5. In the Table Styles group, click the **More** button ▼. The Table Styles gallery opens.

6. In the Medium section, click **Table Style Medium 20** (the third table style in the sixth column). The table styles in the gallery show the formatting applied to the current table elements. See Figure 2-31.

Figure 2-31   **Revised table style**

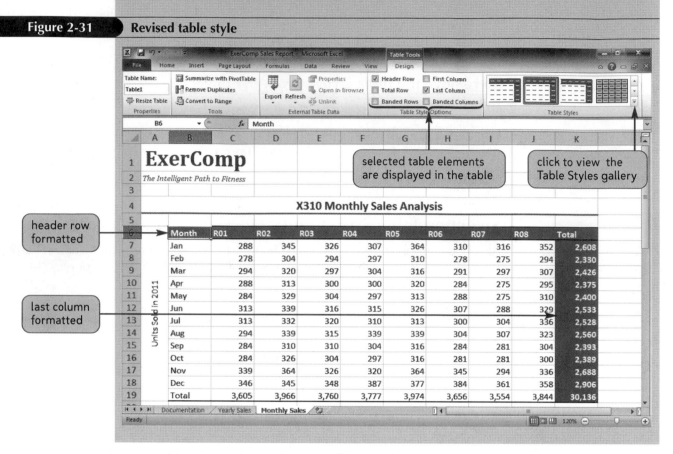

A table style might not format a table exactly the way you want. For example, Tom wants the column titles in the header row to be centered and the Total row to have a single top border and a double bottom border. Because the table style you used does not include either of these formats, you'll add these formats to the table cells. You can use cell styles and the formatting tools you've used with individual cells and ranges to format Excel tables.

To format the header row and the Total row:

1. Select the range **C6:K6**. You'll change the alignment of the header row.

2. Click the **Home** tab on the Ribbon, and then click the **Center** button ≣ in the Alignment group. The column titles are centered.

3. Select the range **B19:K19**. You'll apply a different cell style to the Total row.

4. In the Styles group, click the **Cell Styles** button, and then click **Total** (the sixth cell style) in the Titles and Headings section.

5. Click cell **A5** to deselect the range. The Total row is formatted in bold with a single top border and a double bottom border.

Tom likes the formatting of the first table, and wants you to format the other two tables similarly. You cannot use the Format Painter to copy table formats, and you must format each range as a table separately.

To format the other two tables:

1. Select the range **B21:K34**.

2. In the Styles group on the Home tab, click the **Format as Table** button, click **Table Style Medium 6** (the sixth table style in the first row of the Medium section), and then click the **OK** button in the Format As Table dialog box. The range is formatted as a table.

3. Click the **Data** tab on the Ribbon, and then click the **Filter** button in the Sort & Filter group to turn off the filter arrows.

4. Click the **Design** tab on the Ribbon, and then, in the Table Style Options group, click the **Banded Rows** check box to remove the check mark and click the **Last Column** check box to insert a check mark. The banded rows are removed and the last column is formatted.

5. In the Table Styles group, click the **More** button, and then click **Table Style Medium 20** (the sixth table style in the third row of the Medium section). The table is quickly reformatted with a new style.

6. Select the range **C21:K21**, click the **Home** tab on the Ribbon, and then click the **Center** button ≣ in the Alignment group. The column headings are centered.

7. Select the range **B34:K34**; in the Styles group, click the **Cell Styles** button, and then click **Total** (the sixth cell style in the Titles and Headings section). The Total row is formatted.

8. Select the range **B36:K49** and repeat Steps 2 through 5, select the range **C36:K36** and repeat Step 6, and then select the range **B49:K49** and repeat Step 7. The third table is formatted to match the first two tables.

Highlighting Cells with Conditional Formats

The formatting you have applied to the workbook has made the content more readable. However, Tom also wants this worksheet to highlight important trends and sales values of interest. For example, Tom is interested in knowing which regions and months have the highest sales or showed the highest increase between 2011 and 2012.

You can answer these kinds of questions using conditional formats, in which the format applied to a cell depends upon the value or content of the cell. For example, a conditional format can make negative numbers red and positive numbers black. Conditional formats are dynamic, so that if the cell's value changes, the cell's format also changes as needed. Each conditional format has a set of rules that define how the formatting should be applied and under what conditions the format will be changed.

REFERENCE

Highlighting a Cell Based on Its Value

- Select the range in which you want to highlight cells that match a specified rule.
- In the Styles group on the Home tab, click the Conditional Formatting button, point to Highlight Cells Rules or Top/Bottom Rules, and then click the appropriate rule.
- Select the appropriate options in the dialog box, and then click the OK button.

Excel has four conditional formats—data bars, highlighting, color scales, and icon sets. In this tutorial, you will apply cell highlighting, which changes the cell's font color or background color based on the cell's value. Figure 2-32 describes some of the ways that cells can be highlighted with conditional formats.

Figure 2-32 **Highlighting rules**

Rule	Highlights
Greater Than	Cells that are greater than a specified number
Less Than	Cells that are less than a specified number
Between	Cells that are between two specified numbers
Equal To	Cells that are equal to a specified number
Text That Contains	Cells that contain specified text
A Date Occurring	Cells that contain a specified date
Duplicate Values	Cells that contain duplicate or unique values

Tom wants to highlight sales regions that showed an increase in sales from 2011 to 2012. With all of the data on the Monthly Sales worksheet, this information can be difficult to locate. To make this data stand out, you will use a conditional format to display worksheet cells with a positive value using a different font or fill color than cells containing zero or a negative value.

To highlight the positive sales numbers:

1. Select the range **C37:J48**. This range shows the difference in sales by region and month for 2011 and 2012.

2. In the Styles group on the Home tab, click the **Conditional Formatting** button, point to **Highlight Cells Rules**, and then click **Greater Than**. The Greater Than dialog box opens. You want to highlight those regions and months in which sales increased, which means that they are greater than zero.

3. Type **0** (a zero) in the Format cells that are GREATER THAN box, click the **with** arrow, and then click **Green Fill with Dark Green Text**. This rule formats any cells that display a number greater than zero in a green font with a green background.

4. Click the **OK** button to apply the highlighting rule.

5. Click cell **A35** to deselect the range. Cells with positive numbers are highlighted in green. See Figure 2-33.

Figure 2-33   **Conditional format highlights positive cell values**

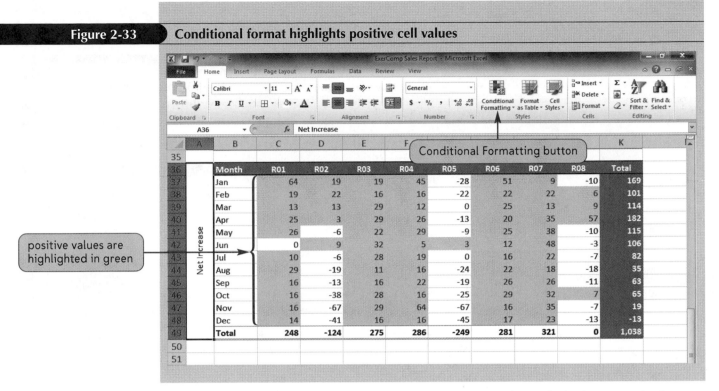

Conditional Formatting button

positive values are highlighted in green

From the highlighting, you can tell that most regions and months had increased sales in 2012. Most of the declines occurred in regions R02, R05, and R08. Tom wonders if some months or regions had particularly strong sales increases. You'll first clear the current highlighting. Note that clearing a conditional format doesn't affect the contents of the cells.

To clear a conditional format:

1. Select the range **C37:J48**.

2. In the Styles group on the Home tab, click the **Conditional Formatting** button, point to **Clear Rules**, and then click **Clear Rules from Selected Cells**. The current highlighting is removed.

Now add a conditional format that highlights the regions and months that rank in the top 10 percent in terms of net sales increase from 2011 to 2012.

To highlight the top 10 percent in sales increase:

1. Make sure the range **C37:J48** is still selected.

2. In the Styles group, click the **Conditional Formatting** button, point to **Top/Bottom Rules**, and then click **Top 10 %**. The Top 10% dialog box opens.

3. Verify that **10** is entered in the % box, click the **with** arrow, and then click **Green Fill with Dark Green Text**.

4. Click the **OK** button. Cells whose sales increases for 2011 and 2012 were in the top 10 percent are highlighted in green.

5. Click cell **A35** to deselect the range. See Figure 2-34.

Figure 2-34   **Conditional formats highlight the top 10 percent sales increases**

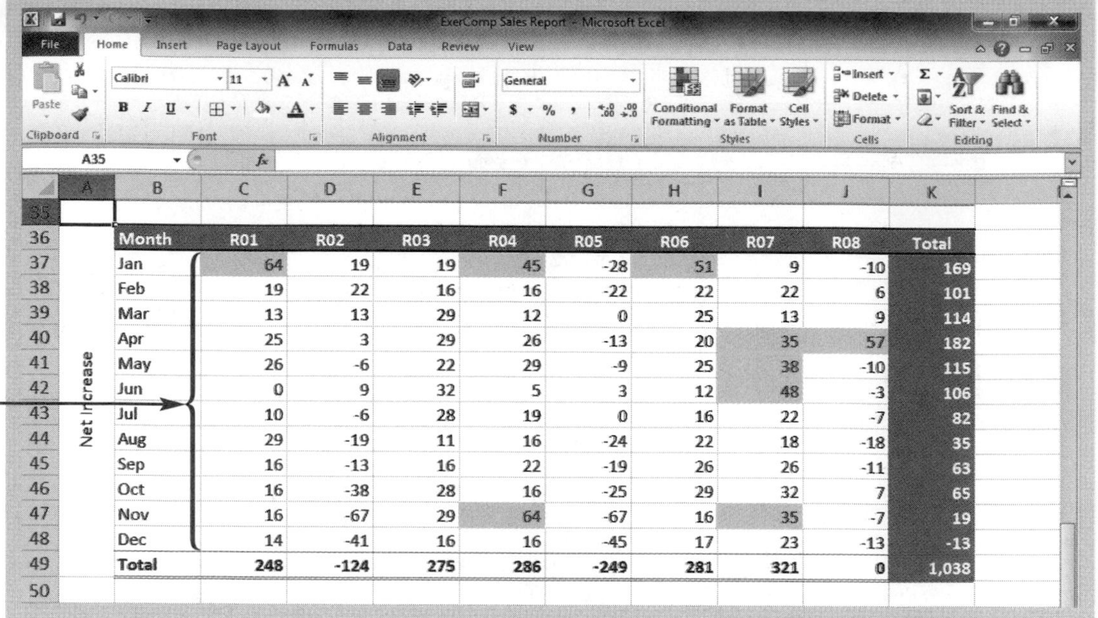

cells highlighted in green rank in the top 10 percent in sales increases

Month	R01	R02	R03	R04	R05	R06	R07	R08	Total
Jan	64	19	19	45	-28	51	9	-10	169
Feb	19	22	16	16	-22	22	22	6	101
Mar	13	13	29	12	0	25	13	9	114
Apr	25	3	29	26	-13	20	35	57	182
May	26	-6	22	29	-9	25	38	-10	115
Jun	0	9	32	5	3	12	48	-3	106
Jul	10	-6	28	19	0	16	22	-7	82
Aug	29	-19	11	16	-24	22	18	-18	35
Sep	16	-13	16	22	-19	26	26	-11	63
Oct	16	-38	28	16	-25	29	32	7	65
Nov	16	-67	29	64	-67	16	35	-7	19
Dec	14	-41	16	16	-45	17	23	-13	-13
Total	248	-124	275	286	-249	281	321	0	1,038

Net Increase

The results provide Tom with some interesting information. For example, region R08, which underperformed for most of the year, had one of the largest sales increases during April (cell J40). In fact, the increase in sales during that one month compensated for the sales declines in other months; so that by the end of the year, region R08 showed no overall decline in sales. Also, region R01 had a large increase in sales during January 2012 but demonstrated the same level of increase for the rest of the year. Finally, four of the nine cells highlighted in the table are from region R07; three of those occurred during the spring months, which are traditionally slow times for the company.

Tom wonders what insights he could gain from highlighting the bottom 10 percent of the table—the regions and months that showed the lowest sales increases in 2012.

To highlight the bottom 10 percent in sales increases:

1. Select the range **C37:J48**.

2. In the Styles group on the Home tab, click the **Conditional Formatting** button, point to **Top/Bottom Rules**, and then click **Bottom 10 %**. The Bottom 10% dialog box opens.

3. Verify that **10** is entered in the % box and **Light Red Fill with Dark Red Text** is selected in the with box.

4. Click the **OK** button. Red cells highlight the regions and months that placed in the bottom 10 percent for sales increases from 2011 to 2012.

5. Click cell **A35** to deselect the range. See Figure 2-35.

Figure 2-35   **Conditional formats highlight the bottom 10 percent of sales increases**

cells highlighted in red rank in the bottom 10 percent in sales increases

Month	R01	R02	R03	R04	R05	R06	R07	R08	Total
Jan	64	19	19	45	-28	51	9	-10	169
Feb	19	22	16	16	-22	22	22	6	101
Mar	13	13	29	12	0	25	13	9	114
Apr	25	3	29	26	-13	20	35	57	182
May	26	-6	22	29	-9	25	38	-10	115
Jun	0	9	32	5	3	12	48	-3	106
Jul	10	-6	28	19	0	16	22	-7	82
Aug	29	-19	11	16	-24	22	18	-18	35
Sep	16	-13	16	22	-19	26	26	-11	63
Oct	16	-38	28	16	-25	29	32	7	65
Nov	16	-67	29	64	-67	16	35	-7	19
Dec	14	-41	16	16	-45	17	23	-13	-13
Total	248	-124	275	286	-249	281	321	0	1,038

Tom immediately sees that the bottom 10 percent come from only regions R02 and R05, and that six of the nine cells highlighted occurred in the most recent months: October, November, and December. Conditional formatting helped Tom isolate and highlight potential problem areas, which he can investigate further.

When you use conditional formatting to highlight cells in a worksheet, you should always include a **legend**, which is a key that shows each color used in the worksheet and what it means, so others know why certain cells are highlighted. You will add a legend to the Monthly Sales worksheet.

To create a conditional formatting legend:

1. In cell D51, type **light red**, and then click cell D51 to make it the active cell. You will use a highlight rule to fill this cell with the light red color used for the bottom 10 percent sales increases.

2. In the Styles group on the Home tab, click the **Conditional Formatting** button, point to **Highlight Cells Rules**, and then click **Text that Contains**. The Text That Contains dialog box opens.

3. Verify that **light red** appears in the Format cells that contain the text box, select **Light Red Fill with Dark Red Text** in the with box, and then click the **OK** button. Cell D51 is filled with the same light red fill color used for the bottom 10 percent values.

4. In cell D52, type **light green**, and then click cell **D52** to make it the active cell. You will use a highlight rule to fill this cell with the green color used for the top 10 percent sales increases.

5. In the Styles group, click the **Conditional Formatting** button, point to **Highlight Cells Rules**, and then click **Text that Contains**. The Text That Contains dialog box opens.

6. Verify that **light green** appears in the Format cells that contain the text box, select **Green Fill with Dark Green Text** in the with box, and then click the **OK** button. Cell D52 is filled with the same light green fill color used for the top 10 percent values.

7. In cell E51, enter **Bottom 10% in terms of sales increase** and then, in cell E52, enter **Top 10% in terms of sales increase**.

8. Select the range **E51:E52**. You'll format these cells with a cell style to distinguish them from the rest of the text in the worksheet.

9. In the Styles group, click the **Cell Styles** button, and then, in the Data and Model section, click **Explanatory** (the third cell style in the first row).

10. Click cell **A35** to deselect the range. The legend is complete. See Figure 2-36.

Figure 2-36	Conditional formatting legend

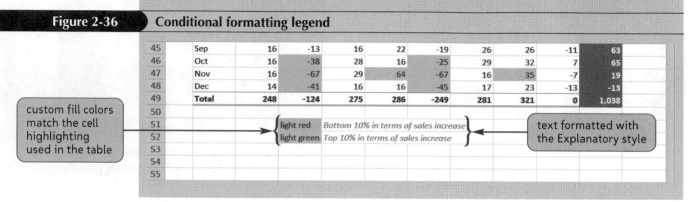

custom fill colors match the cell highlighting used in the table

light red — Bottom 10% in terms of sales increase
light green — Top 10% in terms of sales increase

text formatted with the Explanatory style

The conditional formatting in the Monthly Sales worksheet helps Tom understand how sales of the X310 heart rate monitor changed over the past two years and helps him focus on particular sales regions for additional analysis.

INSIGHT

Using Conditional Formatting Effectively

Conditional formatting is an excellent way to highlight important trends and data values to clients and colleagues. However, it should be used judiciously. An overuse of conditional formatting can sometimes obscure the very data values you want to emphasize. You'll need to make decisions about what to highlight and how it should be highlighted. Keep in mind the following tips as you consider the best ways to effectively communicate your findings to others:

*   **Document the conditional formats you use.** If a bold, green font means that a sales number is in the top 10 percent of all sales, include that information in a legend in the worksheet.
*   **Don't clutter data with too much highlighting.** Limit highlighting rules to one or two per data set. Highlights are designed to draw attention to points of interest. If you use too many, you'll end up highlighting everything—and, therefore, nothing.
*   **Use color sparingly in worksheets with highlights.** It's difficult to tell a highlight color from a regular fill color, especially when fill colors are used in every cell.
*   **Consider alternatives to conditional formats.** If you want to highlight the top 10 sales regions, it might be more effective to simply sort the data with the best-selling regions at the top of the list.

Remember that the goal of highlighting is to provide a strong visual clue of important data or results. Careful use of conditional formatting helps readers to focus on the important points you want to make rather than be distracted by secondary issues and facts.

Hiding Worksheet Data

The Monthly Sales worksheet contains too much data to fit into the worksheet window without drastically reducing the zoom level, which would make the contents too small to read easily. One way to manage the contents of a large worksheet is to selectively hide (and later unhide) those rows and columns containing extraneous information, allowing you to focus your attention on only a select few data points. Hiding rows, columns, and worksheets is a good way to manage a large volume of information; but it should never be used to hide data that is crucial to understanding a workbook. Note that hiding a row or column does not affect the other formulas in the workbook. Formulas still show the correct value even if they reference a cell in a hidden row or column.

Tom wants to view only the third table, which shows the difference in sales between 2011 and 2012, but not the other tables. You'll hide the rows that contain the first two tables and then unhide those rows after Tom has looked at the third table.

To hide and unhide worksheet rows:

1. Select row **6** through row **35** in the Monthly Sales worksheet.

2. In the Cells group on the Home tab, click the **Format** button, point to **Hide & Unhide**, and then click **Hide Rows**. Rows 6 to 35 are hidden, and the row numbers in the worksheet jump from row 5 to row 36. The data in the third table hasn't changed even though its formulas use data from the hidden tables.

3. Select row **5** and row **36**, which are the rows before and after the hidden rows.

4. In the Cells group, click the **Format** button, point to **Hide & Unhide**, and then click **Unhide Rows**. The hidden rows 6 through 35 reappear.

Formatting the Worksheet for Printing

Your final task is to prepare the workbook for the printer. Excel supports a wealth of print options, including the ability to set the page orientation as well as specify whether the page will include headers and footers. Print settings can be applied to an entire workbook or to individual sheets. Because it is likely that other people, such as clients and colleagues, will see the printed version of your spreadsheet, you should take as much care in formatting the printed output as you do in formatting the contents of the electronic file.

Tom wants you to print the analysis of the monthly sales figures. You'll look at the Monthly Sales worksheet in Page Layout view to see how it would currently print.

To view a worksheet in Page Layout view:

1. Click the **Page Layout** button 🔲 on the status bar. The worksheet switches to Page Layout view.

2. Change the zoom level of the worksheet to **70%** to view more of the page layout. See Figure 2-37.

Figure 2-37   **Page Layout view of the Monthly Sales worksheet**

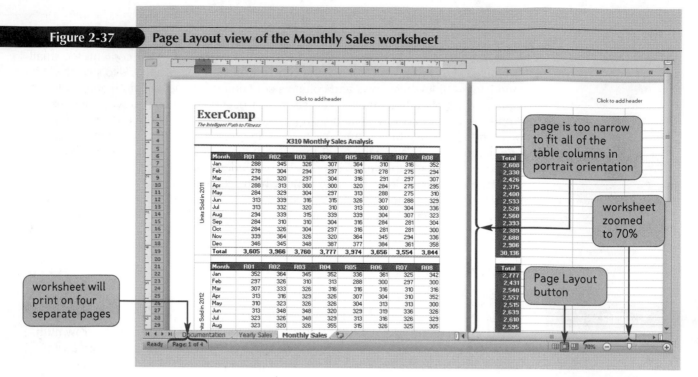

worksheet will print on four separate pages

page is too narrow to fit all of the table columns in portrait orientation

worksheet zoomed to 70%

Page Layout button

In the worksheet's current orientation, its contents do not fit on a single page and the tables break across pages. You'll change the orientation from portrait to landscape so that the page is wide enough to fit all the table columns on one page.

To change to landscape orientation:

1. Click the **Page Layout** tab on the Ribbon.

2. In the Page Setup group, click the **Orientation** button, and then click **Landscape**. The page orientation changes to landscape, making each page wide enough to display all of the columns of each table.

Defining the Print Area

By default, all cells in the active worksheet containing text, formulas, or values are printed. The region that is sent to the printer from the active sheet is known as the **print area**. To print part of a worksheet, you can define the print area, overriding the default setting. A print area can cover an adjacent or nonadjacent range in the current worksheet.

There are many different ways to define the print area, but it's generally easiest to set the print area in Page Break Preview. For example, if Tom wanted to print only the first table in the Monthly Sales worksheet, you could define the print area to cover that range while in Page Break Preview. You will go to Page Break Preview, and then set the print area.

To switch to Page Break preview and set the print area:

1. Click the **Page Break Preview** button ▦ on the status bar.

   Trouble? If the Welcome to Page Break Preview dialog box opens, click the OK button.

2. Change the zoom level of the worksheet to **70%**.

3. Select the range **A1:K19**, which is the range of the first table.

4. In the Page Setup group on the Page Layout tab, click the **Print Area** button, and then click **Set Print Area**. The print area changes to cover only the range A1:K19. The rest of the worksheet content is shaded to indicate that it will not be part of the printout.

5. In the Page Setup group, click the **Print Area** button, and then click **Clear Print Area**. The print area is reset to cover the entire contents of the worksheet.

Inserting Page Breaks

Often the contents of a worksheet do not fit onto a single page. By default, Excel prints as much of the content that fits on single page without resizing the content, and then inserts **automatic page breaks** to continue printing the remaining worksheet content on successive pages. This can result in page breaks that leave a single column or row on a separate page or split worksheet content in awkward places such as within a table.

One way to fix this problem is to scale the printout by reducing the font size to fit on a single sheet of paper. However, if you have more than one or two columns or rows to fit onto the page, the resulting text is often too small to read comfortably. The better fix is usually to split the worksheet into logical segments, which you can do by inserting **manual page breaks** that specify exactly where the page breaks occur. A page break is inserted directly above and to the left of a selected cell, directly above a selected row, or to the left of a selected column.

REFERENCE

Inserting and Removing Page Breaks

To insert a page break:
- Select the first cell below the row where you want to insert a page break.
- In the Page Setup group on the Page Layout tab, click the Breaks button, and then click Insert Page Break.

To remove a page break:
- Select any cell below or to the right of the page break you want to remove.
- In the Page Setup group on the Page Layout tab, click the Breaks button, and then click Remove Page Break (or click Reset All Page Breaks to remove all the page breaks from the worksheet).

Tom wants the three tables in the Monthly Sales worksheet to print on separate pages. You'll insert page breaks to accomplish this.

TIP

In Page Break Preview, a dashed blue line indicates an automatic page break and a solid blue line indicates a manual page break.

To insert page breaks between the tables:

1. Click cell **A20**. With this cell selected, a page break will be inserted between rows 19 and 20.

2. In the Page Setup group on the Page Layout tab, click the **Breaks** button, and then click **Insert Page Break**. A page break separates row 19 from row 20.

3. Click cell **A35**, and then repeat Step 2 to insert a page break that splits the second table from the third. The printout is now three pages. See Figure 2-38.

Figure 2-38 ▸▸▸   **Worksheet in Page Break Preview**

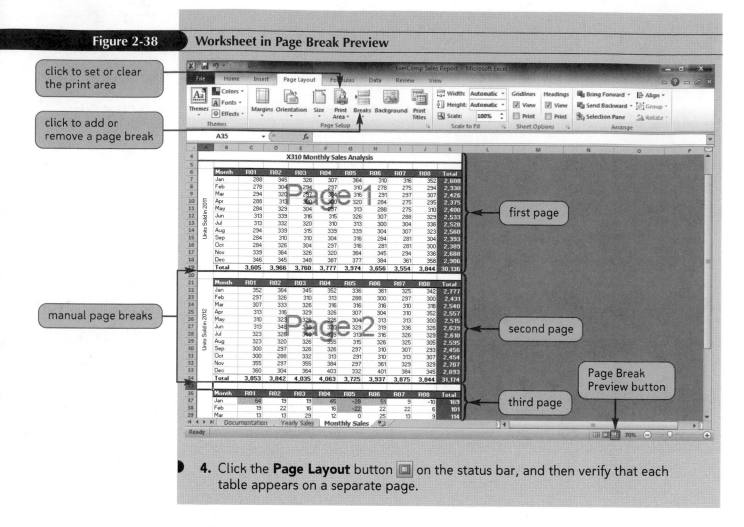

4. Click the **Page Layout** button ▣ on the status bar, and then verify that each table appears on a separate page.

Adding Print Titles

It is a good practice to include descriptive information, such as the company name, logo, and worksheet title on each page of a printout in case a page becomes separated from the other pages. You can repeat information, such as the company name, by specifying which rows or columns in the worksheet act as print titles. If a worksheet contains a large table, you can print the table's column headings and row headings on every page of your printout by designating those initial columns and rows as print titles.

In the Monthly Sales worksheet, the company name, the slogan, and the worksheet title all appear on the first page of the printout, but do not appear on the other two pages. You will define the range that includes this text as a print title. These four rows will then print on each page.

To define the print title for the pages:

1. In the Page Setup group on the Page Layout tab, click the **Print Titles** button. The Page Setup dialog box opens with the Sheet tab displayed.

2. Click the **Rows to repeat at top** box, move your pointer over the worksheet, and then select the range **A1:A4**. A flashing border appears around the first four rows of the worksheet as a visual indicator that the contents of the first four rows will be repeated on each page of the printout. The cell reference $1:$4 appears in the Rows to repeat at top box.

3. Click the **OK** button.

4. Scroll through the second and third pages of the printout in Page Layout view to verify that the company name, slogan, and worksheet title appear on each page. See Figure 2-39.

Figure 2-39 **Third page of the printout**

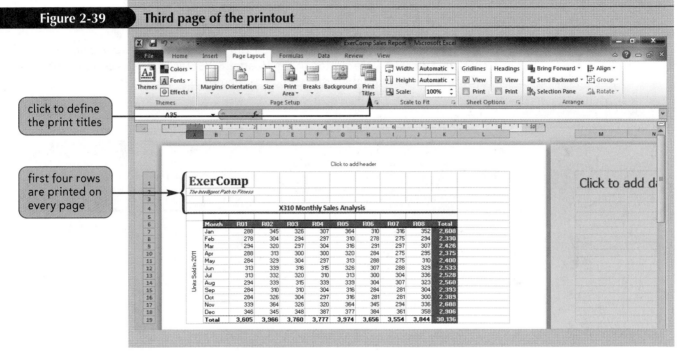

click to define the print titles

first four rows are printed on every page

The Sheet tab in the Page Setup dialog box provides other print options, such as printing the gridlines or row and column headings. You can also print the worksheet in black and white or in draft quality. For a multiple page printout, you can specify whether the pages are ordered by going down the worksheet and then across, or across first and then down.

Creating Page Headers and Footers

Another way to repeat information on each printed page is with headers and footers. Headers and footers contain helpful and descriptive text that is usually not found within the worksheet, such as the workbook's author, the current date, or the workbook filename. If the printout covers multiple pages, you can display the page number and the total number of pages in the printout to help ensure you and others have all the pages.

The header and footer each have three sections: a left section, a center section, and a right section. Within each section, you type the text you want to appear or insert elements such as the worksheet name or the current date and time. These header and footer elements are dynamic; if you rename the worksheet, for example, the name is automatically updated in the header or footer.

Tom wants his printouts to display the workbook's filename in the header's left section and the current date in the header's right section. He wants the center footer to display the page number and the total number of pages in the printout, and the right footer to display your name as the workbook's author.

To insert a header and footer:

1. In Page Layout view, change the zoom level of the worksheet to **90%**.

2. Scroll to the top of the worksheet, and then click the left section of the header directly above cell A1. The Header & Footer Tools contextual tab appears on the Ribbon.

3. Type **Filename:** in the left section of the header, press the **spacebar**, and then, in the Header & Footer Elements group on the Design tab, click the **File Name** button. The code &[File], which displays the filename of the current workbook, is added into the left section of the header.

4. Press the **Tab** key twice to move to the right section of the header, and then click the **Current Date** button in the Header & Footer Elements group. The code &[Date] is added into the right section of the header. See Figure 2-40.

Figure 2-40 Page header with content

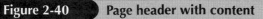

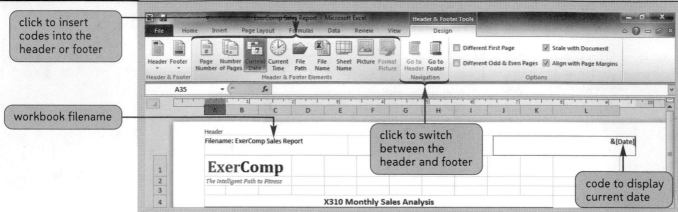

click to insert codes into the header or footer

workbook filename

click to switch between the header and footer

code to display current date

5. In the Navigation group on the Design tab, click the **Go to Footer** button. The right section of the footer is selected.

6. Click the center section of the footer, type **Page**, press the **spacebar**, and click the **Page Number** button in the Header & Footer Elements group.

7. Press the **spacebar**, type **of**, press the **spacebar**, and then click the **Number of Pages** button in the Header & Footer Elements group. The text Page &[Page] of &[Pages] appears in the center section of the footer.

8. Press the **Tab** key to move to the right section of the footer, type **Prepared by:**, press the **spacebar**, and then type your name. See Figure 2-41.

Figure 2-41 Page footer

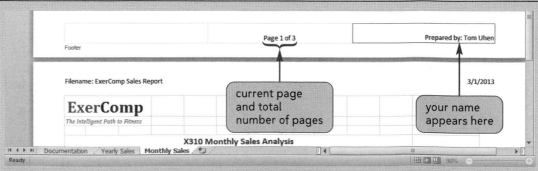

current page and total number of pages

your name appears here

9. Click cell **A1**, and then scroll through the other two pages of the worksheet to verify that the same header appears for each page, and the center section of the footer displays the correct page number and total number of pages.

Defining the Page Margins

Another way to fit a large worksheet on a single page is to reduce the size of the page margins. By default, Excel sets the page margins to between 0.7 and 0.75 inches, and allows for 0.3-inch margins around the page header and footer. You can reduce or increase these margins as needed by selecting from a set of predefined margin sizes or defining your own.

Tom's reports need wide margins to accommodate the page binding. You will change the default margins for the printout.

To set the page margins:

1. Click the **Page Layout** tab on the Ribbon.

2. In the Page Setup group, click the **Margins** button. A menu opens with a list of predefined margins.

3. Click **Wide** to set 1-inch margins around the printed content with 0.5-inch margins around the header and footer. The size of the margins around the page increases, but does not affect the content. Each of the three tables and the print titles still fit on single sheets.

Tom is happy with the appearance of the worksheet and the layout of the printout. You will save the workbook, and then print the Monthly Sales worksheet.

To save the workbook and print the worksheet:

1. Click the **Normal** button ⊞ on the status bar to return the Monthly Sales worksheet to Normal view.

2. Save the workbook.

3. Print the Monthly Sales worksheet, and then close the workbook. Each table is printed on a separate page, and the headers and footers display the filename, current date, page number and total number of pages, and your name.

Tom will distribute the finished report during the upcoming sales meeting.

REVIEW

Session 2.2 Quick Check

1. Discuss two methods of applying the same format to different ranges.
2. Describe the difference between a cell style and a table style.
3. What are the six table style options you can turn on and off?
4. What is a conditional format?
5. How would you highlight the top five values in the range A1:C20?
6. How do you insert a page break into a worksheet?
7. What are print titles?
8. Describe how to add the workbook filename in the center section of the footer on every page of your printout.

Practice the skills you learned in the tutorial using the same case scenario.

PRACTICE

Review Assignments

Data Files needed for the Review Assignments: X410.xlsx, Paper.jpg

ExerComp introduced another heart rate monitor, the X410, two years ago. Tom wants you to format a workbook that compares the sales of the X310 and X410 models during that time. The workbook already has a Documentation sheet, a Model Comparison sheet comparing the total units sold for each model in the eight sales regions, and a Monthly Sales sheet reporting the number of units sold per month.

In the Model Comparison sheet, you will highlight the sales regions that showed the greatest sales increases from 2011 to 2012. In the Monthly Sales sheet, you will calculate the monthly sales totals for both models during 2011 and 2012. Complete the following:

1. Open the **X410** workbook located in the Excel2\Review folder included with your Data Files, and then save the workbook as **X410 Sales Comparison**.

2. In the Documentation sheet, enter your name in cell B4 and the date in the format *mm/dd/yyyy* in cell B5.

3. In the Documentation sheet, set the font color of cells A1 and A2 to blue, format the text in cell A1 in a 26-point Times New Roman font, and then format the text in cell A2 in a 10-point italicized Times New Roman font. In cell A1, change the font color of the text "Comp" to red.

4. In the range A4:A6, set the font color to white and set the fill color to blue. In the range B4:B6, set the fill color to white. In the range A4:B6, add border lines around all of the cells.

5. In cell B5, display the date with the Long Date format and left-align it within the cell.

6. In the Documentation sheet, insert a background image using the **Paper.jpg** image file located in the Excel2\Review folder included with your Data Files.

7. Use the Format Painter to copy the format from the range A1:A2 in the Documentation sheet to the range A1:A2 in the other two sheets. In cell A1, change the font color of the text "Comp" to red.

8. Go to the Model Comparison sheet. In cells E6 and E17, enter **Increase**. In ranges E7:E14 and E18:E25, enter formulas to calculate the increase in sales for each region.

9. In cells F6 and F17, enter the text **% Increase**. In ranges F7:F14 and F18:F25, enter formulas to calculate the percent increase in sales for each region.

10. In cells B15 and B26, enter the text **Total**. In cells C15, D15, C26, and D26, enter formulas to calculate the total units sold per year for each model. In cells E15 and E26, enter formulas to calculate the total increase in sales. In cells F15 and F26, enter formulas to calculate the percent increase in total sales from 2011 to 2012.

11. Merge and center the range A6:A15, center the text vertically, and then change the orientation to vertical text. Center the text in the range C6:F6, and then indent the region labels in the range B7:B14 one character.

12. In the range C7:E15, format the numbers in a Number format using a thousands separator, no decimal places, and negative numbers displayed with a minus symbol. In the range F7:F15, format the numbers in a Percentage format with two decimal places.

13. Apply the Accent1 cell style to the range B6:F6 and the merged cell A6. Change the font of cell A6 to 18 points and bold. Apply the Total cell style to the range B15:F15.

14. In the range E7:E14, apply a conditional format that adds a Top/Bottom Rule to display the highest number in the range in dark green text with a green fill. In the range F7:F14, apply a conditional format that adds a Top/Bottom Rule to display the highest number in the range in dark red text with a light red fill.

15. Use the Format Painter to copy all of the formats from the range A6:F15 to the range A17:F26.

16. In cell D3, enter **highest**, and then apply a conditional format to cell D3 that adds a Highlight Cells Rule to format the cell that contains the text "highest" with Green Fill with Dark Green Text. In cell D4, enter **highest**, and then apply a conditional format to cell D4 that adds a Highlight Cells Rule to format the cell that contains the text "highest" with Light Red Fill with Dark Red Text.

17. In cell E3, enter **Highest increase in units sold**. In cell E4, enter **Highest % increase in units sold**. Format both cells with the Explanatory Text cell style.

18. Go to the Monthly Sales sheet. In cells D5 and I5, enter the text **All Models**. In cells A18 and F18, enter the text **Total**.

19. Enter formulas in the worksheet to calculate the total sales by month, by model, and then over all months and over both models.

20. Merge and center the range A4:D4, merge and center the range F4:I4, and then apply the Heading 1 style to both merged cells. In the range B5:D5;G5:I5, center the text.

21. In the nonadjacent range B6:D18;G6:I18, format the numbers to show a thousands separator (,) with no decimal places to the right of the decimal point.

22. Select the range A5:D18, and then apply Table Style Light 8 (the first table style in the second row of the Light section in the Table Styles gallery). Turn off the filter arrows, and then display only the header row, first column, and last column table style options. In the range A18:D18, apply the Total cell style.

23. Select the range F5:I18, and then repeat Step 22, applying the Total cell style to the range F18:I18.

24. For the Model Comparison and Monthly Sales worksheets, set the page orientation to landscape, display your name in the center section of the header, display the sheet name in the left section of the footer, display the workbook filename in the center section of the footer, and then display the current date in the right section of the footer.

25. Save and close your workbook. Submit the finished workbook to your instructor, either in printed or electronic form, as requested.

Case Problem 1

Data File needed for the Case Problem: Frosti.xlsx

FrostiWear   Linda Young is a sales manager for FrostiWear, a successful new store based in Hillsboro, Oregon. She's tracking the sales figures for FrostiWear's line of gloves. She created a workbook that contains the sales figures from the past year for three glove models. She wants you to help format the sales report. Complete the following:

1. Open the **Frosti** workbook located in the Excel2\Case1 folder included with your Data Files, and then save the workbook as **FrostiWear Sales Report**.

2. In the Documentation sheet, enter your name in cell B3 and the date in cell B4. Set the background color for all the cells in the worksheet to standard blue, and then set the background color for the range B3:B5 to white. Add a border line around each cell in the range B3:B5.

3. Change the font of cell A1 to the Headings font of the current theme, change the font size to 36 points, change the font color to white, and then bold the text. Change the font size of the range A3:A5 to 16 points, change the font color to white, and then bold the text.

4. Go to the Glove Sales worksheet. Add formulas to calculate the total sales for each month and region over the three glove models.

5. Merge and center the range A1:H1, apply the Title cell style, and then increase the font size to 26 points. Merge and center the range A2:H2, apply the Heading 4 cell style, and then increase the font size to 16 points.

6. Merge and center the range A3:A16, set the alignment to Middle Align, rotate the text up, apply the Accent1 cell style, increase the font size to 18 points, and then bold the text.

7. Use the Format Painter to copy the format of merged cell A3 into the two ranges A18:A31 and A33:A46.

8. Center the text in the range C3:H3. Format the range C4:H16 to include thousands separators (,) and no decimal places. Use the Format Painter to copy the formats in the range C3:H16 to the two ranges C18:H31 and C33:H46.

9. In the range B3:H16, apply the Table Style Medium 2 table style. Turn off the filter arrows, and then display the header row, first column, last column, and banded rows. In the range B16:H16, change the fill color of the Total row to standard yellow.

10. Repeat Step 9 for the other two tables in the worksheet.

11. In the Glove Sales worksheet, set the page orientation to landscape, insert manual page breaks at cells A18 and A33, and then repeat the first two rows of the worksheet on every printed page.

12. Display your name in the center header, display the filename in the left footer, display **Page** *page number* **of** *number of pages* in the center footer, and then display the current date in the right footer.

13. Save and close your workbook. Submit the finished workbook to your instructor.

Add formulas and formatting to create a packing slip.

CREATE

Case Problem 2

Data File needed for the Case Problem: GrillRite.xlsx

GrillRite Grills   Brian Simpko is a shipping manager at GrillRite Grills in Hammond, Indiana. He uses an Excel workbook to provide shipping and order information for customer orders and deliveries. You will create and format the worksheet that Brian can use to enter information for packing slips. Complete the following:

1. Open the **GrillRite** workbook located in the Excel2\Case2 folder included with your Data Files, and then save the workbook as **GrillRite Grills Packing Slip**. In the Documentation sheet, enter your name in cell B3 and the date in cell B4.

2. Insert a new worksheet at the end of the workbook, and then rename it **Packing Slip**.

3. In the Packing Slip worksheet, select all of the cells in the worksheet. (*Hint*: Click the Select All button at the intersection of the row and column headings.) Change the font to the Body font of the current theme. For the range A1:D3, set the fill color to black and the font color to white.

4. Set the width of columns A through D to 20 characters. Set the height of row 1 to 36 characters.

5. Merge the range A1:B3, and then left- and top-align the merged cell. Merge the range C1:D3, and then right- and top-align the merged cell.

6. In cell A1, enter the following three lines of text, and then format the first line in a 26-point bold font using the Headings font of the current theme:

GrillRite Grills
200 Commerce Lane
Hammond, Indiana 46324

7. In cell C1, enter **Packing Slip**, and then format the text in a 26-point bold font using the Headings font of the current theme.

8. In the range A5:A7, enter the following three lines of text in a bold font, and then right-align the text and indent the text one character:

 Order Date

 Order Number

 Purchase Order

9. Format cell B5 in the Long Date format. Insert border lines around each of the cells in the range B5:B7.

10. In the range C5:C7, enter the following three lines of text, and then use the Format Painter to copy the formats from the range A5:B7 to the range C5:D7:

 Date

 Sales Rep

 Account Num

11. In cell B9, enter **Ship To**. In cell D9, enter **Bill To**. Format the text in both cells in a bold font.

12. In cell A10, enter **Address** in a bold font, right-align the text, and then indent it one character.

13. Merge the cells in the range B10:B15, left- and top-align the cell contents, and then insert a border around the merged cell. Click the Wrap Text button from the Alignment group on the Home tab to ensure that text within this cell wraps to a new line.

14. In cell C10, enter **Address**. Copy the format from the range A10:B15 into the range C10:D15.

15. Enter the following data into the worksheet:

 Cell A17: **Item**

 Cell B17: **Product No.**

 Cell C17: **Description**

 Cell D17: **Order Quantity**

 cells A18:A27: the numbers from **1** to **10**

⊕ EXPLORE   16. For the range A17:D27, apply Table Style Medium 1, turn off the filter arrows, and display the header row, Total row, and banded rows. In cell D28, select the SUM function from the list.

17. In cell A30, enter **Comments** in a bold font.

18. Merge the range A31:D39, left- and top-align the cell contents, and then add a thick box border around the merged cell.

19. In cell D40, enter **Thank you for your business!** in an italic, 16-point font, and then right-align the cell contents.

20. Enter the packing slip data shown in Figure 2-42.

Figure 2-42   **GrillRite Grills packing slip**

	A	B	C	D	E
1	**GrillRite Grills**			**Packing Slip**	
2	200 Commerce Lane				
3	Hammond, Indiana 46324				
4					
5	**Order Date**	Tuesday, April 30, 2013	**Date**	Friday, May 03, 2013	
6	**Order Number**	GR3985-11	**Sales Rep**	Linda Bingham	
7	**Purchase Order**	GR005-205-11	**Account Num**	188	
8					
9		**Ship To**		**Bill To**	
10	**Address**	Blake Stout	**Address**	Hilltop Hardware	
11		Hilltop Hardware		450 Drake Avenue	
12		450 Drake Avenue		Monroe, WI 53566	
13		Monroe, WI 53566			
14					
15					
16					
17	Item	Product No.	Description	Order Quantity	
18	1	MG304-29	Mini-Grill Set	7	
19	2	TTG044-22	Table Top Grill Box	4	
20	3	GC141-35	Grill Cleanser Box (35)	10	
21	4	GTK412-15	Grill Toolkit (Standard)	8	
22	5	GPK252-29	Grill Parts Kit (Standard)	10	
23	6				
24	7				
25	8				
26	9				
27	10				
28	Total			39	
29					
30	Comments				
31	Please contact shipping manager Brian Simpko (ext. 315) regarding discount shipping rates.				
32					
33					
34					
35					
36					
37					
38					
39					
40				*Thank you for your business!*	

21. Make sure the worksheet's page orientation is set to portrait, and then add a footer that displays your name in the left section, the filename in the center section, and the current date in the right section.

22. Save and close your workbook. Submit the finished workbook to your instructor, either in printed or electronic form, as requested.

Apply conditional formats to create a wind speed grid.

CHALLENGE

Case Problem 3

Data File needed for the Case Problem: Wind.xlsx

Arcadia Wind Farm   Tara Young is a researcher at Arcadia Wind Farm, a government research center near Topeka, Kansas, involved in exploring how to create economical and efficient wind farms. One of Tara's jobs is to record wind speeds from different sectors of the wind farm. Tara has entered the wind speed data into a workbook as a table with wind speed measures laid out in a grid. Because the numbers are difficult to read and interpret, you will color code the wind speed values using a conditional format. Complete the following:

1. Open the **Wind** workbook located in the Excel2\Case3 folder included with your Data Files, and then save the workbook as **Wind Farm**. In the Documentation sheet, enter your name and the date.

2. Go to the Wind Speed Grid worksheet. Merge the range A1:V1, and then apply the Heading 1 style to the merged cell and set the font size to 20 points.

3. Select the range B3:V3, and then change the font style to white text on a black background. Copy this formatting to the grid coordinates in the range A4:A64.

4. Select the range B4:V64. The data in this range comprises the wind speed measures for different sensors in Sector 5.

EXPLORE 5. Create a conditional formatting that highlights cells whose value equals 18 with fill color equal to the RGB color value (99, 37, 35). (*Hint*: In the Equal To dialog box, select Custom Format in the with box to open the Format Cells dialog box. On the Fill tab, in the Background Color section, click the More Colors button, and then click the Custom tab to enter the RGB color value.)

EXPLORE 6. Repeat Step 5 to continue creating conditional formats that set highlight colors for the following wind speed values:

Wind Speed	RGB Color Value
16 m/s	(150, 54, 52)
14 m/s	(218, 150, 148)
12 m/s	(230, 184, 183)
10 m/s	(242, 220, 219)
8 m/s	(242, 242, 242)
6 m/s	(255, 255, 255)
4 m/s	(197, 217, 241)
2 m/s	(141, 180, 226)
0 m/s	(83, 141, 213)

7. In the range B4:V64, reduce the font size of the values to 1 point.

8. Enclose each of the cells in the range B4:V64 in a light gray border.

9. Apply the conditional highlight colors specified in Steps 5 and 6 to the legend values in the cell range X3:X12.

10. Merge the range Y3:Y12, and then center the contents of the merged cell and rotate the text down. Display the text in a bold 18-point font.

11. Set the print area of the page to the range A1:Y64.

EXPLORE 12. On the Page Layout tab, scale the page to fit on a single page. (*Hint*: Use the Width and Height boxes in the Scale to Fit group to force the worksheet to fit on one page.)

13. Add a header to the printed page with your name in the top-left header and the file-name in the top-right header.

14. Save and close your workbook. Submit the finished workbook to your instructor, either in printed or electronic form, as requested.

Case Problem 4

Format a meal-planning worksheet that highlights high-calorie and high-fat foods.

CREATE

Data File needed for the Case Problem: Life.xlsx

Life Managers Kate Dee is a dietician at Life Managers, a company in Kleinville, Michigan, that specializes in personal improvement, particularly in areas of health and fitness. Kate wants to create a meal-planning workbook for her clients who want to lose weight and improve their health. One goal of meal planning is to decrease the percentage of fat in the diet. Kate thinks it would be helpful to highlight foods that have a high percentage of fat as well as list their total fat calories. She already created an Excel workbook that contains a few sample food items and lists the number of calories and grams of fat in each item. She wants you to format this workbook. Complete the following:

1. Open the **Life** workbook located in the Excel2\Case4 folder included with your Data Files, and then save the workbook as **Life Managers Nutrition Table**. In the Documentation sheet, enter your name in cell B3 and the date in cell B4.

2. In the Meal Planner worksheet, add a column that calculates the calories from fat for each food item. Fat contains nine calories per gram.

3. Add a column that calculates the percentage of fat for each food item. This value is calculated by dividing the calories from fat by the total number of calories.

4. Display all values for calories and grams of fat with one decimal place. Display the fat percentages as percentages with one decimal place.

5. Format the rest of the Meal Planner worksheet attractively, but be sure to include at least one example of each of the following design elements:
   - A range merged into a single cell
   - Text centered and rotated within a cell
   - Cell styles applied to one or more elements
   - Borders applied to one or more elements

6. For good health, the FDA recommends that the fat percentage should not exceed 30 percent of the total calories per day. Apply a rule to the fat percentages to highlight those food items that exceed the FDA recommendation. Include a legend to document the highlighting color you used.

7. Add descriptive headers and footers to the printed document. Also insert page breaks and print titles to ensure that the printout is easily read and interpreted.

8. Save and close your workbook. Submit the finished workbook to your instructor, either in printed or electronic form, as requested.

SAM: Skills Assessment Manager

For current SAM information, including versions and content details, visit SAM Central (http://samcentral.course.com). If you have a SAM user profile, you may have access to hands-on instruction, practice, and assessment of the skills covered in this tutorial. Because various versions of SAM are supported throughout the life of this text, check with your instructor for the correct instructions and URL/Web site for accessing assignments.

ENDING DATA FILES

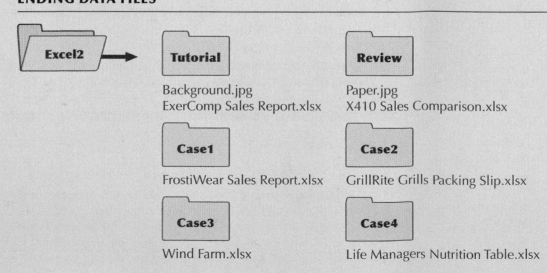

Background.jpg
ExerComp Sales Report.xlsx

Paper.jpg
X410 Sales Comparison.xlsx

FrostiWear Sales Report.xlsx

GrillRite Grills Packing Slip.xlsx

Wind Farm.xlsx

Life Managers Nutrition Table.xlsx

OBJECTIVES

Session 3.1
- Copy formulas
- Build formulas containing relative, absolute, and mixed references
- Review function syntax
- Insert a function with the Insert Function dialog box
- Search for a function
- Type a function directly in a cell

Session 3.2
- Use AutoFill to fill in a formula and complete a series
- Enter the IF logical function
- Insert the date with the TODAY function
- Use the PMT financial function to calculate monthly mortgage payments

EXCEL

Working with Formulas and Functions

Developing a Family Budget

Case | *Drake Family Budget*

Newlyweds Diane and Glenn Drake are trying to balance career, school, and family life. The couple's income and expenses vary throughout the year. Diane works full-time as a legal assistant, but earns less in the summer months when she cuts back her work hours to attend summer courses. Glenn is in a graduate program at a nearby university where he recently was hired as a lab assistant. In the summer, Glenn takes on other work to earn additional income. The couple just moved into a new apartment, but plan to purchase a house within the next several years. Although Glenn and Diane's salaries have grown in the past few years, the couple seems to have less cash on hand. This financial shortage has prompted them to take a closer look at their finances and figure out how to best manage them.

Diane has set up an Excel workbook and entered the monthly income from their two jobs. She has identified and entered expenses the family pays on a monthly basis, such as the rent and grocery bill, as well as other expenses that occur only a few times a year, such as Glenn's tuition and vacations. She wants to calculate how much money they are bringing in and how much money they are spending. She also wants to come up with a savings plan for the down payment on a house they hope to buy in a few years.

You'll help Diane complete the workbook. You will enter formulas to perform the calculations that will provide Diane with a better overall picture of the family's finances. Diane and Glenn will be able to use this information to manage their money more effectively.

STARTING DATA FILES

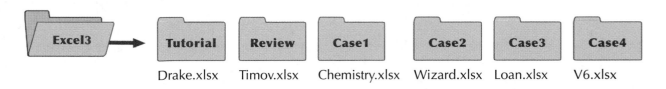

Excel3 →	Tutorial	Review	Case1	Case2	Case3	Case4
	Drake.xlsx	Timov.xlsx	Chemistry.xlsx	Wizard.xlsx	Loan.xlsx	V6.xlsx

SESSION 3.1 VISUAL OVERVIEW

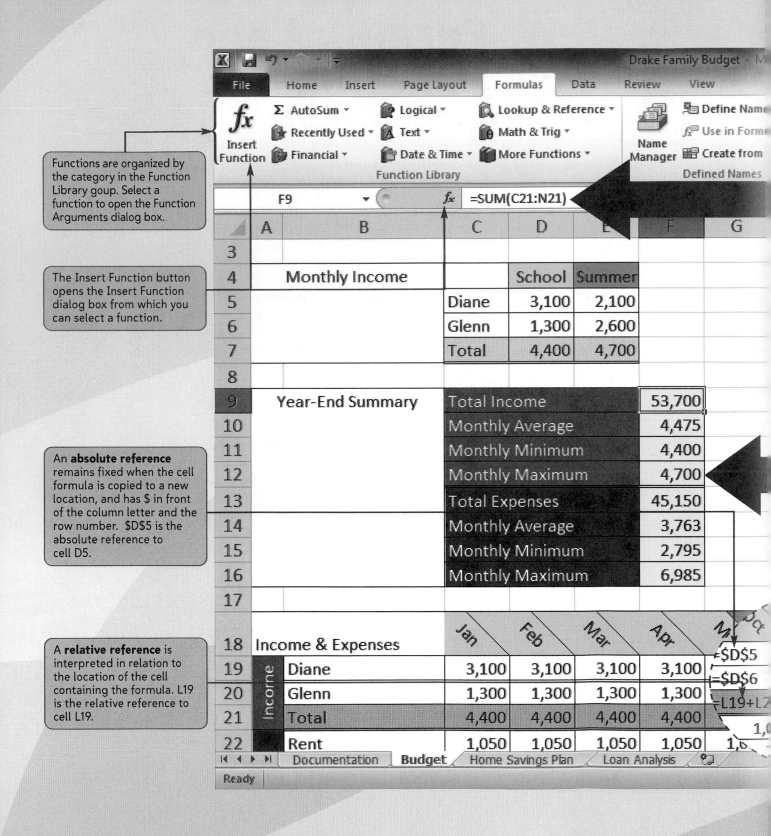

Functions are organized by the category in the Function Library goup. Select a function to open the Function Arguments dialog box.

The Insert Function button opens the Insert Function dialog box from which you can select a function.

An **absolute reference** remains fixed when the cell formula is copied to a new location, and has $ in front of the column letter and the row number. $D$5 is the absolute reference to cell D5.

A **relative reference** is interpreted in relation to the location of the cell containing the formula. L19 is the relative reference to cell L19.

CELL REFERENCES AND EXCEL FUNCTIONS

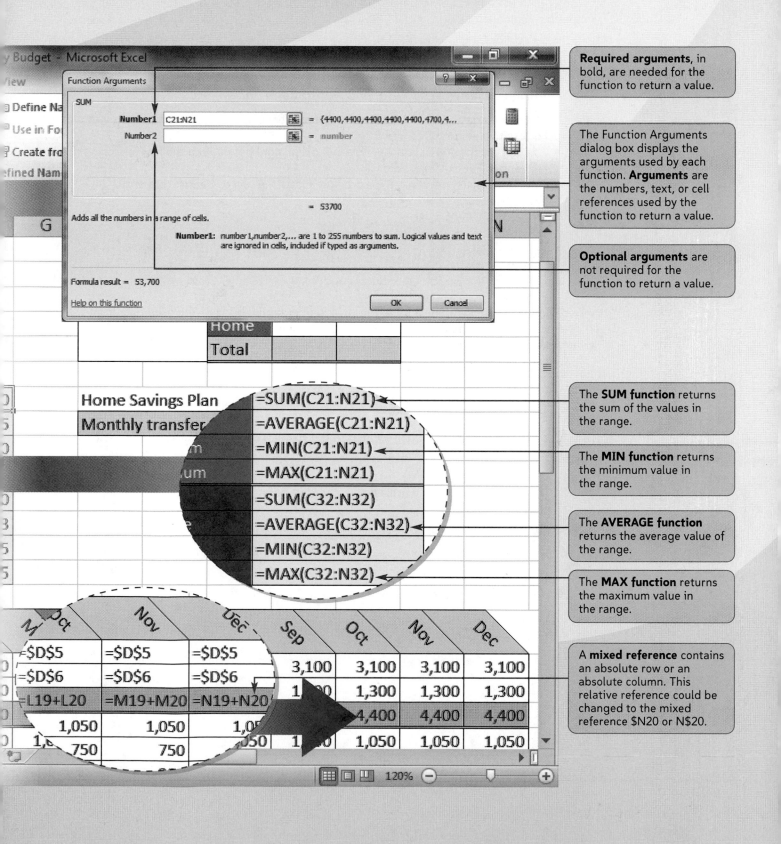

Required arguments, in bold, are needed for the function to return a value.

The Function Arguments dialog box displays the arguments used by each function. **Arguments** are the numbers, text, or cell references used by the function to return a value.

Optional arguments are not required for the function to return a value.

The **SUM function** returns the sum of the values in the range.

The **MIN function** returns the minimum value in the range.

The **AVERAGE function** returns the average value of the range.

The **MAX function** returns the maximum value in the range.

A **mixed reference** contains an absolute row or an absolute column. This relative reference could be changed to the mixed reference $N20 or N$20.

Function Arguments

SUM
Number1 C21:N21 = {4400,4400,4400,4400,4400,4700,4...
Number2 = number

= 53700

Adds all the numbers in a range of cells.

Number1: number1,number2,... are 1 to 255 numbers to sum. Logical values and text are ignored in cells, included if typed as arguments.

Formula result = 53,700

Help on this function   OK   Cancel

Home Savings Plan =SUM(C21:N21)
Monthly transfer =AVERAGE(C21:N21)
=MIN(C21:N21)
=MAX(C21:N21)
=SUM(C32:N32)
=AVERAGE(C32:N32)
=MIN(C32:N32)
=MAX(C32:N32)

	Oct	Nov	Dec	Sep	Oct	Nov	Dec
=$D$5	=$D$5	=$D$5		3,100	3,100	3,100	3,100
=$D$6	=$D$6	=$D$6		1,300	1,300	1,300	1,300
=L19+L20	=M19+M20	=N19+N20			4,400	4,400	4,400
1,050	1,050	1,0					
750	750	50		1,050	1,050	1,050	1,050

120%

Understanding Cell References

Most Excel workbooks are created to record and analyze data. To do this effectively, you enter data in cells in a worksheet, and then reference the cells with data in formulas that perform calculations on that data, such as adding the total of a column of numbers as part of a budget.

REFERENCE

Entering Relative, Absolute, and Mixed References

- To enter a relative reference, type the cell reference as it appears in the worksheet. For example, enter B2 for cell B2.
- To enter an absolute reference, type $ (a dollar sign) before both the row and column references. For example, enter $B$2.
- To enter a mixed reference, type $ before either the row or column reference. For example, enter $B2 or B$2.

or

- Select the cell reference you want to change.
- Press the F4 key to cycle the reference from relative to absolute to mixed and then back to relative.

Diane has already done a lot of the work on her family budget. She used data from the past year to estimate the couple's monthly expenses for the upcoming year and entered this data into an Excel workbook. You will open this workbook and review her estimates of the family's monthly expenses.

To open Diane's workbook:

1. Open the **Drake** workbook located in the **Excel3\Tutorial** folder included with your Data Files, and then save the workbook as **Drake Family Budget** in the same folder.

2. In the Documentation worksheet, enter your name in cell B3 and the date in cell B4.

3. Switch to the Budget worksheet, and then review its contents.

4. Scroll down to view the range A18:N32. This range lists Diane's estimate of her family's monthly expenses by category for the upcoming year. See Figure 3-1.

Figure 3-1   **Monthly expenses for the Drake family**

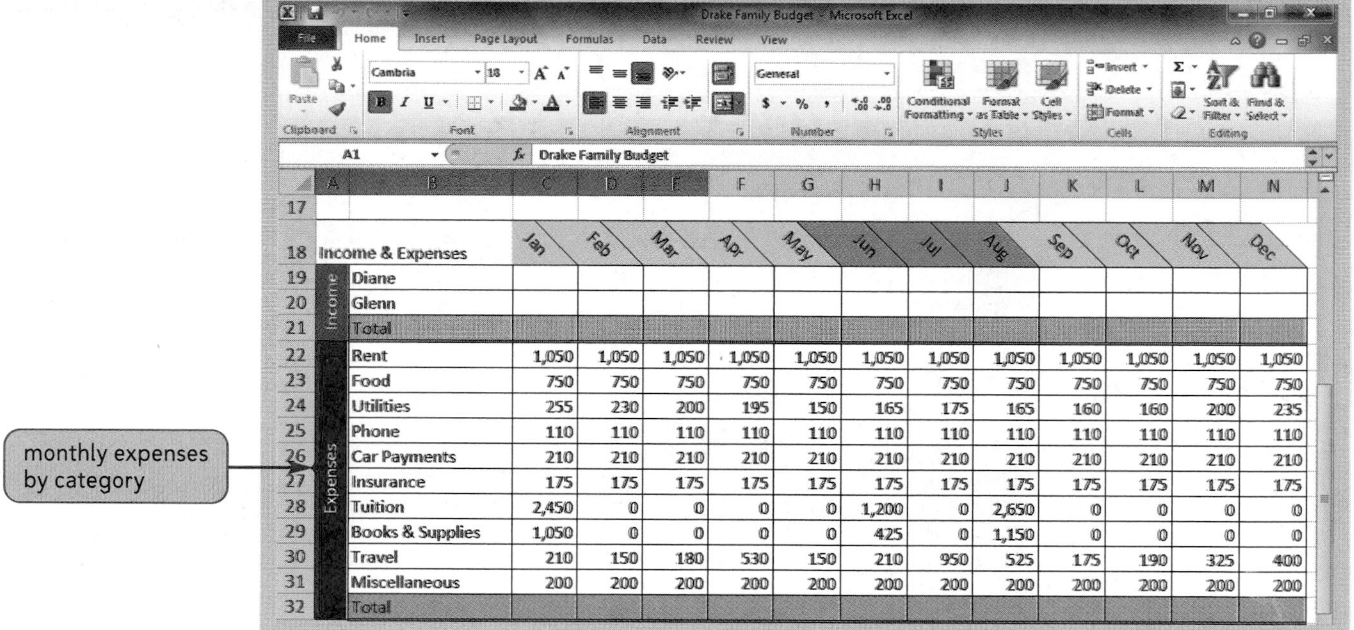

monthly expenses by category

		Jan	Feb	Mar	Apr	May	Jun	Jul	Aug	Sep	Oct	Nov	Dec
18	Income & Expenses												
19	Diane												
20	Glenn												
21	Total												
22	Rent	1,050	1,050	1,050	1,050	1,050	1,050	1,050	1,050	1,050	1,050	1,050	1,050
23	Food	750	750	750	750	750	750	750	750	750	750	750	750
24	Utilities	255	230	200	195	150	165	175	165	160	160	200	235
25	Phone	110	110	110	110	110	110	110	110	110	110	110	110
26	Car Payments	210	210	210	210	210	210	210	210	210	210	210	210
27	Insurance	175	175	175	175	175	175	175	175	175	175	175	175
28	Tuition	2,450	0	0	0	0	1,200	0	2,650	0	0	0	0
29	Books & Supplies	1,050	0	0	0	0	425	0	1,150	0	0	0	0
30	Travel	210	150	180	530	150	210	950	525	175	190	325	400
31	Miscellaneous	200	200	200	200	200	200	200	200	200	200	200	200
32	Total												

Diane wants you to calculate the total expenses for each month. You'll start by inserting the formula to calculate the January expenses and then paste that formula into the remaining months of the year.

To calculate the total monthly expenses:

1. In cell C32, enter the formula **=SUM(C22:C31)** to add the estimated expenses for the month of January. The value 6,460 is displayed in cell C32, indicating that Diane estimates the couple will spend $6,460 in January of the upcoming year.

2. Click cell **C32** to select it.

3. Click the **Home** tab on the Ribbon, if necessary, and then click the **Copy** button in the Clipboard group.

4. Select the range **D32:N32**, and then click the **Paste** button in the Clipboard group. The SUM function is pasted into the selected range, calculating the total expenses for the remaining months of the year. See Figure 3-2.

Figure 3-2   **Total monthly expenses**

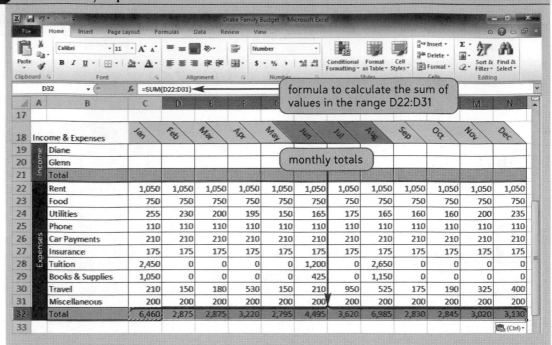

5. Review the total expenses for each month. January and August are particularly expensive months because Glenn has to pay tuition and purchase books for the upcoming semester.

6. Click each cell in the range D32:N32, reviewing the formula entered in the cell. The formulas pasted into the range D32:N32 all calculate the sums of values in different cell references. For example, the formula =SUM(D22:D31) was inserted in cell D32, the formula =SUM(E22:E31) was inserted in cell E32, and so forth.

Using Relative References

When you entered the formula in cell C32 to sum the January expenses, Excel interprets the cell references in that formula relative to the location of cell C32. In other words, Excel interprets the formula =SUM(C22:C31) as adding the values entered in the 10 cells directly above cell C32.

Excel uses this interpretation of the cell references when the formula is pasted into other cells. For example, when you pasted the formula in cell D32, the formula changed to =SUM(D22:D31), which has a different cell reference but the same meaning: adding the values of the 10 cells directly above the active cell. The formulas in the remaining cells of the range D32:E32 were similarly adjusted so that each formula displays the total expenses for the selected month.

The cell references used in these formulas are called relative references because when Excel copies and pastes them, they are always interpreted in relation, or relative, to the location of the cell containing the formula. Figure 3-3 illustrates how a relative cell reference in a formula changes when the formula is copied to another group of cells.

| Figure 3-3 | Formulas using a relative reference |

formula references a cell three rows up and three columns to the left of the active cell

when copied to new cells, each formula still references a cell three rows up and two columns to the left

values returned by each formula

In this figure, the formula =A2 entered in cell D5 displays the value of 10, which is the value entered in cell A2. When pasted to a new location, each of the pasted formulas contains a reference to a cell that is three rows up and three rows to the left of the current cell's location. One of the great advantages of relative references is that you can quickly generate row and column totals without having to worry about revising the formulas as you copy them to new locations.

Using Absolute References

A good practice when designing a workbook is to enter values in their own cells in one location of the worksheet, and then reference the appropriate cells in formulas throughout the worksheets. This reduces the amount of data entry when you need to use the same data in more than one location. It also makes it faster and more accurate when you need to change a data value, as all the formulas based on that cell are updated to reflect the new value.

Next, you will enter the Drakes' monthly income. The couple's income changes in the summer as Diane works fewer hours and Glenn works more. Rather than inserting these same values each month, you'll enter them in cells at the top of the worksheet and then reference those values in the income/expenses table at the bottom of the worksheet. Later, if Diane modifies the monthly income estimates, you'll need to change them in only one location rather than in 12 different locations.

To enter the couple's estimated monthly income:

1. Scroll to the top of the worksheet, and then enter the following data in the specified cells:

   cell D5: **2800**   cell E5: **2100**
   cell D6: **1300**   cell E6: **2600**

2. Select the range **D7:E7**. You'll enter the monthly income totals in these cells.

3. In the Editing group on the Home tab, click the **Sum** button **Σ**. The total estimated income is calculated for the school and summer months. See Figure 3-4.

Figure 3-4   **Monthly income estimates**

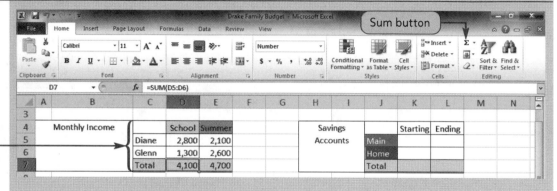

estimated income during the school and summer months

Next, you'll calculate the couple's projected income for January through May by referencing the values you just entered at the top of the worksheet. The couple will have the same income for the next four months as they did in January, so you can copy the formulas from January into February through May.

To insert the monthly income for January through May:

1. Click cell **C19**, type **=D5**, and then press the **Enter** key. The value 2,800, Diane's income for January, appears in cell C19.

2. In cell C20, enter the formula **=D6**. The value 1,300, Glenn's income for January, appears in cell C20.

3. In cell C21, enter the formula **=C19+C20**. This formula calculates the total income for the couple in the month of January, displaying the value 4,100.

4. Select the range **C19:C21**, and then click the **Copy** button in the Clipboard group on the Home tab. The three formulas are copied to the Clipboard.

5. Select the range **D19:G21**, and then click the **Paste** button in the Clipboard group. The formulas are pasted and calculate the couple's income for January through May. See Figure 3-5.

Figure 3-5   **Income values inserted for January through May**

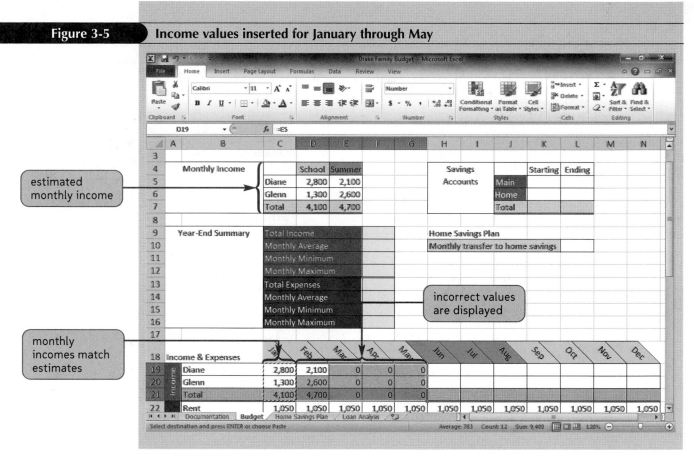

The formulas you copied and pasted from January resulted in incorrect values for February, March, April, and May. The February column show the couple's estimated monthly income for the summer, and the March, April, and May columns display the value 0. What went wrong?

The problem is that the formulas use relative references. For example, the formula in cell C19 is =D5, which references the cell located 14 rows up and 1 column to the right of the current cell. When you pasted that formula to cell G19, Excel inserted the formula =H5, which references the empty cell located 14 rows up and 1 column to the right of cell G19, so that the value displayed in the cell is 0.

Instead of using relative references, you need to use a cell reference that will remain fixed when the formula is copied to a new location. Cell references that remain fixed are called absolute references. In Excel, absolute references have a $ (dollar sign) before each column and row designation. For example, B8 is a relative reference to cell B8, whereas $B$8 is an absolute reference to cell B8. When you copy a formula that contains an absolute reference to a new location, the reference does not change. Figure 3-6 shows an example of how copying a formula with an absolute reference results in the same cell reference being pasted in different cells regardless of their location.

Figure 3-6 Formulas using an absolute reference

formula containing an absolute reference to the sales tax rate in cell A2

	A	B	C	D	E	F
1	Sales Tax Rate		Purchase	Sales Tax	Total	
2	0.05		$24.95	=C2*$A$2	=C2+D2	
3			$122.35			
4			$199.81			
5			$45.40			
6						
7				absolute reference to cell A2	relative references to cells C2 and D2	

when pasted into a new location, the absolute reference remains unchanged

	A	B	C	D	E	F
1	Sales Tax Rate		Purchase	Sales Tax	Total	
2	0.05		$24.95	=C2*$A$2	=C2+D2	
3			$122.35	=C3*$A$2	=C3+D3	
4			$199.81	=C4*$A$2	=C4+D4	
5			$45.40	=C5*$A$2	=C5+D5	
6						(Ctrl) ▾
7						

$A$2 continues to be referenced in the formula

relative references change based on cell location

values returned by the cell formulas

	A	B	C	D	E	F
1	Sales Tax Rate		Purchase	Sales Tax	Total	
2	5%		$24.95	$1.25	$26.20	
3			$122.35	$6.12	$128.47	
4			$199.81	$9.99	$209.80	
5			$45.40	$2.27	$47.67	
6						(Ctrl) ▾
7						

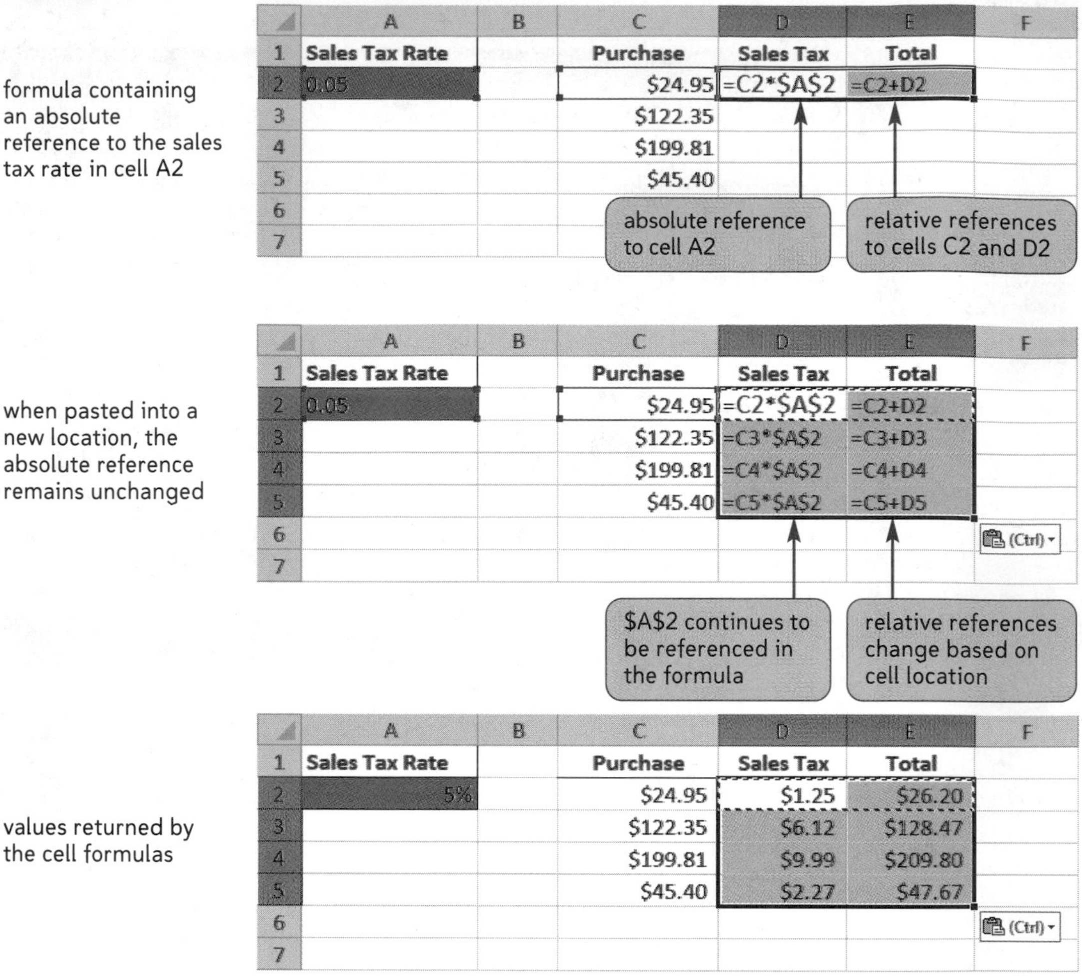

In this figure, the sales tax of different purchases is calculated and displayed. All items have the same 5 percent tax rate applied to the purchase, with the tax rate stored in cell A2. The sales tax and total cost of the first item are calculated in cells D2 and E2, respectively. When those formulas are copied and pasted to the remaining purchases, the relative references in the formulas are modified to point to the new location of the purchase cost; however, the sales tax rate continues to point to cell A2, regardless of the location of the selected cell.

You will modify the formulas in the Budget worksheet so that they reference Diane's income estimates using absolute rather than relative references.

To use absolute references to display the monthly income:

1. In cell C19, enter **=$D$5**. This formula contains an absolute reference to cell D5, which contains Diane's monthly income during the school months.

2. In cell C20, enter **=$D$6**. This formula contains an absolute reference to cell D6, which contains Glenn's monthly income during the school months.

3. Copy the corrected formulas in the range **C19:C20**, and then paste them in the range **D19:G20**. As shown in Figure 3-7, the months of February through May now correctly show the monthly income values for the school months.

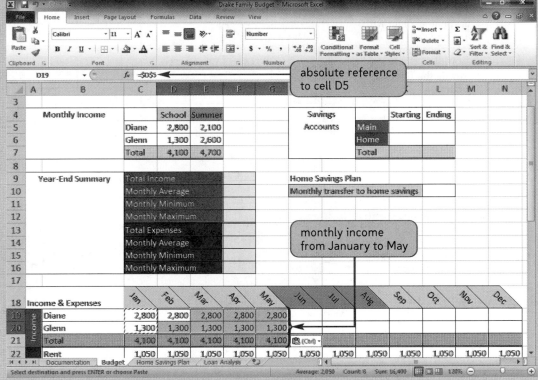

Figure 3-7   Results of formulas with absolute references

4. Click each cell in the range D19:G20 and verify that the formulas =$D$5 and =$D$6 were copied into the appropriate cells.

Using Mixed References

A formula can also include cell references that are mixed. A mixed reference contains both relative and absolute references. For example, a mixed reference for cell A2 can be either $A2 or A$2. In the mixed reference $A2, the column reference to column A is absolute and the reference to row 2 is relative. In the mixed reference A$2, the column reference is relative and the row reference is absolute. As you can see, a mixed reference "locks" one part of the cell reference while the other part can change. When you copy and paste a formula with a mixed reference to a new location, the absolute portion of the cell reference remains fixed and the relative portion shifts.

Figure 3-8 shows an example of using mixed references to complete a multiplication table. The first cell in the table, cell B3, contains the formula =$A3*B$2, which multiplies the first column entry (A3) by the first row entry (B2), returning the value 1. When this formula is copied to another cell, the absolute portions of the cell references remain unchanged and the relative portions of the references change. For example, if the formula is copied to cell E6, the first mixed cell reference changes to $A6 because the column reference is absolute and the row reference is relative, and the second cell reference changes to E$2 because the row reference is absolute and the column reference is relative. The result is that cell E6 contains the formula =$A6*E$2 and returns the value 16. Other cells in the multiplication table are similarly modified so that each entry returns the multiplication of the row and column headings.

Figure 3-8   **A multiplication table using a mixed reference**

original formula with a mixed cell reference that multiplies the first row by the first column

▲	A	B	C	D	E	F	G
1			**Multiplication Table**				
2		1	2	3	4	5	
3	1	=$A3*B$2					
4	2						
5	3						
6	4						
7	5						
8							
9							

formula copied to the B3:F7 range with mixed ranges to multiply the first row entries by the first column entries

▲	A	B	C	D	E	F	G
1			**Multiplication Table**				
2		1	2	3	4	5	
3	1	=$A3*B$2	=$A3*C$2	=$A3*D$2	=$A3*E$2	=$A3*F$2	
4	2	=$A4*B$2	=$A4*C$2	=$A4*D$2	=$A4*E$2	=$A4*F$2	
5	3	=$A5*B$2	=$A5*C$2	=$A5*D$2	=$A5*E$2	=$A5*F$2	
6	4	=$A6*B$2	=$A6*C$2	=$A6*D$2	=$A6*E$2	=$A6*F$2	
7	5	=$A7*B$2	=$A7*C$2	=$A7*D$2	=$A7*E$2	=$A7*F$2	
8							📋 (Ctrl) ▾
9							

values returned by each formula

▲	A	B	C	D	E	F	G
1			**Multiplication Table**				
2		1	2	3	4	5	
3	1	1	2	3	4	5	
4	2	2	4	6	8	10	
5	3	3	6	9	12	15	
6	4	4	8	12	16	20	
7	5	5	10	15	20	25	
8							📋 (Ctrl) ▾
9							

INSIGHT

Understanding When to Use Relative, Absolute, and Mixed References

Part of effective formula writing is knowing when to use relative, absolute, and mixed references. Use relative references when you want to repeat the same formula with cells in different locations on your worksheet. Relative references are commonly used when copying a formula that sums a column of numbers or that calculates the cost of several items by multiplying the item cost by the quantity being purchased.

Use absolute references when you want different formulas to refer to the same cell. This usually occurs when a cell contains a constant value, such as a tax rate, that will be used in formulas throughout the worksheet.

Mixed references are seldom used other than when creating tables of calculated values such as a multiplication table in which the values of the formula or function can be found in the initial rows and columns of the table.

As you develop formulas and worksheets, you might want to quickly switch a cell reference from relative to absolute or mixed. Rather than retyping the formula, you can switch the reference in editing mode by selecting the cell reference and pressing the F4 key. As you press the function key, Excel cycles through the different reference types, starting by changing a relative reference to an absolute reference, then to a mixed reference with the row absolute, then to a mixed reference with the column absolute, and then finally back to a relative reference.

You'll use the F4 key to cycle through the different types of references as you enter the remaining formulas with the income for the summer months.

To insert the remaining references to the couple's monthly income:

▶ **1.** Click cell **H19**, type **=**, and then click cell **E5**. The formula =E5 appears in the cell, which remains in Edit mode. This formula enters Diane's income for the summer months.

▶ **2.** Press the **F4** key. The formula changes to =$E$5, which is an absolute reference.

   Trouble? If the formula shows anything other than the absolute reference, you probably pressed the F4 key too many times. Continue to press the F4 key to loop through all of the cell reference types until the formula returns to =$E$5, which contains the absolute reference.

▶ **3.** Press the **Enter** key. The formula is entered and 2,100 (Diane's monthly income in the summer) appears in cell H19.

▶ **4.** In cell H20, enter the formula **=$E$6**. This formula uses an absolute reference to enter Glenn's monthly income in the summer.

▶ **5.** In cell H21, enter the formula **=H19+H20**. This formula adds Diane and Glenn's income for June; their combined monthly income in the summer is 4,700.

▶ **6.** Copy the range **H19:H21**, and then paste the copied formulas into the range **I19:J21**. The summer take-home pay values appear for the months of June through August.

   You'll complete the monthly income values for the remaining school months.

▶ **7.** Copy the range **C19:C21**, and then paste it into the range **K19:N21**. The couple's monthly income is entered for all months of the year.

Working with Functions

Excel functions provide a quick way to calculate summary data such as the total, average, minimum, and maximum values in a collection of values. You'll use these functions to summarize Diane and Glenn's income and expense data at the top of the Budget worksheet.

Understanding Function Syntax

Every function has to follow a set of rules, or **syntax**, which specifies how the function should be written. The general syntax of all Excel functions is

```
FUNCTION(argument1, argument2, ...)
```

where *FUNCTION* is the name of the function, and *argument1*, *argument2*, and so forth are arguments, which are the numbers, text, or cell references used by the function to return a value. Arguments are always separated by a comma.

Not all functions have arguments. Some functions have optional arguments, which are not required for the function to return a value, but can be included to provide more control over how Excel calculates the returned value. If an optional argument is not included, Excel assumes a default value for it. These tutorials show optional arguments within square brackets along with the argument's default value, as follows:

```
FUNCTION(argument1, [argument2=value2, ...])
```

In this function, *argument1* is required, *argument2* is an optional argument, and *value2* is the default value used for this argument. As you learn more about individual functions, you will learn which arguments are required and which are optional, and the default values used for optional arguments.

The hundreds of available Excel functions are organized into 11 categories. Figure 3-9 describes these different categories.

TIP

Optional arguments are always placed last in the argument list.

Figure 3-9   **Excel function categories**

Category	Functions That
Cube	Retrieve data from multidimensional databases involving online analytical processing or OLAP
Database	Retrieve and analyze data stored in databases
Date & Time	Analyze or create date and time values and time intervals
Engineering	Analyze engineering problems
Financial	Have financial applications
Information	Return information about the format, location, or contents of worksheet cells
Logical	Return logical (true-false) values
Lookup & Reference	Look up and return data matching a set of specified conditions from a range
Math & Trig	Have math and trigonometry applications
Statistical	Provide statistical analyses of a set of data
Text	Return text values or evaluate text

You can learn about each function using the Help system. Figure 3-10 describes some of the more common Math, Trig, and Statistical functions used in workbooks.

| Figure 3-10 | Common Math, Trig, and Statistical functions |

Function	Category	Description
AVERAGE(*number1* [, *number2, number3,* ...])	Statistical	Calculates the average of a collection of numbers, where *number1, number2,* and so forth are either numbers or cell references. Only *number1* is required. For more than one cell reference or to enter numbers directly into the function, use the optional arguments *number2, number3,* and so forth.
COUNT(*value1* [, *value2, value3,* ...])	Statistical	Counts how many cells in a range contain numbers, where *value1, value2,* and so forth are text, numbers, or cell references. Only *value1* is required. For more than one cell reference or to enter numbers directly into the function, use the optional arguments *value2, value3,* and so forth.
COUNTA(*value1* [, *value2, value3,* ...])	Statistical	Counts how many cells are not empty in ranges *value1, value2,* and so forth, or how many numbers are listed within *value1, value2,* and so forth.
INT(*number*)	Math & Trig	Displays the integer portion of a number, *number*.
MAX(*number1* [, *number2, number3,* ...])	Statistical	Calculates the maximum value of a collection of numbers, where *number1, number2,* and so forth are either numbers or cell references.
MEDIAN(*number1* [, *number2, number3,* ...])	Statistical	Calculates the median, or middle, value of a collection of numbers, where *number1, number2,* and so forth are either numbers or cell references.
MIN(*number1* [, *number2, number3,* ...])	Statistical	Calculates the minimum value of a collection of numbers, where *number1, number2,* and so forth are either numbers or cell references.
RAND()	Math & Trig	Returns a random number between 0 and 1.
ROUND(*number, num_digits*)	Math & Trig	Rounds a number to a specified *number* of digits, where number is the number you want to round and *num_digits* specifies how many digits to which you want to round the number.
SUM(*number1* [, *number2, number3,* ...])	Math & Trig	Adds a collection of numbers, where *number1, number2,* and so forth are either numbers or cell references.

For example, the AVERAGE function calculates the average value from a collection of numbers. The syntax of the AVERAGE function is

```
AVERAGE(number1 [, number2, number3, ...])
```

where *number1, number2, number3,* and so forth are either numbers or cell references to numbers. The following formula uses the AVERAGE function to calculate the average of 1, 2, 5, and 8, returning the value 4:

```
=AVERAGE(1, 2, 5, 8)
```

However, functions usually reference values entered in the worksheet. So, if the range A1:A4 contains the values 1, 2, 5, and 8, the following formula also returns a value of 4:

```
=AVERAGE(A1:A4)
```

The advantage of using cell references is that the values used in the function are visible to users and can be easily edited as needed. Functions can be included as part of larger formulas. For example, the following formula, which includes the MAX function, returns the maximum value from the range A1:A100, and then divides that value by 100:

```
=MAX(A1:A100)/100
```

Functions can also be placed inside another function, or **nested**. If a formula contains several functions, Excel starts with the innermost function and then moves outward. For example, the following formula first calculates the average of the values in the range A1:A100 using the AVERAGE function, and then extracts the integer portion of that value using the INT function:

```
=INT(AVERAGE(A1:A100))
```

One challenge of nesting functions is to make sure that you include all of the parentheses. You can check this by counting the number of left parentheses, and making sure that number matches the number of right parentheses. Excel will also display different levels of nested parentheses in different colors to make it easier to match the opening and closing parentheses in the formula. If the number of parentheses doesn't match, Excel will not accept the formula and will offer a suggestion for rewriting the formula so the number of left and right parentheses does match.

PROSKILLS

Problem Solving: Choosing the Right Summary Function

Problem solving involves determining how to best summarize a large sample of data into a few easy-to-use statistics. The field of statistics provides several summary measures, each with its own advantages and disadvantages.

One of the most common statistical approaches is to average the sample data. You can calculate the average in Excel with the AVERAGE function. However, determining an average is not always the best choice. Averages are susceptible to extremely large or small data values. Imagine calculating the average size of homes in a neighborhood that has one huge mansion and several small houses. In this case, the average value is heavily influenced by the size of that single mansion, and might not represent a typical neighborhood house.

When the data includes a few extremely large or extremely small values that have the potential to skew results, it's often better to use the **median**, or middle, value from the sample. For example, in a survey of nine homes, the median would be the size of the fifth largest—or middle-sized—home in the sample. You can calculate the median in Excel with the MEDIAN function.

Another approach is to calculate the most common value in the data, otherwise known as the **mode**. The mode is most often used with data that has only a few possible values, each of which might be repeated several times. Rather than using square feet, you might want to express the value in terms of the number of bedrooms each home contains. The mode would return the most common number of bedrooms in the homes included in the sample. You can calculate the mode in Excel using the MODE function.

By knowing which summary measure best fits your data, you can create useful and precise information that will aid you and others in interpreting the results.

Inserting a Function

Functions are organized in the Function Library group on the Formulas tab on the Ribbon. In the Function Library, you can select a function from a function category or you can open the Insert Function dialog box to search for a particular function. When you select a function, the Function Arguments dialog box opens, listing all the arguments associated with that function. Required arguments are in bold type; optional arguments are in normal type.

You'll use the SUM function to add the total income and expenses for the year in Diane's proposed budget.

To calculate annual income and expenses with the SUM function:

1. Click cell **F9** to select it.

2. Click the **Formulas** tab on the Ribbon.

3. In the Function Library group, click the **Math & Trig** button. An alphabetical listing of all the math and trigonometry functions opens.

> **TIP**
>
> You can click the Collapse Dialog Box button to shrink the Function Arguments dialog box to see more of the worksheet, select the range, and then click the Expand Dialog Box button to restore the dialog box.

4. Scroll down the list, and then click **SUM**. The Function Arguments dialog box opens, listing all of the arguments associated with the SUM function.

5. Click in the worksheet, and then select the range **C21:N21**. The dialog box reduces to its title bar as you select the range. The range reference, which includes all the monthly income amounts, appears as the value of the Number1 argument. See Figure 3-11.

Figure 3-11   **Function Arguments dialog box**

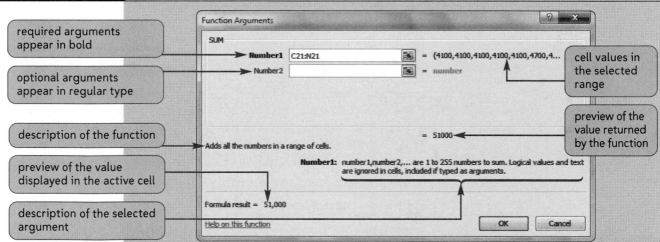

6. Click the **OK** button. The formula =SUM(C21:N21) is inserted into cell F9, which displays the value 51,000. This represents Diane and Glenn's total annual income.

7. Click cell **F13**. This is where you want the SUM function to add the monthly expenses for the year.

8. In the Function Library group on the Formulas tab, click the **Math & Trig** button, and then click **SUM**. The Function Arguments dialog box opens. You'll enter the monthly expenses stored in the range C32:N32 for the argument.

9. Click in the worksheet, and then select the range **C32:N32**.

10. In the Function Arguments dialog box, click the **OK** button. The formula =SUM(C32:N32) is inserted in cell F13, which displays the value 45,150. This represents the total projected expenses for the upcoming year. See Figure 3-12.

Figure 3-12   **Total annual income and expenses**

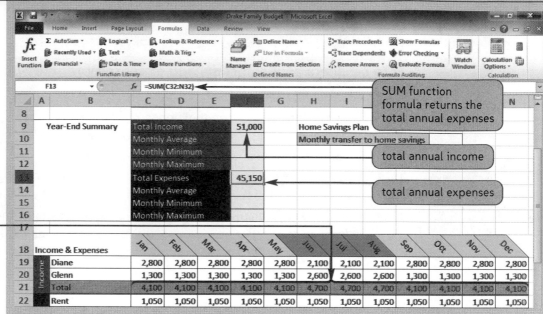

Diane projects that she and Glenn will earn roughly $6,000 more than they will spend throughout the year. It's easier for Diane to plan her budget if she knows how much, on average, the couple earns and spends each month. You can use the AVERAGE function to do this calculation using the same method you used for the SUM function.

If you aren't sure of the function's name or category, you can use the Insert Function dialog box. The Insert Function dialog box organizes all of the functions by category and includes a search feature for locating functions that perform particular calculations.

To calculate the couple's average monthly income:

1. Click cell **F10**. This is the cell in which you want to enter the AVERAGE function formula.

2. In the Function Library group on the Formulas tab, click the **Insert Function** button. The Insert Function dialog box opens.

3. In the Search for a function box, type **Calculate an average value**, and then click the **Go** button. Functions for calculating an average appear in the Select a function box. See Figure 3-13.

Figure 3-13   **Insert Function dialog box**

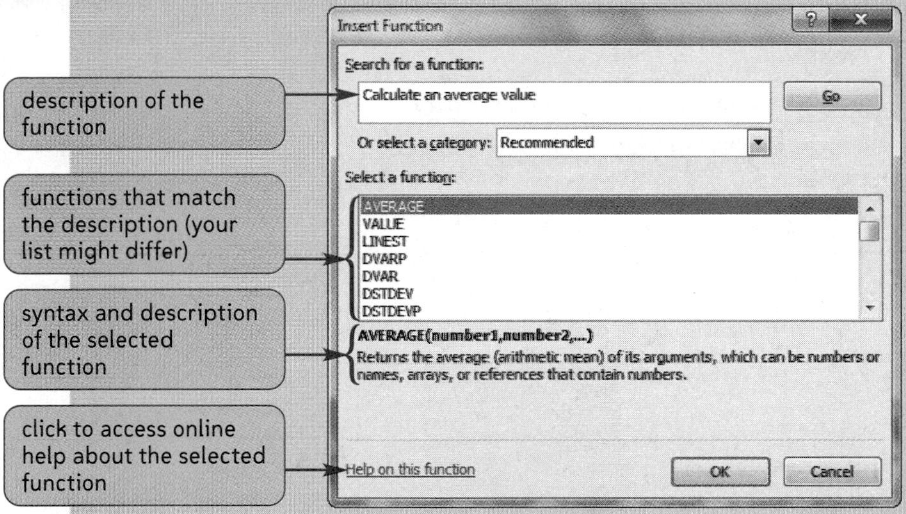

description of the function

functions that match the description (your list might differ)

syntax and description of the selected function

click to access online help about the selected function

▶ **4.** Verify that **AVERAGE** is selected in the Select a function box, and then click the **OK** button. The Function Arguments dialog box opens with the arguments for the AVERAGE function. A range reference for a cell directly above this cell already appears for the Number1 argument.

▶ **5.** Select the range reference in the Number1 argument box, and then select the range **C21:N21** in the worksheet.

▶ **6.** Click the **OK** button. The dialog box closes, and the formula =AVERAGE(C21:N21) is entered in cell F10, which displays the value 4,250—the couple's average monthly income.

How does the couple's average monthly income compare to their average monthly expenses? To find out, you'll use the AVERAGE function again. Because the function has already been used in your workbook, you can select it from a list of recently used functions.

To calculate the average monthly expenses:

▶ **1.** Click cell **F14**. This is the cell where you want to calculate the average monthly expenses.

▶ **2.** On the formula bar, click the **Insert Function** button f_x. The Insert Function dialog box opens.

▶ **3.** If necessary, click the **Or select a category** arrow, and then click **Most Recently Used**. The most recently used functions, sorted in order of recent use, appear in the Select a function box. The AVERAGE function is at the top followed by the SUM function.

▶ **4.** Verify that **AVERAGE** is selected in the Select a function box, and then click the **OK** button.

▶ **5.** Select the range **C32:N32** in the worksheet to insert the range reference C32:N32 in the Number1 box.

▶ **6.** Click the **OK** button. The formula =AVERAGE(C32:N32) is entered in cell F14, displaying the value 3,763. This represents the average expenses per month under Diane's budget. See Figure 3-14.

Figure 3-14 ▶ **Average family income and expenses**

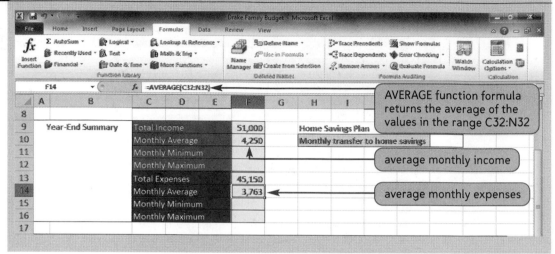

The average monthly expense, 3,763, is displayed to the nearest dollar amount. This is because Diane has formatted the workbook to not display decimal values. The actual value, 3,762.50, is stored in the cell although it is not displayed.

Typing a Function

After you become more familiar with functions, it is often faster to type the functions directly in cells rather than using the Insert Function dialog box or the Function Library. As you begin to type a function name within a formula, a list of functions that begin with the letters you typed appears. For example, when you type *S*, the list shows all of the functions starting with the letter *S*; when you type *SU*, the list shows only those functions starting with the letters *SU*, and so forth. This helps to ensure that you're entering a legitimate Excel function name.

The income and expenses averages show that the couple will bring in about $500 more than they spend each month. That does not leave much money to deal with an unexpected expense, so Diane wants to know how much variation is in the budget. What is the most money she could expect to take home during a single month in the upcoming year? What is the least? And what are the highest and lowest values for the monthly expenses? You'll use the MAX and MIN functions to calculate those values.

To calculate the minimum value for monthly income and expenses:

▶ **1.** Click cell **F11**. This is the cell in which you want to enter the monthly income.

▶ **2.** Type **=M**. As you type a formula, a list with function names starting with *M* opens.

▶ **3.** Type **I**. The list shows only those functions starting with *MI*. See Figure 3-15. As soon as the function you want appears in the list, you can double-click its name to enter it in the cell without typing the rest of its name.

| Figure 3-15 | Function being typed into a cell |

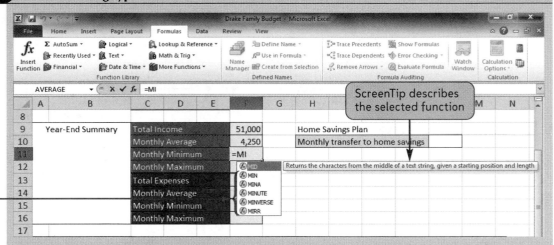

list of Excel functions
starting with *MI*

4. Double-click **MIN** in the list box. The MIN function with its opening parenthesis is inserted into cell F11 and a ScreenTip shows the syntax for the function. At this point, you can either type in the range reference or select the range with your mouse. To avoid typing errors, it's often better to use your mouse to enter range references.

5. Select the range **C21:N21**. The range reference is added to the formula.

6. Type **)** (the closing parenthesis), and then press the **Enter** key. The formula =MIN(C21:N21) is inserted in cell F11, displaying the value 4,100. This is the minimum amount that Diane expects the couple to bring home in a single month for the upcoming year.

Next, you'll calculate the minimum monthly expense projected for the year.

Be sure to end this and all functions with the closing parenthesis) to ensure that Excel interprets the formula correctly.

7. Click cell **F15**, and then repeat Steps 2 through 6 to enter the formula **=MIN(C32:N32)** in cell F15. The cell displays the value 2,795, which is the lowest amount that Diane expects to spend in a single month in the upcoming year.

The final piece of the year-end summary is the maximum monthly value for both income and expenses. Maximum values are calculated using the MAX function.

To calculate the maximum value for monthly income and expenses:

1. Click cell **F12**, and then enter the formula **=MAX(C21:N21)**. The value 4,700 appears in cell F12, indicating that the maximum income the couple can expect in a single month is $4,700.

   Trouble? If #NAME? appears in the cell, you probably mistyped the function name. Edit the formula to correct the misspelling.

2. Click cell **F16**, and then enter the formula **=MAX(C32:N32)**. The value 6,985 appears in cell F16, indicating that the maximum expenses for a single month are projected to be $6,985. See Figure 3-16.

Figure 3-16 **Year-end summary values**

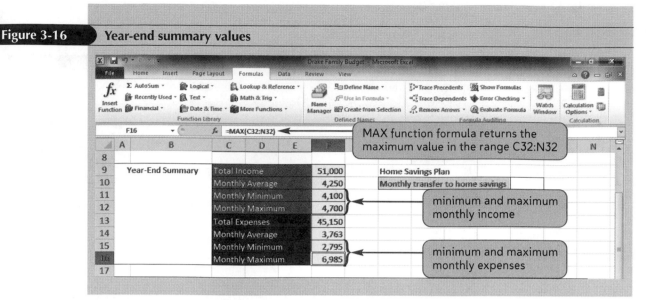

Based on the year-end summary, Diane and Glenn's monthly income will range from a minimum of $4,100 to a maximum of $4,700 with an average of $4,250. Monthly expenses, on the other hand, range from a minimum of $2,795 to a maximum of $6,985 with an average of $3,763. This budget does not have a lot of wiggle room.

Diane has just been promoted at work. Her income will increase to $3,100 per month during the school year. She wants to know how this affects the year-end summary.

To modify Diane's estimated income:

▶ **1.** In cell D5, enter the value **3100**.

▶ **2.** Confirm that Diane's monthly income for January through May and September through December has been automatically updated.

▶ **3.** Review how the year-end summary data has changed. See Figure 3-17.

Figure 3-17 **Revised income projection**

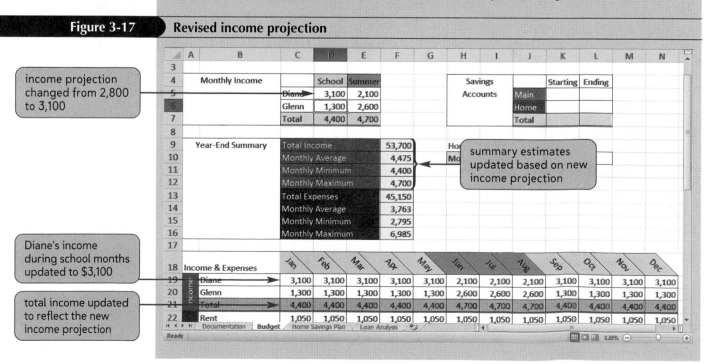

With Diane's promotion, the couple's annual income increases from $51,000 to $53,700 and the monthly average increases from $4,250 to $4,475. The couple's income should exceed their expenses by about $700 per month. The monthly income now ranges from a minimum of $4,400 up to a maximum of $4,700.

Diane now has a better picture of the family's finances for the upcoming year, and she is more confident about how to manage the couple's budget. She and Glenn hope to save enough for a down payment on a house in a few years. With the promotion, this seems like a real possibility. In the next session, you'll help Diane explore the couple's options in planning for the purchase of a house.

Session 3.1 Quick Check

REVIEW

1. You need to reference cell Q57 in a formula. What is the absolute cell reference? What are the two mixed references?
2. Assume that cell R10 contains the formula =R1+R2. What formula is entered if this formula is copied and pasted into cell S20?
3. Assume that cell T10 contains the formula =$T1+T$2. What formula is entered if this formula is copied and pasted into cell U20?
4. Assume that cell V10 contains the formula =AVERAGE($U1:$U5). What formula is entered if this formula is copied and pasted into cell W20?
5. What are optional arguments? What happens if you do not include an optional argument in a function?
6. What function formula can you use to add the numbers in the range X1:X10?
7. The range of a set of values is defined as the maximum value minus the minimum value. What formula with functions can you enter to calculate the range of the values in Y1:Y10?
8. What formula with functions can you enter to calculate the ratio of the maximum value in the range Z1:Z10 to the minimum value?

SESSION 3.2 VISUAL OVERVIEW

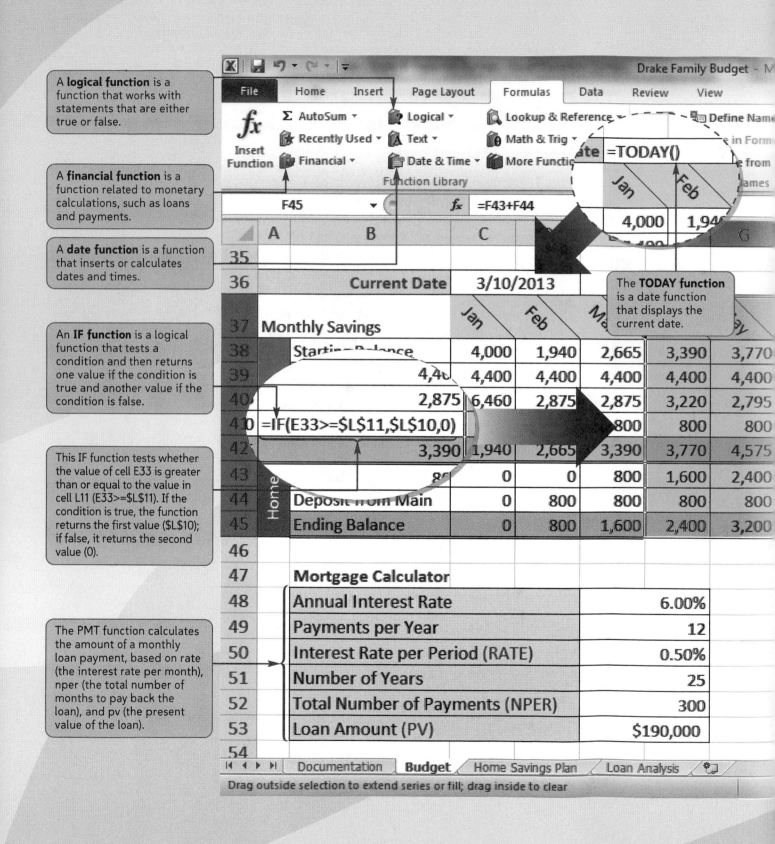

A **logical function** is a function that works with statements that are either true or false.

A **financial function** is a function related to monetary calculations, such as loans and payments.

A **date function** is a function that inserts or calculates dates and times.

An **IF function** is a logical function that tests a condition and then returns one value if the condition is true and another value if the condition is false.

This IF function tests whether the value of cell E33 is greater than or equal to the value in cell L11 (E33>=$L$11). If the condition is true, the function returns the first value ($L$10); if false, it returns the second value (0).

The PMT function calculates the amount of a monthly loan payment, based on rate (the interest rate per month), nper (the total number of months to pay back the loan), and pv (the present value of the loan).

The **TODAY function** is a date function that displays the current date.

Drake Family Budget - M

File   Home   Insert   Page Layout   Formulas   Data   Review   View

Insert Function — AutoSum, Recently Used, Financial, Logical, Text, Date & Time, Lookup & Reference, Math & Trig, More Functions, Define Name

Function Library

=TODAY()

F45   fx   =F43+F44

	A	B	C	Jan	Feb		G
35							
36		Current Date	3/10/2013	4,000	1,940		
37	Monthly Savings			Jan	Feb	M	y
38		Starting Balance		4,000	1,940	2,665	3,390	3,770
39			4,4	4,400	4,400	4,400	4,400	4,400
40			2,875	6,460	2,875	2,875	3,220	2,795
41	=IF(E33>=$L$11,$L$10,0)					800	800	800
42			3,390	1,940	2,665	3,390	3,770	4,575
43		8		0	0	800	1,600	2,400
44	Deposit from Main			0	800	800	800	800
45	Ending Balance			0	800	1,600	2,400	3,200
46								
47	Mortgage Calculator							
48	Annual Interest Rate						6.00%	
49	Payments per Year						12	
50	Interest Rate per Period (RATE)						0.50%	
51	Number of Years						25	
52	Total Number of Payments (NPER)						300	
53	Loan Amount (PV)						$190,000	
54								

Documentation   Budget   Home Savings Plan   Loan Analysis

Drag outside selection to extend series or fill; drag inside to clear

AUTOFILL AND MORE FUNCTIONS

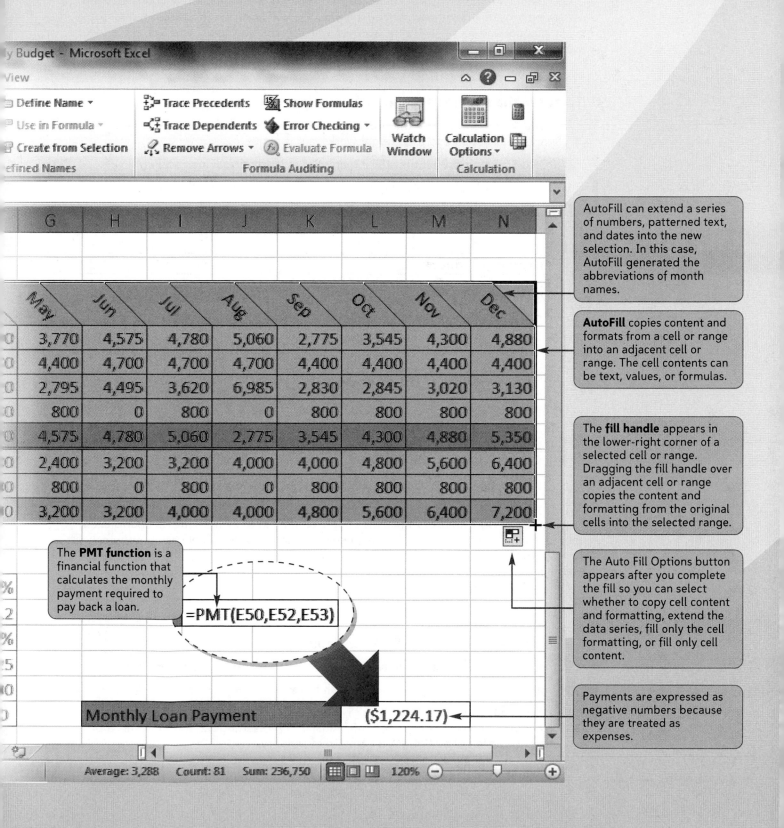

y Budget - Microsoft Excel

View

Define Name ▾   Trace Precedents   Show Formulas
Use in Formula ▾   Trace Dependents   Error Checking ▾   Watch Window   Calculation Options ▾
Create from Selection   Remove Arrows ▾   Evaluate Formula
efined Names   Formula Auditing   Calculation

	G	H	I	J	K	L	M	N
	May	Jun	Jul	Aug	Sep	Oct	Nov	Dec
0	3,770	4,575	4,780	5,060	2,775	3,545	4,300	4,880
0	4,400	4,700	4,700	4,700	4,400	4,400	4,400	4,400
0	2,795	4,495	3,620	6,985	2,830	2,845	3,020	3,130
0	800	0	800	0	800	800	800	800
0	4,575	4,780	5,060	2,775	3,545	4,300	4,880	5,350
0	2,400	3,200	3,200	4,000	4,000	4,800	5,600	6,400
0	800	0	800	0	800	800	800	800
0	3,200	3,200	4,000	4,000	4,800	5,600	6,400	7,200

The **PMT function** is a financial function that calculates the monthly payment required to pay back a loan.

=PMT(E50,E52,E53)

Monthly Loan Payment   ($1,224.17)

Average: 3,288   Count: 81   Sum: 236,750   120%

AutoFill can extend a series of numbers, patterned text, and dates into the new selection. In this case, AutoFill generated the abbreviations of month names.

AutoFill copies content and formats from a cell or range into an adjacent cell or range. The cell contents can be text, values, or formulas.

The **fill handle** appears in the lower-right corner of a selected cell or range. Dragging the fill handle over an adjacent cell or range copies the content and formatting from the original cells into the selected range.

The Auto Fill Options button appears after you complete the fill so you can select whether to copy cell content and formatting, extend the data series, fill only the cell formatting, or fill only cell content.

Payments are expressed as negative numbers because they are treated as expenses.

Entering Data and Formulas with AutoFill

Diane and Glenn hope to purchase a home in the next three years. Currently, they have $4,000 in their main savings account, and they plan to open a second account reserved for saving toward a down payment on a home. You will enter the initial balance for the main account and set up the home account with an initial balance of $0 into the Budget worksheet.

To enter the savings account information:

1. If you took a break after the previous session, make sure the Drake Family Budget workbook is open and the Budget worksheet is active.

2. In cell K5, enter **4,000** (the starting amount in the main savings account).

3. In cell K6, enter **0** (the starting amount in the home savings account).

4. In cell K7, enter the formula **=K5+K6** to sum the total initial amount in both accounts. See Figure 3-18.

| **Figure 3-18** | **Savings account information** |

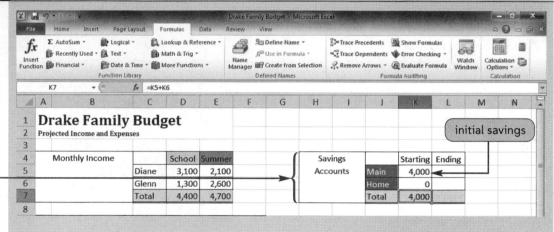

savings will be divided into a Main account and a Home account

Diane wants to learn how much the couple could add to their savings accounts each month. To find out, you must first determine the couple's monthly net cash flow, which is equal to the amount of money they earn each month after paying all of their expenses. You will start by formatting the cells where you'll enter this data and calculating the net cash flow during the month of January.

To calculate the net cash flow for January:

1. Merge and center the range **A33:B33**, and then right-align the cell contents.

2. In the merged cell A33, enter **Net Cash Flow**.

3. In cell C33, enter the formula **=C21–C32**. This formula subtracts total expenses from total income for the month of January. The resulting –2,060 indicates a projected shortfall of $2,060 for the month of January.

4. Apply conditional formatting to cell C33 to highlight the cell with a red fill and red text if the value in the cell is less than 0. Months with negative cash flow will be highlighted on the worksheet. See Figure 3-19.

Figure 3-19   January net cash flow

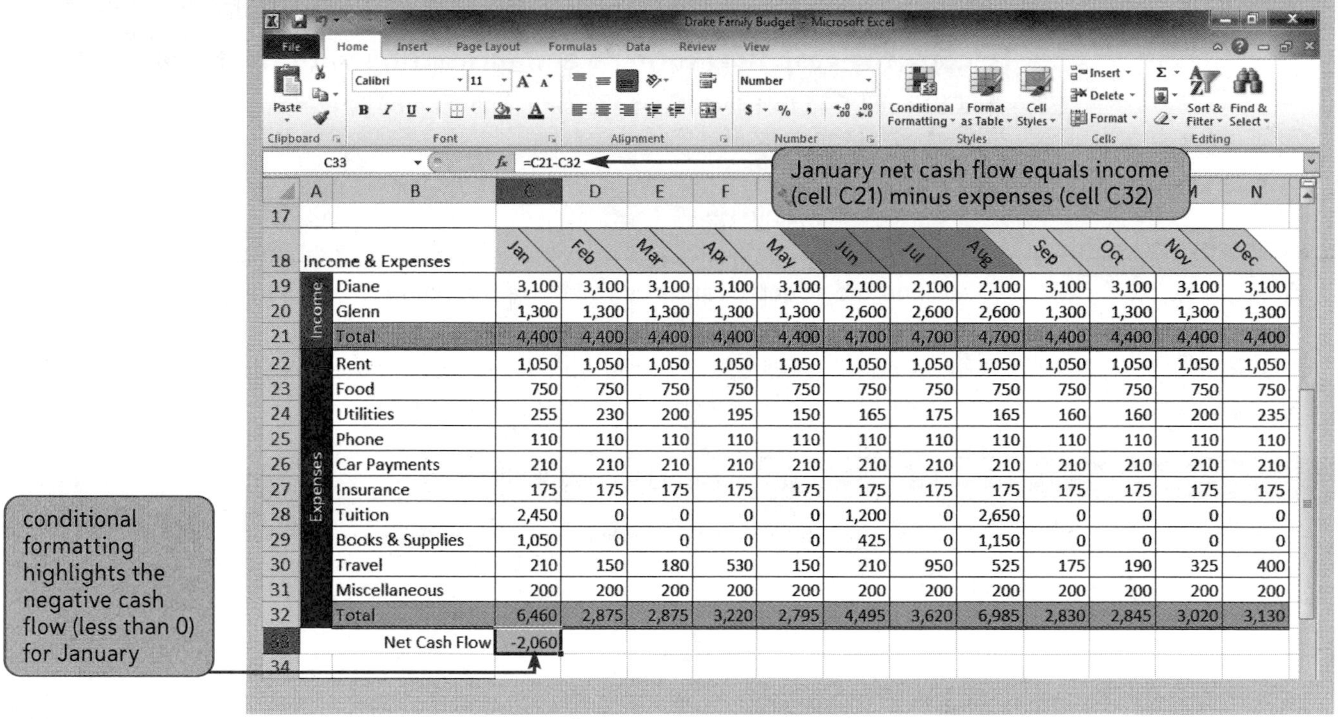

Your calculations show that the couple's expenses will exceed their income by more than $2,000 in January. This is due to the cost of tuition that must be paid that month. You could copy and paste the formula and formatting from cell C33 into the rest of the row to calculate the net cash flow for the other months, as you've done before, but AutoFill is faster.

Using the Fill Handle

After you select a range, the fill handle appears in the lower-right corner of the selection. When you drag the fill handle over an adjacent range, Excel uses AutoFill to copy the content and formats from the original cell into the adjacent range. This process is often more efficient than the two-step process of copying and pasting.

REFERENCE

Copying Formulas and Formats with AutoFill

- Select the cell or range that contains the formula or formulas you want to copy.
- Drag the fill handle in the direction you want to copy the formula(s) and then release the mouse button.
- To copy only the formats or only the formulas, click the Auto Fill Options button and select the appropriate option.

or

- Select the cell or range that contains the formula or formulas you want to copy.
- In the Editing group on the Home tab, click the Fill button.
- Select the appropriate fill direction and fill type.

or

Click Series, enter the desired fill series options, and then click the OK button.

You will use the fill handle to copy the formula and conditional formatting you entered in cell C33 into the remaining cells in the Net Cash Flow row.

To copy the cash flow formula and formatting with the fill handle:

1. Click cell **C33** to select it, if necessary. The fill handle appears in the lower-right corner of the cell.

2. Position the pointer over the fill handle in the lower-right corner of the cell. The pointer changes to **+**.

3. Click and drag the fill handle over the range **D33:N33**. A dotted outline appears around the selected range as you move the pointer.

4. Release the mouse button. The selected range is filled in with the formula and formatting from cell C33, and the Auto Fill Options button appears in the lower-right corner of the selected cells. See Figure 3-20.

TIP

With AutoFill, formulas can easily be copied into the wrong range; if that happens, click the Undo button and try again.

Figure 3-20 Formulas and formatting pasted with AutoFill

formula to calculate the January net cash flow

conditional formatting highlights months of negative cash flow

the formulas and formats in cell C33 are filled into the selected range

Auto Fill Options button

fill handle

		Jan	Feb	Mar	Apr	May	Jun	Jul	Aug	Sep	Oct	Nov	Dec
18	Income & Expenses												
19	Diane	3,100	3,100	3,100	3,100	3,100	2,100	2,100	2,100	3,100	3,100	3,100	3,100
20	Glenn	1,300	1,300	1,300	1,300	1,300	2,600	2,600	2,600	1,300	1,300	1,300	1,300
21	Total	4,400	4,400	4,400	4,400	4,400	4,700	4,700	4,700	4,400	4,400	4,400	4,400
22	Rent	1,050	1,050	1,050	1,050	1,050	1,050	1,050	1,050	1,050	1,050	1,050	1,050
23	Food	750	750	750	750	750	750	750	750	750	750	750	750
24	Utilities	255	230	200	195	150	165	175	165	160	160	200	235
25	Phone	110	110	110	110	110	110	110	110	110	110	110	110
26	Car Payments	210	210	210	210	210	210	210	210	210	210	210	210
27	Insurance	175	175	175	175	175	175	175	175	175	175	175	175
28	Tuition	2,450	0	0	0	0	1,200	0	2,650	0	0	0	0
29	Books & Supplies	1,050	0	0	0	0	425	0	1,150	0	0	0	0
30	Travel	210	150	180	530	150	210	950	525	175	190	325	400
31	Miscellaneous	200	200	200	200	200	200	200	200	200	200	200	200
32	Total	6,460	2,875	2,875	3,220	2,795	4,495	3,620	6,985	2,830	2,845	3,020	3,130
33	Net Cash Flow	-2,060	1,525	1,525	1,180	1,605	205	1,080	-2,285	1,570	1,555	1,380	1,270
35	Monthly Savings												
36	Starting Balance												

5. Review the monthly net cash flows to confirm that AutoFill correctly copied the formula and conditional formatting into the selected range.

These calculations provide Diane with a better picture of how the couple's net cash flow varies from month to month. Only in January and August, when Glenn's tuition payments are due, do the couple's expenses exceed their income. In most months, their income exceeds expenses by about $1,500. In June, however, the net cash flow, while positive, is projected to be only $205.

Using the Auto Fill Options Button

By default, AutoFill copies both the content and the formatting of the original range to the selected range. However, sometimes you might want to copy only the content or only the formatting. The Auto Fill Options button that appears after you release the mouse button lets you specify what is copied. As shown in Figure 3-21, clicking this button provides a list of Auto-Fill options. The Copy Cells option, which is the default, copies both the content and the formatting. The Fill Formatting Only option copies the formatting into the selected cells but not any content. The Fill Without Formatting option copies the content but not the formatting.

Figure 3-21 **Auto Fill Options button**

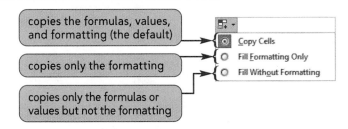

copies the formulas, values, and formatting (the default)

copies only the formatting

copies only the formulas or values but not the formatting

Filling a Series

AutoFill can also be used to create a series of numbers, dates, or text based on a pattern. To create a series of numbers, you enter the initial values in the series in a selected range and then use AutoFill to complete the series. Figure 3-22 shows how AutoFill can be used to insert the numbers from 1 to 10 in a selected range. You enter the first few numbers in the range A1:A3 to establish the pattern for AutoFill to use, consecutive positive integers in this example. Then, you select the range and drag the fill handle over the cells where you want the pattern continued. In Figure 3-22, the fill handle is dragged over the range A4:A10 and Excel fills in the rest of the series.

Figure 3-22 **AutoFill extends a numeric sequence**

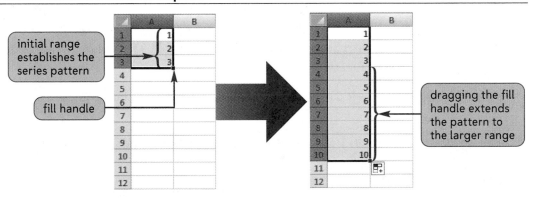

initial range establishes the series pattern

fill handle

dragging the fill handle extends the pattern to the larger range

AutoFill can extend a wide variety of series, including dates and times and patterned text. Figure 3-23 shows examples of some series that AutoFill can generate. In each case, you must provide enough information for AutoFill to identify the pattern. AutoFill can recognize some patterns from only a single value, such as Jan or January, to create a series of month abbreviations or names, or Mon or Monday, to create a series of the days of the week. A text pattern that includes a text string and a number such as Region 1, Region 2, and so on can also be automatically extended using AutoFill.

Figure 3-23 AutoFill applied to values, dates and times, and patterned text

Type	Initial Pattern	Extended Series
Values	1, 2, 3	4, 5, 6, …
	2, 4, 6	8, 10, 12, …
Dates and Times	Jan	Feb, Mar, Apr, …
	January	February, March, April, …
	15-Jan, 15-Feb	15-Mar, 15-Apr, 15-May, …
	12/30/2013	12/31/2013, 1/1/2014, 1/2/2014, …
	12/31/2013, 1/31/2014	2/28/2014, 3/31/2014, 4/30/2014, …
	Mon	Tue, Wed, Thu, …
	Monday	Tuesday, Wednesday, Thursday, …
	11:00AM	12:00PM, 1:00PM, 2:00PM, …
Patterned Text	1st period	2nd period, 3rd period, 4th period, …
	Region 1	Region 2, Region 3, Region 4, …
	Quarter 3	Quarter 4, Quarter 1, Quarter 2, …
	Qtr3	Qtr4, Qtr1, Qtr2, …

For more complex patterns, you can use the Series dialog box. To do so, enter the first value of the series in a worksheet cell, select the entire range that will contain the series, click the Fill button in the Editing group on the Home tab, and then click Series. The Series dialog box opens. From the Series dialog box you can specify a linear or growth series for numeric values; a Date series for dates that increase by day, weekday, month, or year; or an AutoFill series for patterned text. With numeric values, you can also specify the step value (indicating how much each numeric value increases over the previous entry) and a stop value (to specify the endpoint for the entire series).

REFERENCE

Creating a Series with AutoFill

- Enter the first few values of the series into a range.
- Select the range, and then drag the fill handle of the selected range over the cells you want to fill.

or

- Enter the first few values of the series into a range.
- Select the entire range into which you want to extend the series.
- In the Editing group on the Home tab, click the Fill button, and then click Down, Right, Up, Left, Series, or Justify to set the direction in which you want to extend the series.

Diane wants to see how the monthly balances in the main savings account are affected by the couple's changing income and expenses. She wants to make sure that the balance doesn't drop too low after months with particularly high expenses—such as January and August. You'll add data to the worksheet to display the monthly savings balance, starting with the month labels.

To use AutoFill to enter a series of months:

▶ **1.** In cell C35, enter **Jan**. This is the first value in the series. Because "Jan" is a common abbreviation for January, Excel recognizes it as a month and you don't need to type "Feb" for the next month in the series.

▶ **2.** Select cell **C35**, if necessary.

▶ **3.** Drag the fill handle over the range **D35:N35**. As you drag the fill handle, ScreenTips show the month abbreviations for the selected cell.

▶ **4.** Release the mouse button. AutoFill enters the remaining three-letter abbreviations for each month of the year.

▶ **5.** Select the range **C18:N18**, and then click the **Format Painter** button 🖌 in the Clipboard group on the Home tab. You'll apply this formatting to the entries in the range C35:N35.

▶ **6.** Click cell **C35** to apply the format to the range C35:N35, and then click cell **A35** to deselect the column titles. See Figure 3-24.

Figure 3-24	Month labels and formatting

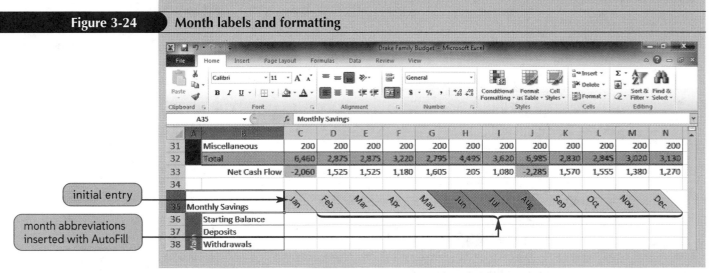

Next, you'll enter formulas to calculate the changing balance in the couple's main savings account. The main savings account balance at the end of each month is determined by four factors:

1. The balance at the beginning of the month
2. Money deposited from the couple's paychecks at the beginning of the month
3. Money withdrawn to pay for expenses
4. Money transferred into a home savings account reserved for a down payment on a mortgage. (Diane and Glenn have not yet decided how much they want to transfer into this account, so you'll leave that value blank for now.)

You'll start by calculating the balance in the couple's account at the end of January.

To calculate the January balance in the savings account:

▶ **1.** In cell C36, enter the formula **=K5**. The formula references the balance in the main savings account at the beginning of the year, which is stored in cell K5.

▶ **2.** In cell C37, enter **=C21** to retrieve the couple's January income. The relative reference will change when you copy the formula to other months.

3. In cell C38, enter **=C32** to retrieve the January expenses. The relative reference will change when you copy the formula to other months. You'll leave cell C39 blank because, at this point, you won't assume that any money will be transferred from the main savings account to the home savings account.

4. In cell C40, enter **=C36+C37−C38−C39**. This formula calculates the ending balance for the main savings account, which is equal to the starting balance plus any deposits minus the withdrawals and transfers. Cell C40 displays 1,940, which is the projected balance in the main savings account at the end of January.

5. Format the range C36:C39 to add borders around all of the cells.

6. Use the Format Painter to copy the formatting from cell C32 to cell **C40**, and then change the fill color to **Blue, Accent 1, Lighter 60%** (the fifth color in the third row of the Theme Colors section) to change the background color of the cell.

7. Click cell **A35**. Figure 3-25 shows the formatted January savings values.

| Figure 3-25 | January savings |

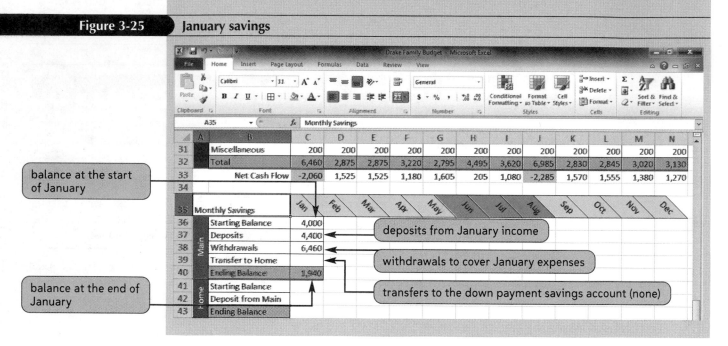

At this point, the couple's projected savings at the end of January will be $1,940, which is $2,060 less than their starting balance of $4,000 at the beginning of the year. The savings formulas for the remaining months are the same as for January except that their starting balances are based on the ending balance of the previous month. You will calculate the activity in the couple's main savings account for the remaining months of the year.

To calculate the remaining balances in the main savings account:

1. Select the range **C36:C40** and drag the fill handle over the February savings in the range **D36:D40**.

2. Change the formula in cell D36 to **=C40** so that the February starting balance for the main savings account is based on the January ending balance.

3. Select the range **D36:D40**, and then drag the fill handle over the range **E36:N40**. The formulas and formatting from February are copied into the remaining months of the year.

4. Click cell **A35** to deselect the main savings account data. See Figure 3-26.

| Figure 3-26 | January through December savings |

savings balance at the end of each month

5. In cell L5, enter the formula **=N40**. The ending balance of the main savings account in December—12,550—appears in cell L5. Diane can quickly see that the couple's savings in the main account will increase by $8,550 in the upcoming year.

Developing a Savings Plan

Under her current budget projections, Diane expects to have $12,550 in the main savings account at the end of the next year but nothing in the home savings account. She wants to transfer money into the home savings account each month. Because the home savings account is used for longer-term savings, Diane cannot withdraw money from it without penalty. So, she wants to make sure the main savings account always has enough money to meet monthly expenses and any unexpected bills without relying on money from the home savings account.

Diane needs to balance her desire to keep a reasonable amount in the main savings account and her desire to save enough for a down payment on a home mortgage. To achieve this balance, she needs to determine her overall savings goal and how soon she and Glenn want to meet that goal.

Diane wants to know how much money the couple can save if they transfer $500 to $1,000 into the home savings account each month for the next three years. You'll create a table that shows the total amount saved in one, two, and three years from deposits starting at $500 that increase in $100 increments through $1,000.

To create a table for different savings plans:

1. Go to the **Home Savings Plan** worksheet.

2. Merge and center the range **B3:G3**, enter **Savings Deposit per Month** in the merged cell, and then format the merged cell using the **Heading 2** cell style.

3. In cell A4, enter **Months**, and then format the cell in bold.

4. In cell B4, enter **500** and then, in cell C4, enter **600**. You entered the first two values in the series so that you could extend the numeric series.

5. Select the range **B4:C4**, and then drag the fill handle to cell **G4**. The values entered in the series—500, 600, 700, 800, 900, and 1000—are the different amounts the Drakes might transfer into their home savings account each month.

   Trouble? If the number 600 was entered in each cell instead of the series, you probably did not select both cells B4 and C4 before dragging the fill handle. Repeat Step 5, being sure to select both cells before filling.

6. In the range A5:A7, enter the values **12**, **24**, and **36**. These monthly values are equal to one year, two years, and three years, respectively. You entered the years in months because Diane and Glenn plan to deposit money into their home savings account each month. So, they would make 12 deposits in one year, they would make 24 deposits in two years, and they would make 36 deposits in three years.

7. Format the nonadjacent range B4:G4;A5:A7 with the **Input** cell style.

Next, you'll enter formulas to calculate the amount of money saved under each plan. The amount saved is equal to the number of months of savings multiplied by the deposit per month. You'll create this table using the same formulas with mixed cell references discussed earlier in Figure 3-8.

To enter formulas with mixed references to calculate the savings amounts:

1. In cell **B5**, enter **=$A5*B$4**. This formula uses mixed references to calculate the amount of savings generated by saving $500 per month for 12 months. The calculated value 6000 is displayed in the cell.

2. Select cell **B5** and drag the fill handle over the range **C5:G5** to calculate total savings over 12 months for deposits of $500 to $1,000 per month.

3. With B5:G5 still selected, drag the fill handle down to **G7** to apply the formula to the remaining cells in the multiplication table.

4. Format the values in the range B5:G7 using a thousands separator with no digits to the right of the decimal point, and add a border around each of the cells in the range.

5. Click cell **B5**. Figure 3-27 shows the completed and formatted values.

Figure 3-27 | Savings plan table

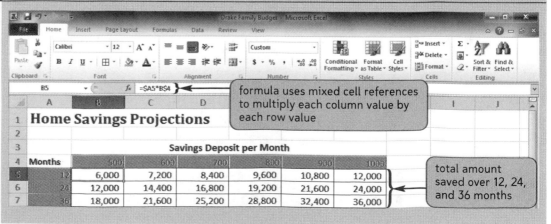

The data shows how increasing the monthly amount that Diane and Glenn save toward a down payment quickly adds up. For example, if they save $800 per month, at the end of three years (36 months), they would have saved $28,800. This is just a little less than the $30,000 they want to save for the down payment. You will add the transfer of $800 from the main savings account to the home savings account each month to the proposed budget. So that Diane can explore the impact of transferring different amounts of money per month, you'll enter the $800 value at the top of the Budget worksheet where it can be easily referenced and modified.

To specify the $800 transfer amount:

▶ **1.** Return to the **Budget** worksheet.

▶ **2.** In cell L10, enter **800**. See Figure 3-28.

Figure 3-28 ▶ **Home savings plan**

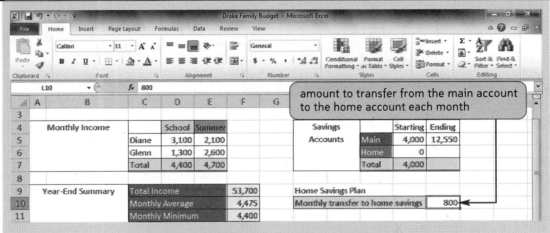

Next, you'll apply this monthly savings goal to Diane's proposed budget. You'll start by calculating the impact of transferring $800 on the January balances in the two savings accounts.

To modify the January balances:

▶ **1.** In cell C39, enter the formula **=$L$10** to insert the amount of money withdrawn from the main savings account in January. The ending balance for the main account falls to $1,140. You used an absolute cell reference so that this formula continues to refer to cell L10 when you copy it into the remaining months of the year.

▶ **2.** In cell C41, enter the formula **=K6** to insert the starting balance ($0) in the home account.

▶ **3.** In cell C42, enter the formula **=C39** to insert the amount deposited from the main account into the home account.

▶ **4.** In cell C43, enter the formula **=C41+C42** to calculate the ending balance in the home account.

▶ **5.** Use the Format Painter to copy the formatting from the range **C38:C40** to the range **C41:C43**.

6. Change the fill color of cell C43 to **Orange, Accent 6, Lighter 60%** (the last color in the third row of the Theme Colors section).

7. Click cell **C43** to select it, if necessary. See Figure 3-29.

Figure 3-29   **Ending January balances in the Main and Home accounts**

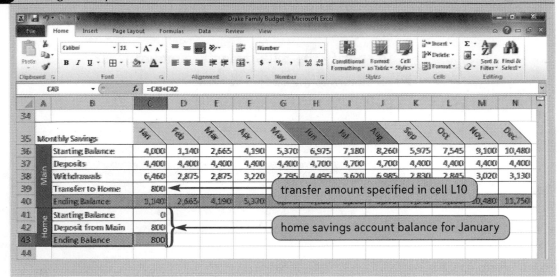

Now you'll insert the savings balances for the remaining months of the year, transferring $800 each month from the main savings account to the home savings account. As you did for the main savings account, you need to modify the formulas in row 41 so that the starting balance for February through December is taken from the ending balance of the previous month.

To complete the formulas for the home savings account:

1. Click cell **C39**, and then drag the fill handle over the range **D39:N39**. The formula =$L$10 is inserted in each cell in the range. The ending balance for December drops to $2,950, which is the final balance in the main account after transferring $800 per month.

2. Copy the range **C41:C43**, and then paste it into the range **D41:D43**. The formulas and formatting from January are entered for February. The starting balance for February shows the initial balance in the home savings account, $0, rather than the ending balance from January, $800.

3. Change the formula in cell D41 to **=C43** so that the February starting balance is taken from the January ending balance. Cell D41 correctly shows the February starting balance of 800, and cell D43 displays the value 1,600, the ending balance for February.

4. Select the range **D41:D43**, and then drag the fill handle over the range **E41:N43**. The formulas and formatting from February are copied to the remaining months of the year.

5. Click cell **N43** to deselect the range. Figure 3-30 shows the monthly balances for both accounts from January through December.

| Figure 3-30 | Projected monthly savings balances for the year |

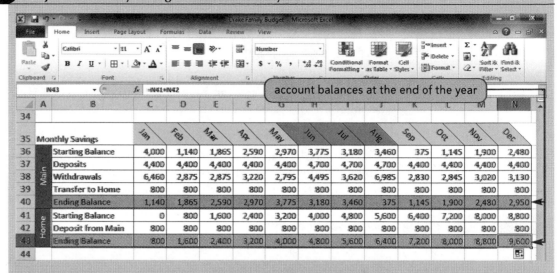

6. In cell L6, enter the formula **=N43**. The savings plan table at the top of the work-sheet displays 9,600, which is the year-end balance for the home account.

7. In cell L7, enter the formula **=L5+L6** to calculate the total savings amount from both accounts at the end of the year. Under Diane's current plan, the couple will have $2,950 in the main savings account and $9,600 in the home savings account at the end of the year.

Working with Logical Functions

Although Diane is pleased that $9,600 will be moved into the home savings account in the next year, she's concerned about the amount of money left in the main savings account. Even more troubling are the month-to-month balances in that account. For example, the balance in the main savings account will be only $375 at the end of August and will remain well below $2,000 for several months of the year. Diane is concerned that this savings plan will leave the couple with insufficient funds in the main savings account to handle unforeseen expenses.

Part of the problem is that the couple's net cash flow is negative during several months of the year. If they continue to transfer $800 into the home savings account during those months, the main savings account might fall below an acceptable level. Diane wants to modify her savings plan so that money is not transferred into the home savings account unless the net cash flow for that month is greater than or equal to $1,000. You need a formula that can "choose" whether to transfer the funds. You can build this kind of decision-making capability into a formula through the use of a logical function.

A logical function is a function that works with statements that are either true or false. Consider a statement such as "cell A5 = 3". If cell A5 is equal to 3, this statement has a value of true; if cell A5 is not equal to 3, this statement has a value of false. Excel supports many different logical functions, one of which is the IF function.

Using the IF Function

The IF function is a logical function that returns one value if a statement is true and returns a different value if that statement is false. The syntax of the IF function is

```
IF(logical_test, [value_if_true,] [value_if_false])
```

where *logical_test* is a statement that is either true or false, *value_if_true* is the value returned by the IF function if the statement is true, and *value_if_false* is the value returned by the function if the statement is false. For example, the following formula tests whether the value in cell A1 is equal to the value in cell B1. If it is, the formula returns a value of 100; otherwise it returns a value of 50.

```
=IF(A1=B1, 100, 50)
```

In many cases, however, you will not use values directly in the IF function. The following formula uses cell references, returning the value of cell C1 if A1 equals B1; otherwise, it returns the value of cell C2:

```
=IF(A1=B1, C1, C2)
```

The = symbol in these formulas is a comparison operator. A **comparison operator** is a symbol that indicates the relationship between two values. Figure 3-31 describes the comparison operators that can be used within a logical function.

Figure 3-31   **Comparison operators**

Operator	Statement	Description
=	A1 = B1	Tests whether the value in cell A1 *is equal to* the value in cell B1
>	A1 > B1	Tests whether the value in cell A1 *is greater than* the value in cell B1
<	A1 < B1	Tests whether the value in cell A1 *is less than* the value in cell B1
>=	A1 >= B1	Tests whether the value in cell A1 *is greater than or equal to* the value in cell B1
<=	A1 <= B1	Tests whether the value in cell A1 *is less than or equal to* the value in cell B1
<>	A1 <> B1	Tests whether the value in cell A1 *is not equal to* the value in cell B1

The IF function also works with text. For example, the following formula tests whether the value of cell A1 is equal to YES. If the value of cell A1 is equal to YES, the formula returns the text DONE; otherwise, it returns the text RESTART.

```
=IF(A1="YES", "DONE", "RESTART")
```

In addition, you can nest other functions inside an IF statement. The following formula first tests whether cell A5 is equal to the maximum of values within the range A1:A100. If it is, the formula returns the text "Maximum"; otherwise, it returns no text.

```
=IF(A5=MAX(A1:A100), "Maximum","")
```

In Diane and Glenn's budget, you will use an IF function for each month to test whether the net cash flow for that month is $1,000 or greater. If it is, Diane wants to transfer some of it into the home savings account. On the other hand, if the net cash flow is less than $1,000, she does not want to transfer any of it into the home account. You'll start creating this function by entering the minimum net cash flow into the worksheet.

To specify the minimum net cash flow:

1. In cell H11, enter the label **Minimum required net cash flow**.

2. In cell L11, enter **1000**. This is the minimum cash flow amount.

3. Use the Format Painter to copy the formatting from the range **H10:L10** to the range H11:L11.

Next, you'll enter a formula to determine how much to transfer each month. For the month of January, the formula to determine how much money is transferred is:

```
=IF(C33>=$L$11, $L$10, 0)
```

Cell C33 contains the net cash flow for the month of January, cell L11 contains the minimum net cash flow needed before Diane will transfer the money between accounts, and cell L10 contains the amount of money that Diane wants to transfer when the net cash flow meets or exceeds the minimum. For the current worksheet, this function tests whether the net cash flow for the month of January (cell C33) is greater than or equal to 1000 (cell L11). If it is, the formula returns 800 (cell L10) as the amount to transfer from the main savings account into the home savings account. Otherwise, it returns 0 and no money will be transferred that month.

This logical test uses both relative and absolute references. The C33 reference is relative because you will copy this formula into cells for the remaining months of the year. The $L$11 and $L$10 references are absolute so that the expression always references the minimum net cash flow specified in cell L11 and the amount to transfer specified in cell L10.

You'll replace the formula in cell C39 with this IF function.

To insert the IF function to determine the monthly transfer amount:

1. Clear the contents of cell **C39**.

2. Click the **Formulas** tab on the Ribbon, if necessary.

3. In the Function Library group, click the **Logical** button, and then click **IF** in the list of logical functions. The Function Arguments dialog box for the IF function opens.

4. In the Logical_test box, enter **C33>=$L$11**. This tests whether the net cash flow for January is greater than or equal to the value in cell L11 (1000).

5. In the Value_if_true box, enter **$L$10**. If the value in cell C33 is greater than or equal to the value in cell L11, the formula returns the value in cell L10 (800).

6. In the Value_if_false box, enter **0**. If the value in cell C33 is less than the value in cell L11, the formula returns 0 and no money will be transferred from the main savings account into the home savings account that month. See Figure 3-32.

> **TIP**
>
> When you type the IF function directly in the cell, remember that the *value_if_true* argument comes before the *value_if_false* argument.

| Figure 3-32 | Function Arguments dialog box for the IF function |

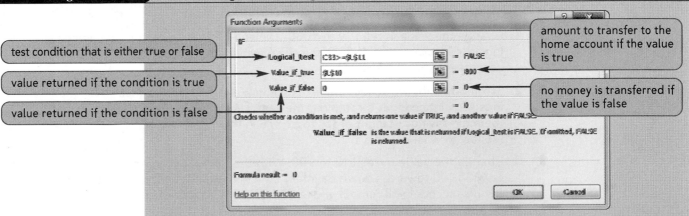

test condition that is either true or false

value returned if the condition is true

value returned if the condition is false

amount to transfer to the home account if the value is true

no money is transferred if the value is false

7. Click the **OK** button. A value of 0 is displayed in cell C39. Because the net cash flow for January is –2,060, no money will be transferred from the main savings account into the home savings account that month.

8. Drag the fill handle for cell C39 over the range **D39:N39** to copy this formula with the IF function into the remaining months of Diane's proposed budget.

9. Click cell **N40** to deselect the range. The new savings account balances are shown in Figure 3-33.

Figure 3-33 Monthly savings account balances

click to view logical functions

net cash flow is >= $1,000 every month except January, June, and August

$800 is transferred every month except January, June, and August

N40   fx =N36+N37-N38-N39

	A	B	C	D	E	F	G	H	I	J	K	L	M	N
31		Miscellaneous	200	200	200	200	200	200	200	200	200	200	200	200
32		Total	6,460	2,875	2,875	3,220	2,795	4,495	3,620	6,985	2,830	2,845	3,020	3,130
33		Net Cash Flow	-2,060	1,525	1,525	1,180	1,605	205	1,080	-2,285	1,570	1,555	1,380	1,270
34														
35	Monthly Savings		Jan	Feb	Mar	Apr	May	Jun	Jul	Aug	Sep	Oct	Nov	Dec
36		Starting Balance	4,000	1,940	2,665	3,390	3,770	4,575	4,780	5,060	2,775	3,545	4,300	4,880
37		Deposits	4,400	4,400	4,400	4,400	4,400	4,700	4,700	4,700	4,400	4,400	4,400	4,400
38	Main	Withdrawals	6,460	2,875	2,875	3,220	2,795	4,495	3,620	6,985	2,830	2,845	3,020	3,130
39		Transfer to Home	0	800	800	800	800	0	800	0	800	800	800	800
40		Ending Balance	1,940	2,665	3,390	3,770	4,575	4,780	5,060	2,775	3,545	4,300	4,880	5,350
41		Starting Balance	0	0	800	1,600	2,400	3,200	3,200	4,000	4,000	4,800	5,600	6,400
42	Home	Deposit from Main	0	800	800	800	800	0	800	0	800	800	800	800
43		Ending Balance	0	800	1,600	2,400	3,200	3,200	4,000	4,000	4,800	5,600	6,400	7,200
44														

With this savings plan, the ending balance in the main savings account remains above $3,000 for most months of the year, and $800 is transferred from the main savings account into the home savings account in nine months of the year. Only in January, June, and August will Diane not transfer money into the home account. By the end of the year, the couple will have $5,350 in the main savings account and $7,200 in the home savings account.

Diane wants to explore what would happen if she increases the monthly transfer from $800 to $1,000. How would that affect the monthly balance of the main savings account?

To change the conditions of Diane's savings plan:

1. Change the value in cell L10 to **1000**. The end-of-year balance in the home savings account increases to $9,000 (cell L6) while the main savings account balance decreases to $3,550 (cell L5).

2. Scroll down the worksheet and examine how the monthly balance in the main savings account changes throughout the year. Under this revised plan, the balance in the main savings account drops to $1,775 in the month of August. This is a little too low for Diane.

3. Change the value in cell L10 to **900**. With this savings plan, the couple will save $8,100 toward a down payment on a home, and the balance in their main savings account will remain above $2,000 every month except January, when it dips to $1,940.

Diane feels that this revised savings plan is a good compromise between the need to save money for their future home while still maintaining a decent balance in their main savings account.

PROSKILLS

Decision Making: Using the IF Function to Explore Financial Options

Decision making is the process of choosing between possible courses of action. No decisions should be made until after the analysis of all potential alternatives is complete.

With financial decisions, you will often explore the impact of alternative scenarios on a projected outcome. Budget planning should not be limited to a single budget projection, but instead include several possible budgets. Your decision is then based on the evaluation of these different budgets. The budget you choose should prepare you to deal with shortages in future revenue or ways to take advantage of better-than-expected revenue.

Using Excel to manage your finances allows you to quickly explore these multiple scenarios. You can quickly examine how changing one or more values will affect such outcomes as income, expenses, and cash flow. You can use logical functions such as the IF function to help you explore these what-if scenarios because you can set the outcome of one value only if certain conditions are met. Different scenarios can be coded with names such as Option1, Option2, and Option 3. By using these scenario names as input values to an IF function, you can set up the worksheet to display the results specific to each scenario. In a well-designed workbook, you can quickly switch between scenarios simply by changing a few values in the worksheet.

By applying Excel's logical functions, you can more easily plan for different outcomes, and avoid the problems associated with unexpected occurences.

Working with Date Functions

To be effective, budgets need to be monitored and updated as conditions change. In the upcoming year, Diane plans to use this workbook to enter her and Glenn's actual salaries, expenses, and savings. This will enable Diane to track how well her projected values match the actual values. Because Diane will be updating the workbook throughout the year, she wants the worksheet to always display the current date so she can tell how far she is into her budget projections. You can accomplish this using a date function. Seven date functions supported by Excel are described in Figure 3-34. You can use these functions to help with scheduling or to determine on what days of the week certain dates occur.

Figure 3-34 | **Date and time functions**

Function	Description
DATE(*year, month, day*)	Creates a date value for the date represented by the *year*, *month*, and *day* arguments
DAY(*date*)	Extracts the day of the month from the *date* value
MONTH(*date*)	Extracts the month number from the *date* value where 1=January, 2=February, and so forth
YEAR(*date*)	Extracts the year number from the *date* value
WEEKDAY(*date*, [*return_type*])	Calculates the day of the week from the *date* value, where 1=Sunday, 2=Monday, and so forth; to choose a different numbering scheme, set the optional *return_type* value to "1" (1=Sunday, 2=Monday, ...), "2" (1=Monday, 2=Tuesday, ...), or "3" (0=Monday, 1=Tuesday, ...)
NOW( )	Displays the current date and time
TODAY( )	Displays the current date

TIP

If you don't want the date and time to change, you must enter the date and time value directly in the cell.

Perhaps the most commonly used date function is the TODAY function, which returns the current date. The syntax of the TODAY function is:

```
=TODAY()
```

The TODAY function doesn't have any arguments. Neither does the NOW function, which returns both the current date and the current time. The values returned by the TODAY and NOW functions are updated automatically whenever you reopen the workbook or enter a new calculation.

Diane wants the Budget worksheet to display the current date.

To display the current date:

1. In cell I1, enter the label **Current Date**.

2. Merge cells **I1** and **J1**, left-align the merged cell, and change the cell's fill color to **Tan, Background 2** (the third color in the first row of the Theme Colors section).

3. Click cell **K1**. You'll enter the TODAY function in this cell.

4. Click the **Formulas** tab on the Ribbon.

5. In the Function Library group, click the **Date & Time** button, and then click **TODAY** in the date functions list. The Function Arguments dialog box opens, with a description of the function and a reminder that there are no arguments for the TODAY function.

6. Click the **OK** button. The Function Arguments dialog box closes, and the =TODAY() function is inserted into cell L1.

7. Merge and center the range **K1:L1**, and then add a border around each of the cells in the range I1:L1.

8. Click cell **K1** to deselect the range. See Figure 3-35.

Figure 3-35   TODAY function displays the current date

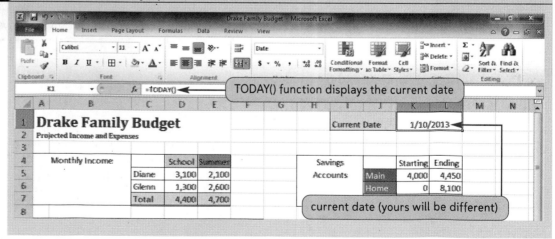

Working with Financial Functions

Excel provides a wide range of financial functions related to loans and interest payments. One of these is the PMT function, which can be used to calculate a payment schedule required to completely pay back a mortgage or loan. Figure 3-36 describes the PMT function and some of the other financial functions often used to develop budgets. These financial functions are the same as those widely used in business and accounting to perform various financial calculations, such as depreciation of an asset, the amount of interest paid on an investment, and the present value of an investment.

Figure 3-36	Financial functions for loans and investments

Function	Description
FV(rate, nper, pmt, [pv=0] [,type=0])	Calculates the future value of an investment, where *rate* is the interest rate per period, *nper* is the total number of periods, *pmt* is the payment in each period, *pv* is the present value of the investment, and *type* indicates whether payments should be made at the end of the period (0) or the beginning of the period (1)
PMT(rate, nper, pv, [fv=0] [,type=0])	Calculates the payments required each period on a loan or investment, where *fv* is the future value of the investment
IPMT(rate, per, nper, pv, [fv=0] [,type=0])	Calculates the amount of a loan payment devoted to paying the loan interest, where *per* is the number of the payment period
PPMT(rate, per, nper, pv, [fv=0] [,type=0])	Calculates the amount of a loan payment devoted to paying off the principal of a loan
PV(rate, nper, pmt, [fv=0] [,type=0])	Calculates the present value of a loan or investment based on periodic, constant payments
NPER(rate, pmt, pv, [fv=0] [,type=0])	Calculates the number of periods required to pay off a loan or investment
RATE(nper, pmt, pv, [fv=0] [,type=0])	Calculates the interest rate of a loan or investment based on periodic, constant payments

The cost of a loan to the borrower is largely based on three factors: the principal, the interest, and the time required to pay back the loan. **Principal** is the amount of money being loaned, and **interest** is the amount added to the principal by the lender. You can think of interest as a kind of "user fee" because the borrower is paying for the right to use the lender's money for a period of time. A few years ago, Diane and Glenn borrowed money to buy a second car and are still repaying the bank for the principal and interest on that loan. On the other hand, Diane and Glenn have also deposited money in their main savings account and receive interest payments from the bank in return.

Interest is calculated either as simple interest or as compound interest. In **simple interest**, the interest is equal to a percentage of principal for each period that the money has been lent. For example, if Diane and Glenn deposit $1,000 at a simple interest rate of 5 percent, they will receive $50 in interest payments each year. After one year their investment will be worth $1,050, after two years it will be worth $1,100, and so forth.

With **compound interest**, the interest is applied not only to the principal but also to any accrued interest. If Diane and Glenn deposit $1,000 in a bank at 5 percent annual interest compounded every year, they will earn $50 in the first year, raising the value of the account to $1,050. If they leave that money in the bank for another year, the interest payment in the second year rises to 5 percent of $1,050 or $52.50, resulting in a total value of $1,102.50. So they earn more money the second year because they are receiving interest on their interest.

Compound interest payments are divided into the period of time in which the interest is applied. For example, an 8 percent annual interest rate compounded monthly results in 12 interest payments per year with the interest each month equal to 1/12 of 8 percent, or about 0.67 percent per month.

Another factor in calculating the cost of a loan is the length of time required to pay it back. The longer it takes to pay back a loan, the more the loan costs because the borrower is paying interest over a longer period of time. To save money, loans should be paid back quickly and in full.

INSIGHT

Using Functions to Manage Personal Finances

Excel has many financial functions to manage personal finances. The following list can help you determine which function to use for the most common personal finance problems:

- To determine how much an investment will be worth after a series of monthly payments at some future time, use the FV (future value) function.
- To determine how much you have to spend each month to repay a loan or mortgage within a set period of time, use the PMT (payment) function.
- To determine how much of your monthly loan payment is used to pay the interest, use the IPMT (interest payment) function.
- To determine how much of your monthly loan payment is used for repaying the principal, use the PPMT (principal payment) function.
- To determine the largest loan or mortgage you can afford given a set monthly payment, use the PV (present value) function.
- To determine how long it will take to pay off a loan with constant monthly payments, use the NPER (number of periods) function.

For most loan and investment calculations, you need to enter the annual interest rate divided by the number of times the interest is compounded during the year. If interest is compounded monthly, divide the annual interest rate by 12; if interest is compounded quarterly, divide the annual rate by 4. You must also convert the length of the loan or investment to the number of interest payments per year. If you will make payments monthly, multiply the number of years of the loan or investment by 12.

Using the PMT Function

Diane and Glenn plan to purchase a house in the next several years. Diane wants to know how large of a mortgage she and Glenn could afford given their current income and expenses. To calculate the costs associated with a loan or mortgage, you need the following information:

- The amount being borrowed
- The annual interest rate
- The number of payment periods per year
- When loan payments are due
- The length of the loan in terms of the number of payment periods

In Diane and Glenn's neighborhood, starter homes are selling for about $240,000. If Diane and Glenn can keep to their savings plan, they will have saved $8,100 by the end of the year (as shown in cell L6 in the Budget worksheet). If they save this same amount for the next three years, they will have $24,300 in their home savings account to put toward the down payment. Based on this, Diane estimates that she and Glenn will need a home loan of almost $215,000.

Diane wants to know how much a mortgage of this size would cost in monthly payments. To determine this, you'll use the PMT function, which has the syntax

```
PMT(rate, nper, pv, [fv=0] [type=0])
```

where *rate* is the interest rate for each payment period, *nper* is the total number of payment periods required to pay off the loan, and *pv* is the present value of the loan or the amount that needs to be borrowed. For Diane and Glenn, the present value of the proposed loan is $215,000.

The PMT function has two optional arguments: *fv* and *type*. The *fv* argument is the future value of the loan. Because the intent with most loans is to pay them off completely, the future value is equal to 0 by default. The *type* argument specifies when the interest is charged on the loan, either at the end of the payment period (*type=0*), which is the default, or at the beginning of the payment period (*type=1*).

For most mortgages, the payment period is one month. This means that Diane and Glenn must make a payment on the loan every month, and interest on the loan is compounded every month. The annual interest rate on home loans in Diane and Glenn's area is 6.0 percent. To determine the interest rate per month, you divide the annual interest rate by 12. For Diane and Glenn, the interest rate each month is 6 percent divided by 12, or about 0.5 percent per month.

Diane and Glenn want to pay off their home loan in 20 years, or 240 months (20 years multiplied by 12 months per year). Putting all of this information together, you can calculate the monthly payment for the couple's home loan with the following formula:

```
=PMT(0.06/12, 20*12, 215000)
```

This formula returns a value of –$1,540.33. The value is negative because the payment is considered an expense, which Excel treats as a negative value. If you want to display this value as a positive number in a worksheet, enter a minus sign directly before the PMT function as follows:

```
=-PMT(0.06/12, 20*12, 215000)
```

Based on these calculations, Diane and Glenn would have to pay the bank $1,540.33 every month for 20 years before the loan and the interest are completely paid. Right now, the couple is spending about $1,050 per month on rent. So this home loan would be a significant increase over their current expenses.

Diane wants you to calculate the monthly payment for a home loan under other possible scenarios. You'll start by examining the costs associated with a $200,000 loan.

To create a loan payment worksheet:

1. Go to the **Loan Analysis** worksheet. You will do the loan calculations in this worksheet.

2. In cell B3, enter **6.00%**. This is the annual interest rate for the loan.

3. In cell B4, enter **12** for the number of payments per year.

4. In cell B5, enter the formula **=B3/B4** to calculate the interest per period, which is 0.50% per month.

5. In cell B6, enter **20** for the length of the mortgage in years.

6. In cell B7, enter the formula **=B4*B6** to calculate the total number of monthly payments, which is 240.

7. In cell B8, enter **$200,000** for the amount of the loan. All the values for the loan are entered.

The Loan Analysis worksheet includes all the data you need to calculate the monthly payment required to pay off the mortgage in 20 years at 6 percent interest compounded monthly. You will enter the PMT function to calculate this value.

To use the PMT function to calculate the monthly payment:

1. Click cell **B10** to select it.

2. In the Function Library group on the Formulas tab, click the **Financial** button, and then click **PMT** in the list of financial functions. The Function Arguments dialog box opens.

3. In the Rate box, enter the cell reference **B5**, which is the cell with the interest rate per month.

4. In the Nper box, enter the cell reference **B7**, which is the cell with the total number of monthly payments required to pay back the loan.

5. In the Pv box, enter the cell reference **B8**, which is the cell with the present value of the loan. See Figure 3-37.

TIP

Be sure to enter the interest rate per month for the Rate argument and not the annual interest rate for any loan or investment that has monthly payments.

| Figure 3-37 | Function Arguments dialog box for the PMT function |

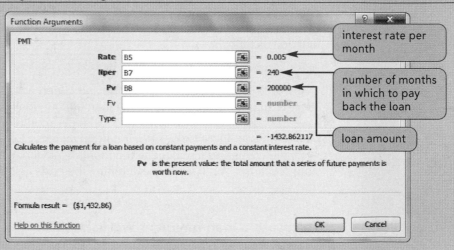

6. Click the **OK** button. The value $1,432.86 is displayed in parentheses in cell B10 to indicate a negative currency value. See Figure 3-38.

Figure 3-38 | Money payments to pay back a $200,000 loan

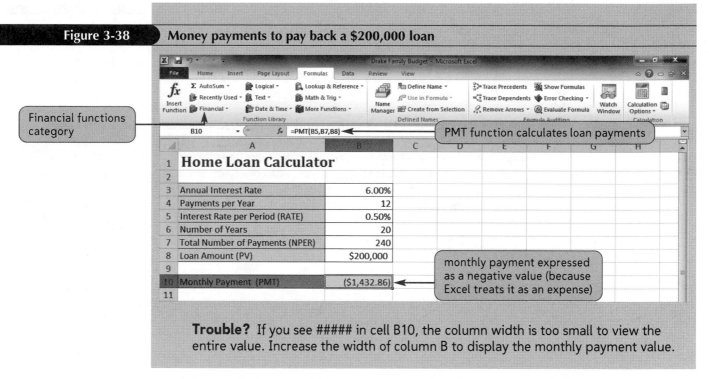

Financial functions category

B10 · =PMT(B5,B7,B8) ◄ **PMT function calculates loan payments**

	A	B
1	**Home Loan Calculator**	
2		
3	Annual Interest Rate	6.00%
4	Payments per Year	12
5	Interest Rate per Period (RATE)	0.50%
6	Number of Years	20
7	Total Number of Payments (NPER)	240
8	Loan Amount (PV)	$200,000
9		
10	Monthly Payment (PMT)	($1,432.86)
11		

monthly payment expressed as a negative value (because Excel treats it as an expense)

Trouble? If you see ##### in cell B10, the column width is too small to view the entire value. Increase the width of column B to display the monthly payment value.

Diane and Glenn would have to pay more than $1,400 per month for 20 years to repay a $200,000 loan at 6 percent interest. This is still too high. Diane is interested in other possibilities. Because you already set up the worksheet, you can quickly try other scenarios without having to reenter any formulas. Diane wonders whether extending the length of the loan would reduce the monthly payment by a sizeable margin. She asks you to calculate the monthly payment for different loan options.

To analyze other loan options:

1. Change the value in cell B6 to **30**. The amount of the monthly payment drops to $1,199.10, which is a decrease of $200 per month.

2. Change the value of cell B8 to **175,000**. For this smaller home loan, the monthly payment drops even further to $1,049.21 per month. This is almost exactly equal to what the couple is currently paying in rent.

3. Save the workbook, and then close it.

You've completed your work on Diane and Glenn's budget. Your analysis has shown Diane several important things. Her projected budget allows the couple to transfer enough money to the home savings account to make a down payment on a home in about three years. This savings plan leaves enough funds in the main savings account to cover their monthly expenses. Finally, the possible monthly mortgage payments for a loan will not be substantially more than what Diane and Glenn are currently paying in rent. So, not only will Diane and Glenn be able to save enough to make the initial down payment, their monthly income should also cover the monthly payments. Of course, all budgets must be revised periodically to meet changing expenses and income, and many different options exist in the home mortgage market. For example, Diane and Glenn could receive a mortgage with a lower interest rate or one that requires a smaller down payment. Your work has given Diane and Glenn enough information to make informed choices about their immediate financial future.

PROSKILLS

Written Communication: Presenting a Budget

In business, government, and personal lives, budgets play a key role in making sound financial decisions. However, a well-organized budget is only the first step. The budget must also convey information that is easily grasped by your audience or clients. Keep in mind the following guidelines as you work on budget spreadsheets:

- **Plan the budget around a few essential goals.** What is your budget trying to achieve? Be specific and focused.
- **Pick out a few important measures or "bottom lines" that can convey whether the proposed budget will meet your goals.** Are you trying to pay off a debt, raise money, or achieve a specific level of savings?
- **Look at your financial history to aid you in creating budget projections.** Search for important trends and take into account other factors such as inflation in your projections.
- **When explaining the budget, describe the results in terms of everyday examples.** Avoid the temptation of overwhelming your audience with raw facts and figures; rather, interpret what those facts and figures mean in terms of your bottom line measures.

You want your budget spreadsheet to remain current as new data and projections become available. This means continually updating the budget. But, do not just overwrite or delete the old budget spreadsheets. Keep earlier budgets easily accessible so you can access the original assumptions and goals when preparing the next budget. By keeping an audit trail of your past work, you can make your future budgets more accurate and reliable.

Session 3.2 Quick Check

REVIEW

1. How do you use AutoFill to copy a set of cell values, but not the formatting?
2. If the first three selected values in a series are 3, 6, and 9, what are the next three values that will be inserted using AutoFill?
3. If cell P5 contains the text "Mon," and then you select the cell and drag the fill handle over the range P6:P8, what text will be entered into those cells?
4. If cell Q3 is greater than cell Q4, you want to display "OK"; otherwise, you want to display "RETRY". Write the formula that accomplishes this.
5. Write the formula to display the current date.
6. Write the formula to display the current date and time.
7. You want to take out a loan for $130,000. The interest on the loan is 5 percent compounded monthly. You intend to pay back the loan in 20 years. Write the formula to calculate the monthly payment required to pay off the loan under those conditions.
8. What financial function do you use to determine how many payment periods are required to pay off a loan?

Practice the skills you learned in the tutorial using the same case scenario.

PRACTICE

Review Assignments

Data File needed for the Review Assignments: Timov.xlsx

Sergei and Ava Timov, friends of Diane and Glenn, ask you to create a similar workbook for their family budget. The Timovs want to purchase a new home. They are considering two houses with different mortgages. They want the budget worksheet you create to display the impact of monthly mortgage payments on the couple's cash flow. They also want to be able to quickly switch between one mortgage plan and another to observe the impact of each plan on their budget. The couple has already designed the workbook and entered estimates of their income and expenses for the upcoming year. You need to set up the formulas. Complete the following:

1. Open the **Timov** workbook located in the Excel3\Review folder included with your Data Files, and then save the workbook as **Timov Family Budget**.

2. In the Documentation sheet, enter your name in cell B3. Use the TODAY function to display the current date in cell B4.

3. In the Family Budget worksheet, in the range C18:N18, use AutoFill to replace the month numbers with the abbreviations **Jan** through **Dec**.

4. In the range C21:N21, calculate the couple's total income. In the range C27:N27, calculate the couple's total monthly expenses. In the range C28:N28, calculate the monthly net cash flow (equal to the total income minus the total expenses).

5. In cell C7, enter a formula to calculate the sum of Sergei's monthly income for the entire year. In cell D7, calculate Sergei's average monthly income. In cell E7, calculate Sergei's maximum monthly income. In cell F7, calculate Sergei's minimum monthly income.

6. Complete the Year-End Summary table by first selecting the range C7:F7. Use AutoFill to copy the formula in the range C7:F7 into the range C7:F16. Use the Auto Fill Options button to copy only the formulas into the selected range and not both the formulas and the formats. (*Hint*: Because you haven't yet entered any mortgage payment values, cell D14 will show the value #DIV/0!, indicating that Excel cannot calculate the average mortgage payment. You'll correct that problem shortly.)

7. In the range K2:K7, enter the following loan and loan conditions of the first mortgage:

   a. In cell K2, enter **6.7%** as the annual interest rate.

   b. In cell K3, enter **12** as the number of payments per year.

   c. In cell K4, calculate the monthly interest rate.

   d. In cell K5, enter **30** as the number of years in the mortgage.

   e. In cell K6, calculate the total number of months to repay the loan.

   f. In cell K7, enter **395,000** as the loan amount.

8. In cell K8, use the PMT function to calculate the monthly payment required to repay this loan.

9. Edit the formula in cell K8, adding a minus sign directly before the PMT function to make the value returned by the formula positive rather than negative.

10. In the range K10:K15, enter the following conditions of the second mortgage plan, and calculate the monthly interest rate and the total number of months to repay the loan:

    • The annual interest rate is **6.7%**.

    • The interest rate is compounded **12** times a year (or monthly).

    • The mortgage will last **20** years.

    • The loan amount (or value of the principal) is **$300,000**.

11. In cell K16, enter the PMT function to calculate the monthly payment needed to pay off this loan, and then edit the formula to make the value displayed in the cell positive by placing a negative sign in front of the PMT function.

12. Sergei and Ava want to be able to view their monthly cash flow under both mortgage plans. The mortgage being applied to the budget will be determined by whether 1 or 2 is entered into cell E3. To switch from one mortgage to another, do the following:

    a. In cell C26, enter an IF function that tests whether cell E3 equals 1. If it does, return the value of cell K8; otherwise, return the value of cell K16. Use absolute cell references for all references in the formula.

    b. Use AutoFill to copy the formula in cell C26 into the range D26:N26.

    c. Verify that the values in the range C26:N26 match the monthly payment for the first mortgage condition. (Note that the worksheet will display the monthly payment amount to the nearest dollar.)

13. In cell E3, change the value from 1 to **2**. Verify that the monthly payment for the second mortgage appears in the range C26:N26.

14. Sergei and Ava want to maintain an average net cash flow of at least $1,000 per month. Is this achieved on either mortgage plan?

15. Save and close the workbook, and then submit the finished workbook to your instructor, either in printed or electronic form, as requested.

Case Problem 1

APPLY

Data File needed for this Case Problem: Chemistry.xlsx

Chemistry 303 Karen Raul is a professor of chemistry at a community college in Shawnee, Kansas. She has started using Excel to calculate the final grade for students in her Chemistry 303 course. The final score is a weighted average of the scores given for three exams and the final exam. One way to calculate a weighted average is by multiplying each student's exam score by the weight given to the exam, and then totaling the results. For example, consider the following four exam scores:

Exam 1 = 84   Exam 2 = 80   Exam 3 = 83   Final Exam = 72

If the first three exams are each given a weight of 20 percent and the final exam is given a weight of 40 percent, the weighted average of the four scores is:

84*0.2 + 80*0.2 + 83*0.2 + 72*0.4 = 78.2

Karen has already entered the scores for her students and formatted much of the workbook. You will enter the formulas and highlight the top 10 overall scores in her class. Complete the following:

1. Open the **Chemistry** workbook located in the Excel3\Case1 folder included with your Data Files, and then save the workbook as **Chemistry 303 Final Scores**.

2. In the Documentation sheet, enter your name in cell B3 and the date in cell B4.

3. In the First Semester Scores worksheet, in cell F17, enter a formula to calculate the weighted average of the first student's four exams. Use the weights found in the range C8:C11, matching each weight with the corresponding exam score. Use absolute cell references for the four weights.

4. Use AutoFill to copy the formula in cell F17 into the range F18:F52.

5. In cell B5, use the COUNT function to calculate the total number of students in the class.

6. In cell D8, calculate the median score for the first exam.

7. In cell E8, calculate the maximum score for the first exam.

8. In cell F8, calculate the minimum score for the first exam.

9. In cell G8, calculate the range of scores for the first exam, which is equal to the difference between the maximum and minimum score.

10. Repeat Steps 6 through 9 for each of the other two exams, the final exam, and the overall weighted score.

11. Use conditional formatting to highlight the top 10 scores in the range F17:F52 in a light red fill with dark red text.

12. Insert a page break at cell A14, repeat the first three rows of the worksheet in any printout, and verify that the worksheet is in portrait orientation.

13. Save and close the workbook, and then submit the finished workbook to your instructor, either in printed or electronic form, as requested.

Use formulas and functions to create an order form for a fireworks company.

APPLY

Case Problem 2

Data File needed for this Case Problem: Wizard.xlsx

WizardWorks   Andrew Howe owns and operates WizardWorks, an online seller of fireworks based in Franklin, Tennessee. Andrew wants you to help him develop an order form for his business. The form needs to contain formulas to calculate the charge for each order. The total charge is based on the quantity and type of items ordered plus the shipping charge and the 5 percent sales tax. Orders can be shipped using standard 3- to 5-day shipping for $3.99 or overnight for $10.99. Andrew is also offering a 4 percent discount for orders that exceed $200. Both the shipping option and the discount need to be calculated using formulas based on values entered into the worksheet. Complete the following:

1. Open the **Wizard** workbook located in the Excel3\Case2 folder included with your Data Files, and then save the workbook as **WizardWorks Order Form**.

2. In the Documentation sheet, enter your name in cell B3 and enter the date in cell B4.

3. In the Order Form worksheet, in cell C4, enter the customer name, **Kevin Kemper**. In cell C6, enter the order number, **28314**. In the range C9:C13, enter the following address:

Address 1:   **315 Avalon Street**
City: **Greenfield**
State: **IN**
Zip: **46140**

4. In cell C5, enter a function that displays the current date.

5. In the range B20:E22, enter the following orders:

Item	Name	Price	Qty
BF001	**Bucket of Fireworks**	**$45.75**	**1**
NAF	**Nightair Fountain**	**$12.95**	**4**
MR20B	**Mountain Rockets (Box 20)**	**$55.25**	**2**

6. In cell C15, enter **overnight** to ship this order overnight.

⊕ EXPLORE

7. In cell F20, enter an IF function that tests whether the order quantity in cell E20 is greater than 0 (zero). If it is, return the value of cell E20 multiplied by cell D20; otherwise, return no text by entering **""**. AutoFill this formula into the range F21:F25.

8. In cell F27, calculate the sum of the values in the range F20:F25.

9. In cell F28, enter an IF function that tests whether cell F27 is greater than 200. If it is, return the value of cell F27 multiplied by the discount percentage in cell F12; otherwise, return the value 0 (zero).

10. In cell F29, subtract the discount value in cell F28 from the subtotal value in cell F27.

11. In cell F31, calculate the sales tax by multiplying the after discount value in cell F29 by the sales tax percentage, 0.05.

⊕ **EXPLORE**

12. In cell F32, determine the shipping charge by entering an IF function that tests whether cell C15 equals "standard". If it does, return the value in cell F9; otherwise, return the value in cell F10.

13. In cell G32, display the value of cell C15.

14. In cell F34, calculate the total of the after discount value, the sales tax, and the shipping fee.

15. Reduce the quantity of Mountain Rockets boxes from 2 to **1**, and then verify that the discount is changed to 0 for the order.

16. Change the shipping option from overnight to **standard**, and then verify that the shipping fee is changed to the fee for standard shipping.

17. Save and close the workbook, and then submit the finished workbook to your instructor, either in printed or electronic form, as requested.

Explore how to use relative and absolute references and the PMT function to create a loan table.

CHALLENGE

Case Problem 3

Data File needed for this Case Problem: Loan.xlsx

Eason Financial Services Jesse Buchmann is a finance officer at Eason Financial Services in Meridian, Idaho. She works with people who are looking for home mortgages. Most clients want mortgages they can afford, and affordability is determined by the size of the monthly payment. The monthly payment is determined by the interest rate, the total number of payments, and the size of the home loan. Jesse can't change the interest rate, but homebuyers can reduce their monthly payments by increasing the number of years to repay the loan. Jesse wants to give her clients a grid that displays combinations of loan amounts and payment periods so that they can select a loan that best meets their needs and budget. Jesse already entered much of the layout and formatting for the worksheet containing the loan payment grid. You will enter the PMT function. Complete the following:

1. Open the **Loan** workbook located in the Excel3\Case3 folder included with your Data Files, and then save the workbook as **Loan Grid**.

2. In the Documentation sheet, enter your name and the date.

3. In the Loan Calculation worksheet, in cell E3, enter a monthly payment of **$1,750**.

4. In cell E5, enter the annual interest rate of **5.75%**. In cell E6, enter **12** to indicate that the interest payment is compounded 12 times a year, or monthly.

5. In the range C10:C20, use AutoFill to enter the currency values **$250,000** through **$350,000** in increments of $10,000. In the range D9:H9, use AutoFill to enter the year values **15** through **35** in increments of 5 years.

⊕ **EXPLORE**

6. In cell D10, use the PMT function to calculate the monthly payment required to repay a **$250,000** loan in **15** years at **5.75%** interest compounded monthly. Use absolute references to cells E5 and E6 to enter the annual interest rate and number of payments per year. Use the mixed references D$9 and $C10 to cells D9 and C10, respectively, to reference the number of years to repay the loan and the loan amount. Place a minus sign before the PMT function so that the value returned by the function is positive rather than negative.

⊕ **EXPLORE**

7. Using AutoFill, copy the formula in cell D10 into the range E10:H10, and then copy that range of formulas into the range D11:H20.

⊕ **EXPLORE**

8. Conditionally format the range D10:H20 to highlight all of the values in the range that are less than the value in cell E3 in a dark green font on a green fill.

9. Add a second conditional format to the range D10:H20 to highlight all of the values in the range that are greater than the value in cell E3 in a dark red font on a red fill.

✛EXPLORE 10. Change the value in cell E3 from $1,750 to **$1,800**. If this represents the maximum affordable monthly payment, use the values in the grid to determine the largest mortgage for payment schedules lasting 15 through 35 years. Can any of the home loan values displayed in the grid be repaid in 20 years at $1,800 per month?

11. Save and close the workbook, and then submit the finished workbook to your instructor, either in printed or electronic form, as requested.

Create a workbook that automatically grades a driving exam.

CREATE

Case Problem 4

Data File needed for this Case Problem: V6.xlsx

V-6 Driving Academy   Sebastian Villanueva owns and operates the V-6 Driving Academy, a driving school located in Pine Hills, Florida. In addition to driving, students must take multiple-choice tests offered by the Florida Department of Motor Vehicles. Students must answer at least 80 percent of the questions correctly to pass each test. Sebastian has to grade these tests himself. Sebastian could save a lot of time if the test questions were in a workbook and Excel totaled the test results. Sebastian has already entered a 20-question test into a workbook. You will format this workbook and insert the necessary functions and formulas to grade a student's answers. Complete the following:

1. Open the **V6** workbook located in the Excel3\Case4 folder included with your Data Files, and then save the workbook as **V6 Driving Test**.

2. In the Documentation sheet, enter your name in cell B3 and enter the date in cell B4.

3. In the Exam1 worksheet, format the questions and possible answers so that the worksheet is easy to read. The format is up to you. At the top of the worksheet, enter a title that describes the exam, and then enter a function that returns the current date.

4. Add a section somewhere on the Exam1 worksheet where Sebastian can enter each student's name and answers to each question. Design the workbook so that Sebastian can always go back and review any student's completed exam.

5. The answers for the 20 questions are listed below. Use this information to write functions that will grade each answer, giving 1 point for a correct answer and 0 otherwise. Assume that all answers are in lowercase letters; therefore, the function that tests the answer to the first question should check for a "c" rather than a "C".

Question	Answer	Question	Answer	Question	Answer
1	c	8	a	15	b
2	a	9	c	16	b
3	b	10	b	17	b
4	a	11	c	18	b
5	c	12	b	19	b
6	b	13	b	20	c
7	c	14	a		

6. At the top of the worksheet, insert a formula to calculate the total number of correct answers for each student.

7. Insert another formula that divides the total number of correct answers by the total number of exam questions on the worksheet. Display this value as a percentage.

8. Enter a logical function that displays the message "PASS" on the exam if the percentage of correct answers is greater than or equal to 80 percent; otherwise, the logical function displays the message "FAIL".

9. Test your worksheet with the following student exams. Which students passed and which failed? What score did each student receive on the exam?

Juan Marquez

Question	Answer	Question	Answer	Question	Answer
1	a	8	a	15	b
2	b	9	c	16	b

Question	Answer	Question	Answer	Question	Answer
3	b	10	b	17	a
4	a	11	c	18	b
5	c	12	b	19	b
6	b	13	a	20	c
7	c	14	a		

Kurt Bessette

Question	Answer	Question	Answer	Question	Answer
1	a	8	a	15	c
2	a	9	b	16	b
3	b	10	c	17	a
4	a	11	c	18	b
5	c	12	a	19	a
6	b	13	b	20	c
7	c	14	a		

Rebecca Pena

Question	Answer	Question	Answer	Question	Answer
1	c	8	a	15	c
2	a	9	c	16	b
3	b	10	a	17	b
4	a	11	c	18	b
5	c	12	b	19	b
6	b	13	b	20	b
7	c	14	a		

10. Format the worksheet so that it prints nicely with no questions crossing over a page break, and the names of the students and the name of the driving academy at the top of each page.

11. Save and close the workbook, and then submit the finished workbook to your instructor, either in printed or electronic form, as requested.

SAM: Skills Assessment Manager

ASSESS

For current SAM information, including versions and content details, visit SAM Central (http://samcentral.course.com). If you have a SAM user profile, you may have access to hands-on instruction, practice, and assessment of the skills covered in this tutorial. Since various versions of SAM are supported throughout the life of this text, check with your instructor for the correct instructions and URL/Web site for accessing assignments.

ENDING DATA FILES

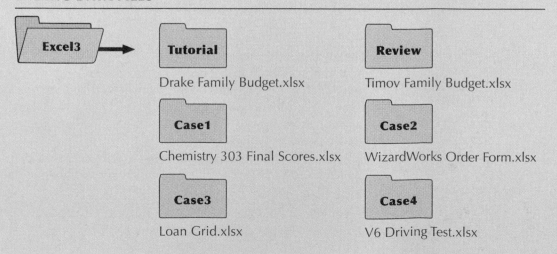

Excel3 → Tutorial

Drake Family Budget.xlsx

Review

Timov Family Budget.xlsx

Case1

Chemistry 303 Final Scores.xlsx

Case2

WizardWorks Order Form.xlsx

Case3

Loan Grid.xlsx

Case4

V6 Driving Test.xlsx

Enhancing a Workbook with Charts and Graphs

Charting Financial Data

EXCEL

OBJECTIVES

Session 4.1
- Create an embedded chart
- Create and format a pie chart
- Work with chart titles and legends
- Create and format a column chart

Session 4.2
- Create and format a line chart
- Modify a chart data source
- Create and format a combined chart
- Create a 3-D chart
- Create and format sparklines and data bars
- Create a chart sheet

Case | *Seaborg Group*

Ajita Gupte is a financial assistant for the Seaborg Group, a financial consulting agency located in Providence, Rhode Island. One of her duties is to prepare financial reports on the investments the Seaborg Group makes for its clients. These reports go into a binder containing the financial status of each client's different investments. The client receives the binder at annual meetings with his or her financial advisor, and receives updates on the status of the investments periodically throughout the year.

Many of the company's clients invest in the New Century Fund, a large growth/large risk mutual fund that has been operating for the past 10 years. Ajita needs to create a report that summarizes the fund's financial holdings as well as its 10-year performance record. She already entered the financial data into an Excel workbook, but needs help finishing the report. Because many clients are overwhelmed by tables of numbers, Ajita wants to include charts and graphs in the report that display the current and past performance of the New Century Fund. You will help Ajita to create these charts.

STARTING DATA FILES

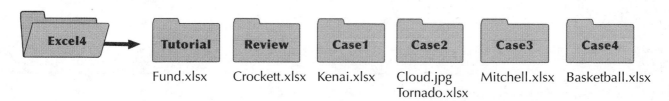

Excel4 →	Tutorial	Review	Case1	Case2	Case3	Case4
	Fund.xlsx	Crockett.xlsx	Kenai.xlsx	Cloud.jpg Tornado.xlsx	Mitchell.xlsx	Basketball.xlsx

SESSION 4.1 VISUAL OVERVIEW

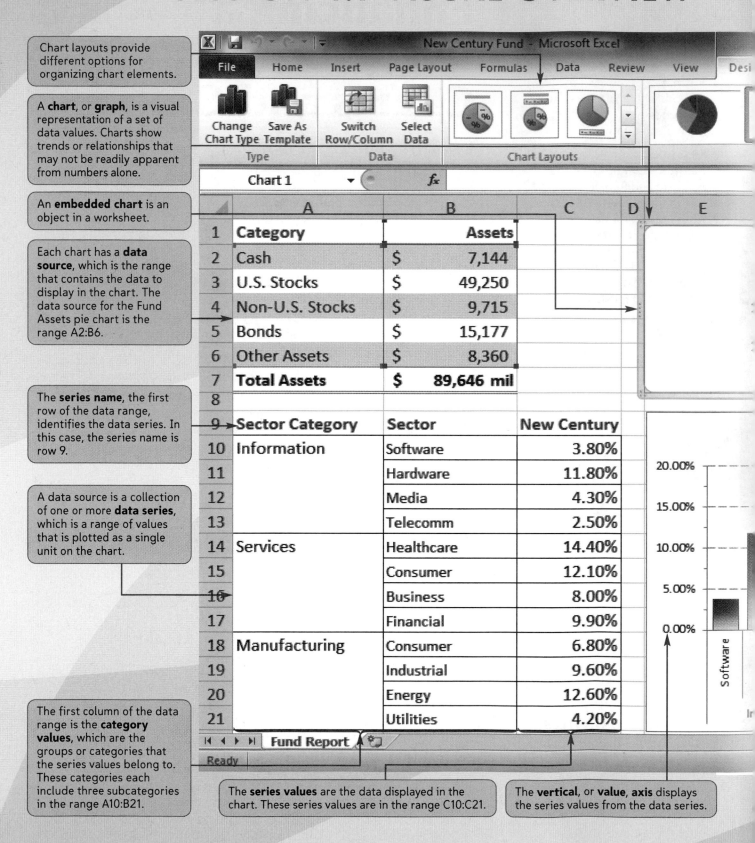

Chart layouts provide different options for organizing chart elements.

A **chart**, or **graph**, is a visual representation of a set of data values. Charts show trends or relationships that may not be readily apparent from numbers alone.

An **embedded chart** is an object in a worksheet.

Each chart has a **data source**, which is the range that contains the data to display in the chart. The data source for the Fund Assets pie chart is the range A2:B6.

The **series name**, the first row of the data range, identifies the data series. In this case, the series name is row 9.

A data source is a collection of one or more **data series**, which is a range of values that is plotted as a single unit on the chart.

The first column of the data range is the **category values**, which are the groups or categories that the series values belong to. These categories each include three subcategories in the range A10:B21.

The **series values** are the data displayed in the chart. These series values are in the range C10:C21.

The **vertical**, or **value**, **axis** displays the series values from the data series.

New Century Fund - Microsoft Excel

File   Home   Insert   Page Layout   Formulas   Data   Review   View   Desi

Change Chart Type   Save As Template   Switch Row/Column   Select Data

Type   Data   Chart Layouts

Chart 1

	A	B	C	D	E
1	**Category**	**Assets**			
2	Cash	$ 7,144			
3	U.S. Stocks	$ 49,250			
4	Non-U.S. Stocks	$ 9,715			
5	Bonds	$ 15,177			
6	Other Assets	$ 8,360			
7	**Total Assets**	**$ 89,646 mil**			
8					
9	**Sector Category**	**Sector**	**New Century**		
10	Information	Software	3.80%		
11		Hardware	11.80%		
12		Media	4.30%		
13		Telecomm	2.50%		
14	Services	Healthcare	14.40%		
15		Consumer	12.10%		
16		Business	8.00%		
17		Financial	9.90%		
18	Manufacturing	Consumer	6.80%		
19		Industrial	9.60%		
20		Energy	12.60%		
21		Utilities	4.20%		

20.00%
15.00%
10.00%
5.00%
0.00%

Software

Fund Report

Ready

CHART ELEMENTS

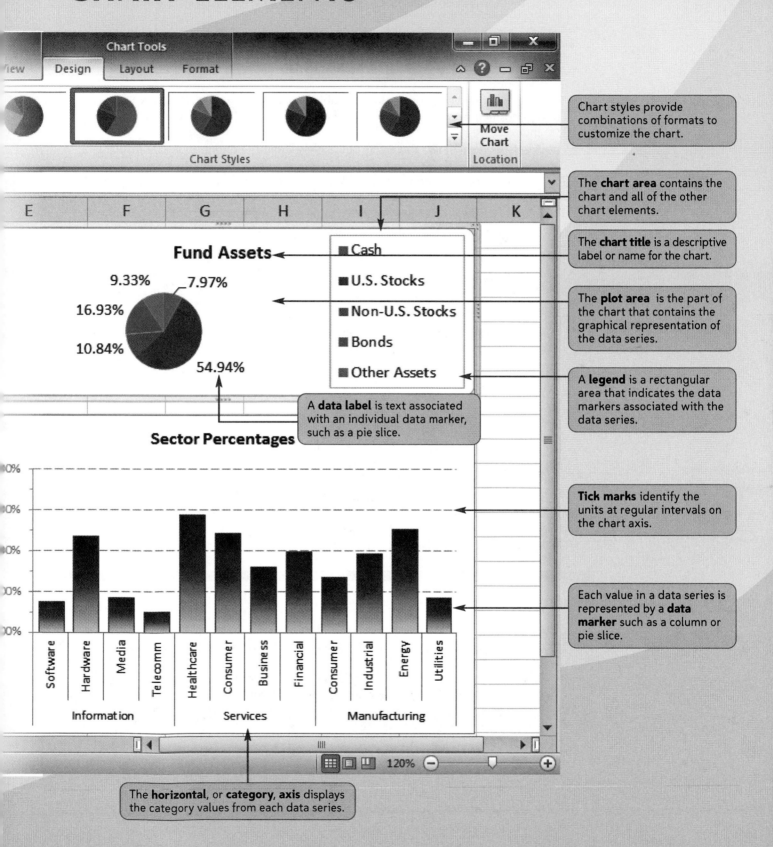

Chart styles provide combinations of formats to customize the chart.

The **chart area** contains the chart and all of the other chart elements.

The **chart title** is a descriptive label or name for the chart.

The **plot area** is the part of the chart that contains the graphical representation of the data series.

A **legend** is a rectangular area that indicates the data markers associated with the data series.

A **data label** is text associated with an individual data marker, such as a pie slice.

Tick marks identify the units at regular intervals on the chart axis.

Each value in a data series is represented by a **data marker** such as a column or pie slice.

The **horizontal**, or **category**, **axis** displays the category values from each data series.

Creating an Excel Chart

Ajita already created a workbook in which she entered and formatted data that describes the New Century Fund. In addition to the Documentation sheet, the New Century Fund workbook contains the following five worksheets:

- The Summary Report worksheet includes summary data and facts about the New Century Fund.
- The Fund History worksheet provides a table that shows how well the New Century Fund performed over the past 10 years compared to a similar fund and the S&P 500 index.
- The Assets worksheet lists the assets of the New Century Fund grouped by investment categories.
- The Sectors worksheet shows the economic sectors in which the New Century Fund invests.
- The Sector History worksheet provides a table showing how each of the economic sectors in the New Century Fund has performed in the last 10 years.

You'll begin by opening this workbook and reviewing its contents.

To open and review Ajita's workbook:

1. Open the **Fund** workbook located in the **Excel4\Tutorial** folder included with your Data Files, and then save the workbook as **New Century Fund** in the same folder.

2. In the Documentation sheet, enter your name in cell B3 and the date in cell B4.

3. Take some time to review the contents of the workbook.

Charts show trends or relationships in data that are more difficult to see by simply looking at numbers, such as the range of months in which the New Century Fund performed exceptionally well. Ajita wants financial data from the Fund History, Assets, and Sectors worksheets displayed in the Summary Report worksheet as charts, or graphs. In the summary report, she wants one chart that shows the performance of the New Century Fund compared to two similar funds, and she wants two charts that show how money in the New Century Fund is currently invested. The final Summary Report worksheet will be a single page that includes all of the information Ajita wants her clients to see.

REFERENCE

Inserting a Chart

- Select the data source with the range of data you want to chart.
- In the Charts group on the Insert tab, click a chart type, and then click a chart subtype in the Chart gallery.
- In the Location group on the Chart Tools Design tab, click the Move Chart button to place the chart in a chart sheet or embed it into a worksheet.

Selecting a Data Source

Each chart has a data source. After you select a range to use as the chart's data source, Excel uses the first row of the selected range as the series name, the first column as the category values, and the remaining columns as the series values. If the data source is organized in rows rather than in columns, the first row contains the category values, the remaining rows contain the data values for each data series, and the first column of each series row contains the series names.

The first chart you will create is based on data in the Assets worksheet that indicates how the New Century Fund's holdings are divided among different investment categories. The data source you will select has only one data series that shows the assets for five investment categories.

To select the data source for the assets chart:

▶ **1.** Click the **Assets** sheet tab to make the Assets worksheet active.

▶ **2.** Select the range **A3:B8**. The data source in this range has one data series, named Assets. Its category values in the range A4:A8 list the different asset categories, and its series values in the range B4:B8 contain the data to be charted. See Figure 4-1.

Figure 4-1   Data source selected for the assets chart

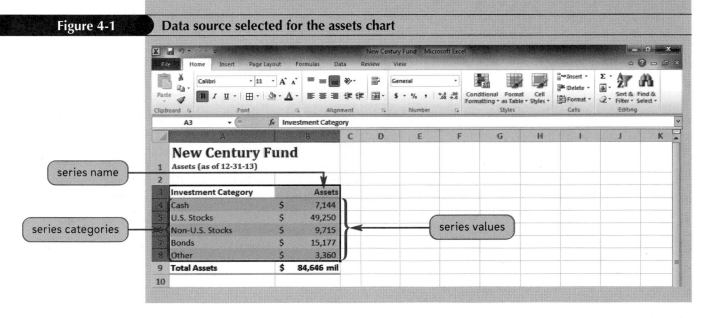

Selecting a Chart Type

You can apply a wide variety of chart types to the selected data source. Excel supports 73 built-in charts organized into 11 categories, which are described in Figure 4-2. You can also create custom chart types based on the built-in charts.

Figure 4-2   **Excel chart types**

Chart Type	Description
Column	Compares values from different categories. Values are indicated by the height of the columns.
Line	Compares values from different categories. Values are indicated by the height of the line. Often used to show trends and changes over time.
Pie	Compares relative values of different categories to the whole. Values are indicated by the areas of the pie slices.
Bar	Compares values from different categories. Values are indicated by the length of the bars.
Area	Compares values from different categories. Similar to the line chart except that areas under the lines contain a fill color.
Scatter	Shows the patterns or relationship between two or more sets of values. Often used in scientific studies and statistical analyses.
Stock	Displays stock market data, including the high, low, opening, and closing prices of a stock.
Surface	Compares three sets of values in a three-dimensional chart.
Doughnut	Compares relative values of different categories to the whole. Similar to the pie chart except that it can display multiple sets of data.
Bubble	Shows the patterns or relationship between two or more sets of values. Similar to the XY (Scatter) chart except the size of the data marker is determined by a third value.
Radar	Compares a collection of values from several different data sets.

You should select the type of chart that best represents the data. For example, a pie chart provides the best way to show the breakout of the asset data you selected. A **pie chart** is a chart in the shape of a circle (like a pie) that shows data values as a percentage of the whole. Each value in the data series represents a slice of the pie. The larger the value, the larger the pie slice. For the asset data, each slice will represent the percentage of the total assets from each investment category in the New Century Fund.

Pie charts are most effective with six or fewer slices, and when each slice is large enough to view. The pie chart of the asset data will have five large slices, representing the five asset categories—Cash, U.S. Stocks, Non-U.S. Stocks, Bonds, and Other. The Total Assets row, which you did not select as part of the data source, is not an asset category and should not be included in a pie chart.

TIP

The data source for a pie chart should include only the category labels and data values and not row or column totals because Excel will treat those totals as another category to be graphed.

To insert a pie chart:

1. Click the **Insert** tab on the Ribbon. The Ribbon displays the insert options.

2. In the Charts group, click the **Pie** button. The Pie Charts gallery opens.

3. In the 2-D Pie section, click **Pie** (the first pie chart in the first row). The pie chart is inserted in the Assets sheet, and three new tabs appear on the Ribbon with a label identifying them as Chart Tools contextual tabs. See Figure 4-3.

Figure 4-3   **Pie chart inserted into the Assets sheet**

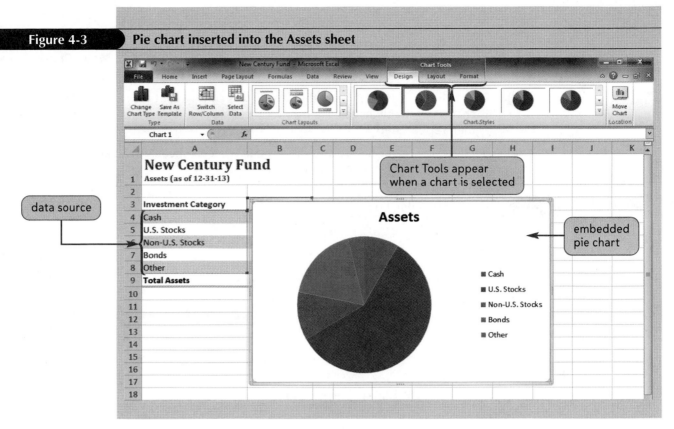

Each slice in the pie chart you just created is a different size based on its value in the data series. The biggest slice of the pie represents U.S. Stocks, which is the category that has the largest value in the data series. The smallest slice of the pie represents the Other category, which has the smallest value in the data series.

When you create or select a chart, three Chart Tools contextual tabs appear on the Ribbon. The Design, Layout, and Format tabs provide additional commands for working with the chart's content and appearance. On the Design tab, you set the chart's overall design. On the Layout tab, you work with individual elements of the chart, such as the chart's title. On the Format tab, you format graphic shapes found in the chart, such as the chart's border or markers placed in the chart. When you select a worksheet cell or another object that is not a chart, the Chart Tools contextual tabs disappear until you reselect the chart.

Moving a Chart to a Different Worksheet

By default, a chart is inserted as an embedded chart. The advantage of an embedded chart is that you can display the chart alongside any text or graphics that can explain the chart's meaning and purpose. However, an embedded chart covers worksheet cells, which might contain data and formulas. You'll learn how to move and resize an embedded chart in this section.

You can move an embedded chart to a different worksheet in the workbook or you can move it into a chart sheet (a sheet that contains only the chart and no worksheet cells). Likewise, you can move a chart from a chart sheet and embed it in any worksheet you select. The Move Chart dialog box provides options for moving charts between worksheets and chart sheets. You can also cut and paste a chart to a new location in the workbook.

The assets pie chart was embedded in the Assets worksheet by default. Ajita wants the chart embedded in the Summary Report worksheet. You will move the chart.

To move the embedded pie chart to the Summary Report worksheet:

▶ **1.** In the Location group on the Chart Tools Design tab, click the **Move Chart** button. The Move Chart dialog box opens.

    Trouble? If you don't see the Chart Tools contextual tabs on the Ribbon, the chart is probably not selected. Click the chart in the Assets sheet to select it, and then repeat Step 1.

▶ **2.** Click the **Object in** arrow to display a list of worksheets in the active workbook, and then click **Summary Report**. See Figure 4-4.

Figure 4-4	Move Chart dialog box

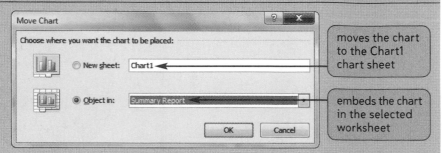

▶ **3.** Click the **OK** button. The embedded pie chart moves from the Assets worksheet to the Summary Report worksheet, and remains selected.

Moving and Resizing Charts

An embedded chart might cover other data in the worksheet or be placed in an awkward location. You can fix this by moving or resizing the embedded chart. To do so, first select the chart, which displays a **selection box**, which is a box surrounding the chart object that is used to move or resize the object. To move the chart, drag the selection box to a new location in the worksheet. To resize the chart, drag a **sizing handle**, which is a square or dot on the selection box that is used to change the object's width and height.

You will move and resize the assets pie chart so that it does not cover the data on the Summary Report worksheet.

To move and resize the assets pie chart:

Be sure to click the chart area; otherwise, elements in the chart might move.

▶ **1.** Move the pointer over an empty area of the selected chart until the pointer changes to ⁺ and the "Chart Area" ScreenTip appears.

▶ **2.** Drag the chart down and to the left until its upper-left corner is in cell **A13**, and then release the mouse button. The chart moves to a new location, but it still covers some data.

    Trouble? If the pie chart resizes or does not move to the new location, you probably didn't drag the chart from the chart area. Press the Ctrl+Z keys to undo your last action, and then repeat Steps 1 and 2, being sure to drag the pie chart from the chart area.

TIP

To retain the chart's proportions, hold down the Shift key as you drag the sizing handle.

▶ **3.** Move the pointer over the sizing handle in the lower-right corner of the chart until the pointer changes to ⬉, and then drag the sizing handle up to cell **E21**. The chart resizes to cover the range A13:E21 and remains selected. See Figure 4-5.

Figure 4-5   **Moved and resized pie chart**

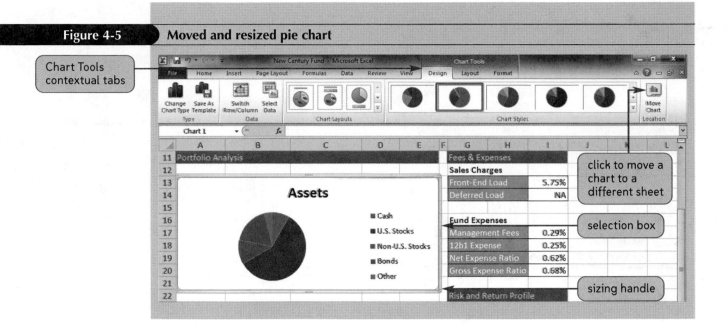

Designing a Pie Chart

Charts include individual elements that can be formatted, including the chart area, the chart title, the plot area, data markers, and a legend. You can choose which of these elements to include in the chart as well as how each element looks. You can make these changes using a built-in style that formats the entire chart or by selecting and formatting an individual element.

To apply formatting to an individual chart element, you can double-click that chart element to open a dialog box with format options specific to the selected element. You can also open the dialog box by clicking the appropriate element button on the Layout tab.

Choosing a Chart Style

A chart style is similar to a cell style or a table style in that it applies several formats to the chart at one time. When you create a chart, Excel applies the default chart style for that chart type. For example, the default pie chart style applies a solid color to each slice. You can quickly change the appearance of the entire chart by selecting a different chart style in the Chart Styles gallery.

Ajita wants you to use a style that gives each pie slice a rounded, three-dimensional look.

To apply a different chart style to the assets pie chart:

▶ 1. Click the **Chart Tools Design** tab on the Ribbon, if necessary. The design options for charts appear on the Ribbon.

▶ 2. In the Chart Styles group, click the **More** button to open the Chart Styles gallery, and then click **Style 26** (the second style in the fourth row). Each pie slice now has a rounded, raised look. See Figure 4-6.

Figure 4-6   **Pie chart with the Style 26 chart style applied**

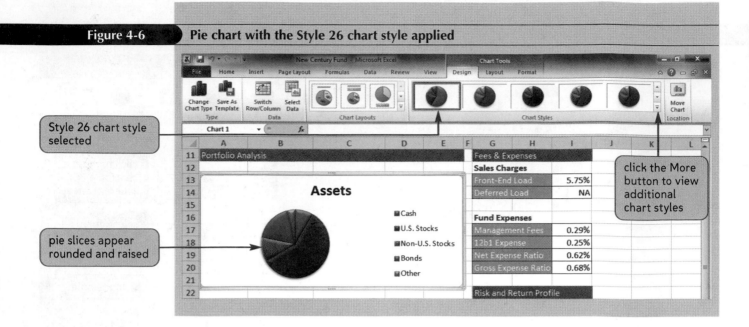

Style 26 chart style selected

click the More button to view additional chart styles

pie slices appear rounded and raised

Choosing a Chart Layout

The built-in chart layouts specify which chart elements are displayed and how they are formatted. The chart layouts include some of the most common ways of displaying different charts. Each chart type has its own collection of layouts. Depending on the pie chart layout you choose, you can hide or display the chart title, display a chart legend or place legend labels in the pie slices, and add percentages to the pie slices.

To clarify the relationship between the pie slices in the assets pie chart, Ajita wants each slice to display its percentage of the whole. You'll do this by changing the chart layout.

To apply the Layout 6 chart layout to the assets pie chart:

1. In the Chart Layouts group on the Chart Tools Design tab, click the **More** button to open the Chart Layouts gallery.

2. Click **Layout 6** (the third layout in the second row). Percentages appear on or next to the slices in the pie chart, and the chart title and legend remain in their original locations. See Figure 4-7.

TIP

Percentages appear on pie slices large enough to fit the number; otherwise, percentages appear next to the slices in the chart area.

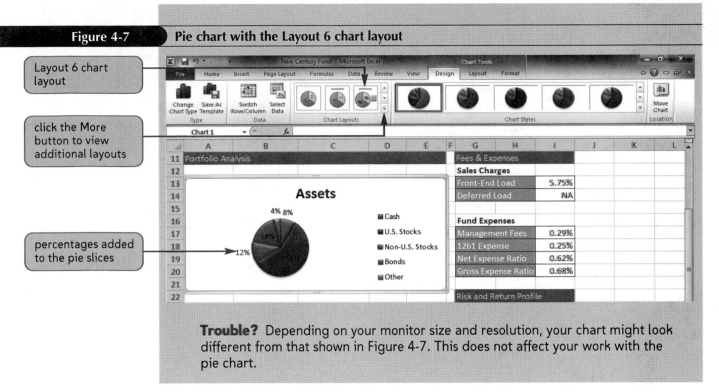

Figure 4-7   **Pie chart with the Layout 6 chart layout**

Layout 6 chart layout

click the More button to view additional layouts

percentages added to the pie slices

Trouble? Depending on your monitor size and resolution, your chart might look different from that shown in Figure 4-7. This does not affect your work with the pie chart.

With the percentages displayed on the pie chart, clients can quickly see how the assets of the New Century Fund are allocated. For example, 58 percent of the New Century Fund is invested in U.S. stocks and 12 percent in non-U.S. stocks. To fit the percentages, Excel reduced the size of the pie chart in the plot area. You'll format some of the other chart elements smaller to make more space for the pie.

Formatting the Chart Title

The chart title provides a description of the chart. By default, Excel uses the series name for the chart title. You can edit or replace the default chart title. You can also format the text of the chart title just like you can any other text in the workbook.

Ajita wants a more descriptive chart title. You'll also reduce the title's font size to make more room for the pie chart.

To change and resize the chart title:

TIP

You can revise the title text rather than replacing it by double-clicking the chart title to place the insertion point in the text, and then editing the text.

1. Click the **chart title** to select it. A selection box appears around the chart title.

2. Type **Allocation of Assets**. The new chart title appears in the formula bar, but no changes are made to the title in the chart itself.

3. Press the **Enter** key. The chart title is updated with the entry and remains selected.

4. Click the **Home** tab on the Ribbon.

5. In the Font group, click the **Font Size arrow**, and then click **12**. The chart title shrinks from 18 points to 12 points, and the pie chart increases in size to fill the extra space. See Figure 4-8.

Figure 4-8 **Chart title updated and formatted**

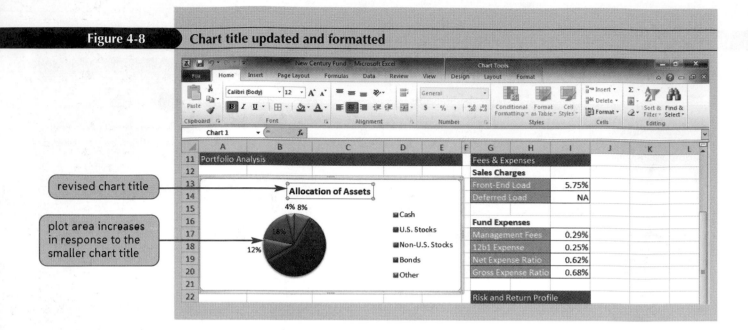

revised chart title

plot area increases in response to the smaller chart title

Formatting the Chart Legend

The chart legend identifies each of the data series in the chart. With a pie chart, the legend shows the colors used for each slice and the corresponding category values. In this case, the category values are the different asset groups. As with the other elements, you can choose the location of the legend and format it using tools on the Chart Tools Layout tab.

Ajita wants you to move the legend to the left side of the chart and add an orange border around the legend text to distinguish it from the rest of the chart.

To format the chart legend:

1. Click the **Chart Tools Layout** tab on the Ribbon.

2. In the Labels group, click the **Legend** button, and then click **Show Legend at Left**. The legend moves to the left side of the chart.

3. In the Labels group, click the **Legend** button, and then click **More Legend Options**. The Format Legend dialog box opens, providing more advanced options to format the element's appearance.

4. Click **Border Color** in the list on the left side of the dialog box. The Border Color options appear on the right side of the dialog box.

5. Click the **Solid line** option button. Two options related to border colors appear in the dialog box.

6. Click the **Color** button ![color button] to open the color palette, and then click **Orange, Accent 6, Lighter 40%** (the last color in the fourth row) in the Theme Colors section. See Figure 4-9.

Figure 4-9   Border Color options in the Format Legend dialog box

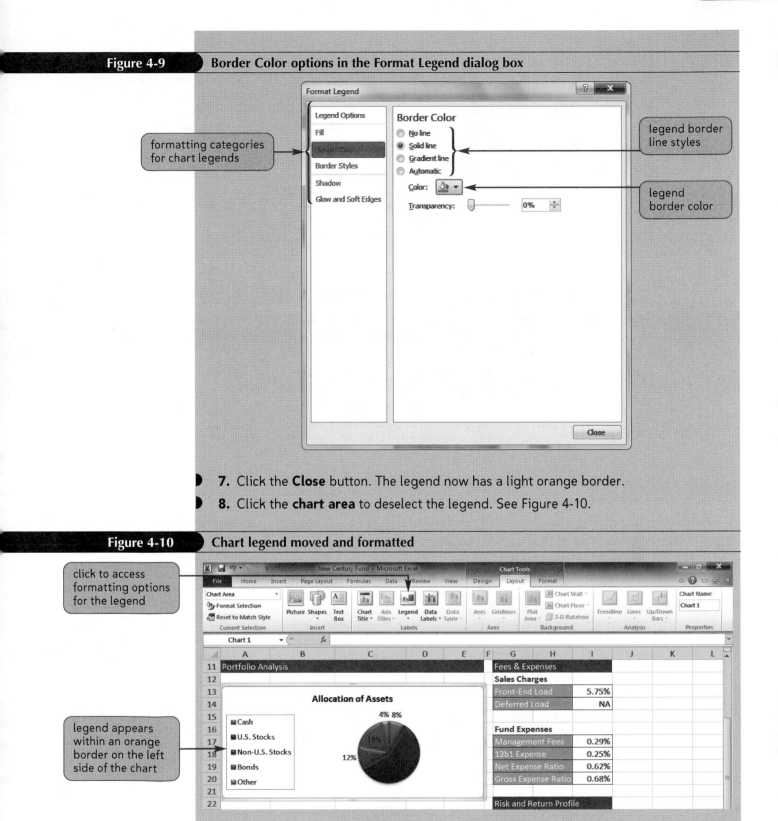

7. Click the **Close** button. The legend now has a light orange border.

8. Click the **chart area** to deselect the legend. See Figure 4-10.

Figure 4-10   Chart legend moved and formatted

Formatting Data Labels

Data labels provide descriptive text for the individual data markers, such as pie slices. When you use a chart layout that shows data labels, each label is placed where it best fits—either on the pie slice or along its side. You can use this placement to specify that all data labels appear next to their pie slices. Labels placed outside of the pie might appear far from their slices. In those cases, **leader lines**, lines that connect each data label to its corresponding data marker, can be added. Note that a leader line disappears when enough space exists in the chart area to place a label next to its slice.

You added data labels to the assets chart when you selected the Layout 6 chart layout. These percentage values were placed where they best fit in relation to the pie slices. For some asset categories, the label appears within the pie slice; for others, the label appears next to the slice. For consistency and for ease of reading, Ajita wants all the data labels to appear outside the pie chart. You'll show leader lines for the labels.

To format the pie chart's data labels:

1. In the Labels group on the Chart Tools Layout tab, click the **Data Labels** button, and then click **More Data Label Options**. The Format Data Labels dialog box opens with the Label Options displayed.

2. In the Label Position section, click the **Outside End** option button. In the Label Contains section, the Percentage and the Show Leader Lines check boxes are already checked because these were included in the chart layout you applied earlier. These options set the data labels to display percentages outside the pie chart and use leader lines when needed to connect the labels with their corresponding pie slices. See Figure 4-11.

Figure 4-11 Label Options in the Format Data Labels dialog box

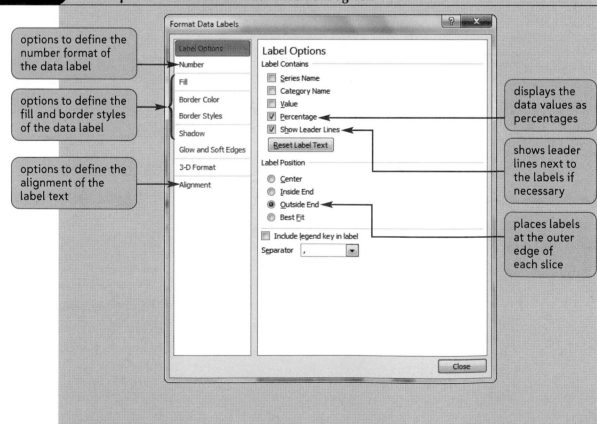

options to define the number format of the data label

options to define the fill and border styles of the data label

options to define the alignment of the label text

displays the data values as percentages

shows leader lines next to the labels if necessary

places labels at the outer edge of each slice

> **3.** Click **Number** in the list on the left side of the dialog box. The options related to number formats appear in the dialog box.

> **4.** Click **Percentage** in the Category box, and then verify that **2** appears in the Decimal places box. The percentage values for each slice show two decimal places for more accuracy.

> **5.** Click the **Close** button. The data labels appear as percentages on the outer edges of the slices. Note that leader lines don't appear in the pie chart because the chart area has enough space to place the labels close to their slices. See Figure 4-12.

Figure 4-12 **Formatted data labels**

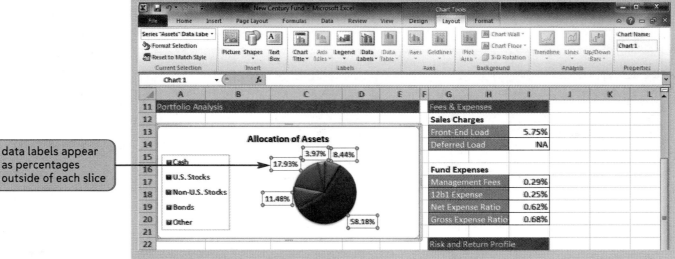

data labels appear as percentages outside of each slice

Changing Pie Slice Colors

Pie slice colors should be as distinct as possible to avoid confusion. Using distinct colors is especially important for adjacent slices. Depending on the printer quality or the monitor resolution, similarly colored slices might be difficult to distinguish in the final report. You can change the colors used for each slice. Because each slice in a pie chart represents a different value in the series, you must format each slice rather than the entire data series.

In the assets pie chart, the slices for Cash, Bonds, and Other have similar colors. You'll change the fill color of the Other and Cash slices.

To select and format pie slices in the assets pie chart:

> **1.** Click the pie to select the entire data series.

> **2.** Click the light blue **Other** slice, which represents 3.97 percent of the pie. Only that value, or slice, is selected.

> **3.** Click the **Home** tab on the Ribbon.

> **4.** In the Font group, click the **Fill Color button arrow** 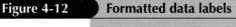, and then click **Yellow** (the fourth color in the Standard Colors section). The Other slice and legend marker change to yellow.

> **5.** Click the dark blue **Cash** slice, which covers 8.44 percent of the pie.

6. In the Font group, click the **Fill Color button arrow** 🎨▾ , and then click **Light Blue** (the seventh color in the Standard Colors section). The Cash slice and legend marker change to light blue. Each slice of the pie now has a distinct color. See Figure 4-13.

Figure 4-13 **Pie slices with new colors**

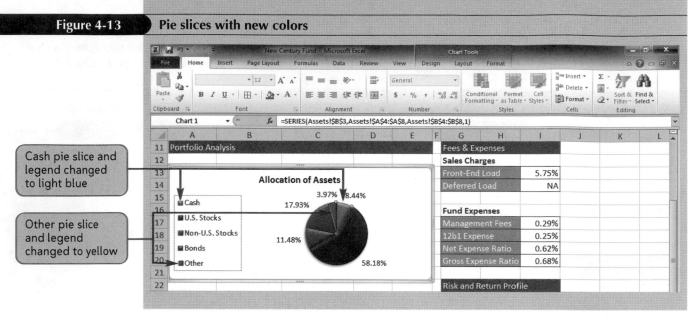

Cash pie slice and legend changed to light blue

Other pie slice and legend changed to yellow

The pie chart in the summary report clearly shows that most assets of the New Century Fund are allocated toward U.S. stocks.

INSIGHT

Exploding a Pie Chart

Pie slices do not need to be fixed within the pie. An **exploded pie chart** moves one slice away from the others as if someone were taking the piece away from the pie. Exploded pie charts are useful for emphasizing one category above all of the others. For example, to emphasize how much of the New Century Fund is allocated toward U.S. stocks, you could explode that single slice, moving it away from the other slices in the pie.

To explode a pie slice, select that slice from the pie chart and then drag the slice away from the pie. You can also explode multiple slices by selecting each slice and dragging them away. To explode all of the slices, select the entire pie and drag the pointer away from the pie's center. Each slice will be exploded and separated from the others. Although you can explode more than one slice, the resulting pie chart is rarely effective as a visual aid to the reader.

Creating a Column Chart

A **column chart** displays values in different categories as columns; the height of each column is based on its value. Related to the column chart is the **bar chart**, which is a column chart turned on its side so that the length of each bar is based on its value.

Column and bar charts are superior to pie charts when the number of categories is large or the categories are close in value. It is easier to compare height or length than area. Figure 4-14 displays the same data as a pie chart and a column chart. As you can see, it's more difficult to determine which pie slice has the largest area and by how much. This is much simpler to determine with the column chart.

Figure 4-14	Comparing pie charts and column charts

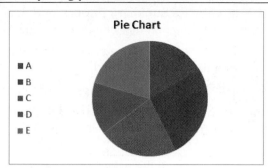

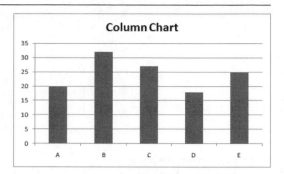

Column and bar charts can also be applied to a wider range of data than pie charts. For example, you can demonstrate how a set of values changes over time, such as the value of the New Century Fund over several years. You can also include several data series in a column or bar chart, such as the value of three funds over several years. The values from different data series are displayed in columns side by side. Pie charts usually show only one data series.

Inserting a Column Chart

The process for creating a column chart is the same as for creating a pie chart. First, you select the data source. Then, you select the type of chart you want to create. After the chart is embedded in the worksheet, you can move and resize the chart as well as change the chart's design, layout, and format.

The next part of the summary report lists the type of stocks being purchased by the fund. Each mutual fund invests in different kinds of stocks. Some funds are heavily invested in information technology, others in the service industry, and still others in manufacturing. Diversification (the distribution of investments among a variety of companies or sectors to limit losses in the event one company or sector has an economic downturn) is important, so all funds are invested to some degree in multiple economic sectors. The New Century Fund is invested in 12 different economic sectors, organized into the categories of information, services, and manufacturing.

Ajita wants you to create a chart that shows how the New Century Fund is distributed among the 12 sectors in which it is invested. A pie chart cannot display 12 categories effectively, so you will create a column chart to display this economic sector data. The columns will represent only one data series, so you'll use the 2-D Clustered Column chart type. A clustered column chart uses vertical rectangles to compare values across categories.

To create a column chart from the sector data:

1. Go to the **Sectors** worksheet, and then select the range **A3:C15**. This range covers the New Century Fund data that you want to include on the column chart.

2. Click the **Insert** tab on the Ribbon.

3. In the Charts group, click the **Column** button, and then click the **Clustered Column** chart (the first chart in the 2-D Column section). The column chart is inserted in the Sectors worksheet, and the Chart Tools Design tab on the Ribbon is selected.

4. In the Location group on the Chart Tools Design tab, click the **Move Chart** button. The Move Chart dialog box opens. You'll move the chart to the Summary Report worksheet.

5. Click the **Object in** arrow, click **Summary Report**, and then click the **OK** button. The column chart moves to the Summary Report worksheet.

6. In the Summary Report worksheet, click a blank spot in the chart area of the column chart to make sure the chart is selected.

7. Drag the selected column chart down so its upper-left corner is in cell **A23**.

8. Drag the sizing handle in the lower-right corner of the chart until the chart covers the range **A23:E37**. The chart is resized smaller. See Figure 4-15.

| Figure 4-15 | Column chart of investment sectors in the New Century Fund |

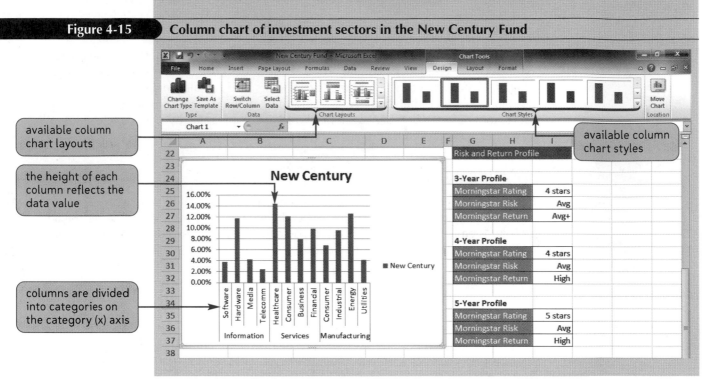

The column chart shows that the New Century Fund is most heavily invested in hardware information technology, healthcare and consumer services, and energy manufacturing. On the other hand, the fund does not invest much in software, media, and telecommunications.

Formatting a Column Chart Title and Legend

The Design tab provides a gallery of column chart layouts and a gallery of column chart styles. As with the pie chart you created, you can design the appearance of a column chart by selecting one of the chart styles or formatting individual chart elements. The default column chart layout includes a title and legend. When a chart has only one data series—such as the column chart you just created—the chart title and legend are redundant.

You will remove the legend, and then edit and format the chart title to provide a more descriptive title.

To remove the legend and format the chart title of the column chart:

▶ 1. Click the **Chart Tools Layout** tab on the Ribbon.

▶ 2. In the Labels group, click the **Legend** button, and then click **None**. The chart legend is removed from the chart, and the column chart resizes to fill the available space.

▶ 3. Click the chart title to select it, and then click the **Home** tab on the Ribbon.

▶ 4. In the Font group, click the **Font Size arrow**, and then click **12**. The chart title is reduced to 12 points, and remains selected.

▶ 5. Type **Sector Percentages** as the new chart title, and then press the **Enter** key.

Editing the Axis Scale and Text

The vertical or value axis shows the range of series values, and the horizontal or category axis shows the category values. The range of values, or **scale**, of an axis is based on the values in the data source. The default scale usually ranges from 0 (if the data source has no negative values) up through the maximum value. If the scale includes negative values, it ranges from the minimum value up through the maximum value. Excel divides the scale into regular intervals, which are marked on the axis with tick marks and labels. For example, the scale of the vertical axis for the Sector Percentages chart ranged from 0.00 percent up to 16.00 percent in increments of 2.00 percent. Having more tick marks at smaller intervals could make the chart more difficult to read because the tick mark labels might start to overlap. Likewise, having fewer tick marks at larger intervals could make the chart less informative. Major tick marks identify the main units on the chart axis. You can also add minor tick marks to identify smaller intervals between the major tick marks. Gridlines extend the tick marks across the plot area.

Some charts involve multiple data series that have vastly different values. In those instances, you can plot one data series against a **primary axis**, which usually appears along the left side of the chart, and the other against a **secondary axis**, which is usually placed on the right side of the chart. The two axes can use different scales and labels.

By default, no titles appear next to the value and category axes. This is fine when the axis labels are self-explanatory; otherwise, you can add descriptive axis titles. In general, you should avoid adding extra chart elements such as axis titles when that information is easily understood from other parts of the chart.

Ajita thinks that the value axis scale is too crowded and wants tick marks placed at 5 percent intervals, ranging from 0 percent to 25 percent. You will modify the scale of the value axis.

To change the scale of the vertical axis:

▶ 1. Click the **Chart Tools Layout** tab on the Ribbon.

▶ 2. In the Axes group, click the **Axes** button, point to **Primary Vertical Axis**, and then click **More Primary Vertical Axis Options**. The Format Axis dialog box opens with the Axis Options displayed. The value axis options are set to Auto, which causes Excel to set the values.

▶ 3. Next to Maximum, click the **Fixed** option button, and then type **0.25** in the box. The maximum value will be 25 percent.

▶ 4. Next to Major Unit, click the **Fixed** option button, and then enter **0.05** in the box. The major tick marks will appear at 5 percent intervals. See Figure 4-16.

Figure 4-16   **Axis options in the Format Axis dialog box**

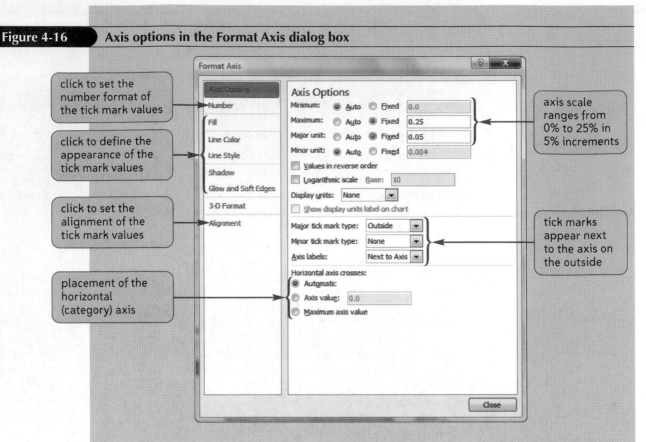

click to set the number format of the tick mark values

click to define the appearance of the tick mark values

click to set the alignment of the tick mark values

placement of the horizontal (category) axis

axis scale ranges from 0% to 25% in 5% increments

tick marks appear next to the axis on the outside

5. Click **Number** on the left side of the dialog box, make sure **Percentage** is selected in the Category box, and then type **0** in the Decimal places box. The percentage values in the vertical axis will show no decimal places.

6. Click the **Close** button. The percentages on the value axis range from 0 percent to 25 percent in 5 percent intervals with no decimal places.

These changes make the value axis easier to read. Ajita also thinks that the font size of both the value axis and the category axis is too large, dominating the rest of the graph. You will reduce the font size of the axes so that more of the chart area is available for the column chart itself.

To modify the font size of the axis titles and labels:

1. Make sure that the vertical axis is still selected, and then click the **Home** tab on the Ribbon.

2. In the Font group, click the **Font Size arrow**, and then click **8**. The values displayed in the vertical axis are smaller, leaving more room for the data series.

3. Click anywhere within the **category axis** to select it, and then change the axis font size to **8** points. The revised column chart is easier to read. See Figure 4-17.

Figure 4-17   Formatted chart axes

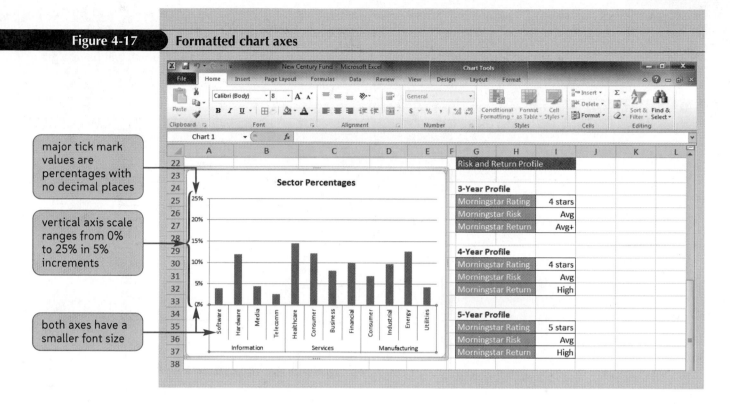

major tick mark values are percentages with no decimal places

vertical axis scale ranges from 0% to 25% in 5% increments

both axes have a smaller font size

Formatting the Chart Columns

In a pie chart, each slice or data marker has a different format. In a column chart, all of the columns usually have a common format because the columns are distinguished by height, not color. (However, you can format individual columns in a data series to high-light a particular column value.) You can modify the appearance of the data markers in a column chart using a variety of formatting options.

Ajita thinks that the columns are spaced too widely and could be formatted more attractively. You will reduce the gap between the columns, and change their fill color and appearance to make the columns stand out.

TIP

You can also select a data series by clicking any of its columns in the column chart.

To format the chart columns:

1. Click the **Chart Tools Layout** tab on the Ribbon, and then click the **Chart Elements arrow** in the Current Selection group. The list includes each element you can select in the column chart.

2. Click **Series "New Century"**. All the columns for the data series in the chart are selected.

3. In the Current Selection group, click the **Format Selection** button. The Format Data Series dialog box opens with the Series Options displayed.

4. Drag the Gap width slider to **50%** to reduce the gap between adjacent columns. The columns become wider to fill the space.

   Trouble? If you cannot drag the Gap width slider to exactly 50%, type 50 in the Gap width box below the slider.

5. Click **Fill** on the left side of the dialog box, and then click the **Gradient fill** option button to fill the columns with a gradually changing mix of colors.

6. Click the **Direction** button [icon] to open a gallery of fill directions, and then click **Linear Right** (the fourth fill direction in the first row). The columns will have a gradient fill that blends to the right. See Figure 4-18.

Figure 4-18 Fill options in the Format Data Series dialog box

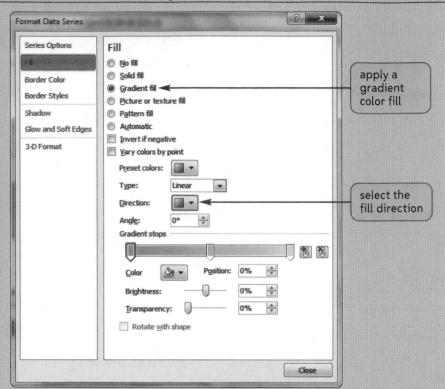

apply a gradient color fill

select the fill direction

7. Click the **Close** button, and then click cell **A38** to deselect the chart. See Figure 4-19.

Figure 4-19 Formatted chart columns

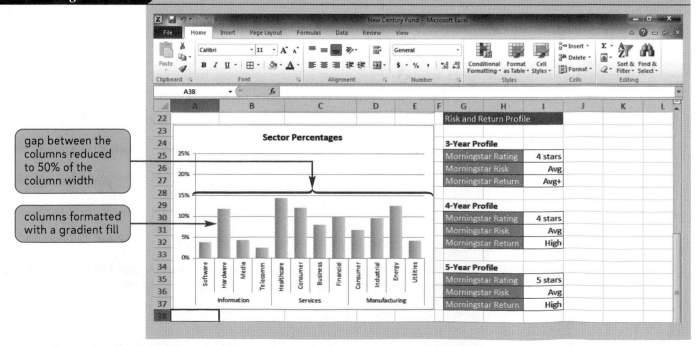

gap between the columns reduced to 50% of the column width

columns formatted with a gradient fill

PROSKILLS

Written Communication: Communicating Effectively with Charts

Studies show that people interpret information easier in a graphic form than in a tabular format. As a result, charts can help communicate the real story underlying the facts and figures you present to colleagues and clients. A well-designed chart can illuminate the bigger picture that might be hidden by viewing only the numbers. However, poorly designed charts can mislead readers and make it more difficult to interpret data.

To create effective and useful charts, keep in mind the following tips as you design charts:

- **Keep it simple.** Do not clutter a chart with too many graphic elements. Focus attention on the data rather than on decorative elements that do not inform.
- **Focus on the message.** Design the chart to highlight the points you want to convey to readers.
- **Limit the number of data series used in the chart.** Line charts and column charts should display no more than three or four data series. Pie charts should have no more than six slices.
- **Use gridlines in moderation.** Gridlines should be used to provide only approximate values for the data markers. Having too many gridlines can obscure the data being graphed.
- **Choose colors carefully.** Display different data series in contrasting colors to make it easier to distinguish one series from another. Modify the default colors as needed to make them distinct on the screen and in the printed copy.
- **Limit your chart to a few text styles.** Use a maximum of two or three different text styles in the same chart. Having too many text styles in one chart can distract attention from the data.

The goal of written communication is always to inform the reader in the simplest, most accurate, and most direct way possible. When creating worksheets and charts, everything in the workbook should be directed toward that end.

Ajita is pleased with the two charts you've created and formatted. In the next session, you'll create a line chart and you'll explore options for creating 3-D charts, chart sheets, and sparklines.

REVIEW

Session 4.1 Quick Check

1. What are the three components of a data series?
2. In what two locations can a chart be placed?
3. What is the difference between the chart area and the plot area?
4. A data series contains values divided into 10 categories. Would this data be better displayed as a pie chart or a column chart? Why?
5. What are major tick marks, minor tick marks, and gridlines?
6. What is a bar chart?
7. How do you change the scale of a chart axis?

SESSION 4.2 VISUAL OVERVIEW

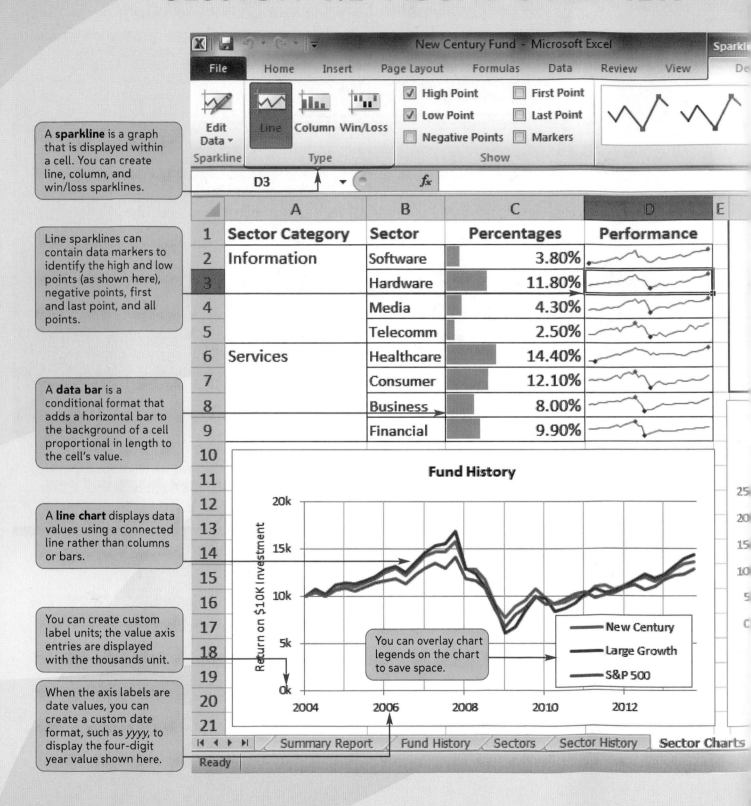

A **sparkline** is a graph that is displayed within a cell. You can create line, column, and win/loss sparklines.

Line sparklines can contain data markers to identify the high and low points (as shown here), negative points, first and last point, and all points.

A **data bar** is a conditional format that adds a horizontal bar to the background of a cell proportional in length to the cell's value.

A **line chart** displays data values using a connected line rather than columns or bars.

You can create custom label units; the value axis entries are displayed with the thousands unit.

When the axis labels are date values, you can create a custom date format, such as *yyyy*, to display the four-digit year value shown here.

New Century Fund - Microsoft Excel

File   Home   Insert   Page Layout   Formulas   Data   Review   View

Edit Data ▾   Line   Column   Win/Loss

☑ High Point   ☐ First Point
☑ Low Point   ☐ Last Point
☐ Negative Points   ☐ Markers

Sparkline   Type   Show

D3

	A	B	C	D	E
1	**Sector Category**	**Sector**	**Percentages**	**Performance**	
2	Information	Software	3.80%		
3		Hardware	11.80%		
4		Media	4.30%		
5		Telecomm	2.50%		
6	Services	Healthcare	14.40%		
7		Consumer	12.10%		
8		Business	8.00%		
9		Financial	9.90%		

Fund History

Return on $10K Investment

20k
15k
10k
5k
0k

2004   2006   2008   2010   2012

You can overlay chart legends on the chart to save space.

— New Century
— Large Growth
— S&P 500

Summary Report   Fund History   Sectors   Sector History   **Sector Charts**

Ready

CHARTS, SPARKLINES, AND DATA BARS

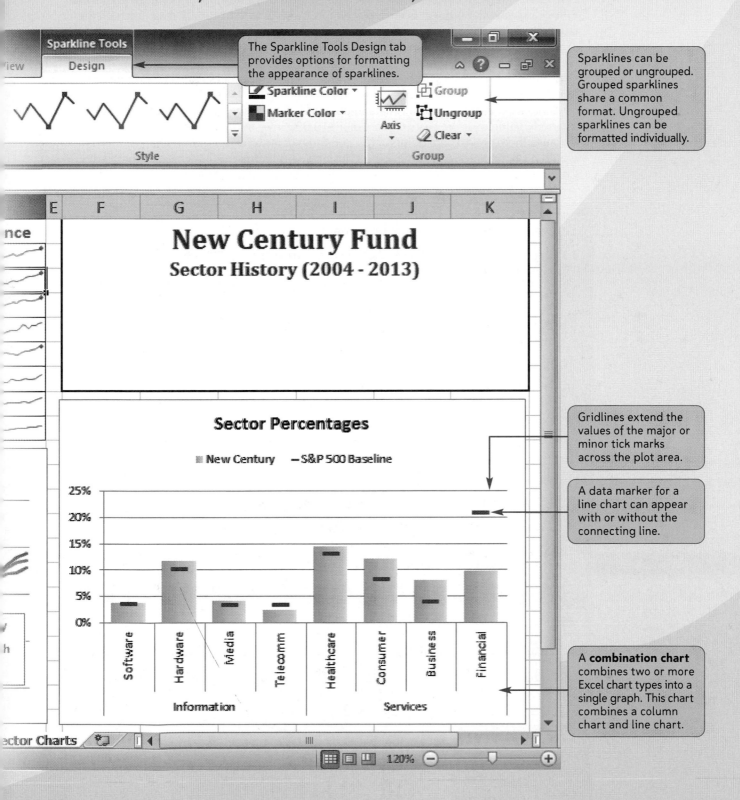

The Sparkline Tools Design tab provides options for formatting the appearance of sparklines.

Sparklines can be grouped or ungrouped. Grouped sparklines share a common format. Ungrouped sparklines can be formatted individually.

Gridlines extend the values of the major or minor tick marks across the plot area.

A data marker for a line chart can appear with or without the connecting line.

A **combination chart** combines two or more Excel chart types into a single graph. This chart combines a column chart and line chart.

Creating a Line Chart

Line charts are typically used when the data consists of values drawn from categories that follow a sequential order at evenly spaced intervals, as with historical data in which the data values are recorded periodically such as monthly, quarterly, or yearly.

Ajita wants the summary report to include a chart of the performance history of the New Century Fund against two other investments: a large growth fund and the S&P 500. (The Standard and Poor's 500 is an index of 500 blue chip stocks that is commonly used to measure the performance of stocks and funds.)

Ajita has already entered this data in the Fund History worksheet. She calculated the quarterly value over the past 10 years of a $10,000 investment in each of the three funds. Because there are 40 data points across the three data series, a column chart of this data would be difficult to read and interpret. Instead, you'll create a line chart for the New Century Fund performance, plotting the value of the three investments against time.

To create the fund history line chart:

1. If you took a break at the end of the previous session, make sure that the New Century Fund workbook is open.

2. Go to the **Fund History** worksheet, and then select the range **A4:D44**. This range contains the data for the value of the New Century Fund, the average value of large growth funds, and the value of the S&P 500 for each quarter of 2004 through 2013.

3. Click the **Insert** tab on the Ribbon.

4. In the Charts group, click the **Line** button, and then click the **Line** chart (the first chart in the 2-D Line section). A line chart is embedded in the Fund History worksheet.

5. In the Location group on the Chart Tools Design tab, click the **Move Chart** button. The Move Chart dialog box opens.

6. Click the **Object in** arrow, and then click **Summary Report**.

7. Click the **OK** button. The line chart moves to the Summary Report worksheet.

8. Move and resize the chart to cover the range **D1:I9**. See Figure 4-20.

| Figure 4-20 | Line chart moved and resized |

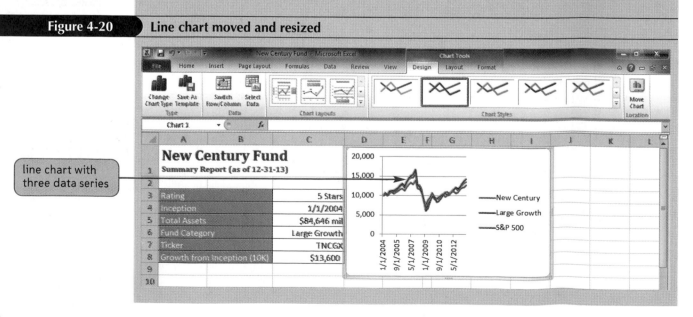

line chart with three data series

The line chart includes three data series—the New Century Fund, a competing large growth fund, and the S&P 500. Each series has a different line color. The line chart is crowded by the default size of the legend and axis labels. You'll reduce the font size of the axis and legend, and then add a chart title that describes the chart's content.

To edit the fund history line chart:

▶ **1.** Click the **Chart Tools Layout** tab on the Ribbon.

▶ **2.** In the Labels group, click the **Chart Title** button, and then click **Above Chart**. A chart title appears above the line chart surrounded by a selection box.

▶ **3.** Type **Fund History**, and then press the **Enter** key. The new, descriptive title appears above the chart.

▶ **4.** Click the **Home** tab on the Ribbon.

▶ **5.** In the Font group, click the **Font Size arrow**, and then click **10**. The chart title is reduced to 10 points.

▶ **6.** Click the **value axis** to select it, and then set its font size to **8** points.

▶ **7.** Click the **category axis** to select it, and then set its font size to **8** points.

▶ **8.** Click the **chart legend** to select it, and then set its font size to **8** points. The line chart resizes to fill the space left by the smaller chart titles, axes, and chart legend.

Next, you will change the scale used in the value axis so that the values range from $0 to $20,000 in $5,000 increments.

To modify the value axis scale:

▶ **1.** Double-click the **value axis** to open the Format Axis dialog box.

▶ **2.** Next to Maximum, click the **Fixed** option button, and then type **20000** in the box.

▶ **3.** Next to Major Unit, click the **Fixed** option button, and then type **5000** in the box.

▶ **4.** Click the **Close** button. The scale of the vertical axis ranges from $0 to $20,000 in $5,000 increments.

Formatting Date Labels

In addition to numbers, a scale can be based on dates, as the category axis in the Fund History line chart is. As with numerical scales, you can set the minimum and maximum dates to use in the scale's range. You can also set the major and minor units as days, months, or years to use for the scale's interval.

Ajita is more interested in the general trend from year to year than the exact dates on which the fund values were calculated. Because of this, she wants the scale of the category axis to show only years. You can save space by showing the labels every other year. To do this, you'll set the major tick marks to appear at two-year intervals, and then set the minor tick marks to appear at one-year intervals, even though you won't display the minor tick marks on the chart until later.

To format the category axis labels:

1. Double-click the **category axis** to open the Format Axis dialog box with the Axis Options displayed.

2. Next to Major unit, click the **Fixed** option button, type **2** in the box, and then select **Years** in the list. The major tick marks are set to every two years.

3. Next to Minor unit, click the **Fixed** option button, type **1** in the box, if necessary, and then select **Years** in the list. The minor tick marks are set to every year. See Figure 4-21.

Figure 4-21   Date intervals for tick marks

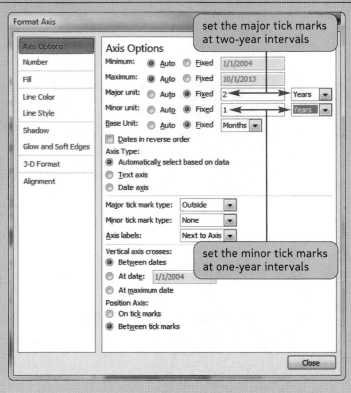

Next, you'll format the category labels to show the four-digit year value rather than the complete date. Excel does not have a built-in format to display only four-digit year values, but you can create a custom format to accomplish this.

Custom date formats use combinations of the letters "m", "d", and "y" for months, days, and years, respectively. The number of letters controls how Excel displays the date, as follows:

- With months, *m* or *mm* displays the one- or two-digit month number, *mmm* displays the month's three-letter abbreviation, and *mmmm* displays the month's full name.
- With days, *d* or *dd* displays the one- or two-digit day value and *dddd* displays the day's full name.
- With years, *yyyy* displays the four-digit year value.

For example, a custom format of *mmm-dd* displays a three-letter month abbreviation followed by a hyphen and a two-digit day number (such as Apr-05). The current date format used in the category axis is *m/d/yyyy*, which—for example—displays March 14, 2013 as 3/14/2013.

You'll create a custom format for the category axis that displays only the four-digit year.

To create a custom format for the four-digit year:

1. Click **Number** on the left side of the Format Axis dialog box.

2. Type **yyyy** in the Format Code box, which is the code for displaying only years. See Figure 4-22.

Figure 4-22   Custom date format

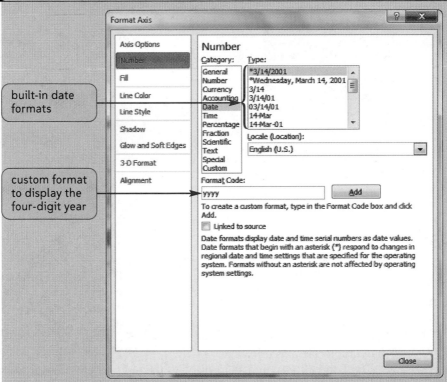

3. Click the **Add** button. The four-digit year format code is added to the list of custom formats and is selected.

4. Click the **Close** button. The Format Axis dialog box closes, and the category axis labels show values for every other year on the major tick marks. See Figure 4-23.

Figure 4-23   **Rescaled vertical and horizontal axes**

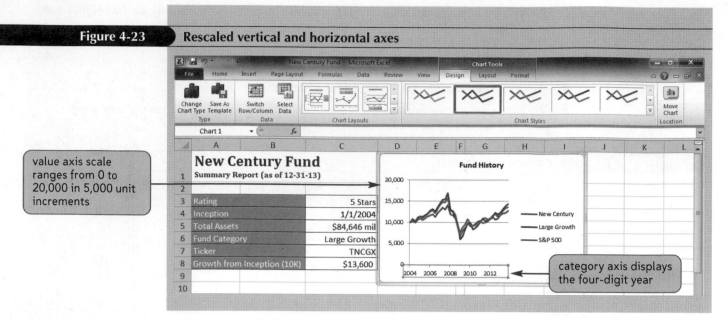

value axis scale ranges from 0 to 20,000 in 5,000 unit increments

category axis displays the four-digit year

The category axis shows four-digit year values for 2004, 2006, 2008, 2010, and 2012. Because fewer years are included on the axis, there is enough room to display the labels horizontally instead of vertically.

Setting Label Units

When a chart involves large numbers, the axis labels can take up a lot of the available chart area and be difficult to read. You can simplify the chart's appearance by displaying units of measure more appropriate to the data values. For example, you can display the value 20 to represent 20,000 or 20,000,000. This is particularly useful when space is at a premium, such as in an embedded chart confined to a small area of the worksheet. When you select the display units, such as Thousands, you can choose to show the display unit in the axis title.

The Fund History line chart displays data in tens of thousands of dollars. Rather than displaying a large value such as 20,000, Ajita wants to save space by displaying numbers in units of thousands. You will change the display units for the value axis but not show the units in the axis title.

To set the display unit for the value axis:

1. Double-click the **value axis** to open the Format Axis dialog box with the Axis Options displayed.

2. Click the **Display units** arrow, and then click **Thousands**.

3. Move the dialog box so you can see the line chart's value axis. The scale of the value axis changed from 0 to 20,000 in intervals of 5,000 to 0 through 20 in intervals of 5. The axis title "Thousands" indicates that the values are expressed in units of 1000. To save space, you'll remove this title from the chart.

4. Click the **Show display units label on chart** check box to remove the check mark. The axis title is removed from the chart.

You can apply custom formats to numbers just as you did earlier with dates. One application of custom formats is to add text to a number. This is often used to include the units of measure alongside the value, such as 10k to indicate 10,000. To add text to a value, you use the custom format *value"text"*, where *value* is the number format applied to the value and *text* is the text to include next to the value. The text must be placed within quotation marks.

Without the Thousands title, the Fund History line chart provides no indication of what the value axis numbers mean. Ajita suggests you add the letter "k" to each number, displaying the values as 10k, 20k, and so forth. To do this, you'll create a custom format. Excel uses the format #,##0 to display integers, so you'll change this format to #,##0"k" to display the letter "k" at the end of the value.

TIP

Use Excel Help to learn more about custom format codes.

To create a custom format showing the thousands unit:

1. Click **Number** on the left side of the Format Axis dialog box.

2. Click in the Format Code box after the number format, and then type **"k"** to make the format code #,##0"k".

3. Click the **Add** button. This format code is added to the list of custom formats in the Type box.

4. Click the **Close** button. The Format Axis dialog box closes, and the value axis labels are revised, with the letter "k" added after each value. See Figure 4-24.

Figure 4-24	Custom value axis label units

value axis labels use the letter "k" to represent thousands as the display units

Overlaying a Chart Legend

Chart elements, such as titles and legends, overlay the chart area, which means they are placed on top of the chart. Overlaying chart elements is a way to make more space for the plot area because the chart does not resize to make room for that element. After you overlay an element, you might want to format it to make it easier to read.

Ajita thinks the legend takes up too much space on the right side of the chart. You will overlay the legend, leaving more room in the chart area for the chart itself, and then format it.

To overlay and format the chart legend:

1. Double-click the **legend** to open the Format Legend dialog box.

2. Click the **Show the legend without overlapping the chart** check box to remove the check mark. The size of the chart increases, and the legend is now overlaying the chart. The plot and the legend intersect, and the plot area shows through the legend.

3. Click **Fill** on the left side of the Format Legend dialog box, and then click the **Solid fill** option button.

4. Click the **Color** button [🎨 ▼], and then click **white** (the first color in the Theme Colors section). The legend now has a solid white background, making it easier to read.

5. Click **Border Color** on the left side of the Format Legend dialog box, and then click the **Solid line** option button.

6. Click the **Color** button [🎨 ▼], and then click **Blue** (the eighth color in the Standard Colors section).

7. Click the **Close** button. The Format Legend dialog box closes, and the reformatted legend overlays the chart.

An overlaid chart element floats in the chart area and is not fixed to a particular position. This means that you can drag the chart element to a new location. This is helpful because when you overlay a chart element, it might overlap some of the chart contents, as the legend does. You'll drag the overlaid legend down a bit so that it doesn't obscure any of the data in the line chart.

To move the chart legend:

1. Position the pointer over a blank spot in the chart legend so the pointer changes to ⁺↕ and "Legend" appears in a ScreenTip.

2. Drag the legend to the lower-right corner of the plot area so the bottom of the legend is on the horizontal axis.

3. Click and drag the upper-left sizing handle of the legend down a few pixels until the legend no longer overlaps the lines on the chart. See Figure 4-25.

Figure 4-25   Legend overlaid, moved, and resized

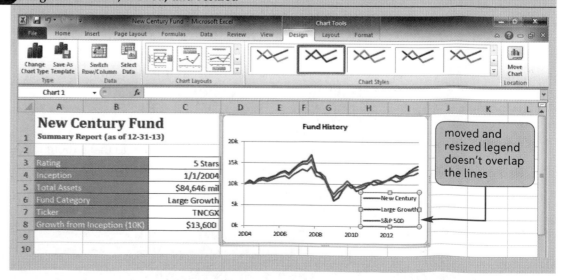

Adding Gridlines

By default, Excel places horizontal gridlines on line charts and column charts. Each gridline is aligned with a major tick mark on the value axis. You can change the gridlines so that they appear for only the minor units, appear for both the major and minor units, or do not appear at all. The category axis has these same gridline options.

Ajita wants you to add vertical gridlines at the minor tick marks on the category axis.

To add vertical gridlines to the chart:

 1. Click the **Chart Tools Layout** tab on the Ribbon.

 2. In the Axes group, click the **Gridlines** button.

 3. Point to **Primary Vertical Gridlines**, and then click **Minor Gridlines**. Vertical gridlines appear on the chart at each minor tick mark (in this case, every year).

Adding an Axis Title

An axis title is descriptive text that appears next to the axis values. An axis title can provide additional information that is not covered in the chart title. It can include information about the source of the data and the units in which the data is measured.

The values in the chart represent the return that the investor would have enjoyed from a $10,000 investment starting in 2004. Because this fact is not obvious from the chart, Ajita wants you to add the title "Return on $10K Investment" to the vertical axis.

To add a title to the vertical axis:

 1. In the Labels group on the Chart Tools Layout tab, click **Axis Titles**, point to **Primary Vertical Axis Title**, and then click **Rotated Title**. A title rotated 90 degrees is added to the axis.

 2. Type **Return on $10K Investment**, and then press the **Enter** key. The descriptive title is entered, but doesn't fit well in the chart area.

 3. Click the **Home** tab on the Ribbon.

 4. In the Font group, click the **Font Size button arrow**, and then click **8**. The font size is reduced to 8 points.

 5. In the Font group, click the **Bold** button **B** to remove the boldface from the axis title.

 6. Click cell **A9** to deselect the chart. The final version of the line chart is easier to read than the unformatted version, and highlights how the New Century Fund has performed over the past 10 years compared to the two benchmarks. See Figure 4-26.

Figure 4-26   Final line chart

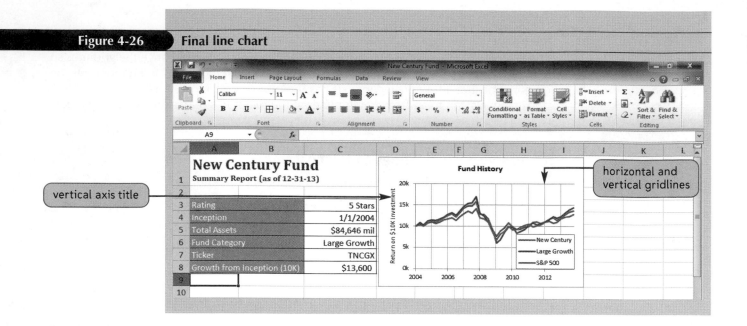

Editing and Revising Chart Data

Chart data can be edited and revised at any time. You do this by modifying the data range that the chart is based on, not by directly modifying the data in the chart. The change can be as simple as updating a specific value within the data source. Or it can be as involved as adding another data series to the chart.

Changing a Data Value

Charts remain linked or connected to their data sources, even if they appear in different worksheets. If you change any values or labels in the data source, the chart is automatically updated to show the new content. One advantage of Excel charts is that you can quickly see how changing one or more values affects a graph.

Ajita found a data entry error in the Assets worksheet—the amount of assets in the Other category entered in cell B8 should be $8,360, not $3,360. She also wants the label "Other" to be changed to "Other Assets." This change also needs to be reflected in the Allocation of Assets pie chart you created based on this data. Because both the asset values and the asset labels are linked to the pie chart, when you make these changes in the Assets worksheet, they will automatically be reflected in the pie chart.

To edit the data source for the assets pie chart:

1. Go to the **Assets** worksheet.

2. In cell A8, edit the text to **Other Assets**.

3. In cell B8, change the value to **8360**.

4. Go to the **Summary Report** worksheet, and then verify that the pie chart was updated with the new data value and category name. Note that the percentage values for each category were recalculated based on the new data. As a result, the Other Assets slice increased in size to reflect its larger percentage of the whole, and the remaining slices decreased in size. See Figure 4-27.

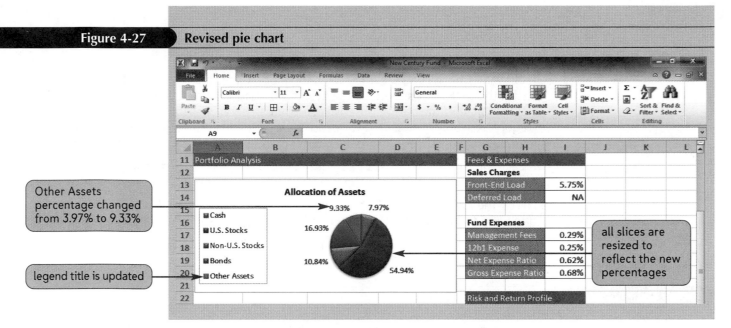

Figure 4-27   **Revised pie chart**

Other Assets percentage changed from 3.97% to 9.33%

legend title is updated

all slices are resized to reflect the new percentages

Occasionally, you will want a chart to show a "snapshot" of the data at a certain time. Before updating the values in the data source, copy and paste the chart as a picture. Select the chart, copy it as usual, click the Paste button arrow, and then click Picture. The chart is pasted as a picture without any connection to its data source.

Adding a Data Series to an Existing Chart

You can also modify a chart by adding a new data series. The new data series appears in the chart with a different set of data markers in the same way that the line chart you created had different data markers for each of the three different series.

REFERENCE

Adding a Data Series to a Chart

- Select the chart to which you want to add a data series.
- In the Data group on the Chart Tools Design tab, click the Select Data button.
- Click the Add button in the Select Data Source dialog box.
- Select the range with the series name and series values you want for the new data series.
- Click the OK button in each dialog box.

The column chart you created shows the distribution of stocks in the New Century Fund. Ajita wonders how this distribution compares to the distribution in the S&P 500 index. For example, does the New Century Fund invest more in the information sector, and is that why it outperformed the S&P 500 for the past 10 years? Ajita included the sector percentages for the S&P 500 in the Sectors worksheet. You will add this information to the column chart you've already created.

To add a data series to the existing column chart:

▶ 1. Click the **Sector Percentages** column chart to select it.

▶ 2. Click the **Chart Tools Design** tab on the Ribbon, and then, in the Data group, click the **Select Data** button. The Select Data Source dialog box opens. The left side lists all of the data series displayed in the chart. The right side lists the category axis labels associated with each data series. You can add, edit, or remove any of these data series from the chart.

▶ 3. Click the **Add** button. The Edit Series dialog box opens. In this dialog box, you specify the name of the new data series and its range of data values.

▶ 4. With the insertion point in the Series name box, click the **Sectors** sheet tab, click cell **D3**, and then press the **Tab** key. The cell with the series name is entered and the insertion point moves to the Series values box.

▶ 5. Select the range **D4:D15**. See Figure 4-28.

Figure 4-28	Edit Series dialog box

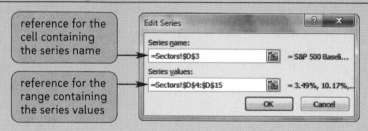

reference for the cell containing the series name

reference for the range containing the series values

▶ 6. Click the **OK** button. The Select Data Source dialog box reappears with the S&P 500 data added to the list of data series in the chart. See Figure 4-29.

Figure 4-29	Select Data Source dialog box

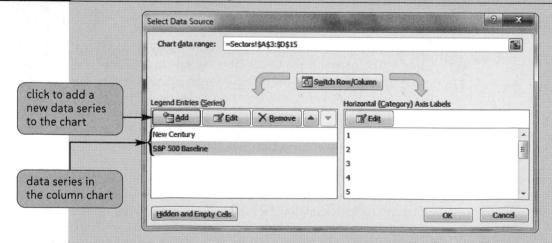

click to add a new data series to the chart

data series in the column chart

▶ 7. Click the **OK** button. The S&P 500 sector values appear as red columns in the chart. See Figure 4-30.

| Figure 4-30 | Column chart with added data series |

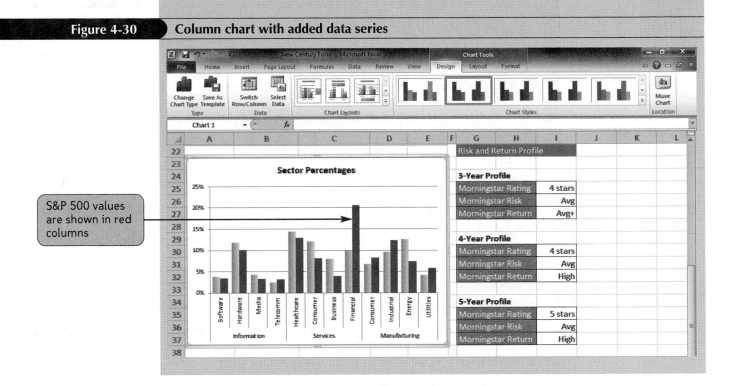

S&P 500 values are shown in red columns

Understanding the Series Function

If you select a chart's series and look at the formula bar, the formula being displayed uses the SERIES function. The SERIES function describes the content of a chart data series and has the syntax

```
=SERIES(name, categories, values, order)
```

where *name* is the name that appears in the chart, *categories* are the labels that appear on the category axis of the chart, *values* are the values that Excel plots for the data series, and *order* is the order in which the series appears in the chart. For example, a data series might be represented by the following SERIES function:

```
=SERIES(Sheet1!$D$1,Sheet1!$A$2:$A$9,Sheet1!$D$2:$D$9,3)
```

In this function, the name of the series is in cell D1 of the Sheet1 worksheet, the labels are in the range A2:A9 in the Sheet1 worksheet, the data values are in the range D2:D9 in the Sheet1 worksheet, and the series is the third data series in the chart.

Note that although you can edit the SERIES function within the formula bar to make quick changes to your chart, the function is tied to an existing chart. It cannot be used within a worksheet cell or referenced from another Excel formula.

Creating a Combination Chart

A combination chart is a chart that combines two or more chart types in a single graph, such as a column chart and a line chart. To create a combination chart, you select a data series in an existing chart, and then apply a new chart type to that series, leaving the other data series in its original format.

Creating a Combination Chart

• Select a data series in an existing chart that you want to appear as another chart type.
• In the Type group on the Chart Tools Design tab, click the Change Chart Type button, and then click the chart type you want.
• Click the OK button.

With so many columns in the Sector Percentages column chart, the data is difficult to read and interpret. Ajita suggests you separate the S&P 500 values from the New Century Fund values by plotting them as lines rather than columns. To do that, you'll create a chart that is a combination of a column and a line chart.

To apply the line chart type to the S&P 500 data series:

1. Click the **Chart Tools Layout** tab on the Ribbon.

2. In the Current Selection group, click the **Chart Elements arrow**, and then click **Series "S&P 500 Baseline"** to select the data series.

3. Click the **Chart Tools Design** tab on the Ribbon, and then click the **Change Chart Type** button in the Type group. The Change Chart Type dialog box opens.

4. In the Line section, click **Line with Markers** (the fourth Line chart type).

5. Click the **OK** button. The S&P 500 values change to a line chart with markers. See Figure 4-31.

Figure 4-31   **Combination chart**

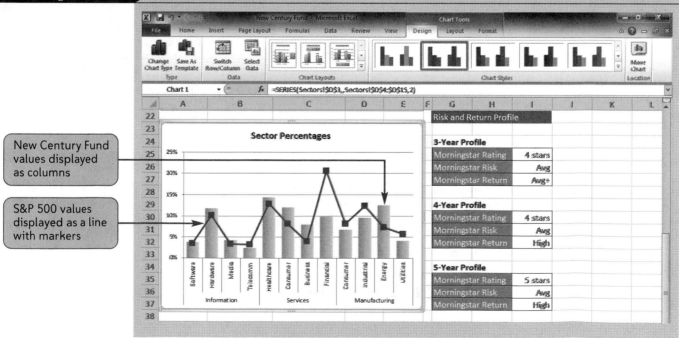

New Century Fund values displayed as columns

S&P 500 values displayed as a line with markers

As noted earlier, line charts are appropriate when the categories can be ordered sequentially such as the Fund History line chart in which the categories represented dates. In Figure 4-31, the sector categories do not have a sequential order and the lines connecting the different categories have no meaning. You'll remove these lines from the chart to avoid confusing Ajita's clients. Also, you'll change the square markers to horizontal line markers at each data point.

To remove the lines and edit the markers in the line chart:

▶ **1.** Click the line for the S&P 500 data series to select it, if necessary.

▶ **2.** Click the **Chart Tools Layout** tab on the Ribbon, and then click **Format Selection** in the Current Selection group. The Format Data Series dialog box opens.

▶ **3.** Click **Line Color** on the left side of the dialog box, and then click the **No line** option button to remove the line from the line chart.

▶ **4.** Click **Marker Options** on the left side of the dialog box, and then click the **Built-in** option button. You can now select the type and size of the marker.

▶ **5.** Click the **Type arrow**, and then click the horizontal line marker (the seventh marker in the list).

▶ **6.** Click the **Size** up arrow until 10 appears in the box. See Figure 4-32.

| Figure 4-32 | Marker Options in the Format Data Series dialog box |

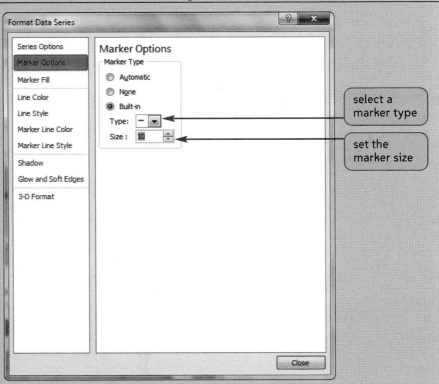

▶ **7.** Click the **Close** button. The S&P 500 values appear only as data markers.

Because the chart now has two data series, you'll add a legend to the top of the chart to identify them.

To add a legend to the combination chart:

1. In the Labels group on the Chart Tools Layout tab, click the **Legend** button, and then click **Show Legend at Top**. The legend appears above the chart.

2. Click the **legend** to select it.

3. Click the **Home** tab on the Ribbon, and then reduce the font size of the legend to **8** points.

4. Click cell **A38** to deselect the chart. See Figure 4-33.

Figure 4-33	Completed combination chart

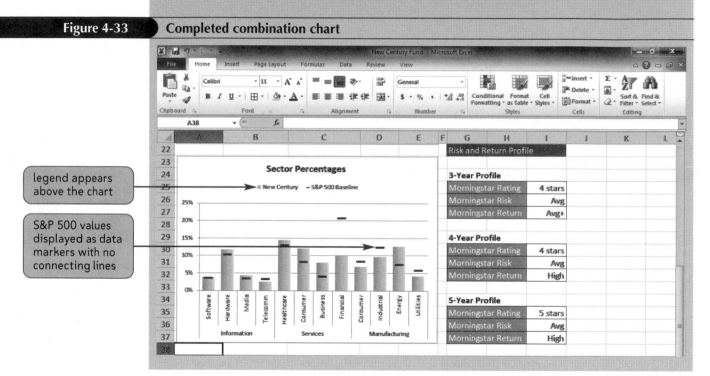

legend appears above the chart

S&P 500 values displayed as data markers with no connecting lines

The combination chart effectively shows that the New Century Fund invests less than the S&P 500 in sectors from the financial service industry, and invests more in other sectors such as energy, consumer services, and hardware. This might account for the higher performance of the New Century Fund.

Decision Making: Choosing the Right Chart

Excel supports a wide variety of charts and chart styles. Deciding which type of chart to use requires evaluating your data and determining the ultimate purpose or goal of the chart. Consider how your data will appear with each type of chart before making a final decision.

In general, pie charts should be used only when the number of categories is small and the relative sizes of the different slices can be easily distinguished. If you have several categories, use a column or bar chart.

Line charts are best for categories that follow a sequential order. Be aware, however, that the time intervals must be a constant length if used in a line chart. Line charts will distort data that occurs in irregular time intervals, making it appear that the data values occurred at regular intervals when they did not.

Pie, column, bar, and line charts assume that numbers are plotted against categories. In science and engineering applications, you will often want to plot two numeric values against one another. For that data, use **XY scatter charts**, which show the patterns or relationship between two or more sets of values. XY scatter charts are also useful for data recorded at irregular time intervals.

If you still can't find the right chart to meet your needs, you can create a custom chart based on the built-in chart types. Third-party vendors also sell software to allow Excel to create charts not built into the software.

Choosing the right chart and chart style can make your presentation more effective and informative.

Creating a 3-D Chart

You can add visual interest to charts by using 3-D (three dimensional) effects. The 3-D effects provide the illusion of depth and distance, which makes the charts appear to stand out on the page. You'll change the format of the Allocation of Assets pie chart to a 3-D style.

To change the assets pie chart to 3-D:

1. Click the **Allocation of Assets pie chart**, and then click the **Chart Tools Design** tab on the Ribbon.

2. In the Type group, click the **Change Chart Type** button. The Change Chart Type dialog box opens.

3. In the Pie section, click **Pie in 3-D** (the second Pie chart type).

4. Click the **OK** button. The pie chart is now a 3-D chart, and has a slight shadow along its lower edge.

To create a 3-D effect, Excel adds three spatial dimensions to the chart, which it labels the x-, y-, and z-axes. The **x-axis** represents the length of the object. The **y-axis** represents the height of the object. The **z-axis** represents the object's depth. These Excel definitions of the x-, y-, and z-axes might not match what you have learned in math classes about 3-D charting.

Currently, the 3-D pie chart does not look very different from the 2-D version because you are looking straight down on the chart from "above," directly along the y-axis. To increase the 3-D effect, you need to rotate the chart. You can only rotate the chart horizontally or vertically. Increasing the rotation horizontally spins the chart clockwise (as seen from above); increasing the rotation vertically raises the user's viewpoint higher above the chart. Often you'll need to experiment to find the right angles for a 3-D chart by rotating the chart in different directions until it looks good without distorting the data.

Excel charts cannot be rotated around the z- or depth axis, but you can specify the chart's depth. Depth values can range from 0 to 2000 units. The larger the value, the thicker or deeper the chart appears to extend away from the viewer. You can also change the chart's **perspective**, which controls how fast the chart appears to recede from the viewer's eye. Perspective values range from 0 degrees to 90 degrees. A 90 degree perspective value exaggerates the 3-D effect, making distant objects appear very small, whereas perspective values near 0 degrees minimize this effect. Excel immediately applies your choices for depth and perspective, so you can try different depth and perspective values to determine which work best for your chart.

You'll rotate the Allocation of Assets pie chart along the horizontal axis so that the largest slice is on the left side of the pie. You'll also orient the chart so that the viewer's eye level is slightly above the chart. You will not change the chart's perspective or depth.

To rotate and reorient the 3-D pie chart:

1. Click the **Chart Tools Layout** tab on the Ribbon.

2. In the Background group, click the **3-D Rotation** button. The Format Chart Area dialog box opens with the 3-D Rotation options displayed.

3. In the Rotation section, type **90** in the X box, and then type **20** in the Y box. See Figure 4-34.

| Figure 4-34 | Format Chart Area dialog box with 3-D Rotation options |

4. Click the **Close** button. The pie chart rotates based on the new x-axis and y-axis values. See Figure 4-35.

Figure 4-35

| Figure 4-35 | Rotated 3-D pie chart |

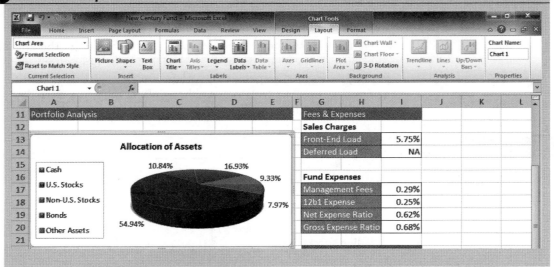

The horizontal and vertical rotation has a significant impact on the way the chart looks. The pie chart was rotated clockwise one-quarter of the way around the circle so that the largest slice, the red U.S Stocks slice, is in the front. The vertical rotation turned the pie chart so that the viewer is looking down on the chart at a lower angle above the horizontal axis. Ajita is pleased with the 3-D effect you added.

INSIGHT

Creating Effective 3-D Charts

Although 3-D charts are visually attractive, they can obscure the relationship between the values in the chart. This is especially true when an exaggerated perspective obscures the relative sizes of different chart elements, such as pie slices.

Because of the visual distortion that can result with 3-D representations, you should include data labels with all 3-D charts. Also, try to avoid extreme viewing angles that elongate chart elements and might cause the viewer to misread the data. Although 3-D charts can be eye-catching, do not use this effect if it overrides the main purpose of a chart, which is data interpretation.

Adding Sparklines and Data Bars

For more compact graphing, you can insert charts within worksheet cells. Excel provides two tools to do this—sparklines and data bars. Both convey graphical information about worksheet data without occupying a lot of space.

Creating Sparklines

A sparkline is a mini chart that is displayed within a worksheet cell. Because sparklines are compact in size, they don't include chart elements such as legends, titles, gridlines, or axes. The goal of a sparkline is to convey the maximum amount of graphical information within a very small space. As a result, sparklines are useful when you don't want charts to overwhelm the rest of your worksheet or take up valuable page space.

Excel supports the following three types of sparklines:

- A line sparkline for highlighting trends
- A column sparkline used for column charts
- A win/loss sparkline for highlighting positive and negative values

Figure 4-36 shows examples of each type of sparkline. The line sparklines show the sales history of each department and all four departments for a computer manufacturer. From glancing at the sparklines, you can quickly see the recent sales history within and across departments. Notice that although total sales rose steadily during the year, peripheral sales lagged for the first two-thirds of the year before increasing in the final third.

Figure 4-36 **Types of sparklines**

line sparklines

	A	B	C
1	**Sales by Department** (sales in millions)		
2	Department	Current	1-Year
3	Laptops	$ 29.4	
4	Printers	$ 13.2	
5	Monitors	$ 13.0	
6	Peripherals	$ 11.5	
7	All Departments	$ 67.1	

column sparklines

	A	B	C
1		Temperature Record	
2	City	Yearly	Monthly
3	Seattle	37.7°C	
4	Buenos Aires	54.0°C	
5	Moscow	14.3°C	
6	Melbourne	47.4°C	

win/loss sparklines

	A	B	C
1	Team	Record	Season
2	Cutler Tigers	10 - 2	
3	Apsburg Hawks	8 - 4	
4	Central City Spartans	6 - 6	
5	Liddleton Lions	3 - 9	

The column sparklines present a record of monthly temperature averages for four cities. Temperatures above 0°C are presented in blue columns; temperatures below 0°C are presented in red columns that extend downward.

Finally, the win/loss sparklines reveal a snapshot of the season results for four sports teams. Wins are displayed in blue; losses are in red. From the sparklines, you can quickly see that the Cutler Tigers finished their 10-2 season with six straight wins and the Liddleton Lions finished their 3-9 season with four straight losses.

To create a set of sparklines, you first select a data range containing the data you want to graph, and then you select a location range where you want the sparklines to appear. Note that the cells in which you insert the sparklines need not be blank. Sparklines are added as part of the cell background and do not replace any cell content.

Creating and Editing Sparklines

- In the Sparklines group on the Insert tab, click the Line, Column, or Win/Loss button.
- In the Data Range box, enter the range for the data source of the sparkline.
- In the Location Range box, enter the range into which to place the sparkline.
- Click the OK button.
- To edit a sparkline's appearance, click the Sparkline Tools Design tab.
- In the Show group, click the appropriate check boxes to specify which markers to display on the sparkline.
- In the Group group, click the Axis button, and then click Show Axis to add an axis to the sparkline.

Ajita wants to add graphs to the Sectors worksheet to indicate how each of the 12 investment sectors performed during the last 10 years. Rather than create a separate chart for each sector, you'll conserve space in the worksheet by creating sparklines.

To insert sparklines in the Sectors worksheet:

1. Go to the **Sectors** worksheet.

2. In cell E3, enter **10-Year History**, and then apply the **Heading 4** cell style to the cell and center the text within the cell.

3. Select the range **E4:E15**. This is the location range, the cells in which you want to insert the sparklines.

4. Click the **Insert** tab on the Ribbon, and then click the **Line** button in the Sparklines group. The Create Sparklines dialog box opens. The location range is already entered because you selected it before opening the dialog box.

5. With the insertion point in the Data Range box, click the **Sector History** sheet tab, and then select the data in the range **B6:M45**. This is the range that contains the data you want to chart in the sparklines. See Figure 4-37.

Figure 4-37 **Create Sparklines dialog box**

the range B6:M45 on the Sector History worksheet contains the data for the sparklines

the range E4:E15 on the current worksheet is the location to place the sparklines

6. Click the **OK** button. Sparklines are inserted into each cell in the selected range. See Figure 4-38.

Figure 4-38   Line sparklines created for each sector

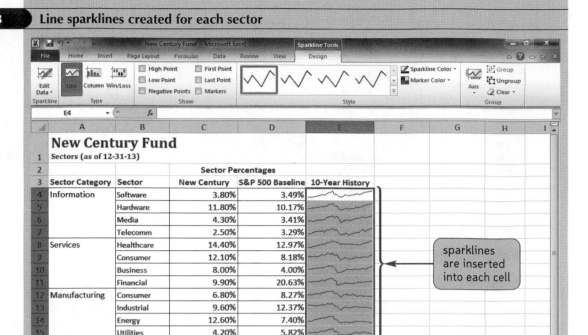

Ajita quickly notices from the sparklines that all of the investment sectors experienced a sharp decline mid-way through the previous decade. The stocks in the information sector category recovered from that loss to post gains during the second half of the decade. However, the manufacturing stocks showed little or no increase after that mid-decade decline. The stocks in the service category showed a moderate increase in the second half of the decade.

Adding and Formatting Sparkline Markers

As with other charts, Excel provides built-in styles for sparklines. Because of the compactness of sparklines, you can specify only the line color and the marker color. For line sparklines, you can create markers for the following points: the highest value, the lowest value, all the negative values, the first value, and the last value. You can also create markers for all data points regardless of their value or position in the data source.

Ajita wants you to add data markers for the high and low points within each sparkline so that she can more easily track the progress each sector made during the decade and locate the decade's maximum and minimum values.

To add high and low markers to the sparklines:

1. Click the **Sparkline Tools Design** tab on the Ribbon, if necessary. The tab contains options associated with the selected sparklines—in this case, line sparklines.

2. In the Show group, click the **High Point** and **Low Point** check boxes to display markers for the high and low points within each sparkline.

3. In the Style group, click the **More** button to open the Style gallery, and then click **Sparkline Style Colorful #2** (the second style in the last row). The color of the high and low point markers changes to reflect the selection. See Figure 4-39.

TIP

You can change the sparkline color by clicking the Sparkline Color button in the Style group on the Sparkline Tools Design tab. You can change the marker color by clicking the Marker Color button.

Figure 4-39   **Data markers added to sparklines**

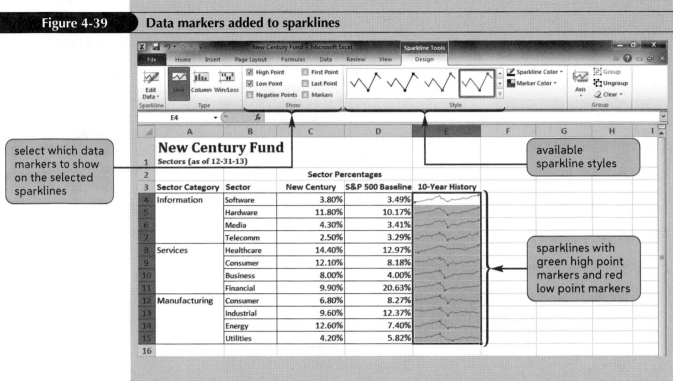

4. Click cell **A2** to deselect the location range containing the sparklines. You can more clearly see that the formatted sparklines use a green marker for the high points and a red marker for the low points.

The only other feature you can add to a sparkline is an axis. The sparkline axis is simply a horizontal line that separates positive values from negative values. To add an axis to a sparkline, click the Axis button in the Group group on the Sparkline Tools Design tab, and then click Show Axis. You won't add an axis to the 10-Year History sparklines because all of the fund values are positive and an axis would not add any information to the charts.

INSIGHT

Sparkline Groups

When you create sparklines, all the sparklines in the location range are part of a single group. Clicking any cell in the location range selects all of the sparklines in the group. Similarly, any formatting you apply affects all the sparklines in the group. This ensures that all the sparklines for related data are formatted consistently.

In some instances, you might want to differentiate one sparkline from others in its group. You can do this by applying a different format to that sparkline. To format an individual sparkline, select the sparkline you want to format, and then click the Ungroup button in the Group group on the Sparkline Tools Design tab. The selected sparkline is split from the rest of the sparklines in the group. You can then apply a unique format to the selected sparkline. To regroup the sparklines, select all of the cells in the location range containing sparklines, and then click the Group button in the Group group.

One advantage of breaking up a sparkline group is that Excel can display each sparkline based on the maximum and minimum values associated with the individual sparkline's data series. This becomes an important consideration if your data source contains multiple data series covering vastly different ranges.

Creating Data Bars

A data bar is a conditional format that adds a horizontal bar to the background of a cell containing a numeric value. When applied to a range of cells, the data bars have the same appearance as a bar chart with each cell containing one bar.

The lengths of data bars are based on the value of each cell in the selected range. Cells with larger values have longer bars; cells with smaller values have shorter bars. Data bars are dynamic, which means that if one cell's value changes, the lengths of the data bars in the selected range are automatically updated.

Data bars differ from sparklines in that the bars are always placed in the cells containing the value they represent and each cell represents only a single bar from the bar chart. By contrast, a column sparkline can be inserted anywhere within the workbook and can represent data from several rows or columns. However, like sparklines, data bars can be used to create compact graphs that can be easily integrated alongside the text and values stored in your worksheet cells.

Ajita wants you to add data bars to the sector percentage values in the Sectors worksheet. The data bars will provide a visual picture of how the New Century Fund and the S&P 500 compare in their investments in different sectors.

To add data bars to the sector percentages:

▶ 1. In the Sectors worksheet, select the range **C4:D15**.

▶ 2. Click the **Home** tab on the Ribbon.

▶ 3. In the Styles group, click the **Conditional Formatting** button, and then point to **Data Bars** to display the Data Bars gallery.

▶ 4. In the Solid Fill group, click **Blue Data Bar** (the first data bar style). The data bars are added to the selected cells.

▶ 5. Click cell **A2** to deselect the sector percentages range. See Figure 4-40.

Figure 4-40   Data bars added to the Sectors worksheet

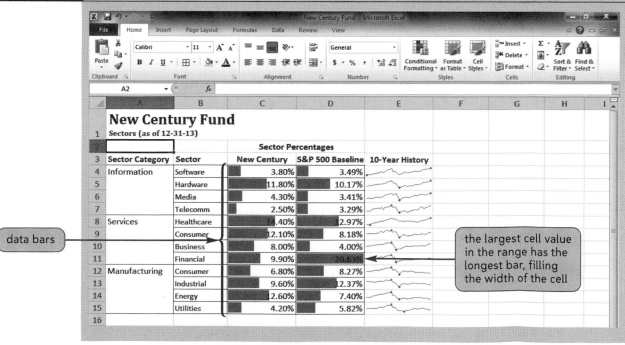

data bars

the largest cell value in the range has the longest bar, filling the width of the cell

The data bars shown in Figure 4-40 present essentially the same information as the combination column and line chart you created earlier. However, the data bars have the advantage of being compact in size and integrated with the values in the Sector Percentages table.

Modifying a Data Bar Rule

The lengths of the data bars are determined based on the values in the selected range. The cell with the largest value contains a data bar that extends across the entire width of the cell, and the lengths of the other bars in the selected range are determined relative to that bar. In some cases, this means that the longest data overlaps the cell's data value, making it difficult to read. You can modify the length of the data bars by altering the rules of the conditional format.

In the Sector Percentages data, cell D11 contains the largest value (20.63 percent) in the range C4:D15 and has the longest data bar. The data bar in cell D5, representing 10.17 percent, fills only half the cell width by comparison. Ajita does not want data bars to overlap the cell values. You will modify the data bar rule to proportionally reduce the lengths of the data bars so that the longest of them only fills less than half of a cell rather than an entire cell.

TIP

When data bars are used with negative values, the data bars originate from the center of the cell with negative bars extending to the left and positive bars extending to the right.

To modify the data bar rule:

1. Select the range **C4:D15**, which contains the data bars.

2. In the Styles group on the Home tab, click the **Conditional Formatting** button, and then click **Manage Rules**. The Conditional Formatting Rules Manager dialog box opens, displaying all the rules applied to any conditional format in the workbook.

3. Make sure **Current Selection** appears in the Show formatting rules for box. You'll edit the rule applied to the current selection, the data bars in the Sectors worksheet.

4. Click the **Edit Rule** button. The Edit Formatting Rule dialog box opens. You want to modify this rule so that the maximum value for the data bar is set to 0.40, or 40 percent. All data bar lengths will then be defined relative to this value.

5. In the Type row, click the **Maximum** arrow, and then click **Number**.

6. In the Value row, type **0.40** in the Maximum box. See Figure 4-41.

| Figure 4-41 | Edit Formatting Rule dialog box |

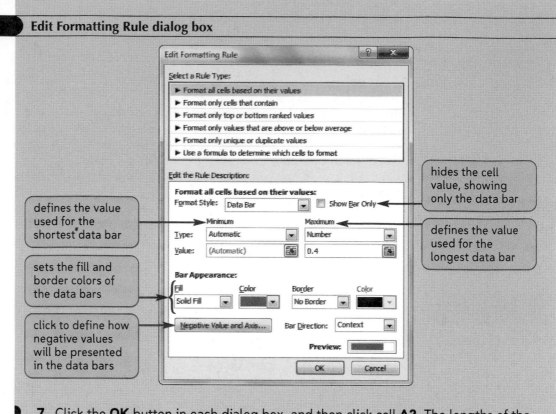

defines the value used for the shortest data bar

sets the fill and border colors of the data bars

click to define how negative values will be presented in the data bars

hides the cell value, showing only the data bar

defines the value used for the longest data bar

7. Click the **OK** button in each dialog box, and then click cell **A2**. The lengths of the data bars are reduced so that the longest bar covers less than half the cell width. See Figure 4-42.

| Figure 4-42 | Revised data bars |

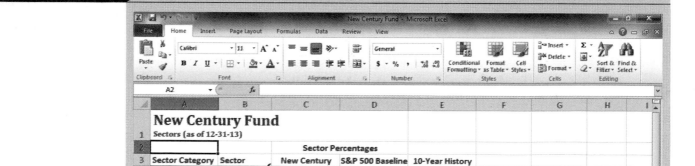

data bar lengths are expressed relative to a maximum value of 40%

the longest data bar covers less than half of the cell and doesn't overlap the cell value

INSIGHT

Edward Tufte and Chart Design Theory

Any serious study of chart design will include the works of Edward Tufte, who pioneered the field of information design. One of Tufte's most important works is *The Visual Display of Quantitative Information* in which he laid out several principles for the design of charts and graphics.

Tufte was concerned with what he termed as "chart junk," in which a proliferation of chart elements—chosen because they look "nice"—confuse and distract the reader. One measure of chart junk is Tufte's data-ink ratio, which is the amount of "ink" used to display quantitative information compared to the total ink required by the chart. Tufte advocated limiting the use of non-data ink. Non-data ink is any part of the chart that does not convey information about the data. One way of measuring the data-ink ratio is to determine how much of the chart you can erase without affecting the user's ability to interpret the chart. Tufte would argue for high data-ink ratios with a minimum of extraneous elements and graphics.

To this end, Tufte helped developed sparklines, which convey information with a high data-ink ratio within a compact space. Tufte believed that charts that can be viewed and comprehended at a glance have a greater impact on the reader than large and cluttered graphs, no matter how attractive they might be.

Creating a Chart Sheet

TIP

You can also embed charts in a chart sheet, enabling you to display several charts in a single chart sheet.

Chart sheets are helpful for detailed charts that need more space to be seen clearly or when you want to show a chart without any worksheet text or data. Some reports require large expansive charts rather than compact graphs to provide more detail and make them easier to view and share. In those situations, you may want to devote an entire sheet to a graph rather than embed it within a worksheet. To create a larger version of a chart that covers an entire sheet, you move the chart to a chart sheet. Chart sheets are used for graphic elements like charts and images, and do not contain worksheet cells for calculating numeric values.

Ajita asks you to create a chart sheet for the workbook that shows a 3-D image of the performance of the New Century Fund over the past 10 years. In this case, the chart sheet is purely decorative; Ajita plans to use it as a cover page for the New Century Fund report.

To create the chart sheet for the New Century Fund report:

1. Go to the **Fund History** worksheet, and then select the range **A4:B44**. This range contains the data you want to use in the chart.

2. Click the **Insert** tab on the Ribbon.

3. In the Charts group, click the **Line** button, and then click the **3-D Line** chart type. The 3-D line chart is embedded in the Fund History worksheet. You'll move this chart to a chart sheet.

4. In the Location group on the Chart Tools Design tab, click the **Move Chart** button. The Move Chart dialog box opens.

5. Click the **New sheet** option button, and then type **Cover Sheet** in the box as the name for the new chart sheet.

6. Click the **OK** button. A chart sheet named "Cover Sheet" that contains the 3-D line chart is inserted in the workbook.

7. Drag the **Cover Sheet** sheet tab to the right of the Documentation sheet tab. The Cover Sheet appears before the Summary Report worksheet and the worksheets that contain the detailed data used to create the summary report. See Figure 4-43.

Figure 4-43   **3-D chart in a chart sheet**

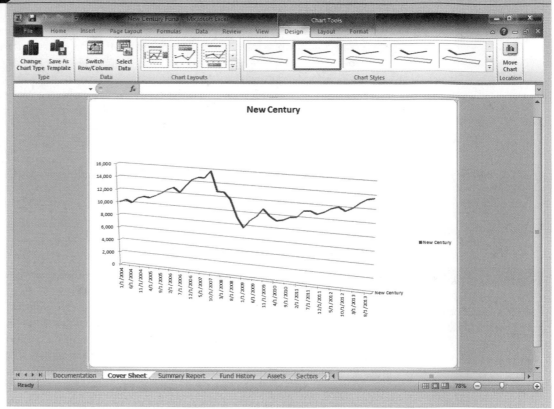

You can format a chart in a chart sheet using all the same options and tools as you do to format a chart embedded in a worksheet. You'll remove the axis labels and legend from the chart and rotate the chart in three dimensions. To increase the 3-D effect, you'll widen the chart's base from 100 to 1000 points.

To format the chart in the chart sheet:

1. In the Chart Styles group on the Chart Tools Design tab, click the **More** button, and then click **Style 40** (the last style in the fifth row in the Chart Styles gallery).

2. Click the **Chart Tools Layout** tab on the Ribbon.

3. In the Labels group, click the **Legend** button, and then click **None** to turn off the legend.

4. In the Axes group, click the **Axes** button, point to **Primary Horizontal Axis**, and then click **None** to remove the horizontal axis.

5. In the Axes group, click the **Axes** button, point to **Primary Vertical Axis**, and then click **None** to remove the vertical axis from the chart.

6. In the Axes group, click the **Axes** button, point to **Depth Axis**, and then click **None** to remove the depth axis.

7. In the Background section, click the **3-D Rotation** button. The Format Chart Area dialog box opens, displaying the 3-D Rotation options.

8. In the Rotation section, change the X value to **60°**, change the Y value to **20°**, and then change the Perspective value to **80°**. These settings rotate the chart.

9. In the Chart Scale section, change the Depth (% of base) value to **1000**. This setting exaggerates the 3-D effect, making the chart appear thicker.

10. Click **Fill** on the left side of the dialog box, and then click the **Gradient fill** option button. The background color of the chart area is set to a gradient fill.

11. Click the **Preset colors** button ▣ ▾, and then click **Daybreak** (the fourth color in the first row).

12. Click the **Direction** button ▣ ▾, and then click **Linear Down** (the second direction in the first row).

13. Click the **Close** button to return to the chart sheet. See Figure 4-44.

| Figure 4-44 | Rotated 3-D chart with exaggerated perspective |

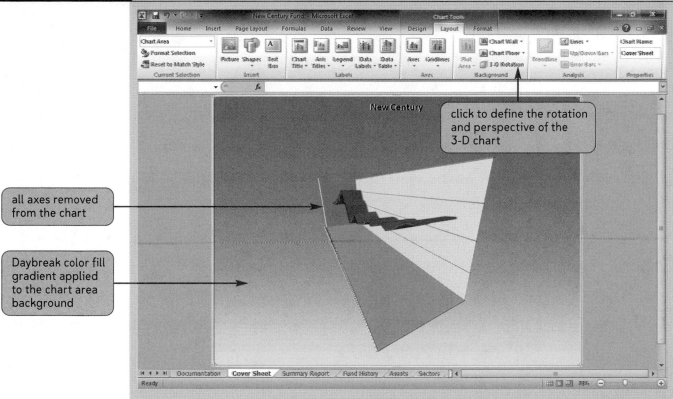

To complete the chart sheet, you'll overlay the chart title "The New Century Fund" over the chart and format it in a 48-point white font.

To overlay and format the chart title:

1. In the Labels group on the Chart Tools Layout tab, click the **Chart Title** button, and then click **Centered Overlay Title**. The chart title is overlaid above the chart. The chart expands to fill the extra space in the chart area.

2. Type **The New Century Fund**, and then press the **Enter** key. The new title is entered.

3. Click the **Home** tab on the Ribbon, and then change the font size to **36** points and the font color to **white**.

4. Click outside of the chart to deselect it. The cover sheet is final. See Figure 4-45.

Figure 4-45 | **Final cover sheet**

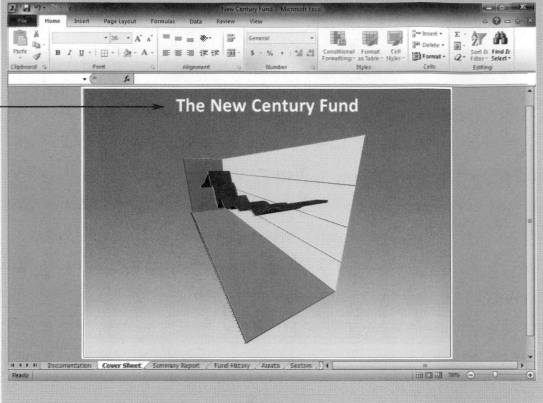

formatted chart title is overlaid above the chart area

The New Century Fund

5. Save the workbook, and then close it.

Ajita is pleased with the work you've done adding charts and graphics to the workbook. She will present the workbook with all of its different charts to her clients to provide them a concise report on the performance of the New Century Fund.

Session 4.2 Quick Check

REVIEW

1. When should you use a line chart in place of a column chart?
2. How do you overlay a chart legend?
3. How do you add a data series to an already existing chart?
4. What is a combination chart? Describe how to create a combination chart.
5. Explain how 3-D charts can lead to a false interpretation of the data. What can you do to correct this problem?
6. What are sparklines? Describe the three types of sparklines.
7. What are data bars? Describe how data bars differ from sparklines.
8. How do you create a chart sheet?

Practice the skills you learned in the tutorial using the same case scenario.

PRACTICE

Review Assignments

Data File needed for the Review Assignments: Crockett.xlsx

Ajita has to create a report on the investment portfolio for Brian and Tammy Crockett. She wants to add charts that display where the couple's money is currently being invested and how their portfolio has performed in recent years. She's already entered the data. You will complete the report by adding the charts and a decorative cover sheet. Complete the following:

1. Open the **Crockett** workbook located in the Excel4\Review folder included with your Data Files, and then save the workbook as **Crockett Portfolio**. In the Documentation sheet, enter your name in cell B3 and the date in cell B4.

2. In the Composition worksheet, select the range A3:B8, and then insert the first 2-D pie chart. Move and resize the embedded pie chart to cover the range D1:G9 in the Portfolio Report worksheet.

3. Move the legend to the left side of the chart area. Change the chart title to **Investment Categories** and set its font size to 11 points. Change the fill color of the Cash slice to yellow. Add data labels that show the percentage of each pie slice to two decimal places outside of the pie chart, and then set the font size of the labels to 8 points.

4. Change the pie chart to a 3-D pie chart and set the 3-D rotation of the x-axis to 230° and the y-axis to 40°.

5. In the Sectors worksheet, select the range A3:D15, and then insert a 2-D clustered column chart. Move and resize the embedded chart to cover the range A12:D25 in the Portfolio Report worksheet.

6. Change the font size of the axis labels and legend to 8 points. Insert the chart title **Sector Percentages** above the plot and set its font size to 11 points. Change the format of the percentages in the vertical axis to display no decimal places. Overlay the legend at the top of the chart, and then change its fill color to white and insert a solid border around the legend.

7. Change the chart type of the S&P 500 series to a line chart, remove the line connecting the markers in the chart, and then change the marker type to a solid horizontal line of size 10.

8. Change the fill color of the columns for the Portfolio data series to the theme color Purple, Accent 4, Lighter 60%. Set the gap width of the columns in the Portfolio data series to 30%.

9. In the Portfolio History worksheet, select the range A3:B127, and then insert a line chart. Move and resize the chart to cover the range D29:G37 in the Portfolio Report worksheet. (*Hint*: Scroll down the Portfolio Report worksheet to locate the embedded chart.)

10. Remove the chart legend. Set the font size of the chart title to 11 points, and then set the font size of the axis labels to 8 points.

11. Set the major tick mark interval for the category axis at two years and the minor tick mark interval at one year. Use a custom format that displays the category axis date values as four-digit year values. Insert vertical gridlines for the minor tick marks.

12. Change the scale of the value axis to range from $200,000 to $350,000. Add major tick marks every $50,000. Add minor tick marks every $25,000. Insert horizontal gridlines for every minor tick mark.

13. In cell B32, insert a line sparkline for the data range C4:C127 of the Portfolio History worksheet to describe the growth of the portfolio over consecutive three-month periods. Mark the high point and the low point with green and red markers, respectively.

14. In cell B37, insert a line sparkline for the data range D4:D127 of the Portfolio worksheet to show the growth of the portfolio over consecutive one-year periods. Add high/low data markers and an axis to this sparkline to match the first sparkline.

15. In cell B42, insert a line sparkline showing the growth of the portfolio over consecutive three-year periods using the data range E4:E127 of the Portfolio worksheet. Format the sparkline to match the other two sparklines.

16. Add solid blue data bars to the values in the range G13:G20. Modify the data bar rule so that the maximum length of the data bar corresponds to a number value of 1.8. Repeat to create data bars for the area values in the range G23:G25.

17. Select the range A3:B127 in the Portfolio History worksheet, and insert a line chart. Move the embedded chart to a new chart sheet named **Cover Sheet**. Move the Cover Sheet worksheet directly after the Documentation sheet.

18. Change the chart style to Style 34 (the second style in the fifth row of the Chart Styles gallery). Remove the display of the horizontal, vertical, and depth axes. Remove the chart legend.

19. For the 3-D rotation, set the x-axis to 60°, the y-axis to 10°, the perspective to 15°, and the depth of the base to 2000.

20. Change the chart title to **Crockett Family Portfolio**. Set the font size of the chart title to 40 points.

21. Save and close your workbook, and then submit the finished workbook to your instructor, either in printed or electronic form, as requested.

Case Problem 1

APPLY

If you have a SAM 2010 user profile, your instructor may have assigned an autogradable version of this assignment. If so, log into the SAM 2010 Web site at www.cengage.com/sam2010 to download the instructions and start files.

Data File needed for this Case Problem: Kenai.xlsx

Kenai Fjords National Park   Maria Sanford is the chief of interpretation at Kenai Fjords National Park. Part of her job is to report on park usage at the visitor centers. She wants to create a chart sheet that displays the park usage data. She has recorded last year's usage data in an Excel workbook. She asks you to present this data in a 3-D column chart for an upcoming meeting with her supervisor. She wants the chart to show the monthly usage totals organized by visitor center. She also wants a 3-D pie chart superimposed on the column chart and a table of park usage data. Complete the following:

1. Open the **Kenai** workbook located in the Excel4\Case1 folder included with your Data Files, and then save the workbook as **Kenai Fjords Park**. In the Documentation sheet, enter your name in cell B3 and the date in cell B4.

2. In the Park Usage Data worksheet, select the range A3:D15, and then insert the 3-D Column chart (the last chart in the 3-D Column section in the Charts gallery).

3. Move the chart to a chart sheet named **Monthly Visits**. Place the Monthly Visits chart sheet directly after the Documentation sheet.

4. Change the style of the chart to Style 42 (the second style in the sixth row in the Chart Styles gallery).

5. Insert a chart title using the centered overlay title format, change the title to **Kenai Fjords National Park 2013 Census**, and then set its font size to 24 points. Remove the legend from the chart.

6. Add the title **Monthly Visitors** to the vertical axis. Rotate the title 90° and set the font size to 14 points.

7. Rotate the 3-D chart using the following parameters: x-axis rotation 30°, y-axis rotation 20°, perspective 25°, and depth 130. (*Hint*: Uncheck the Right Angle Axes check box in the Chart Scale section to make the Perspective box active.)

⊕ EXPLORE   8. Modify the depth axis so that the values are displayed in reverse order. (*Hint*: Use the Axes button in the Axes group on the Chart Tools Layout tab to modify the depth axis.)

⊕ EXPLORE   9. Insert a data table without legend keys below the 3-D chart to provide the data values for the different columns. (*Hint*: Use the Data Table button in the Labels group on the Chart Tools Layout tab.)

10. Change the fill color of the Visitor Center series to orange.

11. In the Park Usage Data worksheet, select the range B3:D3;B16:D16, and then insert a 3-D pie chart.

12. Move the embedded chart to the Monthly Visits chart sheet.

13. Insert the chart title **Total Visits** above the pie chart, and set its font size to 16 points and its color to white.

14. Change the color of the Visitor Center slice to orange.

15. Remove the chart legend from the pie chart.

16. Add data labels to the inside of each slice, displaying the slice's value.

17. Change the fill color of the chart area to none (removing the fill color) and change the border color to no line (removing the border). Resize the embedded pie chart and move it to the lower-left of the column chart.

18. Go to the Park Usage Data worksheet, and then add data bars to the range B4:D15. Modify the rule for the data bars so that the maximum data bar length matches a value of 100,000.

19. Save and close your workbook, and then submit the finished workbook to your instructor, either in printed or electronic form, as requested.

Create a combination chart describing tornado events.

APPLY

Case Problem 2

Data Files needed for this Case Problem: Tornado.xlsx, Cloud.jpg

Midwest Tornado Institute   Joyce Bishop is a meteorologist at the Midwest Tornado Institute located in Decatur, Illinois. Joyce is preparing for a talk she is giving to a local civic group on the possible effects of global warming on tornados. She has collected data on minor, moderate, and major tornado sightings in five-year periods during the second half of the twentieth century and wants you to create a graph for her talk showing her data. She's already entered this data into an Excel workbook. Complete the following:

1. Open the **Tornado** workbook located in the Excel4\Case2 folder included with your Data Files, and then save the workbook as **Tornado Sightings**. In the Documentation sheet, enter your name in cell B3 and the date in cell B4.

2. In the Sightings History worksheet, select the range A3:E13, and then insert a 2-D clustered column chart. Move the embedded chart to a chart sheet named **Sightings Chart**.

3. Change the chart style to Style 32 (the last chart style in the fourth row of the Chart Styles gallery).

4. Insert the chart title **Tornado Sightings: 1950–1999** at the top of the chart, and then change the font size to 24 points.

5. Add the vertical axis title **Sightings** in a 14-point font with horizontal orientation. Add the horizontal axis title **Years** in a 14-point font.

6. Move the legend to the bottom of the chart, and then set its font size to 14 points.

⊕EXPLORE   7. Change the line style of the horizontal gridline from a solid line to a dashed line. (*Hint*: Use the Dash type button in the Line Style options in the Format Major Gridlines dialog box.)

8. Add vertical gridlines to the major tick marks in the chart. Display the gridlines as dashed lines.

9. Change the chart type of the All data series from a column chart to a 2-D line chart. Change the color of the line to standard blue.

⊕EXPLORE   10. Select the plot area and change the fill to a picture fill, using the **Cloud.jpg** file located in the Excel4\Case2 folder included with your Data Files. (*Hint*: Open the Format Plot Area dialog box. In the Fill options, click the Picture or texture fill option button, click the File button, and then locate and select the picture file.)

11. Go to the Sightings History worksheet, and then insert orange data bars in the range B4:D13. Insert blue data bars in the range E4:E13. Note that the meaning of the lengths of the two sets of data bars is different because they are applied to different ranges.

12. In cell B2, insert a sparkline for the data in the range B4:B13 (do *not* include the total in cell B14). Repeat to insert a sparkline in each cell in the range C2:E2.

13. Save and close your workbook, and then submit the finished workbook to your instructor, either in printed or electronic form, as requested.

Explore how to use Excel to chart stock market data.

CHALLENGE

Case Problem 3

Data File needed for this Case Problem: Mitchell.xlsx

Hardin Financial   Kurt Lee is a financial analyst for Hardin Financial, a consulting firm in Owatonna, Minnesota. As part of his job, he records stock market activity in Excel workbooks. One workbook contains the recent stock market activity of Mitchell Oil. He wants your help in creating a chart displaying the stock values. The chart should display the stock's opening, high, low, and closing values, and the number of shares traded for each day of the past few weeks. The volume of shares traded should be expressed in terms of millions of shares. Complete the following:

1. Open the **Mitchell** workbook located in the Excel4\Case3 folder included with your Data Files, and then save the workbook as **Mitchell Oil**. In the Documentation sheet, enter your name in cell B3 and the date in cell B4.

⊕ EXPLORE   2. In the Stock Values worksheet, select the range A3:F33, and then insert a Volume-Open-High-Low-Close stock chart. (*Hint:* Click the Other Charts button in the Charts group on the Insert tab to locate the stock charts.) Move the embedded chart to the chart sheet named **Stock History**.

3. Insert the chart title **Mitchell Oil** above the chart area, and then set the font size of the chart title to 18 points. Remove the chart legend.

4. Add the title **Date** to the primary horizontal axis, and then set its font size to 14 points. Add the title **Shares Traded** to the primary vertical axis, set its font size to 14 points, and then rotate the title 270°.

⊕ EXPLORE   5. Add the title **Stock Value** to the secondary vertical axis, set its font size to 14 points, and rotate the title 90°. (*Hint:* Open the Format Axis Title dialog box for the secondary vertical axis and use the Text direction button found in the Alignment category.)

6. Set the font size of all axis values to 12 points.

7. Display the horizontal and vertical gridlines using a dashed line style. Set the interval between major tick marks on the primary horizontal axis to 7 days.

8. For the primary vertical axis, display the values in units of one million, change the number format to two decimal place accuracy, and then set the maximum value of the axis scale to 2,000,000.

9. For the secondary vertical axis, set the minimum value of the scale to 10.

10. Decrease the gap width between the columns in the plot to 30% and change the fill color to light blue.

11. Change the fill color of the plot area to light yellow.

⊕ EXPLORE   12. In a stock market chart, the daily chart values will show either an increase or a decrease from the previous day. Increases are shown with an up bar displayed in white and decreases are shown with a down bar displayed in black. Select the data series for the up bars and change their fill colors to light green. Select the data series for the down bars and change their fill colors to red.

EXPLORE 13. Go to the Stock Values worksheet. Add a column sparkline to cell B2 to display the Shares Traded values in the range B4:B33.

14. Add a line sparkline to cell F2 to display the closing values of the stock over the range F4:F33.

15. In the range G3:G33, create a new column of values named **Difference** that is equal to the difference between the stock's closing value and its opening value on each day. Display the difference values using the same format as in column F.

EXPLORE 16. Add a win/loss sparkline to cell G2 that indicates the days that the stock gained value and the days that the stock lost value.

17. Save and close your workbook, and then submit the finished workbook to your instructor, either in printed or electronic form, as requested.

Create an Excel workbook to provide a report on a sporting event.

CREATE

Case Problem 4

Data File needed for this Case Problem: Basketball.xlsx

Blowout Sports   Steve Eagan is the owner and operator of Blowout Sports, a sports information and scouting company located in Lexington, Kentucky. One of Steve's jobs is to provide detailed graphical reports and analysis of college basketball games for the media, coaches, and interested fans. Steve has been placing box score data and game logs into an Excel workbook. He wants to summarize this data in one worksheet using charts and graphs. He's asked you to help develop the workbook. Steve has a sample workbook containing the results of a recent basketball game for you to work on. Complete the following:

1. Open the **Basketball** workbook located in the Excel4\Case4 folder included with your Data Files, and then save the workbook as **Basketball Report**. In the Documentation sheet, enter your name in cell B3 and the date in cell B4.

2. The Game Log worksheet contains the minute-by-minute score of the game. Use the data in this worksheet to create a line chart describing the ebb and flow of the game that is embedded in the Game Report worksheet. The format of the chart is up to you, but it should include titles for the chart and the axes, a chart legend overlay, vertical gridlines spaced at 4-minute intervals, and horizontal gridlines at 5-point intervals. (*Hint*: To display vertical gridlines at 4-minute intervals, you must turn off the multi-level category labels.)

3. The Box Score worksheet contains statistical summaries of the game. Use the data in this worksheet to create two column charts describing the points scored by each player on the two teams. Embed the charts in the Game Report worksheet. The format of the charts is up to you, but it should include titles for the chart and axes, and gradient fill colors for the columns.

4. The Box Score worksheet also contains team statistics. Use this data to create several pie charts that compare the two teams. Embed the pie charts in the Game Report worksheet. The final pie charts should include data labels for the pie slices and slice colors that match the team's colors (red for Wisconsin, gold for Iowa).

5. The Season Record worksheet contains a record of each team's season including wins and losses. Use this data to create a win/loss sparkline displayed on the Game Report worksheet alongside each team's season record.

6. Create a chart sheet for the report that will be a cover sheet. The cover sheet should include a 3-D chart of some of the data in the workbook. The format of the chart and chart sheet is up to you.

7. Save and close your workbook, and then submit the finished workbook to your instructor, either in printed or electronic form, as requested.

SAM: Skills Assessment Manager

For current SAM information, including versions and content details, visit SAM Central (http://samcentral.course.com). If you have a SAM user profile, you may have access to hands-on instruction, practice, and assessment of the skills covered in this tutorial. Since various versions of SAM are supported throughout the life of this text, check with your instructor for the correct instructions and URL/Web site for accessing assignments.

ENDING DATA FILES

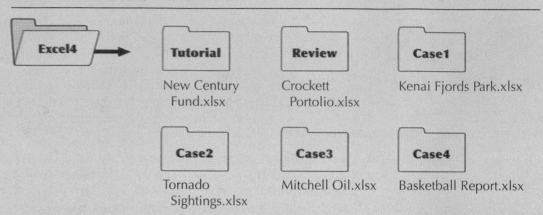

Excel4 →

Tutorial
New Century
Fund.xlsx

Review
Crockett
Portolio.xlsx

Case1
Kenai Fjords Park.xlsx

Case2
Tornado
Sightings.xlsx

Case3
Mitchell Oil.xlsx

Case4
Basketball Report.xlsx

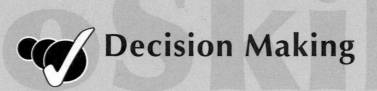

Decision Making

Creating a Budget Worksheet to Make Financial Decisions

Decision making is the process of choosing between alternative courses of action, usually in response to a problem that needs to be solved. Having an understanding of decision-making processes will lead to better decisions and greater confidence in carrying out those decisions. This is especially important when making financial decisions.

Gather Relevant Information

Begin by collecting data and information related to the decision you need to make. This information can include data expressed as currency or numbers, as well as data that cannot be measured numerically. For example, when creating a budget, numerical data includes your income and expenses, current savings, future savings and purchases, and so on. Other data might include the amount of savings you need to feel comfortable before making a large purchase, such as buying a car or paying tuition.

Evaluate the Gathered Information and Develop Alternatives

Evaluate the data you collected and determine potential alternatives. Excel workbooks are well suited to evaluating numerical data. You can also use workbooks to evaluate potential outcomes based on other data by assigning numerical weights to them. For example, you can enter your monthly income and fixed expenses into a worksheet along with variable expenses to determine your cash flow. You can then consider this information along with your current savings to determine how much money to contribute to savings or earmark for a purchase. Based on these results, you can develop alternatives for how to distribute your available money among variable expenses (such as entertainment), savings, and a large purchase.

Select the Best Alternative

Carefully evaluate the alternatives you developed based on your analysis. Before making a decision, be sure to take into account all factors. Consider such questions as:

- Does this alternative make sense for the long term? For example, does this budget allow you to achieve all your financial goals?
- Can you realistically carry out this alternative? For example, does this budget provide enough for necessities such as food and housing as well as for luxuries such as entertainment?
- Will this alternative be acceptable even if its outcome is not perfect or some unconsidered factors emerge? For example, will this budget cover unforeseen expenses such as car repair or an unexpected trip?
- How comfortable are you with this decision? For example, does this budget relieve or add stress about managing your finances?

After analyzing all the factors, one alternative should begin to emerge as the best alternative. If it doesn't, you might need to develop additional alternatives.

ProSkills

Prepare an Action Plan

After making a decision, you need to plan how to implement that decision. Consider what steps you need to take to achieve the final outcome. For example, do you need to open a bank account or change services to reduce expenses (such as switching to a less expensive cell phone plan)? Determine a reasonable time table. When do you want start? How long will each task take? What tasks must be completed before others start? Can tasks be performed at the same time? Develop milestones to track the success of your plan. For example, one milestone might be to see your savings increase by 10 percent in three months. Finally, identify what resources you need to be successful. For example, do you need to talk to a financial advisor at your bank?

Take Action and Monitor the Results

After you develop the action plan, the actual plan begins. For example, you can open bank accounts, change telephone services, and so forth as outlined in your action plan. Be sure to check off completed tasks and assess how well those actions produce the desired outcome. For example, is the budget achieving the financial goals you set? If so, then continue to follow the established plan. If not, you may need to modify the action plan or reevaluate your decision.

PROSKILLS

Develop a Budget Worksheet

Excel is valuable to a wide audience of users: from accountants of *Fortune 500* companies to homeowners managing their budgets. An Excel workbook can be a complex document, recording data from thousands of financial transactions, or it can track a few monthly household expenses. Anyone who has to balance a budget, track expenses, or project future income can use the financial tools in Excel to help them make good financial decisions about their financing and future expenditures.

In this exercise, you will use Excel to create a sample budget workbook that will contain information of your choice, using Excel skills and features presented in Tutorials 1 through 4. Use the following steps as a guide to completing your workbook.

Note: Please be sure *not* to include any personal information of a sensitive nature in any workbooks you create to be submitted to your instructor for this exercise. Later, you can update the workbooks with such information for your personal use.

1. Gather the data related to your monthly cash inflows and outflows. For example, how much do you take home in your paychecks each month? What other sources of income do you have? What expenses do you have—rent, utilities, gas, insurance, groceries, entertainment, car payments, and so on?
2. Create a new workbook for the sample financial data. Use the first worksheet as a documentation sheet that includes your name, the date on which you start creating the workbook, and a brief description of the workbook's purpose.
3. Plan the structure of the second worksheet, which will contain the budget. Include a section to enter values that remain consistent from month to month, such as monthly income and expenses. As you develop the budget worksheet, reference these cells in formulas that require those values. Later, you can update any of these values and see the changes immediately reflected throughout the budget.

ProSkills

4. In the budget worksheet, enter realistic monthly earnings for each month of the year. Use formulas to calculate the total earnings each month, the average monthly earnings, and the total earnings for the entire year.

5. In the budget worksheet, enter realistic personal expenses for each month. Divide the expenses into at least three categories, providing subtotals for each category and a grand total of all the monthly expenses. Calculate the average monthly expenses and total expenses for the year.

6. Calculate the monthly net cash flow (the value of total income minus total expenses).

7. Use the cash flow values to track the savings throughout the year. Use a realistic amount for savings at the beginning of the year. Use the monthly net cash flow values to add or subtract from this value. Project the end-of-year balance in the savings account under your proposed budget.

8. Format the worksheet's contents using appropriate text and number formats. Add colors and line borders to make the content easier to read and interpret. Use cell styles and themes to provide your worksheet with a uniform appearance.

9. Use conditional formatting to automatically highlight negative net cash flow months.

10. Insert a pie chart that compares the monthly expenses for the categories.

11. Insert a column chart that charts all of the monthly expenses regardless of the category.

12. Insert a line chart or sparkline that shows the change in the savings balance throughout the 12 months of the year.

13. Insert new rows at the top of the worksheet and enter titles that describe the worksheet's contents.

14. Examine your assumptions. How likely are certain events to occur? Perform several what-if analyses on your budget, providing the impact of (a) reducing income with expenses remaining constant, (b) increasing expenses with income remaining constant, (c) reducing income and expenses, and (d) increasing income and expenses. Discuss the different scenarios you explored. How much cushion does your projected income give you if expenses increase? What are some things you can do in your budget to accommodate this scenario?

15. Think of a major purchase you might want to make—for example, a car or a computer. Determine the amount of the purchase and the current annual interest rate charged by your local bank. Provide a reasonable length of time to repay the loan, such as five years for a car loan or 20 to 30 years for a home loan. Use the PMT function to determine how much you would have to spend each month on the payments for your purchase. You can do these calculations in a separate worksheet

16. Add the loan information to your monthly budget and evaluate the purchase of this item on your budget. Is it affordable? Examine other possible loans you might pursue and evaluate their impact on your budget. Come up with the most realistic way of paying off the loan while still maintaining a reasonable monthly cash flow and a cushion against unexpected expenses. If the payment exceeds your budget, reduce the estimated price of the item you're thinking of purchasing until you determine the monthly payment you can afford under the conditions of the loan.

ProSkills

17. After settling on a budget and the terms of a loan that you can afford, develop an action plan for putting your budget into place. What are some potential pitfalls that will prohibit you from following through on your proposed budget? How can you increase the likelihood that you will follow the budget? Be specific, and write down a list of goals and benchmarks that you'll use to monitor your progress in following your financial plan.

18. With the worksheet set up and your budget in place, you can take action and monitor your results. You will want to update your worksheet each month as income or expense items change to be sure you remain on track to meet your goals. You will also want to confirm that you made a good decision. If not, evaluate your budget and determine what new action you need to take to get yourself back on track.

19. Format the worksheets for your printer. Include headers and footers that display the workbook filename, the workbook's author, and the date on which the report is printed. If the report extends across several pages, repeat appropriate print titles on all of the pages and include page numbers and the total number of pages on every printed page.

20. Save and close your workbook, and then submit the completed workbook to your instructor, in printed or electronic form, as requested.

GLOSSARY/INDEX

TASK REFERENCE

TASK	PAGE #	RECOMMENDED METHOD
Absolute reference, change to relative	EX 118	*See* Reference box: Entering Relative, Absolute, and Mixed References
Action, undo or redo	EX 40	Click 🔙 or 🔜 on Quick Access Toolbar
AutoFill, copy formulas	EX 142	Select cell with formula, click and drag fill handle over adjacent range
AutoFill, create series	EX 143	Enter first few entries in series, drag fill handle over adjacent range
AutoSum feature, enter function with	EX 35	Click cell, click Σ ▾ in Editing group on Home tab, click function, verify range, press Enter
Border, add to cell	EX 76	Select range, click ▦ ▾ in Font group on Home tab, click border
Cell contents, align horizontally within a cell	EX 72	Click ▤, ▤, or ▤ in Alignment group on Home tab
Cell contents, rotate	EX 75	Click ◈ ▾ in Alignment group on Home tab, click rotation angle
Cell, change fill color	EX 64	Click ◈ ▾ in Font group on Home tab, click color
Cell, clear contents of	EX 20	Right-click cell, range, column, or row; click Clear Contents
Cell, delete	EX 20	Select cell or range, click Delete button in Cells group on Home tab
Cell, edit	EX 38	Double-click cell, enter changes
Cell, go to	EX 7	Click Find & Select button in Editing group on Home tab, click Go To
Cell, move or copy	EX 26	*See* Reference box: Moving or Copying a Cell or Range
Cell reference, change	EX 118	*See* Reference box: Entering Relative, Absolute, and Mixed References
Cells, merge and center	EX 74	Select adjacent cells, click ▦ in Alignment group on Home tab
Cells, select all in worksheet	EX 24	*See* Reference box: Selecting Ranges
Chart, add axis title to	EX 201	Select chart, click Axis Titles button in Labels group on Chart Tools Layout tab, point to axis, select option
Chart, add data label	EX 182	Select chart, click Data Labels button in Labels group on Chart Tools Layout tab, Click More Data Label Options, select options, click Close
Chart, add data series	EX 203	*See* Reference box: Adding a Data Series to a Chart
Chart, add gridlines	EX 201	Select chart, click Gridlines button in Axes group on Chart Tools Layout tab, select option
Chart, change data	EX 202	Enter new values in chart's data source
Chart, change layout	EX 178	Select chart, click layout in Chart Layout group on Design tab
Chart, change style	EX 177	Select chart, click chart style in Chart Styles group on Design tab
Chart, change to 3-D	EX 209	Select chart, click Change Chart Type button in Type group on Chart Tools Design tab, select 3-D chart type
Chart, create	EX172	*See* Reference box: Inserting a Chart
Chart, format data marker	EX 207	Click data marker, click Format Selection in Current Selection group on Chart Tools Layout tab, format as needed
Chart, move	EX 176	Select chart, drag to new location
Chart, move to another sheet	EX 175	Select chart, click Move Chart button in Location group on Design tab
Chart, resize	EX 176	Select chart, drag sizing handle
Chart, select	EX 176	Click empty area of chart ("Chart Area" ScreenTip appears)

TASK	PAGE #	RECOMMENDED METHOD
Chart legend, add or remove	EX 186	Select chart, click Legend button in Labels group on Chart Tools Layout tab, click option
Chart title, change	EX 179	Click chart title, type new chart title, press Enter
Column, change width	EX 15	*See* Reference box: Changing the Column Width or Row Height
Column, insert	EX 19	*See* Reference box: Inserting a Column or Row
Column, select	EX 17	Click column heading
Columns, select	EX 17	Click first column heading, hold down Shift, click last column heading
Combination chart, create	EX 206	*See* Reference box: Creating a Combination Chart
Conditional format, clear	EX 97	Select cell, click Conditional Formatting button in Styles group on Home tab, point to Clear Rules, click Clear Rules from Selected Cells
Conditional format, use to highlight cells	EX 96	*See* Reference box: Highlighting a Cell Based on Its Value
Data bars, create	EX 216	Select range, click Conditional Formatting button in Styles group on Home tab, point to Data Bars, select data bar style
Data series, add to chart	EX 203	*See* Reference box: Adding a Data Series to a Chart
Date, enter into cell	EX 12	Click cell, type date, press Enter or Tab
Date, insert current	EX 155	Enter TODAY() or NOW() function in cell
Dates, fill using AutoFill	EX 144	Enter first few dates, drag fill handle over adjacent range
Excel, start	EX 5	Click ●, click All Programs, click Microsoft Office, click Microsoft Excel 2010
Fill handle, use	EX 141	*See* Reference box: Copying Formulas and Formats with AutoFill
Font, change color	EX 62	Click **A** ⁃ in Font group on Home tab, click color
Font, change size	EX 61	Click Font Size arrow in Font group on Home tab, click point size
Font, change style	EX 61	In Font group on Home tab, click **B**, *I*, or U̲
Font, change typeface	EX 61	Click Font arrow in Font group on Home tab, click font
Format, copy using Format Painter	EX 79	Select range with original formatting, click ✍ in Clipboard group on Home tab, select range to format
Format, find and replace	EX 40	Click Find & Select in Editing group on Home tab, click Replace
Format Cells dialog box, open	EX 77	Click Dialog Box Launcher in Number group on Home tab
Formula, enter	EX 31	*See* Reference box: Inserting a Formula
Formula view, switch to	EX 46	Press Ctrl+`
Function, insert	EX 131	Click function category in the Function Library group on Formulas tab, click a function, enter arguments, click OK
Gridlines, add to chart	EX 201	Select chart, click Gridlines button in Axes group on Chart Tools Layout tab, select option
Header or footer, create	EX 105	Click button in Header & Footer Elements group on Header & Footer Tools Design tab
Margins, set	EX 107	Click Margins button in Page Setup group on Page Layout tab, select margin size
Number format, apply accounting	EX 68	Click $ in Number group on Home tab
Number format, apply long date	EX 71	Click Number Format arrow in Number group, click Long Date
Number format, apply percent	EX 68	click % in Number group on Home tab

TASK	PAGE #	RECOMMENDED METHOD
Number format, apply thousands separator	EX 68	Click ⬚ in Number group on Home tab
Page break, insert or remove	EX 103	*See* Reference box: Inserting and Removing Page Breaks
Pie chart, change slice color	EX 183	Click pie, click slice, click ⬚▾ in Font group on Home tab, click color
Print area, set	EX 102	Select range, click Print Area button in Page Setup group on Page Layout tab, click Set Print Area
Range, insert or delete	EX 29	*See* Reference box: Inserting or Deleting a Range
Range, move or copy	EX 26	*See* Reference box: Moving or Copying a Cell or Range
Range, select adjacent or nonadjacent	EX 24	*See* Reference box: Selecting Ranges
Relative reference, change to absolute	EX 118	*See* Reference box: Entering Relative, Absolute, and Mixed References
Row, change height	EX 15	*See* Reference box: Changing the Column Width or Row Height
Row, hide	EX 101	Select rows to hide, click Format button in Cells group on Home tab, point to Hide & Unhide, click Hide Rows
Row, insert	EX 19	*See* Reference box: Inserting a Column or Row
Row, select one or more	EX 20	Click row heading, hold down Shift and click last row heading
Row, unhide	EX 101	Select rows above and below hidden rows, click Format button in Cells group on Home tab, point to Hide & Unhide, click Unhide Rows
Rows, repeat in printout	EX 104	Click Print Titles button in Page Setup group on Page Layout tab, click Rows to repeat at top, select range, click OK
Series, create with AutoFill	EX 144	*See* Reference box: Creating a Series with AutoFill
Sparklines, add markers	EX 214	Select range with sparklines, click marker check boxes in Show group on Sparklines Tools Design tab
Sparklines, create	EX 213	*See* Reference box: Creating and Editing Sparklines
Spelling, check in worksheet	EX 41	Click Spelling button in Proofing group on Review tab
Style, apply to cell	EX 84	*See* Reference box: Applying a Cell Style
Table, remove filter	EX 93	Click in table, click Filter button in Sort & Filter group on Data tab
Table, select style options	EX 93	Click table, select options in Table Style Options group on Design tab
Text, enter multiple lines in a cell	EX 11	Type first line of entry, press Alt+Enter, type next line
Theme, change for workbook	EX 86	Click Themes button in Themes group on Page Layout tab, click theme
Workbook, preview and print	EX 45	Click the File tab, click Print, click Print button
Workbook, save	EX 21	Click File tab, click Save
Worksheet, add background image	EX 65	Click Background button in Page Setup group on Page Layout tab, click image file, click Insert
Worksheet, change orientation	EX 44	Click Orientation button in Page Setup group on the Page Layout tab, click Landscape or Portrait
Worksheet, change view	EX 43	Click ⬚, ⬚, or ⬚ on status bar
Worksheet, delete	EX 37	Right-click sheet tab, click Delete, click Delete button
Worksheet, insert	EX 37	Click ⬚
Worksheet, move	EX 38	Drag sheet tab to new location
Worksheet, rename	EX 38	Double-click sheet tab, type new name, press Enter
Worksheet, scale for printing	EX 47	Set width and height in Scale to Fit group on Page Layout tab
Worksheets, move between	EX 5	Click sheet tab; or click tab scrolling button and then click sheet tab